Index of Contents

33. Red, Red Wine. Daphne Greece.

34. The Golden Horn. Constantinople Turkey.

35. Big Chopper. Castlecary Scotland.

36. Donut Forsake Me. Alloa Scotland.

37. Brace, Brace. Istanbul Turkey.

38. Most Wanted. US Border Crossings.

39. Haven't I Seen You Somewhere Before. Dharan Saudi Arabia

40. Your Policemen are Wonderful. Chicago USA

41. Topping Off. Karabuk Turkey.

42. Send Me A Postcard. Middle East and West Africa.

43. Is It a Bird, Is it A plane?   US Virgin Islands.

44. Heart of Gold. Dining with Lex UK.

45. Si Si. San Diego USA.

46. A Lovely Pair of Melons. Falkirk Scotland.

47. Going Clubbing. Athens Greece.

48. Dicks Last Stand. Sydney Australia.

49. A Rum Do. Jamaica West Indies.

50. Going Down on Kansas. Emporia Kansas USA.

51. Boing Boing. Teheran Iran.

52. Hubble Bubble Toil and Trouble. Beirut Lebanon.

53. Bammie Barbecue. Kingston Jamaica.

54. Discount Card. Penang Malaysia.

55. Ambush in Athens. Athens Greece.

56. Simply Simon. Singapore and More.

57. To Hell and Back. Scandinavia.

58. The Abominable Snowman. Quebec Canada.

59. Polar Beer. Alaska USA.

60. Grivas Bodily Harm. Nicosia Cyprus.

61. Cuba Libre. Vienna Austria.

62. PA 103. Lockerbie Scotland.

63. The French Connection. Mid Atlantic.

64. Tora, Tora, Tora. Hawaii USA.

65. Mabuhay. Manila Philippines.

66. What's Your Poison? Various Locations.

67. Mortar this than meets the Eye. Hamilton Canada.

68. Tia Maria. Spanish Town Jamaica.

69. Five O Clock Shadow. Kerkyra Greece.

70. Christmas Day. Broken Hill Australia.

71. Blue Uniform. Portland Oregon USA.

72. Happiness Costs Such a Lot. San Francisco USA.

73. Comes the Revolution. Volos Greece.

74. North by Northwest. Galicia Spain.

75. Social Intercourse. York Pa USA.

76. One Careful Owner. Ingliston Edinburgh.

77. Turkish Delight. Eregli Turkey.

78. Rumble in the Jungle. Guinea West Africa.

79. Fort Apache. Teheran Iran.

80. Blue Seas, Blue Booze, Blue Pelicans. Port of Spain Trinidad.

81. Arms Akimbo. Kimbo Guinea.

82. You bet your life. Lake Charles USA.

83. Guy Fawkes. Bucharest Romania.

84. Super Mario. Phoenix Arizona.

85. Soused Herren. Finspång Sweden.

86. Finnish Fun. Helsinki Finland.

87. Michelin Man. Conakry Guinea.

88. Peanuts. Teheran Iran.

89. Public Relations. Gravesend UK.

90. From R&D to A&E. Gravesend UK.

91. Plaka. Athens Greece.

92. Viva Zapata. San Diego USA.

93. Bermuda Triangle. Bermuda.

94. Kelly's Mountain. Sydney Nova Scotia.

95. Sushi. Tokyo Japan.

96. Boothill. Tombstone Arizona USA.

97. Down South. Invercargill New Zealand.

98. All In. Newcastle NSW Australia.

99. Big D. Dallas USA.

100. Visit to Hiroshima. Hiroshima Japan.

101. De Witt. Iowa USA.

102. The Gay Hussar. London UK.

103. Chili Chili Sauce. Douglas USA.

104. Moscow FM. Moscow Russia.

105. Irish Coffee. Limerick Ireland.

106. Kamikazi Karioke. Hiroshima Japan.

107. East Berlin. Berlin Germany.

108. The Good Old Days. Castlecary UK.

109, New Joisey. Rahway NJ USA.

110. Don't Go Down the Mine Daddy. Linlithgow UK.

111. Shy and Retiring. Chester UK.

112. Allo, Allo. Brussels Belgium.

113. Have You Come Far. Heathrow UK.

114. Ouch. Alloa UK.

115. Choo Choo Train. Railways.

116. Russian Ballet. Motherwell UK.

117. Sky High. Tokyo Japan.

118. Idle Rich. JFK USA.

119. Forbidden City. Beijing China.

120. Press Button A. London UK.

121. I Kent his Faither. Denny UK.

122. Just Deserts. Phoenix Arizona USA.

123. Emporia. Kansa USA.

124. Great Wall of China. Beijing China.

125. Three Doors Up. Denny Scotland.

126. Camel Back. Phoenix Arizona USA.

127. I Ran and Ran. Iran.

128. Josi. Johannesburg RSA.

129. Ice Maiden. Iceland.

130. Oh, Lucky Jim. Castlecary UK.

131. Bananarama. Air Travel.

132. Silver Bird in Sky. Cairo Egypt.

133. Roll On, Roll Off. Iceland.

134. Big Olive, Wee Tam. Longcroft UK.

135. George. Castlecary UK.

136. Leith Walk. Edinburgh UK.

137. Diplomatic Service. Worldwide.

138. SCRUFC. Stirling UK.

139. Any Port in A Storm. South Africa.

140. Black Belt. Edinburgh UK.

141. Road Rage Ron. Dunblane UK.

142. In It for the Long Haul. Sao Paulo Brazil.

143. Kai Tak Heart Attack. Hong Kong China.

144. Iron Cross. Savoie France.

145. Do you Remember the 60's? Nostalgia.

146. Close to the Edge. Invercargill South Island New Zealand.

147. California Flakes, Fruits and Nuts. San Francisco USA.

148. Big Easy. New Orleans USA.

159. Cars, Cars and Mair Cars. UK.

160. David and Goliath. Auckland New Zealand.

161. Dan, Dave and Bud. USA and Germany.

162. The Runaway Train. Chicago USA.

163. Don't Rain on My Parade. San Francisco USA.

164. Where There's Smoke. Renfrew to Charlotte.

165. Hallo Sailor. Long Beach California.

166. Look Maw Nae Hauns. Heathrow London.

167. And Don't Come Back. La Guardia New York.

168. Kelly's Mountain. Sydney Nova Scotia.

169. States of Matter. The Great Lakes North America.

170. Hot Cuisine. Various Eateries.

171. Greased Lightning. Havana to Sydney.

172. City of Rain. Rasht Iran.

173. Voodoo You Think you are. Haiti West Indies.

174. C eh N eh D eh. Hudson's Bay Canada.

The Bit at the Beginning

The World Was My Oxter

William Shakespeare said oyster, Arthur Daley lobster, but I'm suggesting it's all too
often oxter. Since the end of the seventeenth century most good stories have started
with "once upon a time in a faraway land". The advantages of this opening being that
there are normally not too many people still around who would be capable of
disputing the tale even if they were disposed to do so. More recently I decided like
many others before me, many of whom inhabited the Fourth Estate, never to let the
facts get in the way of a good story. I firmly believe that I have been greatly
encouraged in this by my late father, Bill, who when he dedicated his first book
claimed in the introduction that it had been written in spite of his wife and family.
Maybe words run in the family as my youngest brother too was both a reporter and
subsequently a subeditor on several UK national daily papers before eventually also
becoming the Father of the Chapel of the NUJ in Scotland based in Glasgow. I forget
now whether his given middle name was "Hyperbole" or "Headline" but I recall some
of his fellow subeditors or others coming out with such epic pronouncements such as
"McArthur Flies Back to Front", "Foot Heads Arms Body", "Churchill Puts Anus on
the Cabinet", as well as " Safety Meeting Ends in Accident" and "Latest Statistics
Show That Teen Pregnancies Drop Off After 25".

Here are multiple examples of what I sincerely hope may be regarded as good stories
occasionally unencumbered by an excess of the aforementioned fact. All of these very
many anecdotes span more than eighty years in total but are definitely not in precise
chronological order. They also occur in over fifty countries but are also not listed in
alphabetical order either. Some of the countries mentioned have changed their names
since the events chronicled and so have most of the people in order to preserve their
anonymity. Possibly as a result, this book might be regarded as being like super glue
in that you may find it difficult to put down, but hopefully very much more enjoyable.
If nothing else it must highlight the differences between recent generations. My young
grandson is inserting emojis in WhatsApp at six years old. My son has to be surgically
removed from his Smartphone every night and I still read the Daily Mail newspaper.
Maybe my great grandson won't meet many people to interact with but will spend the
whole time in virtual reality. That is unlikely actually, because with a population now
over 7.5 billion globally expanding at 1% per annum there won't even be elbow room
to work a phone, or even fart so that no one will know who it was. Maybe it is a bit
like when my son says "Dad tell us again about when you were young and you had to
walk all the way across the room to change the TV channel" to which my reply is
"Well if old black and white TV technology baffles you then these modern devices
and apps must really soften your brain". Little does he realise, that in fact I used to
cross the room to change over the program on the dial of a big wooden radio from the
Home Service to the Light Program and back again just to hear Dick Barton Special
Agent every night at 6.45. Perhaps there is no need to feel sorry for me. As Del Boy
said "next year we will be millionaires my son" so the likelihood would seem to be
that I will be both posthumously rich and famous no doubt at all from the proceeds of
this very epic bestseller. What more could one want from life or indeed from death?

The following are a selection of anecdotes of personal experiences as I recall they might have happened, did happen or could have happened if I had not managed to get away and make my escape in good time.

Sun and Air

The role of the Chairman's son and heir and my very minor role in his eventual downfall played out over a number of years. For the record his downfall consisted of being handed millions of pounds when the company was eventually sold off. While engaging with this former boss in earnest conversation one day I eventually plucked up the temerity to ask him to consider an increase in my salary. His brow furrowed a bit in perplexity and he was obviously struggling to find an appropriate response. After a bit he brightened up perceptibly and then announced "Wait a minute, you may not actually get very much money but you do have all of the perks of extensive foreign travel". Well I have to say to you, to be absolutely fair to him, that he was half right. I did not really get much money! For a considerable time now, I have been trying very hard to figure out what some of the so-called perks of these international travels were in those days of old. Perhaps in fact, things are even worse today than they were earlier when journeys can even actually take longer and be more complicated than before, due to security issues. There seem to be many more and also very much bigger aircraft flying direct but to many fewer destinations even although they mostly have hugely increased range capabilities. This inevitably means that most passengers are fed into and out of hubs or should that be retail centers at both ends of the trip where they are forced to endure lengthy retail therapy between connections.

The problem was that being the Chairman's son his ideas of the perks of foreign travel and mine were always going to be looked at from a very different perspective. He travelled to places which he wanted to visit and I travelled to places where he or someone else wanted me to visit, although eventually the reins were held very much more loosely. Latterly I made a lot of my own decisions based on the successes that I enjoyed from my own hard work. Some of the destinations that I travelled to were places that I would happily return to many times and usually did although a few of them were countries or locations where one visit was one too many and some have even deteriorated since then. Today having travelled the equivalent of more than fifty times around the world by air and about the same by all other means of transport I have to confess that I disagree with Robert Louis Stevenson who once said that "It is better to travel hopefully than to arrive". This may once have possibly been the case for RLS travelling on the back of a donkey in the South of France but in my travels in tourist class on a Jumbo over mid-Atlantic I tended to view things from a very much different perspective. Maybe someone hit the nail on the head when they said that BOAC could stand for better on a camel.

I am not even completely sure that I agree with the American writer Mark Twain when he wrote "Travel is fatal to prejudice, bigotry, and narrow-mindedness, and many people need it sorely on these accounts". Maybe that's true or maybe it is not. It seems to me that travel can just as easily reinforce preconceptions and prejudices if not actually create them in the first place and many of today's travellers should not really be encouraged to inflict themselves on others around the globe. Perhaps this is why many people's first words in English are "Yankee go home". Still, travel can broaden the bum and narrow the mind or is it the other way around? I forget now.

To paraphrase Benjamin Franklin however "Do something worth writing about then write so that it is interesting to read about". While I did not set out to do that exactly it has sometimes seemed that it was a bit like dialing a wrong number on the telephone. You meet some interesting people and situations quite unexpectedly. I am sure that I have not written all that I remember and I am certain that I have not remembered all that I have written. Neither however have I yet completely stopped all of my writing, remembering or doing. I don't ever plan to get to the stage in my life when I come to the point of regarding my work as a lot less fun and fun as a lot more work than it is.

It's all Greek to Me

It's all Greek to me as Shakespeare claims Julius Caesar once said in Ancient Rome.

Greece was very much in the former category of happy destinations for me and for several happy ouzo and pistachio fueled years I had an office in Athens with its own private accommodation which I used as well as many different hotels when travelling in and around the Levant. My "pied a terre" was in Sikelias Street just off Kallirois Avenue, next to Koudouriti Square. The flat was located only two doors away from one of my very large customers Scalisteri and just a short stone's throw away from the Fix Hellas Brewery on the main road from Athens to Piraeus. During one early visit after the new office was opened, I was accompanied by my boss the chairman's son and heir, who wanted to meet the staff. Milto, the elderly patrician local manager decided to take the opportunity to ask if the company would consider putting a small air conditioner into the office, as he claimed absolutely rightly, that sometimes the temperatures reached 50 degrees centigrade in the noonday summer sun. My boss John was either disbelieving of this, or more likely trying to figure out the cost of supplying and fitting the new equipment and how much profit from how many sales would be needed to cover this, in his view, frivolous expense. It was at this point that he chose to adopt an air of informality and swung one leg up and sat on the edge of the manager's large desk. Unnoticed by him it had a thick stainless-steel metal strip running around its entire top surface perimeter. The sun had been beating down strongly all morning through the large south facing French windows which opened onto the small balcony. I reckon that it took John much less than a second to leap into the air from the desk with an agonized look on his face and not much longer to sign the requisition for the air conditioner. After that little diversion while enquiring after John's health we all trooped downstairs for a Greek coffee in the local taverna while he got some Savlon ointment for his rosy cheeks in the next door Farmacia. Oddly enough he elected to drink his coffee standing up and with a slightly pained look.

It was not John's fault that he had a different perspective from me and I believe that it largely arose from him having an ancestor who in Scotland in 1790 had started the ball rolling in business so that by 1965 most of the straining and sweating had already been done. I can't in all honesty say that the family did not also work hard in their own way over these years. John and his family however were reaping the many benefits that had accrued not only from their investment over nearly two hundred year's but also from "other bugger's efforts". This was not the only family, private or public company that I ever worked for in my long career but it did seem to start me off and to set a pattern for the globetrotting that began in the sixties and lasted until I eventually semi-retired in the second decade of the twenty first century.

Having worked for and with, several UK and foreign companies all over the world while always being domiciled in the UK it was interesting to observe the cultural customs and many differences of so many varied nationalities. It was quite refreshing and in fact also often reassuring to return to the UK more or less in one piece and with yet another local souvenir. At that time of my life I firmly believed that many British people seemed to complain nearly all the time about almost everything. I also firmly believed that in contrast to most of the rest of the world they had relatively little basis for complaint. In those days the first question that you had to ask on arriving at a new destination was if it was safe to drink the water assuming of course that you had first survived the corrupt customs officials, the horde of squabbling airport porters and the license unencumbered taxi drivers to even reach the often unstarred foreign hotel at your chosen destination. The irony was of course that very many of the local people that I met around the world were extremely decent, friendly, helpful people and only those who had floated or fought their way to the top were truly awful obnoxious shits until they were replaced by someone else who it seemed were inevitably even worse.

Bondi or Bust

Autumn came early and winter stayed very late in 1947. In October of each year at that time thousands of older school children were encouraged to volunteer for two weeks "holiday" to go "Tattie Howking" although they did not actually dig out the potatoes as these were always excavated more efficiently by mechanical diggers. The kids just followed along picking up the loose spuds and filling them into baskets prior to then dumping them in larger farm trailers. A couple of times after dark at about five o' clock in the afternoon I went into the fields and rescued a few potatoes that had been overlooked. Since they were cold and wet and I was only seven I only managed a very few which I carried home in the turned up, bottom of my soggy pullover. Once I stumbled across a small turnip which I laid claim to even although it was as hard as a mahogany bowling ball with no finger grips. I seem to recall that it took about three days to thaw out and another three to cook. Winter then seamlessly followed on in November 1947 and was the worst for two hundred years or so I have been told, with snow falling somewhere in the UK for up a period of 55 consecutive days and often reaching a depth of over two meters in some places. With transport, fuel and food supplies disrupted and ice on the inside of the windows every morning Scotland was not a fun place to be. It was so bad that we had no small pieces of coal, no carrots and no scarf to spare for the head of our giant snowman and believe me it is hell when the snow is up over the top of your wellies and the wet tops are smacking your calves making both legs raw. When spring eventually sprung in April 1948 my younger brother and I decided there must be better places to live than central Scotland and were especially interested by the stories of Australia told by our uncle who had been in the Royal Navy for the duration the war. We reckoned that if we traveled on our tricycle with me pedaling and with him standing on the back axle it should be doable although if we came to a hill he might have to get off and walk. We kept these plans quiet from our youngest brother because we were not sure that we could fit him onto the trike as well, and also from our parents who might possibly have raised obstacles as adults often do in these cases. We had decided to emigrate on a Tuesday morning but during the Monday night we were awakened from bed by screams of panic and somebody loudly shouting "Fire, Fire". Our neighbor who had been doing her weekly laundry in the washing house, which was built onto the side of our house had left clothes to dry overnight on a wooden rack and these had caught alight from the heat radiating out of the open fire box. The fire was discovered before it set the whole washing house alight but the Tuesday morning dawn revealed a major problem. Our tricycle was severely damaged by both fire and water and it was definitely not going to provide transport for anyone ever again. Based on something that we had vaguely heard on our utility wooden wartime radio we soon came up with Plan B which involved digging a hole in the garden and reaching Australia by that route. This plan had the added attraction in that it was one in which our younger brother then aged about four could play a full part as we made sure that he even had his own shovel. After a few days however this plan had palled somewhat as the hole had only slowly progressed to a depth of about a foot and enthusiasm definitely waned with what even we could see was turning out to be a lengthy project. It might even need more than three shovelers to complete. On the plus side we did have regular meal breaks for porridge and soup and mince rather than a very meagre supply of jeely pieces which we had planned to sustain us when eaten while "en route" while travelling on the back of the soon to be severely fire damaged trike. Bugger it, I thought, Australia can wait a bit and apparently it did so with equanimity until I made several visits later in life using much more convenient and more efficient modes of travel than the old original ill-fated three-wheeler and the vertical shaft options. Both of these options had very soon proved so very problematical even to three ambitious young kids who however were all unfortunately under ten years old and under resourced at the time.

The Historic Triangle

Landing and disembarking in Newark Liberty International Airport in New Jersey USA from a United DC 10 flight from Manchester on a Saturday afternoon was both uneventful and a lengthy procedure. Our plane was only one of a number of "heavies" from Europe that landed around the same time and as a result there were big queues at immigration which slowly snaked forward for processing. Our luggage was checked through to our final destination but we still had to collect it and trundle it through US customs which helped reduce the time hanging around in what is claimed to be the oldest airport in the United States and which to be honest for the most part did look its considerable age. Sadly, it still does not seem to get many more entirely favourable reviews even today. Up in the main terminal concourse we headed for a cold beer and after settling on stools outside the tavern we looked out of the huge, glass, floor to ceiling windows, over the apron. "Look over there" I said to my wife indicating the view to the Northeast. "Oh yes" she said "it's IKEA". The name IKEA I thought is actually derived from two Swedish words Ika meaning Sunday and Keya meaning flipping ruined. Well, I sensed then that it was going to be another one of these days. "No" I said "if you look past IKEA you will see in the distance the Statue of Liberty and beyond that the downtown Manhattan skyline with the twin towers of the World Trade Centre" which at that time were still standing just east of the Westside Highway not far from Broadway and Wall Street.

After our short stopover we caught our connecting flight to Richmond Virginia and when half way there I pointed out that we were overflying part of Washington DC and that while we were unlikely to see another branch of IKEA we might just possibly catch a glimpse of the White House or even maybe the Pentagon on the starboard side of the aircraft. It continued to remain really bright and clear with no cloud cover to obscure them as we overflew the city in late afternoon on our way to our ultimate destination and we did catch a glimpse of both world famous, Washington landmarks.

Fortunately for me as the driver I found that Richmond airport was ideally situated close to Interstate 64 on the east of the city. It only took us half an hour to rent our Ford Granada which some described as "Fords most successful failure" although to me it was just a bigger posher version of what I drove at home. Then we were on our way to Williamsburg VA with the air conditioning full on to escape what was to my sensitive nose the strong smell of tobacco from the surrounding countryside which seemed to permeate everything on that warm summer's evening. Arriving at the Williamsburg Woodland Inn we checked in at reception and were shown to our suite located on the second floor of a large two storey log cabin type building set deep in the surrounding woods. Shortly afterwards to try and offset our jetlag we wandered down to the main cafeteria style dining room for a light supper of cold beer and warm pretzels and bumped into the company Chairman and some of our other colleagues. Paul warmly welcomed us to the USA and asked if our accommodation was OK to which my wife replied that it was, but that it reminded her strongly of the Bar Wood. Fortunately, this remark passed over the Chairman's head as he was not aware that the Bar Wood was a small Scottish weekend scout camp site with a wooden hut for when it rained. In the succeeding week the company wide symposium and social gatherings which had been organised in private rooms with a huge veranda and floor to ceiling windows overlooking the forest went well. We still had much free time however to explore the area located inside what has become known as "The Historic Triangle".

Jamestown was the first permanent English settlement in North America after two earlier short lived, failed attempts (in Roanoke and Popham) prior to1607 which were said to be due to inclement weather and unfriendly locals. One of the leaders of the later third successful Jamestown expedition, Captain John Smith eventually returned to England with his Indian wife Pocahontas. She is in fact today buried in St Marys Churchyard in Rotherhithe. This is across the very narrow cobbled street from the Mayflower pub which had its own pier and where the Pilgrims are alleged to have originally set sail from in 1606. The pub still does a nice traditional fish supper but at contemporary twenty first century price as bartering for beads has gone out of fashion.

Williamsburg was founded much later in 1632 as a fortified settlement between the James and York rivers and is a curious mixture of historic old buildings and a Disney theme park. It served as the capital of the colony until 1780 when the many American colonists in their revolutionary war backed by a French fleet kicked the English out of the New World at nearby Yorktown. Residents of historic Williamsburg still dress in period costume, live in replica buildings and eat chicken straight off of the bone so I assume that neither IKEA nor Marks and Spencer ever made it to North Virginia although KFC obviously did. To me it is a bit weird to be greeted in the street by someone dressed as Samuel Pepys but talking Olde English like Yogi Bear. It's just as equally odd to be served in a candle lit restaurant by a waitress looking like Nell Gwynne whom Pepys referred to as "pretty witty Nell" and who on hearing my accent enquired as to whether "anything was worn under the kilt". I was immediately able to fully reassure her that luckily everything under the kilt was in perfect working order. She might well have been pretty in a good light and even have been called Nell, but in her case, I am convinced that the wit was remarkably well concealed under her large bonnet.

One of the interests for me was to see the glassworks at Jamestown which was the first industrial activity that took place in the new world. The original furnaces were found and excavated in 1948 and production started again on tourist items like wine decanters and glasses but they definitely cheated because the new furnaces are fired by gas rather than by wood as they were originally since this would have been much too difficult for them to replicate. We also went on board replicas of the pilgrim ships which if built to scale seemed to me to be tiny vessels to have sailed over 3000 miles. I thought to compare these with modern US warships and headed down Interstate 64 to Newport News which is a large city at the end of the peninsula between the James and York rivers with big naval and other military bases. I had read about the ten most interesting things to do and see in town but immediately on getting off the freeway I decided the top three things for me to do were to lock the doors, not stop at traffic lights and get the hell out as fast as possible to see if I could escape again still in one piece. I was obviously on the wrong side of the tracks even although I didn't see any but maybe someone stole them. The brevity of my visit probably means that I have a biased view of the town and as a result am being grossly unfair but I did not stop to chat to any of the people sitting on the kerbs watching me drive by. At first, I thought that it was better in the old days when gangs might have shot at you before strolling off but in West Side Story at least they used to dance with each other first. My second thought was that maybe the dancing wasn't such a good idea either. It seemed that in the good old days whenever they were, Americans had Johnny Cash, Steve Jobs and Bob Hope. Sadly, I have to say that from the appearance of most of the locals, few of them seemed to have cash, jobs or even very much hope as far as I could see. I soon surmised that this must have been the result of the US government reassessing its new defence needs, downsizing its manpower requirements and moving some of its bigger military bases around the country to new locations or maybe even new countries as new and often very different threats were perceived to be arising as time progressed.

You're Nicked

I am told that not every-one who visits Beirut is arrested in Beirut. Ok, it was only for forty-five minutes or so each time, not like Anderson, McCarthy and Waite, who were detained without trial for very lengthy periods but on one occasion it was twice in the same weekend for god's sake and very nearly a third as my chauffeur driven car very narrowly avoided a traffic accident. This qualifies Lebanon so far as I am concerned as having the unique distinction of being the only country in the world which has ever requested me to leave and never return. To be honest my reaction at that time was that I would find no difficulty whatsoever in complying with their request especially since MEA had caused me to break a tooth by not taking the stone out of a black olive in my salad Nicoise when I flew in to the Paris of the Levant. What's wrong with these people I wondered apart from lacking in my well known honed, dry sense of humour.

The first time it happened was when I had been coming back down into the capital from the Bekaa Valley in a car with three friends. We had been at a good restaurant in the mountains and drink had been taken. We were now returning to Beirut late on a Friday night or more accurately early on Saturday morning after copious quantities of the local red wine had been imbibed along with a sampling of the local haute cuisine. As we came into the northern suburbs of the town, on the Rue de Damas where it crosses the Fleuve de Beyrouth near Furn El Chebeck we were stopped by a Lebanese army patrol that obviously mistook us for Syrian Hamas infiltrators. The three other Lebanese in the car with me were quite subdued, since they understood that the army patrol's cocked weapons meant that they were serious. I on the other hand, was not too bothered. I could not speak Arabic and anyway I was Scottish, which must surely confer immunity if not immortality on me since I had found out that the national dish of Lebanon was Haggis, although they seemed to have another peculiar name for it.

The officer in charge of the patrol demanded to see all of our papers and I happily told him that coming from a civilised country I did not carry my passport with me at all times. Fortunately, he did not understand me and my Lebanese hosts gave him a much more diplomatic answer along the lines that I was so terribly sorry but that I had left my passport in my luggage in my hotel in the city. The officer, not to be deflected strode over to a nearby house, banged on the door until the owner appeared and sent his signals sergeant into the house and up onto the flat roof. There he hooked his field telephone into the houses phone line and cranked the handset. The military operator to whom he spoke eventually patched him through to the Night Duty Manager in the Holiday Inn in Beirut who confirmed that yes, they did have a guest with the same name as me and no, the guest was not in his room. The officer reflected and decided that on the balance of probability, I was indeed who I claimed to be. He then advised me via my interpreters to get back to the hotel and into bed toute suite and the touter the sweeter. He obviously thought that all honest burghers should have been in bed in any case at that time in the morning and only one of the members of one of the many warring factions or clans would be entering Beirut from the direction of Damascus.

A few short months later in October 1975 the Holiday Inn was downgraded to have extra air conditioning fitted, courtesy of a large number of 88 mm cannon shells from the Hezbollah artillery and ordinance from the other dozen or so local splinter groups. It was the very tallest white building around on a hilltop near the St George and the Phoenicia Intercontinental Hotels. It was on the coastal hillside overlooking the main Lebanese Christian stronghold to the west of the "Green Line", so it was difficult to miss even when no one was actually aiming directly at it. This collateral damage is said to have pissed off the customers and staff over about a period of more than six months. A number of them were occasionally also taken hostage for short periods in between rocket, mortar fire, sniping and vandalism. It seemed to me that being taken hostage at least removed them from the indiscriminate line of fire but neither option was ideal and certainly not included in the room rates nor in my Lebanese itinerary on any of my several visits to the Paris of the middle east. When his business boomed my friend, Jack moved his offices from the dockside in the port area up into a new multi storey office block in the south east of the city. He was not amused when one of the militias commandeered it because of the wide field of fire from the roof. "C'est la guerre." But that's been the fate of honest burghers in Beirut for a very long time.

Not Again

After a working Saturday, a quiet night in my hotel room watching television with Taggart dubbed into Italian and an early morning call on Sunday, I checked out of the Holiday Inn and was picked up by a colleague for the short but often exciting drive to the airport. This was always a difficult time for me, since local protocol was that if you sat in the front passenger seat and the driver was Arabic he thought that you fancied him whereas if you sat in the back seat and the driver was Christian then he decided that you didn't. It was too complicated to ask them which school they had gone to even if they had all spoken English (or French). To hell with it I thought. I sat in the back, as in my opinion it was better to cause offence than to certainly receive an unwanted offer and then to cause even more offence than the other alternative in the first place.

On the way to the airport we headed south towards Israel on the Saida road, however, the car was almost involved in two crashes, the first on the Corniche and the second one just outside the airport gates, so maybe the driver was upset by my choice of seat.

After fighting my way through the surprisingly large number of passengers and the even larger number of relatives, in the departure hall I side stepped the Airport Tax Visa Desk and went straight to the Middle East Airlines check-in desk. The agent there took my bag but explained that she could not check me in, because, although my ticket was valid, my passport did not have an airport tax visa stamp. Condescendingly, I told her to go ahead and issue my boarding card while I carefully explained the very complex Lebanese immigration regulations to her or at least my interpretation of them

Paragraph four subsection three (a) said that British visitors in transit through the Lebanon, within a seventy-two-hour period did not need to obtain and pay for an exit visa stamp. She smiled sadly and shook her head, as she gave me back all my several documents including seat assignment and luggage claim tags and I wheeled round and headed for the next hurdle at immigration control thinking that I had triumphed and achieved success by sheer force of logic. When I then reached the immigration desk however after a short wait in the queue, the officer flicked through my documents then stopped, and went back to my passport, which he examined more closely. He then curtly informed me that I should not be checked in. I did not have an exit visa stamp and that I should return to the visa desk and purchase a valid exit stamp immediately. I patiently explained to him like an erring child that I had arrived in his delightful country on the previous Friday at noon and that therefore since I was technically in transit, I did not need the visa stamp.

After another close examination of the passport he told me that the entry stamp was smudged and that as a result he could not read the time or date of my arrival and he therefore insisted that money should change hands although the precise nature of the transaction was not spelled out in any detail. I pointed out to him, that it had not been me, but one of his colleagues that had stamped the passport on entry and that it was their responsibility not mine, to ensure that the stamps were both legible and readable. It was somewhere round about then that he appeared to lose interest and signalled for two, armed security guards who came over and marched me away into a grimy little room such as you might expect to find in the Lubyanka in Moscow or in HMRC Centre One tax offices at East Kilbride near Glasgow, although I have never actually been inside the Lubyanka. When the interrogation officer eventually arrived, it did cross my mind to ask him what the airport visa service and an ostrich had in common and then if he were unable to answer, to suggest that it might be that they could both stick their bills up their arse. After looking at his face I thought better of my opening remark and remained silent. Sometime later, however having engaged the officer in earnest discussion on the finer points of Lebanese law which he assured me was based on the Napoleonic Code and the legibility of worn rubber stamps, which was based on official laziness, the senior security officer appeared to tire visibly. He sighed and said, "Your plane leaves in fifteen minutes, make sure that you are on it when it goes". I too had wearied of the fun and my reply was along the lines of "don't worry on that score" as I galloped out to the boarding gate and hurled myself through the ready to be closed front door for the Trident flight to Heathrow. On board I consoled myself later with the thought that although not impressed with the system I had at least refrained from ordering a prolonged mortar attack of the airport, as others had regularly done when their right to be in the country at all was questioned by the multiple local bureaucrats, factions, militias and clans who seemed to abound in the region. Sadly, I do not believe that the situation has even improved with time and the people of the region are beset with new problems on top of the original ones which are currently compounding the misery for everyone to the benefit of absolutely none.

Nanotechnology – Don't Let the Bastards Grind you Down

Today one of the buzz words is Nanotechnology which is used extensively mainly by people who have no idea what it means but which the rest of us of course know means manipulating matter on an atomic, molecular or supramolecular scale. Since a single nanometre is about a billionth of a meter in diameter you won't have seen many of them around unless your eyesight is a lot better than mine You could of course always debate as to how many you could get on the head of pin just like people used to argue about angels in the good old days. You can safely assume however that when we talk Nanotechnology that we are definitely talking extremely tiny particles in a fine dust.

Ball mills on the other hand can be enormous or can be small although every one of them is incredibly noisy. There are few better ways to grind powders very fine if that is what you need to do without resorting to the enormous effort needed to do it in a pestle and mortar. The horizontal cylindrical mill is half filled with coarse powder and it rotates on rollers at fairly high speed. Inside the mill there is also a selection of hardened ceramic balls which pulverise the powder until it is eventually reduced to extremely fine dust. The balls themselves are often almost pure Corundum and are of a similar composition to precious stones like rubies. In fact, these balls can be almost as expensive as gemstones are. Since they are extremely hard however they usually manage to survive for an extremely long period of time in operation and are cost effective as they seldom need replaced during the normal course of their working life.

Kenny was a new start in the lab and had been hired partly because his father was a senior manager in the mine attached to the plant. He was a big lad standing six feet in his stocking feet and he was still only sixteen years old. He was very keen and always went the extra mile to impress the boss with his energy and enthusiasm if not always his grasp of what was needed. On this occasion Charles had instructed Kenny to grind a batch of raw clay to very fine powder for some research work that was just about to commence in the development lab. As the day went on, Charles phoned young Kenny several times to see how the job was progressing. "Not quite finished yet" was the answer even after several hours of the ball mills exceptionally hard noisy operation. Slightly puzzled at how long the job was taking, Charles went back at half past four to see what progress Kenny had really made. Before he even went through the door however he knew immediately that something was badly wrong as the rumble of the ball mill had been replaced by the sharp crack of a heavy hammer. About then a look of horror spread slowly over his face. As Charles bounded into the pilot plant there was Kenny on the floor, on his hands and knees, with a lump hammer in his hand smashing the remains of all the expensive grinding balls to small pieces on a hardened steel plate. "Don't worry boss," he said grinning "I will very definitely have the job finished by five," confirmed Kenny cheerfully as he reduced the last remaining few thousand pounds worth of very expensive grinding media to extremely small pieces before the dumbstruck Charles horrified eyes.

Charlie's face was a picture, in fact it was a horror movie as his brain raced and he tried to figure out what to say and do. It was clear that he very dearly wanted to mix business with pleasure and fire Kenny. A little voice in his head however was clearly obviously reminding him that blaming a giant teenager with a hammer in his hand for the situation that had arisen might not be his best move but just might be his last one. He also remembered that Kenny's dad was a senior manager which was the clincher. Charlie or "OIL our illustrious leader" as Kenny and the other lads usually referred to him decided to go to his office shut the blinds and sit in the darkened room for a short spell to try and calm down and compose himself before attempting to drive home. Tomorrow was another day and he could dream up some other essential task for Ken and one which hopefully would not entail anything expensive, cerebral or dangerously risky like looking for a possible gas leak in the laboratory furnace with a lighted taper.

Boom, Boom- A Load of Balls

Bill worked at Carron Company near the town of Falkirk for a few years in the 50's. Well actually this was is not an entirely true and precise reflection of the situation. He was employed for a time as an apprentice in the large drawing office at the old Carron

Company but did his best, quite successfully it seemed to avoid actual work wherever and whenever it was possible to do so. He claimed that he pretended to work because they pretended to pay him. He did have one unique qualification however and one that definitely played in his favour for working in the drawing office in that usually he and others could read his own handwriting. Medicine's loss was Draughting's gain or so it seemed. He also had an ear just ready made to hold a pencil rather than a Woodbine.

Carron's blast furnaces dominated the Falkirk skyline for two centuries ever since late 1760 and in its heyday the company employed over two thousand people. Carron was the company, whose foundry, had many years before, manufactured Carronades, the guns which were used by the English in their ships against the French at Trafalgar. The remains of these guns are still to be found worldwide usually after having been salvaged from some ship or fort. The original pirates of the Caribbean used them in frequent battles with the British navy so it was usually just a question of who had the biggest or the most balls. As you may know if you have ever visited one of the many Disney sites or the Treasure Island Hotel on the strip at Las Vegas there are still a few on display in sunny climates. The company was even visited by Benjamin Franklin who worked with them on the design of the Franklin or Philadelphia heating stove. On one occasion it was also visited by Robert Burns who when he was refused access and while in a fit of pique scratched a poem on the window of a local pub as of course literate vandals are wont to do.

We cam na here to view your works
In hopes to be mair wise,
But only, lest we gang to Hell,
It may be nae surprise;
But when we tirl'd at your door,
Your porter dought na hear us;
Sae may, should we to Hell's yetts come,
Your billy Satan sair us.

To which a spokesman for the company replied

If you came here to view our works
You should have been more civil
Than to give a fictitious name,
In hopes to cheat the devil,
Six days a week to you and all,
We think it very well;
The other if you go to church,
May keep you out of hell.

The company are also credited with manufacturing many of the original red painted telephone boxes and post boxes most of which are now being scrapped due to smart phones, emails and other developments of the digital world which are thrust upon us.

In one of the Carron buildings there was an all steel floor section for test assemblies. On one occasion Bill happened to be up in a crane gantry as a foreman went through the shop. Bill decided it would be fun to drop a large steel cannonball which he just happened to have with him on the steel floor, a short distance behind the foreman.

This largely accounts for the fact that foremen in Carron Company, for many years wore not only bowler hats, but also brown trousers. Bill left Carron works somewhat hurriedly shortly afterwards and as we all know has never looked back. The foreman however even to the day he retired tended to look back over his shoulder rather a lot.

Nile Be Seeing You - Walking the Plank

I am one of these few Scotsmen who don't really drink Whisky or so I claim as I normally prefer Vodka and Windolene. This does not actually help prevent the same terrible hangovers the following morning but it does keep your eyes bright and shiny.

Gamal didn't drink much of anything either, but he was beside himself with absolute happiness. Jimmy and I had just clinched an enormous order after many months of hard negotiations. Being our agent, Gamal was in for ten per cent of the loot and was ecstatic at the prospect. So much so that he insisted on taking us both onto a famous Nile barge the Omar Khayyam for dinner. This barge was a more or less a floating night club moored to the river bank by ropes fore and aft but the rickety gangplank did not inspire much confidence as it creaked and flexed when we walked up onto the main deck. The sounds of the band wafted up the stairs and out through the wide entry hatchway as we boarded. I remember thinking that main difference between the Omar Khayyam Nile barge and the SS Titanic was probably that the Titanic almost certainly had a better band both from the point of view of dress and musical accomplishment.

As soon as we reached the table in the restaurant on the main deck Gamal ordered a large scotch - in fact a litre of Black Label and three glasses. I protested that I would prefer something else, but he would not listen and went on and on, about toasting our incredible success in "our" national drink. In the end I gave in and agreed to drink a scotch for every scotch he drank and so did Jimmy who was also a fellow Scot. This appeared to make Gamal happy and he set about lowering the boats stock of whisky.

Personally, I have always preferred a full bottle in front of me but Gamal who I guess did not drink soon began to act and sound as if he had had a full-frontal lobotomy. At the end of the meal, Gamal's son turned up "just like that" wearing a red Fez and ran us back to our hotel in his father's new Mercedes before going back for his father who was filling in his time ogling the belly dancer. The last thing mumbled to me was "see you at seven, when I will pick you up to go to the station, for the train to Alexandria."

The following morning which was a Sunday, Gamal did not turn up at seven, or at eight but much later his son arrived and informed me that the trip had been postponed. At first I thought that this was for logistical or business reasons as I had heard that a freight train from Alexandria had been derailed blocking the line After some probing however his son admitted to me that when he had gone back for his father at the night club the previous night he had encountered a slight problem. On leaving Gamal had staggered down the gangplank of the barge, stumbled and fallen into the Nile. It had taken his son and several waiters to rescue him from the water and drag him up the embankment to his new Mercedes with white leather upholstery. By the time they got Gamal home it was difficult to tell which was in worse condition Gamal or the car. The car however appeared to have responded better to treatment by soap and water.

With the day off I was forced to seek a bit of Culture and not fancying the Museum of Antiquities or anything else in central Cairo I headed southwest down El Ahram street for Giza passing the Mena Hotel which Winston Churchill stayed at in 1943 and still features the Churchill Suite with a balcony overlooking some of the many pyramids. Equal or better is the adjacent Montgomery Suite and although it was said to have been occupied by Kings and Queens, I don't think Monty actually stayed there as he was generally otherwise engaged battling the Axis. Just south of there again I spent some time wandering round the Sphinx which is a huge limestone statue of a number of mythical creatures combined together and which is supposed to be the guardian of the Pyramid of Khufu although today it looks more ragged than rugged. It therefore fits into the landscape extremely well as of course nearly all of the adjacent pyramids which have largely lost their outer limestone covering could also do with renovation. Fortunately, none of my crew had been there since after a few Luxor Special Gold Lagers had been necked I am convinced that out of professional pride as bricklayers they could well have set about doing a bit of restoration themselves. That could well have impacted Anglo Egyptian relations and ruined the tourist trade for millennia.

The Man from Del Monte – I Say Yes

The white and blue, Eastern Airlines DC9 rolled to a halt and the pilot quickly shut down the twin, rear mounted Pratt and Whitney jet engines. After a couple of minutes as the whine of the engines subsided some local ground crew pulled a set of rickety steps out from besides the little terminal building and wheeled it over to the aircraft so that the plane's doors could be opened and the few passengers scheduled to disembark at that destination could collect their hand luggage and deplane. A blast of hot humid air rising off the concrete hit me along with the smell of aviation fuel which was being wafted on the gentle breeze of an onshore wind. As Caribbean islands go, the first impressions of Port Au Prince Haiti were not spectacular in any respects at all. The only possible way in which they might have been described as spectacular arose from the sight of several large men in very dark sunglasses wearing ill-fitting off - white suits. These were baggy enough to hide any concealed weapons that they were most certainly carrying. Bienvenu a' Port Au prince Haiti I thought anticipating nothing but hassle from them

Standing next to the foot of the steps were some airline employees, and another rather more distinguished looking gentleman in blue slacks, crisp white shirt with blue and white striped tie. "Never mind the Ton Ton Macoute," he said indicating the large ugly men. "Welcome to Haiti. My name is Duvall". I was definitely pleased but also puzzled. How had the businessman whom I had come meet on the island to interview as a potential agent managed to get right to the steps of the aircraft and also recognise me. He laughed and escorted me through immigration and customs with hardly a pause as we were nodded swiftly through whatever the formalities were. I noted that the less privileged few passengers who had also got off the plane stood and sweated in line. "Don't worry, it's not Voodoo" he said, "it's just that I am the Eastern Airlines agent in Haiti and have privileges of access airside that few others on the island have.

Outside the ramshackle old terminal, we were ushered into a large chauffeur driven air-conditioned Ford limousine. As we rolled sedately into town, avoiding most of the potholes and all of the chickens and goats running about he soon noted my admiring approval of the car and said "Yes not bad but I do represent Avis car rentals in Haiti so obviously I get the first choice of all the vehicles they currently have on the island"

On reaching the Plaza Hotel downtown on the Place de Jean Jaques Dessianes, I was quickly processed through reception and before long I ushered into one of the better rooms, such as it was, facing out onto the square in front of the presidential palace. It was a few hundred metres from the Gothic Gingerbread mansion of the old Olofsson Hotel where Graham Greene hung out and which was used as the basis of the Trianon hotel in The Comedians. It transpired quite by coincidence that Duvall represented an American hotel chain in Haiti which was why I got premium accommodation. We did not dine in the hotel but went back to his apartment and sat on his balcony watching the sun go down and sipping chilled Champagne from crystal glasses as it transpired, he represented Moet et Chandon in Haiti. The claret with the main course was superb and after dinner we had a couple of large Cognacs courtesy of Martell whom he also represented in Haiti. When I declined the offer of a third large cognac lest I suffered a hangover which would interfere with our business discussions next day he laughed and assured me solicitously "don't worry I currently represent Alka Seltzer in Haiti".

I pretty much decided there and then this was the agent for me. "Tomorrow" I told him as I staggered out of his house to the car "you'll represent us in Haiti and though it might not impress people as much some of your other prestigious clients they should be pleased if they ever need bricks for a barbecue built in their back yards".

Country Roads

I liked the Southwest with its mixture of mountains, desert and coast, with its clear air, high temperatures and low humidity, as it was on at least most days during the year. This was still big gold and copper mining country, while not so long ago it had even, very much been Indian country and still had a very large Apache reservation only a few miles to the South of Phoenix Arizona. We all made an early start to get across most of the desert and into the mountains before it got too hot. We drove more than 100 miles south from Phoenix, through Apache Junction and up past the Lost Dutchman Gold mine to Inspiration Copper Arizona. After concluding our business, we returned down from the plant in the afternoon heading for the Copper Mountain Motel in Superior where we were booked in that evening. It had been such a good day that we decided to make a little detour however and stop for a meal on the way back. We pulled into a tiny town which for some reason was called Top of the World on Route 60 perhaps because that was also the name of the trading post located there. We drew past a few of the shacks to park in the shade between the little Post Office and the Crystal Palace Saloon. There were very few people in the saloon when we turned up and although we did not burst through the batwing doors conversation seemed to stop when we three strangers blew into town. We gave all the locals perched in the bar a friendly nod and went straight through into the back room, where a trestle table and some benches, formed the restaurant area. We decided to have steak and baked potato with salad mainly because that was all there was on the menu. To be honest they did not actually have a menu although we took the bartenders word for it that if they did have a menu then those "choices "would be what would definitely be on it every day. For starters we had chilled Coors beer in ice cold pitchers and in frosted pint glasses. The steak was both enormous and a great T bone which well done and was served on big enamel plates. I did wonder however how they got salad or even potatoes on top of a mountain in the middle of a desert area. Maybe they had found the joys of hydroponics or maybe somebody had a pickup and drove to the market.

After the meal we paid in greenbacks and went back through to the bar for a few more Coors. Over in the corner was a very old-fashioned jukebox with its lights twinkling merrily away. While Tony got the drinks in, Mel and I gave the juke box the once over, whereupon we discovered Take Me Home Country Roads, the new John Denver record that we had been hearing on the radio all day, was one of the few selections. This was our first choice to play but it seemed to make Tony's feet itchy so that when we put it on Tony wandered over and asked one of the girls sitting at the bar for a dance. When I say asked her for a dance, I really mean dropped first on one knee and quoted the first line of Shakespeare's 18th Sonnet "Shall I compare thee to a summer's day" and then asked her for a dance. She was quite astonished at this since she may not have studied a lot of Shakespeare at school in Arizona and so surprised by Tony's Yorkshire accent that she agreed. After a bit of Fred and Ginger the record then ended whereupon Tony escorted her back to her seat with another theatrical flourish. When we put another record on, Tony who at five foot six had probably filled both legs with lager since his head was empty decided to try the same stunt once more. This time however the large cowboy sitting on the stool next to the young lady eased himself onto his feet. He must have been over seven feet tall in his boots and Stetson so Tony was a good eighteen inches shorter. I am not saying that Tony was short only that if it had started to rain, he would be one of the last people to know. The huge man asked Tony where he was from and Tony thinking that he had made a new friend smiled broadly and told him "Pennsylvania" since that was where the company was that he worked from. The unexpected reply to that however was that the giant announced in a calm soft voice that he firmly believed that people from Pennsylvania were mostly "a bunch of shit from the south end of a donkey heading north". Tony considered this very seriously for quite a few seconds as he looked up at the big man before gravely announcing "do you know I think that you may very well be right" prior to making his way hurriedly for the door. Mel and I fell about laughing so hard we almost spilled our Coors. We made sure we bought the big man and his partner a drink before we too left for the drive to the hotel chauffeured by our designated driver who amongst the four of us was maybe the only who knew that in Arizona we should drive on the right.

Antonine's Wall

I was born in Falkirk just about a kilometre south of Antonine's Wall on the civilised side within the Holy Roman Empire. I spent the first forty years of my life living five kilometres to the north on the uncivilised side of wall. Not that it shows as I spent so much of that time travelling around the globe having the rough edges smoothed off.

Antonine's wall runs for a total distance of about 40 miles from Carriden, near the port of Grangemouth on the River Forth to Old Kilpatrick near Dumbarton on the Clyde. It was built an average of three metres high over a period of twelve years by Roman subcontractors or slaves as they were more usually referred to. It was a constant source of artefacts such as large forged Roman iron nails like those which might have been used at the crucifixion, as well as lots of coins and weapons. I must be one of the few people who have actually not only been on top of the wall but also underneath the wall as I was involved for a year in sampling and examining in some detail, clays from a shallow drift mine in Bonnybridge which passed directly below it.

After work on the way home at night I used to change busses at the Bonnybridge Toll. This was an education in itself. People thought that the Romans had passed through Bonnybridge in 55BC, built a wall and a fort, (at Castlecary), and that not much had happened since. They were wrong. Bonnybridge may have seemed serene like a swan on the water but under the surface it was paddling very hard. This could be seen as a very different picture around the British Legion Hall, Harris's Cinema, the Cornhill Bar at closing time on a Friday and especially also around the area of Petale's chip shop when the place seemed to look more like Bosnia during the Yugoslav civil war. It may be a complete coincidence but in the last fifty years the inhabitants of "Dirty Bonnybridge" have reported more sightings of UFOs than all the rest of the country put together. Frankly an odd claim to fame. I tend to believe that there may be in most cases and in many ways, a link to the consumption of strong alcoholic beverages by the local population most weekends after a hard week in the foundries or brickworks. Although I have passed through the "Bonnybridge Triangle" many times both by day and by night I have only once ever seen weird lights in the sky and this was when I fell on my head coming down the steeply curving Drove Loan at high speed when my brakes failed on a racing bike which a colleague was trying unsuccessfully to sell me.

During the daylight hours in summer which in this area appeared to be of quite short duration local worthies would often lean against the wall outside the Doctor's surgery. They would usually exhibit such torpor that they would often appear to be in state of suspended animation, more like Jurassic Park than the Bonnybridge Anderson Public Park. One afternoon however a lorry delivery driver slowed, stopped and then wound down his window to enquire of the locals where he might find the world-renowned Smith and Wellstood Foundry, as apparently, he had been given instructions to pick up a load of gas cookers from them. With an almost imperceptible nod of the head and a brief sideways glance, one of the local worthies indicated soundlessly, that if he went around the corner, up the hill and over the Forth and Clyde Canal, he would find his destination there in no time flat. As he drove off the amazed lorry driver shouted back, that he would be prepared to part with half a crown if ever he saw a lazier response to a request for assistance. Easing one buttock very slightly off the wall the local turned very slightly and responded "Just slip it intae ma back poaket pal".

I had not made use of the doctor's surgery when I went arse over tip on the borrowed bike but I had been taken there once after banging my head into a steel girder at work. No doubt concussion explains why I have no recollection of the inside of the surgery and no doubt too this also explains a great deal about me ever since I saw the flashing lights on that clear bright sunlight summers morning and pondered over their origin.

Round the Bend

I sat listlessly on the flagged stone terrace of the Cairo Hilton under a large striped umbrella, sipping slowly on an ice cold but expensive Egyptian beer. There was a magnificent view across the Nile whose turgid brown waters flowed gently past the hotel. Round a bend upstream a typical Egyptian river barge appeared and made its way slowly down the river. It was loaded high with large red terra cotta pots so that it sat very low in the water. Each rough unglazed pot looked like one that Ali Baba and the forty thieves might have smuggled into the Caliph of Baghdad's Palace although I hasten to add that even I know that Baghdad is a very long camel ride from Cairo.

The vessel was travelling with the current and had its mast and sail lowered. It drifted slowly down the wide river, which was slightly swollen, because it was the short rainy season, which confers fertility on the Nile delta. The crew of three were fast asleep on top of the warm pots in the sun and only the Captain was steering the boat with the large rear rudder as he too nodded off and awakened again with a start. Immediately just past the hotel was a three-span bridge with a rather low centre span. As the boat approached the bridge it was obvious from my vantage point on the terrace that it would not have enough clearance to pass below the bridge, due to the enormous load the boat was carrying. Sure, enough the crew slept on blissfully unaware of what was about to happen, until the boat wedged itself gently under the bridge. As it bumped lightly into place the crew were shaken from their perches and their slumbers. They rushed up and down the cargo of pots shouting to each other. After a fierce discussion the Captain ordered them to climb up on top of the pots and throw one or two of them into the river so that the boat could continue its passage. Unfortunately, none of them had ever made the acquaintance either of Archimedes or of his Principle. Every time they threw a pot into the water the boat and its cargo became a little lighter and rose up slightly to ensure that it stayed wedged gently under the bridge. The Captain quickly realised that all he was doing was throwing his profit into the river and after a while he hailed another smaller passing vessel and did a deal with its crew to transfer some of the load to it. Both vessels then sailed under the bridge and the pots were reloaded onto the larger vessel, whereupon it resumed its leisurely journey again and drifted on further down the river while the crew once more fought for the right to at least pretend to be both awake and hard at work in the blazing hot afternoon sun.

The heat for me was pleasant as long as I sat in the shade and sipped beer with a very faint breeze wafting under the canvas umbrella but the same heat almost proved fatal very shortly after. The day before, when I had walked across the nearby 6th of October bridge, there had been a small crowd of people gathered round a hawker whose "piece de resistance" seemed to be that he was frying eggs with a little cooking oil poured on the very hot stone bridge parapet. I decided that although the eggs looked extremely well cooked there was no way that I was purchasing one to eat as I was not that brave. On the Rameses Hilton terrace however, I thought that the hygiene standards were to a sufficiently high level that I could risk a light lunch. I glanced at the menu but did not fancy any of the cooked dishes such as the Kabab wa kofta (grilled meats), or the Sugoq wa Kibdah Iskandarani (Alexandrian sausages and liver), or worse than that perhaps the Hawawshi (Egyptian meat pie) since I was not sure exactly what the meat would be. I opted for the club sandwich because I reckoned that turkey, bacon, lettuce and tomato with mayonnaise would be a safe bet. I lost my bet, the entire contents of my stomach and almost my life with food poisoning. I was forced to spend a couple of days in bed, almost delirious with fever and sweating gallons or at least litres of perspiration. The hotel did not offer any assistance and to be fair I was not making a big song and dance as I was almost comatose. At one point I did manage to summon just enough strength to weakly pick up the antique phone on the side table by my bed in the hotel room and dial the British Embassy to ask if they had a factsheet with any details about repatriating a body – namely mine. Eventually It did not come to that but it was maybe the most ill I had ever been in my life. I still retain a strong aversion to Club sandwiches especially with mayonnaise and if I am really honest even to Cairo.

Win Friends and Influence People

This is an odd story really involving at least three guys all of whom were called Bill. To avoid lengthy and complicated explanations which might confuse even me I will call only the first one of them Bill. The second participant I will refer to as the new Managing Director, while I will refer to the third person only as a colleague or as the host of the soiree on this particularly jolly occasion of which I write.

Bills eyesight was not particularly good. He had worn some quite strong prescription glasses for a number of years and from time to time had other minor problems with his sight. As a result of this situation he had been largely confined to the office while I had travelled widely on his behalf although he retained his title, his office and all of his self-respect. On this occasion we had all been going to a formal company dinner and dance and a number of us had been invited round to another colleague's house with our wives for a drink or three before the main event. Bill had arrived first and had managed to acquire a drink with each of the several new guests as they arrived and should have been quite mellow. The company had recently been involved in a takeover by a larger competitor although this was still referred to optimistically by Bill and some of the other older employees as a merger. Apparently however on this occasion Bill was a bit irritated because the new Managing Director and his wife had still not arrived and time was getting on. Why this should have irritated him I don't know as the drink was free. I suspect however that it was more to do with the lack of any good working relationship between Bill and the new man than the delay itself as nobody else seemed to be bothered at all in the slightest by an extended happy hour.

With a slight sigh of exasperation Bill got up from the couch and went to the toilet. While he was there the new Managing Director and his wife arrived and were both given a libation by the host's wife. The women chatted briefly together by the cocktail cabinet but the Managing Director, spotting two empty seats on the couch that Bill had just vacated sat down in the one at the end. Seconds later Bill returned to his seat on the couch not realising that he was now sitting cheek by jowl as it were with the Managing Director. Bill shook his head in exasperation and tutted his disapproval. Throwing back the last of his drink he said to no one in particular but to the room in general "is that rude bastard not here yet then"? As might well be imagined this was something of a conversation stopper as a silence fell over the group and we all peered intently into the depths of our own glasses. The new Managing Director may not even have realised that he was the subject of the comment as he announced "never mind if somebody is running late, we can go on without them and they can catch up with us". Strangely however Bills career did not seem to make a lot of headway after that. I can't imagine why although on sober reflection next day Bill perhaps thought maybe the new Managing Director was not quite as daft as he sounded on that occasion.

The party went downhill from there, when the master of ceremonies who was totally convinced that he was a stand-up comedian, announced that there would be a display of Scottish country dancing, as the young lady booked as a stripper had been forced to cancel at short notice. To make matters worse one of the directors who may well have had a few tinctures and was not at his most astute at that point responded by saying that he hoped that nothing untoward had befallen the fictitious stripper. Later in the evening as the hilarity drew to a close it was found out that a young employee in the company's new IT department had dressed up as an Arab sheik and amused the last few inebriated revellers by lighting his farts apparently without any injury to himself or close bystanders. Nowadays this would all be classified as sexist, racist and worse.

Do you take Sugar in your Coffee?

Puerto Rico had been inhabited for about three thousand years before I finally arrived there. It had been a Spanish colony until the Americans invaded it just before the turn of the twentieth century. Apparently, they had been short of coffee and the sugar to put in it so they sent their fleet down to the island to do a bit of covert colonisation.

I had visited Puerto Rico before and was starting to make some headway in business. I had a couple of meetings lined up for the next day which was a Friday before having a quiet Saturday and travelling on down to Jamaica on the Sunday afternoon ready for another week in paradise. Yes, I know that it is a tough life but somebody had to do it.

This time however it was a little different as on landing and clearing baggage facilities the Pan Am ground staff told us that there were no taxis into town and that we all had to use the buses which had been specially chartered to take us on the final leg of our journey. As we all climbed aboard the big yellow school buses some of the American passengers started talking to each other, as Americans are always won't to do. It was impossible not to overhear the conversations, which were going on all around me. One loud passenger with louder clothes was announcing to anyone within earshot which effectively meant the whole bus that he had only flown in for the Chilli Soup because it was impossible to get a decent bowl of Chilli in Philadelphia. From his girth I guessed that it may have been because he had eaten it all single handed. His lady friend meanwhile whom I surmised was not either his wife or his daughter hung on his arm as well as his every word while gazing up at him as if he had uncovered some startling revelation that the no one in the world had previously been aware of.

As the bus reached the airport entrance to join the main highway it became very obvious why we were on the bus and not in taxis or hire cars as would normally have been the case. There was a huge crowd of angry taxi drivers picketing the intersection. They were being restrained by the local police but it had to be said were only just being held back. Every so often they surged out onto the road blocking the traffic. It took us some time to run the gauntlet with frequent delays for the police to drag the protesters back onto the sidewalk. It was certainly a long noisy and eventful trip into town that Saturday. "Oh well" I thought, "Somebody's soup is going to be cold by the time he gets to his hotel and gets down to dinner" so a few extra chilis there then.

I was almost late for dinner as well since I was playing with a new multi band radio that I had bought in the duty-free shop in Santo Domingo airport on the way to Puerto Rico. I found that it had some aircraft frequencies on it and since the hotel was very close to the airport, I could pick up most of the transmissions between the tower and local aircraft. The one that fascinated me most was when an Eastern Airlines DC9 had landed and was a bit slow in pulling off the runway onto the taxiway. The controller who must have been observing the plane through binoculars was convinced that the tail of the DC9 could possibly be struck by the wing of the next aircraft which was rapidly approaching the runway. The exchange between the tower and the DC9 got a bit terse and the voices rose in volume and tone as the pilot was advised "to get his ass out of there and I mean now!" A similar type of disaster to this had occurred before in Tenerife although in foggy conditions and possibly in other airports in various types of weather so the air traffic controller was only doing his best to save life and limb.

Later I decided to walk along what was even then just starting to be a hotel beach strip towards Old San Juan. The Castillo San Cristibal, La Fortaleza and the cathedral were interesting but I headed around the corner to the Hotel El Convento. On the night that I was there was most conspicuously short of Nuns unless they had all collectively taken a vow to wear their miniskirts that evening with a crucifix and not much else. The local food was said to be based on "comida criolla" but an American commented that it was nothing like the Creole food in the southern United States for which I was truly grateful. Why do many Americans travel great distances only to announce "It's nothing like this back home" on a wide variety of topics? For me and many others, part of the joys and rationale of travel is surely that it is nothing like this back home otherwise why bother? Anyway, after a few hot dishes interspersed by a few cool drinks I was largely uninterested in any American perspective on anything. In answer to the first question I did not take sugar in my coffee. I took rum although even I have to admit that the rum did come from the distillation of the thick aromatic molasses extract of sugar cane but then I am told that I have always been somewhat unrefined.

On the final leg of that journey to Jamaica the pilot of the American Airlines 727 that I was on must have been getting pretty anxious as well at the potential for disaster in Caribbean skies. On his approach to Ocho Rios he spotted a charter DC9 which was taking off but not yet clear of the runway as we were approaching. I did not hear any part of the conversation relating to that event but the DC9 took off and stayed very low to the flat terrain on the coast while our 727 pulled up really quite sharply and went around for another circuit so that we overflew the DC9 to everyone's great relief. Maybe the Jamaican air traffic control was not quite as sharp as the Puerto Rican had been but the two pilots more than made up for any potential deficiency.

Sometimes on a Sunday evening Peter's two cousins would come around to his small apartment in Kiffissia in central Athens. Big George looked like Costas in Shirley Valentine and was married to Anna. Little George looked like the comedian he was and constantly came under severe pressure from Maria his long suffering, girlfriend to join her in the matrimonial stakes. It appeared however that he had so far successfully managed to avoid giving up what he saw as his freedom and settling down to a life of monogamy which he seemed to equate with monotony although both were derived from the Greek language and at some point in ancient Greece may have been fully interchangeable definitions of the same thing. I think that Maria originally bumped into little George in an Athenian travel agents and she may possibly have confused him with the last resort. He, I am sure was trying to arrange a trip to travel to Bosnia Herzegovina because he possibly mistook this Balkan destination with Eva Herzigová the Wonderbra model that big George had told him that he had drooled over when he had read about her in Playboy magazine. Actually, I believe that it was only pictures so neither would have been academically challenged by trying to read in English.

A couple of Ouzos followed by glasses of yellowish Retsina or reddish Mavrodaphne with the meal with a Metaxa or three to follow made for a relaxing time where no one was going to recognise far less criticise the Moussaka. After dinner the girls sat and gossiped with Peter's wife and her elderly mother who lived in the apartment below while the rest of us sat around the table and more or less played cards. It was the usual unruly card game where no one understood the rules and where everybody appeared to be breaking them all in any case. It was also conducted partly in English partly in Greek and partly in Australian, which was the country where Peter had lived and worked for some years before eventually moving back to Athens. Like most lively social gatherings all over the so called civilised world the women were gossiping about a wide range of topics, which they found fascinating and absorbing while the men were playing cards, drinking beer and scratching themselves almost reflexively while the television set which sat in the far corner of the room droned on unnoticed in the background and was largely ignored by everyone in the room.

Just after nine, during a lull in the scratching I glanced across at the television which was sitting in the corner of the room on my right and noticed that the picture quality was not too good that evening which was distinctly unusual as Athens had good TV reception. The picture on the screen was in black and white and it was distinctly fuzzy unlike the previous mixture of normal coloured programmes and adverts, which had been being served up earlier all night. I thought that it might have been a rerun of the blockbuster "O Agnostos Polemos" (The Unknown War) which held the record for the largest number of viewers ever on any Greek TV broadcast. "Surely it's not another one of your old war movies" I complained "don't you have any decent new TV shows in Greece nowadays. Look at all these guys in their Nazi type tin helmets, storming up the beach and moving into town without very much opposition being apparent from the locals". It wouldn't happen like that in real life I thought as I muttered to no one in particular. "Actually" little George explained to me slightly apprehensively "It's not a war film it's the nine o'clock evening news bulletin and the breaking news is that they are claiming that Argentina has just invaded England".

I was well aware of George's belief that he was a comedian all right but I suspected that his constant stream of cigarettes which he had been chain smoking all night might on this occasion just have contained something stronger than his regular brand of aromatic Greek tobacco. "Don't be daft George" I told him, "they couldn't invade England even if they wanted to as Argentina is almost six thousand miles south west of the UK and they could not reach us even on a nice sunny day with a light following breeze blowing". "Please yourself" he said "but the announcer has just been shouting out loud that Argentinian marines have just captured Port Stanley almost unopposed by the garrison who did not want casualties inflicted on the local innocent civilian population".

I knew then it was just another windup by George, as that even after all of the alcohol that had been imbibed during the course of the pleasant but lengthy evening, I was pretty certain that we didn't have a town called Port Stanley anywhere in the UK.

A Game of Two Halves.

I had driven the road many times before it was all upgraded to motorway status and have done so again many times since that particular journey north in May 1982. The divided carriageways on the M6 between Beck Foot and Tebay Junction, wound through a fairly narrow valley in a series of slow curves between some bare grassy hills sparsely populated by a few hardy sheep. There was very little traffic in either direction at that point but I still carefully scanned the road ahead as well as regularly checking in the rear-view mirror for faster vehicles especially police cars or other emergency vehicles coming up behind me. I had just rounded a curve in the valley and glanced back to see in my mirror a Vulcan nuclear bomber coming up fast behind my car at less than a thousand feet above the same carriageway that I was driving on. Almost as a reflex I transferred my attention back to the road in front of me before the enormity of what I had just seen sank in. Holy shit I thought I hope that he is on our side and that it is not the Cumbrian constabulary's latest addition to their traffic fleet to deter drivers from doing more than 70 mph. As I looked back again the monster aircraft had disappeared and I wondered if I was maybe perhaps dreaming the whole thing but the explanation was of course was that by this time he was over the car and so could not be seen as I had no sunshine roof. A second later it appeared in front of me powering forward still very low and drifting up the valley between the hills at more than three times my own ground speed. About 5 seconds after that the car was caught in the blast from the four enormous Bristol Olympus engines each capable of over 17,000 lbs thrust and I was left in no doubt as to what I was seeing, hearing and feeling. It was quite an effort to concentrate fully on my driving and just stay on the road. As my brain processed all the information crowding in on me, I remembered that I had heard that the Vulcan was due to be retired before the end of the year after a career as a nuclear deterrent force spanning almost twenty-five tumultuous years. This one did not seem to be anticipating retirement anytime soon and it set my mind racing as to why it was simulating what appeared be a low-level bombing run which for a nuclear bomber seemed to me to be akin to suicide. It was only a few weeks later that the full story became clear when it was announced that "Operation Black Buck" had commenced and that a Vulcan had flown from a base on Ascension Island to Port

Stanley in the Falkland Islands dropped twenty tons of bombs on the airport runway and returned safely to its base. This was a round trip of over 6800 miles taking over sixteen hours and requiring a fleet of eleven converted Handley Page Victor tanker aircraft for inflight refuelling along the way. When the Argentinian troops recovered from their shock and disbelief which apparently had exceeded mine and repaired the runway Britain carried out four more successful bombing raids making the airfield unusable to Argentinian jets. The French built Mirage planes of the Argentinian air force were obliged to operate from bases inside Argentina which was at the edge of their operating range and limited British armed forces casualties during the conflict. As it happened none of the Vulcan raids involved the aircraft sneaking up on Port Stanley through the mountains as they all went in at 10,000 feet but the planners were obviously covering for all possible contingencies that might conceivably have arisen.

I thought "yes not too shabby for a plane that had been scheduled for a well-earned retirement". Coincidentally while hammering up the A696 in Northumberland the following week I passed close to the south of Otterburn army training camp and got a close up of a UK Chinook or similar helicopter with some hard-looking troops loaded with all their equipment and weapons abseiling out into the forest. It made me start to wonder what they were rehearsing for and what "argy bargy" they might yet get into when they finally did arrive. That question was also soon answered by TV bulletins

Giza Job

Those of you who have seen a desert or three will know that they can all be different. The one at Giza outside Cairo in Egypt certainly is. It is not very flat but tends to rise unevenly from the river Nile up to a very slightly higher level on a small plateau. The ground is certainly sandy but contains millions of small roughly shaped stones which can make walking difficult even for a camel. I decided that a lot of these had come from the outer layer of the great pyramid of Giza which looked a bit ragged although after 4000 years or so it will probably look better than I will. This however certainly won't worry me in the least because I won't be looking in any mirrors by that time.

The pyramid has about 170,000 tons of rock of two main different types in its large block construction. The main pyramid consists of a large grain pink coloured granite which was mined in Aswan far upriver on the Nile. The outer layer is composed of an off-white sandstone which was quarried from the Wadi Al Jarf which is located a very considerable distance up river from the site of the pyramid itself. The stones were cut into large rectangular blocks each weighing about seventy tonnes and then ferried down the river on specially designed barges rowed and steered by Egyptian boatmen. Since the pyramid is not very close to the river the Egyptian engineers built a short canal and a harbour closer to the site   The blocks were unloaded at the harbour about half a mile from the pyramid and rolled the last half mile or so on big sledges over a system of rollers on wooden rails by teams of forty men. It took about 10,000 men up to thirty years to build the pyramids at Giza so there was a huge city situated roughly where the Sphinx now stands. Some of the small rocks probably come from this construction as well. The track up to the pyramid was restricted at one point by a very short coil of rusty barbed wire with an Egyptian almost recumbent at either end of it.

They were dressed in the remnants of what appeared to be first World War vintage long khaki greatcoats over once white robes. This might have seemed excessive in a temperature of fifty degrees but the coats had no buttons and were flapping open. One of the guardians of the pyramid had a rusty rifle which may not have been used since the battle of Omdurman while the other had a satchel with some rather small greenish soapstone carvings of scarab beetles. I could have walked around the ends of the wire but decided to play the game and haggled for the wire to be withdrawn and for me to buy a couple of beetles for good luck. This then allowed me to approach the base of the pyramid and to scramble over the broken stones up to what was said to be the main entrance about twenty feet from the base. In fact, the main entrance was higher up on the north face but it was difficult and dangerous to try and reach it because the outside surface of the pyramid was not in good shape. I actually entered through a smaller hole in the outer shell lower down nearer to the ground called the Robbers Tunnel. It was the entrance to a passageway with a smooth stone floor which sloped gently down into pitch blackness. Another guardian persuaded me to slither slowly down into the darkness until I reached the flat floor of a large rectangular chamber. I would not have known that it was a large rectangular chamber had it not been for a young boy crouched against the wall who lit a candle on my arrival. This just about illuminated most of the room and dimly showed a few artefacts strewn around the chamber which for maximum dramatic effect were lit by the small flickering flame.

After examining a few items in what was claimed to be the Pharoh Khufu's outer burial chamber I made for the tunnel to climb back up and as soon as I left the main chamber the candle was extinguished once more and the room plunged into compete darkness. This was an early Egyptian form of energy conservation but it also gave a dramatic first view of the chamber to each new arrival so it might have been early Egyptian marketing also. After getting back to ground level without breaking any bones another local appeared from around the corner with a mangy looking camel and offered a trip of a lifetime on his ship of the desert. I don't go for tourist trips of a lifetime. Whoever said of the airline BOAC that it was better on a camel may have seen a picture of one or even seen a real one in a zoo but I can guarantee has never actually been on a camel in real life. After a lot of arguing I did actually get into the saddle and hung on as the camel got back to its feet as only camels can. After a short trot around the base of the pyramid the Cameleer suggested that if I gave him ten pounds, he would belt the camel behind the left knee and the camel would kneel down again to allow me to dismount safely. I suggested to the Cameleer that I give him five pounds or that I jump on top of him to break my fall and his neck. This must have sounded like an offer he could not refuse or else the camel collapsed from exhaustion or boredom around that time in any case. Of course, it could have been that maybe my two lucky scarab beetle carvings were kicking in with good luck after all and I should get back up to town fast and put a tenner on red or black in the Hilton rooftop casino.

Newton's Law

Each Monday afternoon at college immediately after lunch it was once more time for the dreaded thermodynamics lecture and its associated endless calculations. This topic

could not have been set for a worse time. If someone had deliberately set out to try
and achieve the most inappropriate time in the entire timetable of studies this was it.
Most of our band of assorted seekers after knowledge had just returned to the lecture
room from the college canteen where we had usually fallen victim to a quite generous
helping of mince and dough balls or some other dubious item of nouvelle cuisine,
followed by an equally large portion of rhubarb and thick custard. If we were lucky
and still in funds then a large mug of hot sweet tea accompanied by a Tunnock's
cream snowball would inevitably have finished both the meal and us off. At times like
those all of the blood in the entire system was urgently required to help digest the
large lunch and there was little or none left over to service such far away organs as the
brain. I am certain that when the lecturer looked at the assembled group, he saw a
vista of faces all of which were untroubled by even a pretension of serious thoughts
far less thermodynamics. If he was really unlucky, he might also just see the tops of
more than a few heads of the students who had already slumped over their desks with
their heads cradled in their arms and were starting to dream of better things that were
yet to come or perhaps in a very few cases possibly entirely losing the will to live.

Since we were entombed in a very warm poorly lit basement lecture room this weekly
situation became the perfect prelude to an early afternoon siesta but certainly not for
forays into complex issues like Film Coefficients, Prandtl Numbers, Newton's Laws
and Boundary Layer Effects. These were by their very cerebral nature only entirely
unwelcome intrusions. This was especially so at that time because each mammoth
calculation that we had to complete required intensive use of our books of log tables
and antilogarithm tables. Each calculation could take two, hour long sessions spread
over two weeks in the days before computers or even electronic scientific calculators
were in general public use. Logs and Antilogs, had been introduced in a new scientific
paper by James Napier in 1617 and three hundred and fifty years later I for one was
still struggling with their use without even making the faintest attempt to understand
the complex mathematical processes which lay behind the use of the data. Apparently,
it took even Napier fifty-seven pages of description to tell people how his Logs and
Antilogs actually worked out in practice. No wonder he was nicknamed "Marvellous
Merchiston" after his castle home near Edinburgh and was admitted to study at Saint
Salvator's College in Saint Andrews University when he was only thirteen. He also
devised the decimal point in his spare time and even when tired and sleepy I could
just about get to grips with that concept although still did not always get it in exactly
the right place. As the lecture progressed during each weekly session, I found greater
difficulty with the passage of time in following what the lecturer was actually saying.
Eventually on one occasion I had to ask him to speak more clearly because not only
could I not understand what he was saying but neither could I even hear him properly.
I thought I had caught a reference to the fourth power of radiation from a perfect
black body and was struggling to figure out how the lecture had progressed from
thermodynamic minutiae to the at that time incomparable Miss Shirley Bassey.

The lecturer speaking in ever quieter tones however explained to me and the rest of
his less than eager students that he did not wish to wake up Mr Brown in the front row
as he had dozed off. The aforementioned Mr Brown gave every indication that he was
very obviously having a pleasant dream judging by the look on his face. Maybe he

had somehow subconsciously also heard the lecturer's comment about perfect black bodies or more likely it was the mince and tatties that had actually seduced him first.

Some years later I acquired two small computer programmes which today would no doubt be referred to as "apps". These were capable of doing those extremely complex calculations and a lot more besides, very accurately and in a tiny fraction of the time. Great news you may be thinking and you would be right except that in the year 1998 a company you may have heard of called Microsoft introduced a computer operation system called Windows 98 and everything started going downhill yet one more time. The programmes that I had were written in MS Dos and windows rapidly developed to the stage that it could not handle such simple code and each iteration makes it worse. This is what some people call progress and I call a large pain in the gluteus maximus. There are now millions of "apps" most of which do nothing, or nothing of real benefit while worthwhile programmes have to be rewritten and then sold on by commercial enterprises at high profits or sometimes lodged in the cloud to be rented at even higher profit and have someone monitor every calculation that you do. Big brother is alive and well and watching your every keystroke. Do you think that if we tell everyone that their brain is an "app" they might start using it since most bugs used to come in through open windows rather than be a built-in feature of most software?

Starting at the Bottom Still Seems Pretty Ambitious

A local company arranged my first interview with my headmaster at school where I was doing moderately well studying Chemistry and Physics while utterly detesting Mathematics. The company was looking for a technical assistant who was good at would you believe chemistry physics and maths. Well I thought two out of three isn't all that bad and who knows maybe the interviewer could not speak Algebra either.

The Technical Manager who was a tall kindly Orcadian PhD conducted the interview or at least the part of it that mattered. He had to my relief obviously decided that he was going to try to make the situation as easy and as painless as possible for both of us as I had zero experience of job applications even less of job interviews and my work experience had been delivering milk in the morning and groceries at weekends.

His first question was to ask how I would find the apparent density of a brick. I seem to recall saying that I did not really know but that maybe we could ask one of the guys who worked in the lab with him. Undeterred he tried again. He asked me how I would determine the moisture content of sand. I told him again that this was not one of the pieces of information, which I just carried in my head and wondered aloud if in fact this information on damp sand was likely to be of much interest at all to anyone. A slight glaze came over his eyes, as this had clearly never occurred to him in his entire exalted managerial position at the pinnacle of the company's technical R&D effort. With the first sign of desperation creeping into his voice he made one final attempt. He asked me if I could make tea "Of course" I said as long as the company supplies the tea leaves, milk and sugar and the necessary hardware and energy input. This apparently clinched it and I was in. I started on Monday at nine and thus began a meteoric career in the esoteric field of refractories technology whatever that is. The dictionary definition says refractory is unmanageable or difficult so I'll take that.

At twenty-one and after six years' experience of high technology I was ready to launch myself onto an unsuspecting world and started to look in the Thursday Daily Telegraph. For my interview at United Steel in Rotherham I managed to drive two hundred and fifty miles but needed a crutch to get up the stairs of the hotel as I had been involved in a fracas at the judo club a few days before. Dr Jimmy McKenzie seemed reasonably impressed with my qualifications and experience but not by my representation of Long John Silver minus the parrot and I don't think that the parrot was the problem. It was more that his umbrella stand had no room for crutches.

For the interview with Mr George Workman at Steel Company of Wales Port Talbot plant I drove even further but was back on two feet and so looked almost normal. The company ran a battery of tests on a about a dozen applicants together in the morning. In the afternoon we had individual technical interviews and were asked various things about refractories. My session centred on what would constitute the best material to line a blast furnace which was a multi-million-pound question even in those days. It was not one which I imagined would ever in a million years be left to me to answer in any practical situation but still put forward some suggestions for zones of the furnace. These were all knocked back much to my surprise and as I was a bit pissed off, I asked my tormentor to be told what the correct answer was and was informed that it was water of course. It was then that I decided that I did not want to work for the Welsh Water Board. The overnight stay in Porthcawl however did highlight that in a smoked salmon salad not all salmon came in tins, which to a wartime baby was a revelation that was almost worth the long journey in itself. The job offer, sent in the post the following week was declined on the grounds that the boss and I would have had our brains tuned into mostly very different wavelengths most of the time and I did not fancy getting scalded every day at work when the water collapsed and vaporised.

The later interview at Colville's Ravenscraig's large integrated iron and steel plant in Motherwell took only a short time as they rapidly established that my qualifications and experience were precisely what the British steel industry needed and they told me I could start on Monday. That job opened my eyes as to how rapidly the industrial sector which still consumes most refractories could get through thousands of tons each week without hardly trying and without most people even realising that it did. It has also been a source of amazement to me that the British Steel industry reached its zenith in 1965 with a production of 28 million tons. More than 3 million of those tons came from my plant in Scotland and which has since sunk into almost total obscurity after I left them much to their own devices and at the mercy of foreign predators.

The Secret Policeman's Bawl

Shah Reza Pahlavi's smiling face looked down on us from portraits and pictures everywhere. In public buildings, offices, hotels and even in many private homes. To make sure that everybody was happy and smiled back there was a liberal sprinkling of SAVAK secret police everywhere including in the streets and in very many buildings. Come to think of it they were about as secret as the one times multiplication table. In fact, they were pretty obvious (or was it odious) and intended to be so to prove who was in charge even before anyone got round to thinking of asking actual questions.

When we pulled into the security check at Isfahan Steelworks in our bright orange
Paykan taxi which was modelled on the Hillman Hunter that was built at Linwood
near Paisley, there were four of us in the car. We clambered out and quickly presented
ourselves to the guards. After a short scrutiny of our documents, such as the letter of
invitation and the temporary confiscation of our passports, we were waved in through
the gate. Actually, I did not give them my passport as I did not trust the blighters. I
gave them my library card and since they did not read English this was mistaken for
an identity card of some kind for someone who might not rate a passport. As we got
back in to drive to the manager's office, I remember thinking that we had somehow
put on weight but the tight squeeze was explained by the fact that a SAVAK man had
climbed into the back seat with us. "This is cosy," I thought but I supposed he just
wanted a lift to the canteen or something. He proved quite useful however by pointing
the quickest way around the large complex so that we quickly reached our destination.
It became obvious however from the way that he shadowed us very closely that he
was actually our minder while we were in the plant and we were under surveillance.
This did not bother me particularly as I knew that foreigners were always the subject
of close official scrutiny by the Shah's henchmen in the land of the peacock throne.

We soon reached the manager's office, which was on the second floor of a large multi
storey once white building stained red with iron ore. We entered the outer reception
area and were offered tea by his secretary who tried to make us feel welcome. After a
short wait we were ushered into the main office by the secretary who announced us to
her boss. The boss greeted us at the door but barred entry to the secret service man
who was curtly told to remain in the reception area while we had our meeting. At the
conclusion of this the manager ushered us out another door directly into the corridor
and we went back down the stairs to our car. It was only when we reached there that
we realised that we had shaken off our minder without really trying to. Mr SAVAK
was still sitting upstairs in the outer office and probably had not even had a cup of tea.

Ian went back to the swing doors at the foot of the stairs opened them and shouted
loudly in English that we were leaving. There was a short delay then the sound of
running footsteps and a crashing noise as the policeman came down the stairs about
four at a time and burst through the swing doors at the bottom doing about 40 miles
per hour. We thought this was amusing but apparently one of the qualifications for
joining SAVAK is that one has to be totally devoid of a sense of humour. He really
harangued us in Farsi all the way back to the gate where we retrieved our documents
and headed for the airport before he perhaps changed his mind and asked us if would
like to accompany him on an extended tour of the elemental facilities at Evin prison.

 It really was a divided society with a young boy following me for miles in the snow
down Tahkti-e Jamshid Avenue from the Hilton to downtown trying to sell chewing
gum. At the other end of the scale Shah Reza Pahlavi was down in Persepolis an
ancient capital of Persia in a luxury tented village celebrating over two and a half
thousand years of the empire and the Peacock Throne with champers and caviar. This
was founded by the emperor Darius with minimal input from succeeding generations.
All good things come to an end however, in fact everything came to an end it seems
when the exiled Ayatollah Sayyid Ruhollah Musavi Khomeini, cleric, revolutionary
and Iranian politician flew back from Paris some short time later to sort things out.

Open Borders

The American Airlines 727 touched down with barely a thud from its undercarriage and taxied back along the main runway to the small off white one storey concrete terminal building. Only a handful of passengers disembarked with most passengers staying on until the next and final destination in Bogota Columbia. As we very few stragglers walked up the path to the arrivals everyone except me turned left to gain entry to Haiti, the first black republic in the world founded even before Liberia. They headed for the immigration desk manned by one official while I turned right into what served as both the transit and the departure lounge. It was a slight exaggeration to describe it as a lounge since it was a big rectangular concrete room with wooden benches fixed around the walls. It was not windowless as there was one big window looking out over the airport apron although the window was glassless and the entrance was door-less which made it look pretty austere but no doubt saved damage during frequent hurricanes in Autumn and no one would have been kept awake by banging.

The other passengers were quickly processed and then they and the immigration officer if that was what he was disappeared leaving me sitting alone in splendid isolation. It only took about 5 minutes looking out of the window for me to be a bit bored with the view which consisted of what could best be described as an untidy clump of jungle. There was one big sign which proclaimed "My father started the revolution and I will continue the progress that he made" signed Jean Claude Duvalier better known maybe as Baby Doc. For progress read steep decline according to everything I had heard ever since the nineteen-year-old spoiled rich kid had been elected by 2,391,916 votes to one after Papa Doc died in 197. I often wonder about the fate of the one who got his cross in the wrong part of the ballot paper. Baby Doc was never a doctor and was even referred to by his dad as fat and gormless. The fact that he managed to shoot a few people endeared him even less to the local population.

It was my fault that I was having to wait several hours in such a location for a flight connection as I had decided that I was not flying in one of Air Haiti's elderly DC3's although there was no sign of any of them so perhaps one had crashed in the jungle, another crashed in the mountains and the third gone down in the sea. I don't think that they were allowed to operate internationally even across the border to the Dominican Republic anyway so I was waiting for a later LIAT Leeward Island Air Transport plane to Santa Domingo which made up the other two thirds of the isle of Hispaniola. Several hours on a hard bench was unappealing so I wandered out onto the airport concourse which was pretty much deserted in the midday heat and nobody seemed in the least interested even although I was wearing a lightweight suit and had a Scottish pallor which distinguished me from absolutely every other person in the entire island.

It was almost deserted and I decided to fill my time taking a quick taxi ride into the capital which was quickly accomplished. Some of the bigger hotels had little stalls outside selling souvenirs up to and including wooden Voodoo dolls about two feet high although trade was slow. Eventually when arriving back at the airport there was another stall outside the departures area and it was selling one or two of these dolls to departing American tourists. At the check in desk however they quickly discovered that the dolls would not be loaded as hold baggage and the airline staff wanted them to buy a single ticket for each doll and set it into a seat by itself with the seat belt on. The price for this was exorbitant however and the tourists were relieved to sell the dolls back to local traders at a huge discount. While all this fun and games was taking place, I took my passport, ticket and boarding card out of my pocket and slipped back into the departure lounge through the still unattended doorway having decided to tell anyone who asked that I had just popped out for a moment to go to the toilet.

 If Haiti was no oil painting in the early seventies at least it had tourism and was most certainly at least to a visitor a vastly better place than it currently is. This is almost certainly due in large part to the earthquake that devastated Port Au Prince and the surrounding area in 2010. Reports of the disaster stated that about fifty percent of all the old historical buildings had been brought down but looking at TV newsreel it is difficult to tell if fifty percent of all of the building are down or fifty percent of each and every individual building is down. Ironically the Ollofson Hotel appears largely unscathed by the tremors but the nearby massive stone-built cathedral is in ruins. The population of the country seems to have grown considerably but this only exacerbates the poverty in which most of the people live in huge urban slums such as Cite Soleil. Ironically the old airport has been rebuilt and renamed following the earthquake as the intended to be impressive sounding Toussaint Louverture International Airport.

 This new large modern looking structure has a much lower volume of passengers passing through it than might be expected from its appearance and a much-increased rate of aviation accidents than in the good old days so where is the fun in any of that.

Does This Help

I don't know why everyone still immediately always identifies me with being Scottish whenever I meet someone new as I have lived in England now for 36 years and found the people south of the border to be immensely kind and at all times most welcoming.

I initially moved to England on the second of January 1984 and at first stayed in leafy Cheshire at the Old Hall Hotel which was a former coaching inn on the main street of the little market town of Frodsham. At the beginning I suppose that I was a little bit homesick as Frodsham was somewhat different to the area in central Scotland where I had previously lived for many years, while still travelling the world. For the first few days of my exile I had a sticker in the rear window announcing "I miss Glasgow". One morning however on going out to the car, to drive to my new workplace in nearby Runcorn I found that the driver's window was broken, the radio had been stolen and a note had been placed on the seat saying "does this help". Actually, that is not true as I just made it up for a joke. No one had broken the window although in a way they had stolen the radio since they had inserted a wire coat hanger through the front offside window to unlock the driver's door and then stolen the entire vehicle during the night. I had taken dinner in the hotel and then gone up to my room to check some work papers to prepare for some discussions the following day. After phoning home, I was in bed early and had no problem in falling asleep. Sometime around midnight some Scallies had come down from Liverpool taken the car and then used it to load up some small electrical goods like portable TV's, CD players and radios from a shop just along the road which I note is no longer in business. At some point they were disturbed by the local gendarmerie and made off at very high speed in my Cortina Ghia towards the Runcorn bridge and their home somewhere in south east Liverpool. After crossing the Mersey pursued by at least two police cars they got the brilliant idea that they could deter the police or at least perhaps slow their progress by throwing small electrical goods out of the back seat of the car through the rear door window and into the path of the pursuers. This meant that by the time they reached their tower block there was nearly nothing left in the car so they screeched to a halt in the car park and legged it into the dark. This left the traffic police with a nice warm empty car to poke around in for clues. One clue being the matching number plates back and front which allowed them to trace the vehicle reasonably quickly as being registered to Cape Industries in Stirling. My previous boss had been so pleased at me helping him beat his annual budget that he told me that I could hold onto the car for a couple of weeks until I had got myself sorted out with my new employer. The CID then phoned Cape in Stirling and were answered by the night shift security officer in the gatehouse who was asked if he knew anything about a Cortina Ghia and cheerily responded "Oh aye, Dougie telt Davie that he could hing oantae the caur for a wee while". When then asked if he knew where they could find Davie, he supplied my Scottish address in Larbert resulting in the local polis tootling quickly round to my house and banging loudly on the front door. My wife who was in bed responded that if they did not go away, she would call the police resulting in a very lively discussion as to whether or not they actually were the police. Eventually they managed to persuade her that they were and she supplied the name of the hotel that I was staying in resulting in the Frodsham flying squad banging on my door and bursting into my room with the hotel manager at about five in the morning. After another altercation centred around where I had been all night, they accepted that if I had driven to Wavertree, I could not possibly have covered the twenty or so miles back from there to Frodsham and got into bed before they arrived even if I had been Mo Farah. Now that I was awake, I started to get grumpy and asked them where my car was in their crime infested county and when would I get it back in good order. If there is one thing that the plod doesn't like very much it is being asked when they are going to solve the crime of the century and they started to fidget and edge towards the door. Before they made their escape however I managed to finally extract from them the information that I should check for an update at Frodsham Police station when it opened later that morning and at which time I would also be given a crime number for any insurance claims that might needed to be made. This prompted me to ask the Hotel manager for his insurance details so that I could claim against the hotel for anything that might occur to me later on in the day. This got him out of the room as well and my parting shot was that he had better get a complimentary full English on the table by seven thirty. After breakfast I walked along to the police station for nine O' Clock and I eventually was informed that I could pick up the car which was largely undamaged from Liverpool after two in the afternoon when the forensics had dusted it for prints swabbed it for DNA and generally admired the car. I got security from my new company to collect me to go into the office and also to retrieve the car and bring it back for my inspection. The first thing that I noticed when I got it back was that any small electrical goods that had been in the car when the police recaptured it had then subsequently been removed for safekeeping or possibly as evidence or even to throw at the Scallies. I quickly decided there and then that I would get Dougie's car back to him that weekend since his shiny well-maintained Ghia was proving to be such an enormous attraction to so many of the criminal fraternity in North West England.

Nice Dacia, Dacia Nice

Athens airport was vastly improved when they opened the new east terminal building for foreign airlines other than Olympic Airways. Since I knew it so well, we were soon through immigration and passport control and in no time had picked up a spit new gleaming Romanian built Renault Dacia hire car with only delivery mileage on the clock. Speeding through the light evening traffic into the city was easy and we checked into the Hilton within thirty minutes of touching down. Early next morning it was down to see Mr Angelopoulos the owner and manager of at the large integrated Halyvourghiki steel plant situated between the city and the port of Piraeus. When I came out of the steel plant office the gleaming new car was actually bright red from the iron oxide that had been deposited on it while we were in the meeting. The first thought that was in my mind was that I must find a car wash but unfortunately, I was distracted and forgot as we headed to Titan Cement at Patras along the coast towards Corinth. At the end of this meeting we again returned to the car to find that it was now covered in a thick layer of grey cement dust from the nearby rotary kiln. It occurred to me again it really would be a good idea to find a car wash but I could not see one and time was really pressing so we headed north to visit Larco a large factory in Larymna, which was Greece's largest producer of Nickel and Ferro alloys. It was dusk when our meeting ended at Larco and as we climbed back into the car to make for the hotel, I was acutely aware that it was almost jet black from a layer of nickel oxide which had been deposited all over it while we had been parked in the plant. I made up my mind that first thing next day I would definitely make sure that the car was fully washed and cleaned. After a good night's sleep, it was an early start for the north and after driving for nearly two hours found myself on one of the worst roads that I had ever driven on. At one point the car strayed across the unmarked Albanian border until we were intercepted by an Albanian Army patrol on mules and soon pointed in the right direction with the aforementioned pointers being guns. Since the pointing had been done with old-fashioned long barrelled carbines, we waved them a friendly goodbye and headed off round the shoulder of the hill in the direction of Karelia. It was dusty negotiating the rough unsurfaced tracks but there were no carwashes in the mountains to remove the thick brown layer of dust churned up from the small mountain track. Before reaching Karelia, we had a puncture but luckily a local garage repaired it as we suffered further damage to a tyre driving along what resembled a dried up river bed rather than any grade of road that I had ever experienced, before we finally reached Thessaloniki and our welcoming hotel for a good meal and another overnight stop.

Another early start let us complete our business in the huge Thessaloniki Hellenic Petroleum petrochemical plant where the car was subjected to a yellow deposit from a huge sulphur burner while we conducted out business meeting inside the main office in cool, airconditioned comfort. We still reached Euboea early and had a magnificent fish for lunch. The local tradition is to roast a large whole cod and serve it on one huge central plate with boiled potatoes and real Greek salad with feta, olives and tomatoes. The host usually applies liberal quantities of salt and lemon juice before all diving in. The afternoon was taken up by a short detour to Aluminium de Grèce near Aspropitia, where we had discussions in the Alumina plant. Seemingly, their filter plant did not seem to be operating at full efficiency and it was no surprise whatsoever that the car was covered in a thick layer of brilliant white dust when we recovered it.

The airport was finally reached in early evening and there was just time to check in the car and the luggage before rushing to catch the Trident flight back to London. "Was everything all right with the car sir?" said the girl at Hertz as I handed back the car keys and signed the return documents. I assured her it had performed beyond all expectation and that her white Renault Dacia which I had christened Joseph because of its newly applied coats of many colours was parked immediately outside her office. "I really should definitely have made more effort to find a car wash" I thought guiltily as I settled back in the BEA Trident seat 8C in anticipation of a gourmet dinner as we jetted back to Heathrow airport and home again after another long but successful trip.

Big Apple.

Some people rave about New York and others rave at it but to be honest I was never impressed one way or another. To me it was just a big American city that I could take or leave and leaving was generally no hardship at all as I could be in Prestwick in less than 5 hours which included dinner and a comfortable snooze in a BOAC Vickers VC 10 aided by the generous tailwind from the ever prevailing north Atlantic jet stream.

Similarly, I was not impressed with the few hotels such as the Hilton that I stayed in on 6th Avenue in mid-town Manhattan just south of Central Park. It was classed as a luxury hotel but when I was last there many years ago the rooms were quite small and were somehow old fashioned if not actually anachronistic. The thing that really drove me bonkers however was that there was an ice making machine in every bathroom which clattered away all night making ice cubes because I could not figure out how to disable it. Neither was I impressed by the local's aggressiveness in seeking tips at any and every opportunity. Unfortunately, local aggressiveness was not restricted just to demanding tips as an Italian businessman Senor Bottero was stabbed outside the Hotel by three women in March 1971 just the week before I stayed there on one occasion.

The police discounted robbery as a motive for the stabbing as he still carried $25 and 2,500 lire (about $4.15 at that time). They claimed that they thought the women, who surprisingly "all disappeared", were probably prostitutes and that the dispute had been the result of "language difficulties" which to me in New York was a virtual certainty. I firmly resolved not to carry so much money, not to be outside the Hilton hotel at three fifteen in the morning and to learn fuck off in several different foreign languages

Being in New York wasn't just like being at the movies; it was much more like being in the movies. Like something out of Kojak or NYPD Blues or some other TV soap.

The following evening, as we were coming back from a local restaurant and heading over to our abode on the Avenue of the Americas, we had a bizarre little encounter. Because there were about fifteen of us, we had not taken taxis and anyway at that particular time of night there were not too many yellow cabs cruising around where we were. We decided that since it was not very far to the hotel we would just walk. Heading back cross-town we had started to straggle because everybody was walking at their own different pace. I was in front of the group by several yards and was striding out. There were very few other people to be seen around especially in those small dark side streets connecting the main north south avenues. These cross streets with their tall brownstone apartment buildings and garment warehouses were ill lit and litter lay in the gutter and around doorways against the buildings. Wisps of steam rose through cracks in the badly surfaced streets while hot foetid air wafted up out of subway gratings. As I strode along, two dark shadows detached themselves from a doorway. Both figures seemed to have a large hand extended out towards me and I heard the single word spoken in a strong Latino accent. "Money"! "No thanks" I said, "I already have some" and simply carried right on walking. As a judo black belt and a self-defence instructor training several nights a week when at home and occasionally also when travelling I was slightly concerned but not overly worried as they appeared to be completely spaced out and I would not have wanted to injure them too badly.

Out of the corner of my eye I am sure I saw the two shadows turn and look at each other with something akin to disbelief and I just caught one of them asking the other what it was that I had said so maybe there were further language difficulties. The two numpties were the New York equivalent of Scotland's Rab C Nesbit of string vest fame and his sidekick Jamesie. This hapless duo themselves had no doubt probably evolved from the previous generation that followed in the footsteps of the legendary Rank Bajin. Amateur stunts such as this fiasco in the big Apple would never have happened in Glasgow, often referred to by those in the know as "the city of the stare" as well as the "sterrs" which were the only way to get to the top of all the tenements. Amateur criminals in Glasgow were largely now as extinct as dinosaurs even although the city was never struck by an asteroid as far as I know. The Glasgow Herald Diary is reported as recording that one night a wee lad in the east end of town ran into the Easterhouse police station and shouted to the desk sergeant that a lion had escaped from the nearby Calderpark Zoo. The sergeant just shrugged saying "Sorry son I'm just in here on duty tonight myself, so the Lion will just have to fend for itself".

Ice Maiden

Did I mention that I had drink and a meal with Miss Iceland - no? Well to be honest I don't suppose she confided this fact to too many people either as I am certain it did not really register much on the scale of the most memorable thing to have happened to her in the early seventies. George Best is supposed to have said that it was not true that he slept with seven Miss Worlds. He insisted that it was only four because he did not turn up for the other three. In my case it wasn't exactly a candlelit dinner with soft music either since it could more accurately be described as Breakfast. It comprised mainly of a plastic tumbler of BEA orange juice to complement a small plastic tray of sausage with scrambled egg served on the shuttle flight from Glasgow to London. I was sitting in the window seat and she was in the middle seat in my row. The guy sitting on the aisle optimistically asked her for her number at one point and she told him that it was in the telephone directory. He must have pondered that and then told her that he did not know her name either, but she replied that it was in the telephone directory too. As someone who has spent some considerable time wrestling with the Icelandic telephone directory, I can confirm that the odds of him ever getting any of this information from that source were infinitesimal. She was going to Heathrow to change onto Philippine Airlines bound for Manila to take part in the Miss Universe contest. Have you ever noticed how many Miss Universe winners come from earth rather than anywhere else in the multiple galaxies which the title seemed to indicate were eligible to take part in. To be honest I was surprised that it was still such a popular contest since it seemed to have more than its fair share of knockers, but on the other hand that might have been a large part of the attraction. I was going to Heathrow to change onto the Piccadilly line bound for Marble Arch to take part in a selling contest in the Bulgarian embassy as she headed further east to Manila in the Philippines. I consoled myself with the thought that she might come first in the competition but that even lacking in good looks I would surely arrive first in life. I have since noted that the Miss Iceland contest made a definite point of stating that it has nothing whatever to do at all with the Miss Universe contest but that it is affiliated to the Miss World competition. I suppose that this increases the chances of some young woman from Iceland winning at least one of the several beauty competitions although with a total population of less than Chelsea the odds must have been pretty well stacked already. God knows what Miss Iceland made of Manila with her undoubted vast array of thick woolly sweaters and pixie hats with a pompom on the top in her catwalk wardrobe. Maybe she had a woolly bikini as well although I am told that they tend to sag when wet and Manila in the typhoon season does tend to get a little bit humid occasionally.

All of this banter was going on in the middle of the three Cod Wars that Britain had with Iceland between 1952 and 1976 when Iceland repeatedly expanded its territorial waters to exclude foreign fishing boats. Sadly, there was one fatality on the Icelandic side during that period but they also managed to bend a couple of their patrol boats ramming them into UK navy fishing protection vessels. Iceland eventually won the third and final war because they threatened to withdraw from NATO and America piled into the argument behind closed doors because they wanted to keep their huge air base at Keflavik as a front line defence against Russian nuclear cold war bombers. The Icelandic government were communist and were aware that the Americans based a shed load of their own strategic B52 nuclear bombers there for first strike capability. Iceland bought all their oil supplies from Russia and I suppose paid the Russians in US dollars earned as rent for the base. As an American base it also had its own colour TV station with all the Hollywood films and cartoons which Iceland itself did not. A few Icelanders tried to patch their black and white TV sets into the American services although the local communist government severely discouraged this in case it seduced any of the locals away from the path of pure living and righteousness. The base also had a PX where copious volumes of beers and spirits were freely available at highly subsidised military prices. In the island itself the government banned the sale of all alcohol after 12 noon on Wednesdays when a very few people on the base went into

town. The chances of the visitors finding or even being remotely interested in trying
to buy local hooch were infinitesimal but made the locals feel that they were helping
prevent any excessive behaviour from their visitors. This achieved absolutely nothing
for the sobriety of the local population some of whom would have a few jars before
noon and again after midnight or just keep drinking their own moonshine anyway.

That was then and this is now as Icelanders discovered sex and the population grew
exponentially. Many became Kronur billionaires, some bought UK businesses and a
few started banks. The economy was a saga, based on a myth, wrapped in a legend
and we all know how well that turned out for everyone concerned. They also shut
down most of Europe's aviation industry with one of their volcanos. Still if you are
stressed you can always sit in a geothermal hot spa like the Blue Lagoon and try to
forget it all as six months of daylight progresses slowly into six months of darkness.
The twilight can even be extended if you have enough local Aquavit while you read
through some extremely slim illustrated volume such as a guide to Icelandic wines.

Under the Affluence of Incohol

Jim was very precise. Seven-o clock we had agreed and seven-o clock it was when he
knocked on my motel door. As I opened it and picked up my sparse luggage, which
was already packed, I could see him standing there immaculate. He was wearing his
dark suit, white shirt, red polka dot tie and his light raincoat. His shoes gleamed in the
early morning light and so did his eyes in the shadow of the brim of his dark fedora.

We headed down to the car with the cases, but by the time we had covered the short
distance to where it was parked Jim had faltered slightly and seemed a bit unsure of
what he was doing. As he fumbled with the keys in the lock, I offered to help but he
mumbled and kept on trying to open the car door. It only took a few seconds to figure
out that either he was very ill or he was very drunk. I grabbed the keys from him and
told him to get into the car. I knew we had plenty of time and I thought that if I could
get him to the airport and check in, I could fill him with enough black coffee to then
get him on the plane. He seemed annoyed that I was driving but he was not able to do
anything about it as he had about as much muscle control and co-ordination as a big
jellyfish. I told him to sit where he was and checked both of us out of the motel on my
credit card before driving quickly to Sky Harbour airport a few short blocks from the
Ramada. On arrival at the airport terminal I helped him out of the car with his case
and returned the rental car before dragging him to the desk in the main concourse and
checking in our luggage for the flight to El Paso on the Texas Mexican border.

It was then that he turned awkward, or to be more accurate much more awkward. He
refused to go to breakfast and weaved off in the direction of the nearby men's room. I
decided that I would let him cool off and had my meal before heading to the departure
lounge where I expected to see him looking a bit sheepish. When I arrived at the gate,
I was one of the first passengers there and went quickly through the security check
and was allocated a seat. Jim arrived eventually, stopped in his tracks and eyed up the
situation. He then shuffled his feet a little until he was precisely lined up with the
free-standing doorframe, which served as a metal detector. Since the cables had to go
completely around the frame and pass under it, the cables were covered by a very

small ramp which passengers walked over as they went through. When he was ready, he started to accelerate and got up to about two miles an hour by the time he was halfway up the ramp, which was less than three inches high. It was at this point that he stopped and went into reverse with his arms flailing to maintain his balance. The armed security guard was standing there with a look of utter amazement on his face as Jim made two more attempts to beat the obstacle but failed each time. Eventually the guard drew his revolver and demanded to see Jim's ticket. After much fumbling Jim managed to produce it from an inside pocket and the guard scrutinised it before conferring with the ticket agent while I hid behind my Wall Street Journal. The result of their deliberations was that Jim was unwell and should delay his flight until he felt recovered. Since the ticket agent was persuasive and the guard had a large calibre weapon Jim eventually obviously concurred, and staggered off to grab some sleep.

The rest of the journey to El Paso was uneventful although to say that I was annoyed was an understatement as I had spent a lot of money time and effort to prepare for the many meetings on a long and complex trip and the local input of our agents was an integral part of what I wanted to be a positive outcome for everyone. At one stage I thought of phoning the security guard and asking him to shoot Jim or flying back and doing it myself. At El Paso I went to the Alamo desk to pick up the rental car we had reserved. It was the time of severe fuel restrictions however and when the girl learned that I planned to drive to Silver City she strongly advised against it. With only half a tank of gas and little chance of a refill she thought it too much of a risk to undertake such a long journey across an area of semi desert. Realising that she was right I went to the airport Hilton checked in and started conducting as much business as possible by phone from my room with an ice-cold Coors effervescing on the bedside table. I only learned later that Jim had caught the next flight and had gone to the car rental desk where he picked up a large Buick and set off weaving across the desert. About a hundred miles from Silver City he ran out of fuel and was eventually rescued by a trucker who saw this dishevelled figure staggering down the road with his hat and tightly buttoned coat. He was clutching his suitcase with his briefcase clamped under his arm while a large flock of vultures circled lazily overhead in the thermals at around 90 degrees Fahrenheit. What happened to the rental car? Who knows maybe the vultures are still sitting on the rusting hulk although there must be a lot more traffic these days and no doubt the vehicle has also since been stripped to its carcass?

Spanish Flyer

We were starting to be looking like being late for our early appointment, mainly because of the heavy traffic on what would probably have been an almost adequate road if it had not been the morning rush hour on a cool dry but slightly overcast Wednesday morning. Heading west on the E50 coast road out of Bilbao we were making poor time due to congestion, in our aim to reach the integrated iron and steel plant of Altos Hornos de Vizcaya for an early morning meeting with one of their top managers. The plan was to discuss forthcoming capital projects with him where we hoped we might be allowed to be one of the bidders and eventually even a supplier.

George, my colleague and the driver of our car on this occasion, was of Italian descent but had lived and worked in Vizcaya in northern Spain most of his adult life. His Latin temperament however made him particularly unsuited to driving slowly in a long convoy of vehicles on a two-lane highway. He made a few daring attempts to overtake other vehicles but on almost every occasion generally had to pull back in almost immediately, due to oncoming traffic. It was if anything, made worse by the fact that his small Fiat although adequate for city use was not exactly capable of accelerating vigorously at the best of times. In one of these mad manoeuvres he was successful in getting past the car in front but had to cut in again very sharply and very nearly clipped the nose of the car which we had just overtaken. The driver of the car, which we had inadvertently carved up, a large green Renault, was apparently very upset and took it badly as he indicated by blasting his horn angrily. George then responded angrily himself with a sharp beep of the Fiats horn. He also attempted a dismissive wave in reply but had to hang onto the steering wheel with at least one hand. An Italian who can only wave one arm is like a man with a speech impediment. Even this limited gesture however resulted in another fierce blast of the Renaults horn. On looking back very surreptitiously from the passenger seat while trying not to make eye contact, I could see that the very angry driver had his car positioned only a very few metres from our back bumper. I decided to clench my buttocks just in case George had to stop quickly and the driver in the car behind could not, for any reason. For the next 20 km or so it seemed to me that George and the driver of the green Renault did almost everything they could to annoy each other as is required on such occasions. Both men were doing a marvellous and comprehensive job in accelerating, braking, blowing their horns, gesticulating at each other and shouting various curses. My role meanwhile was to shrink back into my seat and attempt to become invisible.

Soon afterwards the more powerful Renault following us managed to get past by taking a few chances and accelerated sharply past our car leaving us once again stuck in the long line of vehicles all heading West on the coast road. Throughout the rest of the journey George was still seething even although I tried to persuade him to calm down. I advised him to forget the whole episode and to get us to our destination in one piece. After about another 15 minutes driving, we reached our destination and turned in to the designated parking lot. We checked in with the security guard who indicated that we should walk over to the main office where we entered the reception area and were asked to take a seat until our host could see us. In only a few minutes a secretary came for us and escorted us to the office where we were to meet Senor Grande for our discussions. As soon as we walked through the door of the manager's office however my heart sank into my boots. There sitting in his big swivel chair at a large mahogany desk enjoying his first coffee of the working day was the driver of the green Renault. A look of astonishment followed by a smile of anticipation slowly spread across his face as he recognised us and realised exactly who we were. "It's all right" I said to his secretary "don't hang my coat up," as I reached the conclusion that this might be one of the shortest business meetings that I had ever taken part in. Not that I was worried at all of course about being thrown out into the car park since I was a true expert at rolling break-falls and in a previous incarnation had been Albert Tatlock's stunt man.

Moscow Mule

Business in Moscow was never easy even when like me one was there as a result of an STD. This was not a sexually transmitted disease but part of a very well organised Scottish Trade Delegation. The BOTB, the Scottish Council, the British Embassy and the Chambers of Commerce as well as Intourist, had all done their best but it was still a hassle. Everyone was preparing for the Olympics but the KGB were just getting into their stride to see how awkward they could make it for visitors who thought that they were going to enjoy their visit to Mother Russia. Twenty delegates like me had all pursued meticulously arranged but separate itineraries for meetings with various state organisations such as Avtoexport, Energomachexport, and Licensintorg in and around the capital of the USSR only a very short time before the Moscow Olympics were due to be held. I had managed eight meetings during the week but when I asked for more, I was told that I had fulfilled my quota and that it was not possible. I tried to help them distinguish between the pronouns as in "their" quota and "my" quota. This was not really successful as Russians could not understand the concept of more but only the concept of less at least in the context of work. I just figured that they were running short of shadows to keep us all under strict observation. A couple of days queuing up outside Lenin's Mausoleum, St Basil's Cathedral, GUM, the Beriozska and queuing every time I wanted a meal at any time of the day soon put me back on schedule.

After fighting this uphill bureaucratic battle for eight fun filled days it was actually a relief to be going home. We had come out on a BEA Trident 111 but were going back on Aeroflot in an Ilyushin complete with glass dome at the front so that the bomb aimer could see what he was aiming at. As we left Russian air space the captain was ill advised enough to inform us of this fact and a ragged cheer went up from all of the Scottish contingent, most of whom had had several vodkas by that time. This got a lot of odd looks from the other passengers most of whom were Russian. It also got a few nervous uncomfortable looks from the cabin crew who were only too well aware that there was normally at least one and sometimes more KGB border guards on board all travelling incognito. I reckoned that they were the well-nourished looking ones in the leather coats and dark glasses with faces like bags of spanners but what would I know.

"Anyway" I said cheerily to the stewardess "what is for dinner?" Her answer stopped me in my tracks" Its fowl!" she said. "I imagine it is foul I said but what exactly is it". "Stop winding her up" said Alastair "you know she means that it is chicken". "No, but you hope she means it is chicken" I replied. In fact, it might well actually have been chicken. After the meal I looked out of the window trying to see the north German coast through the light cloud while Alastair who was on the aisle dozed off to sleep. The stewardess returned however because she was under strict instructions to issue every passenger with an after-dinner mint whether they wanted one or not. I popped mine into my mouth immediately as you do if you like choccies. Since I was looking out of the window and not paying much attention as to what was happening around me, I did not notice that rather than waken Alastair from his slumber and resume a discussion on chickens she had laid his chocolate mint on his knee. Sometime later Alastair awoke. As he regained consciousness, he obviously noticed that something seemed amiss. He shot bolt upright in his seat, looked horrified, screamed and asked if somebody or something had shit on his leg. When he had calmed down slightly he

realised that it was an after eight chocolate mint had melted on the knee of his trousers
With the help of a Swiss army knife, which he had carried, since he was a boy scout
he was able to remove most of the chocolate in the toilet. Nowadays, flourishing a
large knife in the cabin would inevitably result in being overpowered and handcuffed
to the arms of the seat. This of course on some airlines would depend on whether you
had just been shot by one or more Sky Marshalls. At that period in time it was said
that on the flight deck of most Russian passenger aircraft there was a steel box welded
to the "transmission tunnel" which when opened by the captain was seen to contain a
fully loaded Makarov 9mm pistol. The stewardess on this particular occasion however
was completely unfazed. She looked like her off duty hobby might have been shot
putting, or stunning small bears with a blow to the top of the head. In any case, she
had only been carrying out orders and doing her job. One supposes that it might have
meant a spell in Siberia if the passengers had not all been paired up with exactly one
segment of minty chocolate each as per standard operating instructions. I suppose it
could have been worse. She could have poked him with a large polonium poisoned
umbrella and he could have glowed gently pulsating in the early evening dusk of a
summers evening after we landed back in the UK at London Heathrow airport.

Anything to Declare

Anyone under fifty will probably never have been asked the questions "Are these
your bags? Did you pack them yourself? and then have you anything to declare?"

It used to be that the UK and most other countries ran customs checks when people
were entering and occasionally also when leaving the country and at one time
virtually no one escaped the questioning and subsequent search unlike today when
only a minority of the millions of arriving passengers are stopped at customs. On one
occasion when arriving from Greece with my normal luggage and a huge bag of
oranges freshly picked from a grove near Corinth the customs man sent for a syringe
and drew some juice from some of the fruit to check if the oranges were loaded with
alcohol or drugs. In time I was able to assure them that the only drug was Vitamin C.

 At London Heathrow the authorities or more accurately HMRC customs and excise
authorities went to great lengths to keep arriving and departing passengers apart. The
arriving passengers are channelled through immigration and customs without ever
catching sight of a duty-free shop where they might be tempted to purchase items
which are allegedly cheaper than the high street prices. This is a great disappointment
especially for non-Muslim passengers from destinations such as North Africa or the
Middle East more so if they have just flown in on Libyan Arab Airlines or Saudia, or
a few other airlines which do not serve alcohol. It was also rough on Scandinavian
passengers, as the duty-free prices in the UK were only a fraction of their domestic
retail prices. Keflavik airport in Iceland however is different. It had one of the biggest
and best duty-free shops in the world called the Horn of Plenty. Official policy was
not only to allow you to enter it as an arriving passenger but in fact you were forced to
walk through it and encouraged to make purchases before they would open the exit
door. It was obviously something of a modern Valhalla if you were a Viking person.

Most Icelandic flights originated in Copenhagen and put down briefly in Glasgow
before the three hours haul up to Iceland. It was the rule rather than the exception that

returning Icelanders would buy their duty-free allowance at Kastrupp airport and drink it before they reached Glasgow. Those that were then able to get off the plane were allowed to buy their duty-free allowance again and consume it again on the long flight home. Those that were not able to get off the plane had to rely on the copious amounts of alcohol carried in the plane's galley. Some Vikings managed both. By the time they reached Keflavik therefore many passengers had bought and consumed at least two lots of duty-free spirits and still found themselves with nothing to take home to their igloos. Just joking. Most Icelanders lived in wooden houses with very brightly painted tin roofs. For them the Horn of Plenty was a godsend and ensured that they did not go home empty handed or at least empty bottled to their expectant families.

I always worried slightly when I saw the flight crews heading for the Duty-free shops in either Copenhagen or Glasgow and prayed that they had the strength of will not to buy alcohol or if they did, not to drink it. I consoled myself however with the thought that as a NATO base Keflavik airport had one of the longest and widest runways of any airport in the world. It also had one of the best radar systems in the world as it was strategically placed to intercept any Russian first strike nuclear attack aircraft or missiles launched against either Europe or the United States. These factors meant that landing a plane in Iceland generally made for happy landings as the pilot only had to line up more or less in the same direction as the runway to ensure a safe landing. This assumed of course that the rate of descent was not too exciting. Nowadays almost every UK airport forces you to walk through the so-called duty-free shopping area between check in and the departure gates. They also insist that you arrive at least two hours before departure time and that almost every shop is licensed to sell alcohol in some form often 24 hours per day so some passengers are poured onto the plane even if it boards in the very early morning. Airline management complain about the antics of drunken passengers but they insist on selling as much drink on board as they can.

It used to be that anyone smelling of drink would be denied boarding before take-off but now it seems it is almost obligatory and is actually difficult not to join the throng. I suppose that if you are going to be a Ryanair sardine you might as well be soused.

Around the World

Going around the world in a mere eight days meant that I had beaten Jules Verne or Phineas Phogg by seventy-two days. I was tired but pleased to hold the new record.

I set off from Stirling and went via Prestwick, to New York, Los Angeles Honolulu, and Fiji then on to Sydney non-stop, except for the refuelling of the 707 on the way. In the good old days, most airlines even gave you a certificate for crossing the line at the equator although were not much into dressing as Neptune on plying you with free drink. Arrival at Sydney two days after leaving home was odd because Kingsford Smith airport in these days turned out to be an unimpressive wooden building with a sliding door which defeated me for a bit until I figured out what I was doing wrong. I was dead tired but the Immigration officer had still given me a hard time by asking all sorts of questions. One of these was if I had a criminal record and I don't think I may have endeared myself to him when I pointed out that it was no longer necessary to be a felon in order to qualify for transportation to "down under". Another "other thing" which confused me, was that a planeload of eastern Europeans arrived at the same time as I did to be met by thousands more family waiting to greet them outside. The babel of Serbo-Croat made me think that I had landed in Sarajevo rather than Sydney.

After a few days of hectic business, it was back on BOAC which I was assured meant "better on a camel" but which quite impressed me. The flight to Manila, Hong Kong, Delhi, Bahrain and London seemed to never end but finally we reached London Heathrow and I transferred to a BEA Britannia for the last flight to Glasgow. As we roared down the runway and took off, I slumped exhausted against the window and fell asleep. Within a few minutes however I was disturbed by the passenger in the middle seat next to me shouting and agitatedly jumping up and down. Through the haze of tiredness, I could just hear the Captain come on the PA and announce that we were currently experiencing a perfectly normal abnormality and not to worry as we were returning to Heathrow. I opened one eye and peered out of the window to see smoke and flames coming out of the starboard outer engine and thought to myself "OK Biggles get out of that".

The fire seemed to be brought under control by the on-board extinguishers but the passenger next to me was still suffering mild hysterics and did not take kindly to my suggestion that he shut up so that I could get back to sleep. The plane circled gently dumping thousands of litres of aviation spirit over Hounslow. The pilot then made a textbook touchdown, which didn't even wake me, and I missed all the fun of the fire brigades and ambulances rushing along beside the plane as it slowed to an eventual halt. I didn't even have the excitement of using the evacuation slide down the orange inflatable chute to the grass. Since I was so tired, I did not care that it took some time to get everyone and their luggage off of the unserviceable aircraft and on to a spare which in these days BEA had no difficulty in bringing into service immediately.

When this replacement aircraft eventually got airborne and the seat belt signs were switched off, I thought that I would keep mine fastened and resume my interrupted snooze in the hour or so of flying time left before touchdown in Glasgow. This proved impossible however due to the fact that there had been a reallocation of the seats and a little oriental gentleman sitting next to me was persistently tapping me on the arm. When I looked at him, I realised that he was actually sitting cross legged on his seat but that he had taken a cigarette out of a packet and was looking for assistance to light it. In these days some seats were designated for smokers but I had no idea if smoking was allowed where we were in the aircraft and in any case, I had no matches or lighter to help him light up his cancer stick. This was apparently his main problem although neither did he appear to speak English so we did not really have much of a discussion. I thought that his best hope of assistance was if he summoned the help of a stewardess and pointed to the call button located in the rack overhead indicating that he should press it. I was rewarded by a nod of the head and a wide smile as he pressed the red button and then proceeded to put the end of his cigarette against it thinking that like the cigarette lighter in a car this would be the answer to his problem. I could not really believe what I was seeing but fortunately for both of us a stewardess arrived promptly and better still from my point of view advised him that we were in no smoking seats. One burning aircraft per day was one too many as far as I was concerned and as I slept for the rest of the flight did not even notice him fidgeting from nicotine craving.

Red, Red Wine

I could have taken the car but I decided that discretion was most definitely the better part of valour. It was not that I was worried by what the other traffic on the roads in and around Athens later that night might do to me. It was more that I was worried what I might eventually do to the local traffic which had a habit of driving mainly on the other side of the road to which I was more accustomed. I considered taking a bus but to be honest fascinating though it would have been I decided that a being a sardine in a smoky diesel smog is no fun and since life is too short anyway, I hailed a taxi.

Daphne was only about 30 minutes away and I could not wait to meet her although Daphne I should perhaps explain was a far-flung suburb of Athens just off the main road to Corinth. The taxi arrived just before seven o clock and made short work of the journey by using a few shortcuts to avoid most of the heavy traffic. There were still relatively few people about when the driver dropped me off at the entrance gate to a large wooded estate, as it was very early by Athenian standards. This was Daphne in all her glory and tonight was the start of the world famous annual Greek national wine festival. The festival itself was scheduled to run either for a week or until they ran out of wine whichever was the shorter period. The estate in which the event was held was both wooded and hilly with paths meandering amongst the groves of scattered olive and pine trees covering most of the hillside. Coloured lanterns were strung at intervals along the paths through the trees casting a weak glow on the stony unsurfaced paths to let everyone see exactly what it was that they had just tripped over in the gloaming.

Just inside the stone gate was a little booth from which the organisers controlled the entrance to the festivities. To gain admittance it was not necessary to buy a ticket. Visitors were charged by offering them the chance to buy either a rough coloured wine glass with or without a decanter and very luckily for me I decided just to settle for the glass itself. Once inside I roamed around at will and found barrels of wine strategically located just off the pathways and under the pine trees. To my amazement and delight the wine was completely free. I simply had to help myself by filling the glass from a barrel using the little tap provided in each one. When a barrel became empty the organisers seemed to appear as if by magic and quickly trundled another full one into its place. Even to my uncultured taste however I quickly realised that this was not vintage wine in the barrels. Each barrel contained a different wine and each wine appeared to be worse than the last as I got further from the gate. I suspected that the wine was of such a quality that no self-respecting Greek would drink it and that the visiting tourists in attendance were providing a much-needed public service by recycling it. Before total anaesthesia set in, I calculated that the wine was running out at about four pence a litre and as the evening progressed running out appeared to be literally quite accurate as the well dispersed amenities were tested to their limits.

The fame of the festival had obviously spread far and wide however and I could not help but notice that what appeared to be the entire manpower of the U S Seventh fleet which was at that time then stationed in the Mediterranean seemed to have shore leave and to be present. As time passed several hundred officers and ratings were nearly all reduced to a catatonic state and were lying over under or around the barrels so that the organisers could hardly get in to change them. It occurred to me that although the total might of the Russian Black Sea fleet couldn't put a scratch on the US Seventh fleet's massive sea power, a small friendly NATO nation had put them out of action in about a couple of hours without firing a single shot. I suppose if the Russians had had their wits about them, they could have occupied the whole of the eastern Mediterranean. As in fact they could just as easily have invaded Glasgow any Saturday morning when the bulk of the population were still suffering from the excesses of their Friday night's lager and curry. An hour or so later I met up with Leila, Paul and Tony all three of whom like me it seemed had avoided the worst of the wine. The four of us had dinner in the very touristy Taverna restaurant on site. The food was just typically local fare which is pretty much lamb three ways including mince or moussaka as they prefer to call it. Mediterranean food always seems to be lukewarm when served. The official explanation is that the natives used to cook on communal village ovens and the food cooled on the way back home. The oven here was about 5 metres from the table so the waiters must have wafted it like hell with a tea towel. The Bouziki was designed to stun the tourist's senses and keep the wine flowing at a high rate of knots but for me was more than a bit loud for serious conversation, eating and drinking. Leila of course as always wanted to dance and since Paul and Tony worked for me, I instructed them to dance with the lady as requested and this seemed to work just fine for all of us. It most certainly worked well for me as I leaned back tuned out and slowly savoured a few iced ouzos to get rid of the remaining taste of the wine that I had sampled earlier in the evening. This initial response had been before good sense had prevailed over my initial desire to make back the entrance fee by consuming copious quantities of what was on offer in the barrels. At around ten o clock which was a ridiculously early hour for Athens night life to be drawn to any normal conclusion we picked our way over and between what had been the cream of the US seventh fleet and took a taxi back to town and our hotel after dropping Leila back off at her penthouse apartment.

The Golden Horn

I always seemed to stay at the Istanbul Hilton when I was in town because it appeared to be a lot more comfortable than many of the more traditional Turkish hotels which although cheaper often left a lot to be desired at least as far as I was concerned. Even when younger I was not much into sitting cross legged on cushions on the stone floor. It is not essential to sit on cold marble floors to get haemorrhoids but it does seem to speed things up. The hotel itself stood on the top of a hill and the aspect to the south east side gave rise to a splendid panoramic view down on Democracy Park and the very ornate Sultans Dolmabahace Palace with its even much more ornate old Clock Tower. Beyond that there was a view to the south stretching away as far as the Blue Mosque, while to the east one could see out over the entire Bosporus which as usual was teeming with ships. Beyond this yet again there was a slightly more distant but still outstanding view out towards the Asian side of the stretch of water known as the Golden Horn which was only some few kilometres away from the hotel's location.

The outside of the hotel itself was a pretty uninspiring rectangular concrete box which looked as if it could have been designed and constructed in rural Albania but inside it was very well appointed to the usual Hilton international standards of the time. The thing that sticks out most in my mind was not so much the building but the staff in traditional Turkish dress who served Turkish coffee in tiny cups from a heated pot on a brass tray at all hours of night and day. Equally well remembered however were the extortionately high prices that they charged for their coffee although neither ever kept me awake as I tended never to go for a drink that could easily break all of your teeth.

Before Sir Alfred McAlpine built the first bridge over the Bosporus linking Europe with Asia most people made the journey by ferry. The ferries operated all day every day and were always packed with vehicles even although they operated every few minutes in both directions. On approaching the ferry terminal, you were marshalled into tightly packed rows in a large car park by anybody who could wave both arms. It was in the car park during the short wait to board a vessel that the entertainment or the aggravation began depending on your frame of mind. Vendors of almost everything imaginable circulated around the vehicles regarding the drivers and passengers as a captive market. They sold newspapers, clothes, food, postcards, souvenirs, lucky charms, drinks, cigarettes, pets and just about anything else you could think of and a few things that you could not. The lucky charms seemed to be quite effective because they sold very few life jackets and lost even fewer passengers on the way to and fro.

When the cars were on the ferry they were even more tightly packed together and most occupants stayed in the vehicles for the short crossing since it was difficult to get out in any case and there was little to do if you could. At this point after the cars were tightly jammed together on the deck the hawkers were joined by lots and lots of barefooted kids. They swarmed over the cars like ants besieging the occupants inside the vehicles by cleaning the windows or just simply begging for money so that they would go away and swarm over some other vehicle. It was not unusual to see several on one car at the same time distracting the drivers and passengers who often had the windows open because of the heat. One could be selling slices of watermelon; another could be selling doughnuts from a pile of twenty or thirty which he had carefully threaded onto an upturned walking stick and the third could be scrubbing at the car's windscreen. The windscreen cleaners would use the natural sponges, which almost certainly came from the warm seas around southern Turkey. I have even seen an urchin selling the driver of one car who was obviously not a local the sponge that he had used on the windscreen as a souvenir after he had cleaned the window with it.

Maybe the kids all had MBA's and probably BMW's as today this might be called after sales service or follow up. Because of the volume of traffic that poured over each way each day then there were fortunes to be made from this huge captive audience in the queues on either side of the straits as well as from the traffic on board. It did occur to me that someone somewhere was in overall control of all this activity and was collecting a rake off in some way or another from all of these seemingly very small individual amounts of cash constantly changing hands. I certainly had no desire to meet them however as we lived in different worlds and I intended to keep it that way.

Big Chopper

Some might have described George as an "eejit" but this would be unfair to "eejits". George was always doing things for effect and to show his superiority over everyone else. Unfortunately, the effect that he created was seldom the one that he had intended although he consistently and totally failed to realise that this was inevitably the case.

On one occasion George found what he regarded as the perfect opportunity to make a dramatic entrance back at the ranch and by so doing allowing us all to be in total awe. George had invited a successful businessman to visit the office for a short meeting with him knowing that the person in question would almost certainly choose to arrive by helicopter claiming that he had a very tight busy schedule to maintain. The pilot was well enough qualified to file a flight plan and navigate from A to B but George insisted in driving several hundred miles south to the helicopters main base so that he could "show the pilot the way" to the office. This was not a raging success because due to weather conditions the helicopter flew for the entire journey over the fairly low cloud base covering the country and George could have been flying up the Kyber Pass for all he knew or cared in fact. As the helicopter approached the final destination and circled the site the pilot chose to set down in the centre of a large clear concreted area between the office, the lab and the works. This was far enough away from all of the buildings so as not to cause any nuisance or disturbance to the majority of occupants. George however had a totally different idea as this defeated the object of arriving by helicopter if any single person on site was not fully aware of his dramatic appearance. He insisted that the pilot fly around the main office block and eventually touchdown on a large triangular lawn which was lovingly tended every day by the company's own gardener. The advantage of this lawn to George was that the Chairman's office and that of several of the other senior directors directly overlooked this area as did the windows of the IT department and the drawing offices in which he normally resided when he made it into the office at all in between his extensive travels. The lawn and the surrounding gardens actually provided a tranquil oasis of calm and a very pleasant view to many of the people toiling away in the office especially in both spring and summer when the very many flowers and shrubs were in constant and fragrant bloom.

Some of the occupants of the offices were probably a little startled and some possibly terrified when the Bell jet ranger banked sharply over the roof and set down in the middle of the grassy space with its whirling rotor blades only feet from the windows. Most were totally amazed and a few rapidly became completely enraged when the downdraft from the powerful rotors uprooted most of the flowers in the beds around the lawn and dashed them against the office windows with a loud noise like a heavy hailstorm. By the time the rotors stopped completely and George himself stepped triumphantly down from the helicopter he fully expected to be the centre of attraction. He certainly achieved that aim. On looking around however he was confronted by most of the staff staring in horror from the windows at him standing in the middle of a lawn with two large gouges in it and flower beds which not only had no flowers but barely still contained earth. In a very few seconds as his ears adjusted to the different noise levels, he plainly heard roars of rage coming from the building. As it turned out these seemed to be coming mainly from the company chairman and the gardener who were arguing fiercely with each other to see which could get to George first to kill him with their bare hands. The subsequent business meeting was fairly frosty as well as short and did not go well being mainly concerned with the issue of consequential damages. Subsequently George had great difficulty in persuading anyone to give him a lift south to retrieve his car still parked at the helicopter base and travelled by train.

Many years later it was decided to vacate the head office and move to newer larger premises within the main plant at Manuel some twenty-five miles away near to the town of Linlithgow. The lawns and extensive gardens around the office had been fully reinstated and were still absolutely pristine and well cared for to fully complement the building which it was hoped might be sold for use as a hotel or perhaps even as some sheltered accommodation for old age pensioners and other deserving people in the district. George decided that he would request some turf from the extensive lawn for his "little garden at his little bungalow" in Bearsden. The company secretary and the head gardener agreed that this should be possible, both having been given the strong impression and believing that George was merely trying to patch a difficult area in the small lawn of his bungalow They soon discovered however that once again in spite of many previous experiences they had seriously misjudged George and his ambitions. At the weekend when no one including the head gardener was around George turned up with a mechanical digger and an enormous truck. The team proceeded to remove every blade of grass on the lawn by stripping the entire area of the premium grade turf and removing it as quickly as possible. No doubt it was destined for a bowling green or lawn of some large house in the west of Scotland and no doubt it was not supplied free of charge to the eager recipients. Once again there was some spirited discussion in the company as to who was to be allowed to kill George first using only their bare hands. Unfortunately, by that time it was water under the bridge or more accurately turf under the railway bridge by which the truck had exited the site on its way west into the sunset. Neither George nor the lawn were ever seen again by any of us. It was in fact rumoured that George was keeping an incredibly and unusually low profile as someone in the Glasgow underworld was apparently also seeking to urgently establish George's current precise whereabout for some reason. In the local pub where we all met most days after work, we discussed Georges potential problems and even opened a book on his eventual fate. Over a pint or three everyone unanimously agreed that had the old office remained open as intended and had we been given a clear choice between George and the lawn we would all most definitely have missed the lawn.

Donut Forsake Me

The president told me to take them donuts. He had been over from America and was accompanied by the chairman for a board meeting at their UK subsidiary where I was appointed a director of another subsidiary much to my astonishment but satisfaction. He was in a good mood as was the chairman since the MD had performed the annual ritual of letting them both beat him at Golf at the Royal Liverpool club in Hoylake. It was an order as Presidents seldom regard their utterances to colleagues as only mere helpful suggestions to be considered along with any other possible options that sprang to mind. I initially regarded the donuts as an amusing suggestion but looking round the table I decided that as the MD was duty bound to countersign any expenses and the Finance Director was duty bound to reimburse me I was duty bound to buy a very large box of donuts crammed full of freshest dairy cream and luscious raspberry jam.

We had been discussing a potentially difficult meeting and accompanying technical presentation that I had set up for the following day at the Chocolate Factory in Alloa. The chocolate factory centred around a very large Herreschoff multi hearth furnace. Its eleven large hearths were about six metres in diameter and each weighed at least thirty tons. They were constructed from specially shaped high temperature bricks to each form shallow domes measuring nearly half a metre thick at their thickest part. Filtered sewage sludge from a large catchment area was fed into the furnace at the top. As it was conveyed downwards to each lower hearth it was first dried, then it was almost totally incinerated to emerge at the bottom as a light brown fine warm powder which we decided had the appearance and consistency if not the actual taste of cocoa.

Brian and I drove north the following morning and made reasonable time reaching Kincardine at about one o clock in the afternoon. Our destination, Alloa was only half an hour further away which gave us plenty of time to search Kincardine for a baker. We screeched to a halt outside Baynes the bakers in the high street and rushed in to check out what was available. Sure enough, there were several large freshly baked donuts filled with cream and jam and I bought four which were very soon boxed up.

When we reached the Clackmannan District Council plant side at Forthside we parked up and went onto the office to be warmly greeted by big Alastair and little George both of whom I knew reasonably well from previous encounters. Alastair truly was big and little George was actually the same size as everyone else but looked small when they were seen together. I told Alastair to get the kettle on as I had brought the cakes. Alastair immediately agreed that George would put the kettle on but decided that neither of them could have a donut as he was on a strict diet and was only having a bare couple of spoonsful of sugar in his coffee. George looked crushed so I wafted the open box under Alastair's nose and told him that we would have to eat our cakes otherwise they would spoil and that unfortunately we would need to share his cake between the three of us so as not to create unnecessary waste. Alastair decided that his solemn duty as manager of the waste disposal division of the county council was to put his own problems aside and polish off his cake as we had requested. After this we got down to business which was an urgent repair to one of the intermediate hearths. Because it was urgent and there were no special shaped bricks in stock or available on short delivery, we proposed casting the hearth in one large monolithic piece inside the furnace when it had been cooled down. This was technologically difficult and had never been done previously but because of the urgency it was decided to execute this.

Brian estimated the time, materials and costs and we had the office fax the offer by opening time on the following day. The offer was accepted and we mobilised to start the job as soon as it was cool enough to get inside. Within the allotted time span we had installed the new hearth in a very dense strong temperature resistant concrete and we handed back the furnace for operation on Friday afternoon. Alastair was then also given a recommended drying out and heating up schedule which was approved by his own independent consultant to get the furnace back into operation as soon as possible. This was absolutely essential to process the large quantities of sewage which were no doubt accumulating in some location which might not have been so easy to identify except perhaps by an odour which could no longer be masked by some powerful air freshener. Early on the following Sunday morning there was an enormous explosion as steam pressure which had built up inside the hearth due to too rapid heating, caused it to explode into thousands of small pieces and simultaneously cover Alloa with a layer of very fine light brown powder. It was calculated that in today's prices we had achieved almost about a quarter of a million pounds worth of improvement to the area while giving all of the many local gardens and municipal flower beds a most welcome addition of fertilizer. We obviously also boosted attendances at all of the area's car washes. It did make me reconsider however America's to me odd solution to apply jam donuts to solve all commercial, technical and environmental problems in life.

Brace, Brace, Brace

The first bridge over the Bosporus was said to have been a pontoon bridge built by Xerxes in 480 BC but not surprisingly no trace remains today. I am guessing that the people using it got pretty seasick and more ships sailed over it than sailed under it. The second bridge which is referred to today as the first bridge was opened on 30th October 1973 which was the 50th anniversary of the founding of the Republic of Turkey and spans from Ortakoy on the European side to Beylerbeyi on the Asian side. At 1560 meters long, the Bosporus Bridge was the fourth longest suspension bridge in the world when it opened in 1973 and was the first to connect Europe and Asia. It cost more than a billion dollars to build and it was so popular that more than a billion road vehicles had crossed it by the end of 1997. I believe that David Coulthard even drove a Red Bull racing car from the European side to the Asian side. When he reached the toll plaza at the eastern end, he did a power slide and shot back over to where he had started. After he finally parked his formula one car in the garden of the Dolmabahçe Palace where his journey had commenced he was told that he would be fined 20 euros because his car had been registered by the ANPR system as having passed the toll booths without paying a toll. Unlike him I never crossed the bridge in either direction after it was officially opened but I believe that I may very probably have been in the first car to cross from west to east around August 1973. We didn't pay a toll either as the bridge was not officially opened. To be honest it was not even completely built but we did not know that and it looked as if it was. After a good lunch in Istanbul we set out for a visit to Assan Aluminium in Tusla on the Asian side and we decided that using the ferry would be a waste of valuable time, fun although it had always proved to be previously. The bridge appeared to me to be open although there was no other vehicular traffic and both sides of the roadway was still littered with various plant and equipment as we set off on our shortcut to Asia. We drove safely if somewhat slowly over most of the bridge avoiding all the many obstacles and without attracting any undue attention from the many workers and others on the bridge so that we soon reached the Asian end. In our enthusiasm and with Asia in sight we decided to speed up a little to almost 30 miles per hour. What we did not immediately notice however was that while the European end was complete the Asian end of the bridge was not and the road on the Asian side was about still three inches lower than the road on the bridge as it had not been given its final blacktop. I think that the driver just shut his eyes and I know that I definitely did as well as clenching my buttocks. Although it was not the most violent landing I ever made in Asia it proved very effectively how well engineered and built Mercedes cars really were and the crash did not seem to be very much worse than we were experienced from some of the other potholes on most of the other Turkish roads at the time. We had a vote and took the ferry back as I had had enough of low flying and heavy landings to last me for quite some time. In any case it is easier driving down over a drop than trying to drive up it even with a ramp and even supposing that we had been able to find any suitable planks from the spare building debris strewn around. Sorry Jeremy mate but we definitely beat you and all your top gear team to that one. I have to confess however that we did not quite match up to the exploits of one TFL bus driver just before new year on the 30th December 1952, Albert Gunter was happily going about his day job, driving the number 78 bus sedately over Tower Bridge towards Shoreditch, when, to his utter amazement the road in front of him seemed to vanish from sight entirely giving him an excellent birds eye view of the Thames. He immediately realised that the bridge was in fact opening and that his bus was on a rising bascule! He opted to slam his foot down on the accelerator and the bus managed to jump the gap and successfully landed safely on the other side, before most passengers even realised what was happening. The police then decided that as a precaution, everyone on board would be taken to hospital for a checkup. There was only one reported injury from this bizarre incident and that was the bus conductor, who broke his leg possibly while trying to jump the gap on his own while weighed down by a ticket machine and a bag of old pre-decimal coinage. I don't know if the conductor got compo but the driver was awarded a day off work and a reward of £10 for his unexpected feat. In my case I thought about owning up to it but only briefly and quickly decided not to tell the Turkish authorities about the day that we unexpectedly decided to try and turn a Mercedes into a magic flying carpet.

Most Wanted

I have never been on the FBI most wanted list which over time has now exceeded 500 desperadoes as far as I know. The guy from the currently now defunct Immigration and Naturalisation Service which has now been superseded by the US Department of Homeland Security amongst other organs of the US administration however had me down as possibly being in residence in the lower echelons in the FBI least wanted list. As a result, he was not keen for me to gain entry to the USA when I landed at O'Hare Airport in Chicago on a flight from the UK. The reason eventually turned out to be that he said that I was already in the USA which was patently ridiculous as I was standing at his booth in the overseas arrivals' terminal. I got the usual spiel that "my screen shows that you never left after your last visit and that you have overstayed your visa" I pointed out to him that his screen was wrong and that if he looked at my passport he could see that I was a citizen of the UK, resident in the UK and had since obtained numerous other entry and exit stamps in my passport since last exiting his fair country. I had definitely visited several other countries in the intervening months when he claimed that I had been languishing in the USA and for who knows what nefarious purposes. In the good old days before the heavy use of computerisation almost every country in the world used to stamp the pages of everyone's passport for nearly every single visit. This used to sell a lot of passports as there were not as many pages in each document as there are now and the pages were soon crammed full of exotic stamps in weird languages if you travelled as frequently as I did at that time. Ironically now that there are more pages in the standard passport far fewer countries bother to stamp passports at least in Europe so most passports do now last for ten years as intended. The situation seemed to confuse the agent quite a bit until he was able to figure out somehow that when I left the USA for Canada more than six months before the check in staff had pulled the green visa stub out of my passport but had not lodged it with the INS. Entries and exits between the USA and Canada had never ever been subject to the most stringent of checks. In fact, at one time there was busy casino ship straddling the US Canadian watery border between Detroit and Windsor and one that you could probably have swam to in terms of the distance although not in terms of the ambient temperature. Even with a multi-year, multiple entry visa, it was necessary for me to go through the entire gamut of immigration and customs procedures for every single entry and exit into the USA. This was a slight complication if you wanted to visit Mexico even for a few hours but on two occasions I almost inadvertently slipped through the net. Once was when I crossed from Douglas Arizona to Agua Prieta and back an hour later by foot. I had been in a Mexican cantina for a tequila or three as you do and then bought a couple of banderillas as of course you must always do too. The banderillas were metal spikes in short wooden batons wrapped with bright red and yellow ribbons and designed to cause maximum irritation to a bull if you were able to stick them into the back of its neck. Not that I had any such intention even after a few tequilas had been necked. The immigration officials on both sides of the border were quite relaxed about the visit and only glanced at the passport to make sure that it was valid and neither commented on the weapons imported into the USA.

When I took my wife and son back to almost exactly the same spot at the border many years later everything had changed and not for the better. We went into a major burger joint on Fifth Street just off US highway 191 and were not impressed. The burgers which had formerly been minced and formed into patties from prime US cuts of beef looked distinctly inferior in appearance and to be honest the smell which prevailed in the establishment washrooms could have influenced my overall judgement for the worse. We survived the meal however then headed back over towards the border close to a new Walmart store. Adjacent to the store at that point there was a narrow dirty ribbon of water which appeared to be set in a large concrete drainage ditch with a high wire fence on the Mexican side of what turned out to be the Rio Grande in high summer. The barrier on the American side of the border comprised mainly of a load of disused and apparently abandoned Walmart shopping trolleys left there by various Mexicans returning home from their weekly shop. Naturally, as Scots my son and I checked them all out individually to see if any still had quarters left in the money slot. Unfortunately, the Mexicans seemed to have been even tighter than the Scots on this occasion and levered the quarters all out or more likely maybe never put them in the slots in the first case. On another later occasion when I came out of one of the big copper smelters after some business meetings I crossed back and forward from one side of the border to the other on a secondary unmarked track before I once again regained the main American east west US interstate highway10 and heading back to civilisation. I should add that this was before the days when the Donald decided to build a wall but paid for by the Mexicans and which in most places is actually a fence.

It probably was not before the days when some Mexican, and I have no doubt also some gringo business men were trafficking drugs across the border but I am very happy to report that I did not see any evidence of this activity nor possibly somewhat surprisingly any signs of surveillance of any kind. Maybe I was on satellite TV.

No one was really surprised that it took the usual three hours to clear the formalities at Dharan Airport. It was absolutely scorching hot there in the arrivals hall which had no discernible working air conditioning. There were a couple of big fans in the roof but either they were not working or more likely somebody had decided to impress this batch of the latest arrivals to Saudi Arabia by leaving them off to show who was the boss around here. The immigration officials at the desk obviously subscribed to that part of The Koran which reminds us that "calmness and patient deliberation is from Allah and haste is from Satan." While they were calmly and patiently examining everyone's passport in great detail checking for anyone with an Israeli stamp in it a few religious police or Mutawa were wandering up and down the very straggly line of foreign visitors. The Committee for the Promotion of Virtue and the Prevention of Vice, often assisted by volunteers were tasked with enforcing conservative Islamic norms of public behaviour, as defined from time to time by the Saudi authorities. One or two of the visitors had not heard or perhaps not believed that the import of all alcoholic drinks was totally banned from the country and were clutching plastic duty free bags with their favourite tipple. The Mutaween who were strolling around would whack an unsuspecting visitor on the wrist so that the bag was dropped and the bottle broken. Others were led to the centre of the room which had a slightly dished floor with a drain in the middle. The bottles would then be removed from the bags and the contents poured down the drain in front of the horrified owner and everyone else in the arrivals area. Well it was their country and their laws and they made no secret of the rules but it was most certainly a different way to win friends and influence people. I just thought that maybe they needed to work on honing their interpersonal skills and perhaps they still do. After that it was only half an hour to find a taxi, make it to the hotel, check in and have a Saudi champagne or large cool orange juice on the rocks.

After two days business in Dharan area I took the Saudia jet over to Jeddah and after three days there flew back to Dhahran via Riyadh for the final short hop to Bahrain. As I walked through the airport to the check in desk with my luggage, I noticed that there was an extremely unhappy looking foreigner sitting in a hard-plastic seat against the wall. One of the reasons that I noticed him was because I remembered seeing him sitting in the very same seat three days earlier when I had been first heading over to Jeddah. I nodded to him in friendly fashion since we were two infidels in the land of Islam. When we spoke together, I realised how foreign that he really was. He was in fact from Yorkshire. As we got chatting, he told me that he too had been intending to go to Bahrain but that the planes had been fully booked and that he had been unable to get on one for the last three days and nights. I could not believe what I was hearing. If he stayed where he was much longer, he would need to take out a mortgage on the seat. I gestured for him to follow me and we ambled over in the oppressive heat to the Gulf Airlines desk where I was to check in for my own connecting flight to Bahrain.

I pushed my own and my new found acquaintance's tickets across the check in desk and suggested that we were travelling together to Bahrain. The clerk immediately announced in a very grave voice that unfortunately the next flight was fully booked. Now I knew that he knew that I knew that it wasn't and that what I should have done was to carelessly leave a few banknotes in either the ticket or the passport as I handed them over. To tell the truth however it had been a hard week. I was hot and sticky and I was getting tired of the entire dreary and wholly predictable theatrical performance. I explained very succinctly to the clerk that he should stop being the back end of a one hump camel and just give us both a boarding card, which he duly did with some very considerable bad grace. We then passed through all the rest of the customs formalities and immigration procedures and were ushered through into the small departure lounge where a ceiling fan did now make a desultory but unsuccessful effort to move the air around just a little. My new found acquaintance who was obviously on his first and possibly his last visit to the kingdom was ecstatic. I felt duty bound to explain to him that a Gulfair Boeing had about 180 seats and that the airport staff would issue about 200 boarding cards for the flight so that it would still be slightly premature to start counting his chickens before the plane was actually in the air. As we sat there in the lounge just before boarding, I thought that I heard a Tannoy announcement requesting me to go back out into the main concourse for yet another customs check. It took me less than five seconds to work out that the disgruntled ticket clerk had suggested to the customs men that they should perhaps take another look at my baggage. I was able to figure out in less than another five seconds that this would not be a brilliant idea. In fact, I am sure that he didn't know that I knew that he knew that if I went back out through immigration to customs I would almost certainly be allowed to exit but that I would almost certainly not be allowed back since I only had a single entry and exit visa. This could mean about three or four days in Dhahran to get another visa before I even got back to where I was. Talk about snakes and ladders. I therefore decided that I had certainly misheard the Tannoy and when the flight was called boarded it anyway by elbowing my way through the throng and running like hell across the tarmac to get a seat on board. When the plane reached Bahrain some thirty minutes later then sure enough there was no luggage for me to collect. I filed a lost luggage report however and Gulf Air had it on the next plane within the hour since to them it was merely a lost bag. No doubt Saudi Customs had very quickly realised that there was nothing even remotely interesting in the luggage which consisted mainly of clothing destined for the laundry. Maybe they even went back and congratulated the desk clerk for giving them the extra hassle and work for nothing. Inshallah. One sincerely hopes so.

Your Policemen Are Wonderful

I had mentioned to Ray that I was transiting through Chicago and that I had almost three hours before my connecting flight with TWA to Kansas City. When he received all of my details he emailed back and insisted that he come to O'Hare airport to meet me and that we go out to a nearby neighbourhood restaurant for a very early dinner. The food was good and the beer which in the USA is always chilled was better. It is not always true that American beer is like making love in a canoe although indeed it can be near water. Time passed exceedingly quickly in his good company and with some lively conversation. Suddenly the realisation dawned on Ray that as the time had passed so quickly it was urgent that we were getting back to the TWA terminal at O'Hare to be certain that I could catch my onward connection. In those enlightened days in USA it was possible to board most flights if you reached the door at least ten minutes before the flights scheduled departure. Even so we both realised that we were cutting it rather finer than usual. He quickly paid the bill on his Gold Amex and we sprinted back to the car, which was brought to us by the varlet from the snowy wastes of the restaurant parking lot. When we turned on to the Freeway it was busy but we made good time to the tollgates at the entrance to the airport expressway spur. Ray must have been a former boy scout as he had the money for the toll ready in his hand and as we rolled up to the tollbooth, he tossed the coins at the collection basket. It may have been the fact that the temperature was below zero or it may have been that he simply drove up to the booth too fast. The result was however that he went through the toll before the machine had time to register the coins and the lights change from red to green. Although there was no physical gate to impede the cars progress as the barrier had immediately lifted, the act of driving through before the light changed from red to green triggered an alarm bell to ring and a strobe to flash. Having paid the appropriate toll fee however Ray ignored both and pressed on regardless. Within just a few seconds however a police cruiser had pulled out from a siding and we had the patrol car on our tail in hot pursuit. The state trooper had been sitting in his car at the side of the tolls impatiently waiting for somebody driving through without paying and now he was only a few yards behind with all his bells and whistles going. It felt just a bit like Smokey and the Bandit. The blue and red gumball machine on the police car's roof was flashing madly and his siren was going like a Clydebank air raid warning during the blitz. Ray cursed and pulled over but as the cars came to a stop he jumped out and rushed back to the trooper's car which I imagine was a very risky manoeuvre. He apologised profusely for the alarm and explained that he had paid but had an overseas visitor with him who had less than twenty minutes to catch his flight to Kansas City. The officer smiled, waved and shouted, "Follow me". He then drove to the TWA terminal flat out or as fast as he could weaving his way in between the few cars, which could not get out of his way quickly enough for his liking. When we reached the terminal entrance, Ray screeched to a halt and I leapt out of the car. As I grabbed my brief case and sprinted into the building, I quickly shouted my thanks back to the policeman who had been so helpful. He gave me a half salute unlike today when you are running away from a policeman and could get a full magazine. After sprinting like hell through the terminal I just made it to the plane as they were getting ready to swing the door shut. I offered my boarding card which they could see was from a connecting international flight and I was waved inside. I had barely made it to my seat and fixed my seat belt before the engines fired up and we trundled slowly backwards away from the gate and out to the live runway before any further snow fell.

Next day I phoned back to Chicago to thank Ray for the dinner and to tell him how impressed I had been by the local law enforcement officer's help. Without his prompt assistance I would almost certainly have missed my connection and lost my luggage which was already on board. Ray told me how pleased he was that I had been able to make the flight and had been impressed by the County Mounty. He then confided in me that as soon as I had disappeared into the terminal the trooper had booked him for jumping a red light by speeding through it even although he had paid the toll. He had been fined forty dollars but worse than that because he had an Oregon rather than an Illinois driving licence he could not pay on the spot and had had to go around to the local nick to be checked out and processed for being such a naughty boy. His gold Amex took another hit for the benefit of the Illinois state treasury Christmas fund.

Topping Off

Jimmy was a greatly travelled man and during the course of his very many exotic expeditions he came across lots of what he regarded as interesting people, places and situations. On his return from each of these travels and in the brief interlude before he set out again on his next odyssey, he used to regale us non-stop with his experiences of various adventures, which got better or at least more complicated each time, he told them. Each and every story was narrated dramatically with the full dialogue from start to finish. Inside Jimmy's head he could mimic the accents and the broken English of any people anywhere in the world whether it was black, white, yellow, pink or brown. To the rest of us in his audience however all Jimmy's accents came out in precisely the same broken English to such an extent that one of the lads in the office asked him one day if he had ever lived in any hot countries. Since he was in the middle of a story about Ebbw Vale in Wales at the time at look of bewilderment fleeted across his face before he shook his head ever so slightly and carried right on in full flow again with his tale. The management must have noticed that productivity in the drawing office rose during his absences and fell again by a significant amount on his return. Noting this I am sure that they convened regularly to debate and decide his next trip.

The only time I ever found Jimmy to be completely speechless in the entire time that I knew him was on one occasion when he was invited to be the guest of honour at the major ceremony of Topping Off a blast furnace in an integrated Iron and Steel plant in central Turkey. Jimmy had been working on his speech for weeks. He had written it, rewritten it and polished it by reciting it ad infinitum in front of his bedroom mirror. When he eventually reached the plant site in central Turkey he was ushered in and up to where he found the other assembled dignitaries. They were all crowded onto a small temporary platform on the new structure at about 150 feet above the ground. Various other luminaries had gone on at great length in Turkish no doubt emphasising their own important roles in the project and no doubt about how much of the credit was due to them that this magnificent achievement had come to fruition. During these speeches Jimmy was impatiently waiting for his opportunity to savour his impending 15 minutes of fame. During a short lull in the proceedings when two of the speakers changed over, he had just looked around him and noticed that one of the other visitors had brought a pet. It then very slowly dawned on him that it was not really anyone's pet but was in fact a large sheep on a short leash. The sheep however was standing so unusually still that it could have been stunned by the speeches but more probably had been given some sedatives. He was just reworking his speech in his mind to get in at least one reference or joke about a sleepy sheep counting humans jumping over a furnace when one of the officials handed him a razor-sharp knife and indicated that at the end of the speech, he should cut the sheep's throat. Jimmy was horrified and to calm him down the official confirmed to him that the sheep would be stunned but not apparently as much as Jim was himself. To aid putting the sheep totally at its ease one of the local dignitaries was apparently tasked to turn to the sheep and advise it in the local patois that its time had just come. This not surprisingly put Jimmy right of his stroke and his speech was so disjointed that someone suggested that to reduce the level of suffering overall it would have been much kinder to cut the sheep's throat and indeed every other person's present before he gave his speech rather than after it. He also made his excuses and left dinner prematurely rather than eat his lamb kebabs.

This was not actually the only episode on that trip that caused Jimmy some anguish. All the way over in the plane Jimmy had been going on endlessly about the offer of the month in the flight magazine which was an elegant gold Dunhill cigarette lighter. He finally bought it and then started on at me to buy something no doubt to help him assuage his guilt until in desperation I purchased a Polaroid camera which at that time was newly introduced from the USA. At dinner with the two most important clients after the ceremony Jimmy had been flashing his lighter ostentatiously and it soon became evident that one of the clients had determined that he deserved it more than Jimmy who he reckoned could always put it on his expenses, which he had in any case already determined to do. I could see that it was tearing Jimmy apart but could equally see that if he did not hand over the lighter, we could anticipate many fewer orders in future from our clients which was a situation I clearly did not relish. It only took a few seconds for a compromise solution to suggest itself to me. I told Jimmy that if he gave one client the Dunhill, I would give the other one the Polaroid. That way they could photograph the lighter and he could have the photo immediately to take home and admire at his leisure. He eventually and reluctantly did as suggested, but I can confirm that it's not comfortable watching a grown man cry.

Send Me A Postcard

I could of course be entirely wrong, as I remember one occasion in the distant past when I was also mistaken, but I must assume that Billy Connolly has not spent much time in the Middle East as it just does not compute. If he had, I just don't see how he could possibly have avoided going on at some length about often inevitably sparse and sometimes even non-existent toilet facilities are there. You must know the type that I mean that you encounter, but never unfortunately between oases or otherwise often enough. They usually consist of a twelve-inch diameter hole in the floor with a size 10 footprint on either side to slot your sandals into. The footprints themselves give you a hint as to which way to face not that it matters greatly as holes are often round as we know from our experience of life. The hole sems to go straight to the centre of the earth to judge by the heat and smell which emanate from it and also the fact that it is always impenetrable to light even when the sun is literally overhead. I can confirm too that it is most definitely not a good place to be during any period of volcanic activity which seem to occur with all too increasing frequency around the Arabian plate which keeps inching northwards. I can equally confirm the fact that it is not even a good place to be when it is not a period of volcanic activity. Neither it seems is toilet tissue usually an issue as more often than not there is none. There may occasionally be some loose sand or a sharp-edged rock for the skilful but even these are not guaranteed. This may be one of the reasons why the Boy Scouts left-handed handshake has never caught on in the area the other being the shortage of boy scouts.

Jimmy was forced into using one toilet in Istanbul however and quickly concurred with the recent findings of Swiss scientists who had corelated hot climates and spicy foods with an increased risk of intestinal upset. I never cease to be amazed at the range of projects for which governmental funding is available. In this instance there was not even a tiny shred of recycled paper to hand as it were. He decided to make the ultimate sacrifice and used one of the picture postcards which he had just purchased.

As good luck would have it, he thought in the way of a true Scotsman, he had not yet put a stamp on it but as bad luck would have it the postcard had a serrated edge all the way around. Judging by Jimmy's later description it had wreaked havoc on his gluteus maximus or should it be maximi since it was to both cheeks equally. He reckoned that he would probably have done himself less damage if he had used the type of scraper used to apply tile cement on a wall but had inadvertently left it in his garage at home. Jimmy spent much of the rest of that particular week explaining to anyone who would listen and many who would not, that he really did prefer standing to sitting since he had an extremely sedentary job. Apparently sleeping in the upper missionary position is much more restful for you as well but only if you use a snorkel with the table tennis ball removed so that you can continue to breathe throughout the whole night. I have to admit that I have bought a lot of postcards too and only recently disposed of a couple of hundred otherwise I would probably still have most of them. It was a postcard that I did not buy that caused me most embarrassment some years later however when I was in Guinea. I was nervously sitting landside in the so called, lounge in Conakry airport waiting on my passport and tickets being delivered back to me by the client's private courier service. I was approached by a young child. The child was a small boy who appeared to have no legs and was propelling himself around the terminal floor on what might have been an old skateboard. He could not speak any English but stopped right in front of where I was seated and stared straight at me with big sad brown eyes. He then offered me a selection of postcards to buy. They seemed to be monochrome photos but they were so old and dirty and tattered that it was impossible to see exactly what the subject matter really was. With a slight pang of conscience, I declined on the basis that for all I knew they could have had Ebola on them as well as tattered old photos. The boy said nothing but moved on to another westerner seated a couple of rows away who actually gave him some local currency paper money for the photos and then immediately dumped them in a waste bin. Unknown to him however the kid circled around behind him and retrieved the postcards quickly from the bin before moving on to offer them to someone else. Now that is what I call initiative, minimum investment, high stock turnover, 100% recycling and worth an MBA in anyone's estimate. He maybe even had a shiny limo parked in the shade behind the terminal.

Is It a Bird - Is It a Plane?

I always referred to it San Krawh which of course is how it would be pronounced by one familiar with the diktat of the Academie Francaise. This was probably why no one knew what I was talking about. The Americans I met however and all the locals referred to it as Sint Kroy. I was sorely tempted to fall into line but one must have and indeed retain some standards in life after all, or one is merely judged to be a savage.

The island itself was a paradise and the southernmost of all the Virgin Islands in the eastern Caribbean. It was not large but it was heavily wooded with the hills sweeping down to series of bays on the coast. Inland, hidden from the tourists was a huge scar where large multinational companies quarried and processed the bauxite that provided employment for those not engaged in the tourist trade. This trade was albeit somewhat spasmodic and depended mainly on huge cruise ships, which docked regularly in the main harbour at Christiansted. A good view of these vessels docking could be always be obtained from Jakobsberg, the hill directly overlooking the town. In between cruise ships life could be tough for some of the locals. Prices, which were high whenever the ships were in port, would drop dramatically when they left. It was possible to buy a tee shirt with some tasteful motto such as "**I slept on a Virgin Island**" for about half price when they weighed anchor and sailed off on the rest of the windward island's tourist itinerary. The real test for me was to find a T shirt that was not XXXL size.

I regarded myself as fortunate in being there between cruise ships as these could bring an influx of maybe a couple of thousand raucous tourists for a short frenetic invasion. Instead of fighting such a swarm I was able to obtain one of the best guest rooms in the Caravelle Hotel at the end of Queens Cross Street and at a bargain rate to boot. The large airy well appointed, bedroom looked out through French windows over a tiled balcony, which was almost the size of a small terrace. After unpacking my bag, I took a cool beer out of the fridge and went out onto the terrace to study some notes I had made and to prepare for some meetings the next day. The blue Caribbean lapped gently under the first-floor veranda as the water at high tide came almost right up to the bottom of the wall which was built on some rocks on the shore. It was a European first floor veranda as far as I was concerned as an American first floor is perplexingly to me always on the ground floor. St Croix was an American Island with European themes and Danish names. The capital Charlotte Amalie is actually on St Thomas a neighbouring island if that doesn't sound too Irish but it is still a fact even if it does.

As I looked over towards my right, I saw a few locals lazing about on a little slipway next to the hotel. After a few minutes I was distracted by a faint buzz which sounded like a distant mosquito. The buzz gradually grew louder and squinting into the bright sky I could see a small black dot which slowly took shape as an approaching aircraft. It was quite obviously propeller driven and as it came nearer to me, I could see that it was getting lower and lower. Closer still I could see a short stab of flame at the rear of each of the two engines mounted above the high wing which enabled me to identify it as an old Grumman Goose aircraft. I was a little concerned however as the noise of the engines started to sound to me as a little irregular. It continued its approach getting lower all the time until it banked slightly and appeared to go down into the water only a few hundred metres from the hotel. I jumped to my feet rushed back into the room and grabbed the phone. When the operator answered I quickly blurted out "ring for the coastguard cutter". I then rushed back out onto the balcony to see what disaster might have occurred. It was about then that I realised that the plane was a seaplane with what was a boat shaped hull and with two small stabilising floats at the outer extremities of each wing that I had not noticed as it approached. It had in fact made a text book approach and a perfect landing and was now taxiing towards the hotel with its engines coughing and spluttering as I sat watching the approach with some interest.

The five-o clock Antilles Airboat from Miami and nicknamed the Virgin Streetcar had just landed. Concerned lest I be thought a complete pillock, I rushed back into the room and grabbing the phone again rang the operator back. When she answered I demanded to know when they would "bring my toast and butter". When she confessed that she had not understood a single word of my original garbled message I was very greatly relieved and suggested that it was Ok as I would come down to the bar and toast myself with something perhaps containing a little alcohol perhaps with a hint of rum. As I went out again onto the terrace the seaplane was just pulling right up onto a slipway next to the hotel and deplaned some homecoming Virgin islanders. I thought that If I had been coming into St Croix from Miami, I would have used the service which would have delivered me within 50 yards of the hotel. Since St Croix was a US virgin Island there were no immigration or customs to be gone through. I would have missed the run in from the Islands airport however through some quaintly and some weirdly named parishes. There was Hope, Anna's Hope, Betty's Hope, Upper Love and Lower Love, William's Delight, Envy, Jealousy, Profit, even Slob and Hard Labour, with many more along the road. I was convinced that there were loads of tales to tell arising from amongst that lot. Maybe a large local Cruzan Rum over ice with some lime juice would help research along the way. It was worth trying anyway as I felt that if you are going to do research it is imperative that it is done properly.

Heart of Gold

I mentioned to Lex's wife that I thought that for all his alleged foibles, he had a heart of gold. She regarded me oddly for a moment before she responded by saying "so has a hardboiled egg". But I liked him. He was always helpful and generous and friendly. When he realised that I genuinely admired his considerable skills with a camera, there was nothing that he would not do to help me. At every opportunity he would come out with me to customers and take some stunning shots which I used for many and varied advertising purposes, He not only relished the challenge to his artistic talents but of course he loved every minute of it too just being out of the lab and dark room that he normally worked in. On one occasion at North British Steel in their Bathgate plant in central Scotland he insisted on getting an extremely dramatic shot of the underside of an electric arc furnace roof. This was to provide evidence to prove how the roof bricks had hardly any wear on them even after a record long campaign life in service. It was a very difficult assignment because not even Lex was dumb enough that he would climb into a large steel furnace at over two thousand degrees centigrade along with his expensive Leica camera in case he perhaps damaged the camera. The solution that came to him was that he would cower down on the shop floor while the crane driver in the large overhead crane which ran on rails the length of the building swung the roof off the furnace and over his head briefly to allow him to fire off a few shots that he thought would best illustrate and record the situation for posterity. Had this event taken place today everybody concerned would have been jailed for breaching health and safety regulations or maybe even more relevantly with assisted suicide. The roof duly swung overhead and Lex fired off his shots before the roof was again lifted back onto the furnace. On seeing the roof safely back onto the furnace I turned to find Lex still crouched down on the floor. I noticed however with some amazement that his plastic safety helmet had melted down over his ears and he was protectively holding the camera lens under his jacket. Lex was not the only one in a sweat as we peeled off the distorted helmet but he did get some unique shots of the underside of an EAF roof.

On a subsequent odyssey we both went to dinner in the evening with the customer in the five-star hotel in which we were forcing ourselves to endure staying in overnight. Lex had never been in a hotel quite like it and intended to do it full justice especially so far as the meal was concerned. To start with the waiter brought a large trolley with a magnificent selection of horse's doovers as he referred to them in a strong brummy accent. Lex was beside himself with delight to learn that he could have a portion of anything or indeed in his case everything on the trolley providing only that there was room on his plate. He finished the lot with great gusto although the salted anchovies slowed him down just a little and had him begging for a lager and lime to wash them down. After the main course of steak and chips Lex slowed again for a short breather.

Shortly afterwards he again welcomed the waiter returning to the table but this time with a larger trolley full of deserts of every kind imaginable. Lex's eyes positively lit up in anticipation. This gourmet dining was not nearly as hard as everyone made out it be and he was by then really getting into his stride after a few large glasses of Nuits St Georges. Before anyone else including our customer, who was our guest could even announce their selection Lex took command. "Just give me some of everything," he said "but not too many bananas because they take up far too much room on the plate". As he later weaved his way to his room, I could just imagine him picturing breakfast.

Three of us who ran a PR and promotion's company in our spare time also sometimes used Lex privately to take photographs for us, for brochures and advertising leaflets in the various ventures that we from time to time found ourselves involved in producing. While promoting a range of Scottish knitwear of all types for a very well-respected border company, we had need of some glamour models for a brochure that was being put together. We advertised in several local newspapers and hired a venue which just so happened to be part of Stirling castle for the photoshoot. Quite a lot of girls many with their parents or guardians and friends turned up and we found ourselves with a lot of good potentials to call on as necessary. During the shoot Lex sidled up to me a bit shame faced and informed me that one of the many mother's present had invited him to her home to photograph her two daughters privately for portfolios that they were putting together for a modelling agency. I told him not to worry and that if he wanted to do it, he should proceed on his own with this invitation and not involve us in it at all. Nothing further was heard until sometime later Lex told me the rest of the story of what had subsequently transpired. On reaching his clients large house he was welcomed in and invited to set up his equipment. A comprehensive set of photos were then taken during which the girl's mother kept Lex and herself going with several tots of whisky. After the initial session and while he went to reload for the second time with another new roll of film he realised to his horror that he only had two rolls in his camera bag Undeterred however he apparently just went on for some further time taking shots with no actual film in the camera and drinking shots until even he had reached his limit. He eventually made his excuses and left although apparently with some considerable difficulty as they say in the red tops. On leaving he decided that instead of driving the four or so miles straight back home on main roads he would detour about 25 miles over some small country lanes to reduce the chances of him being spotted weaving his way home by the local constabulary who in those days still patrolled the beat on foot and by bike and even occasionally in little Morris minor cars. It worked for Lex as far as the police were concerned but I understand that he got all hell from his wife on his return. When the shots that he did have were then eventually developed and printed he decided that discretion was the better part of valour at least in his case and posted them first class post to the client along with his invoice rather than deliver them by hand. Maybe it was something his wife said.

Si Si

San Diego has a long tradition of naval history. Not as long as Portsmouth but for the state of California and even for America it certainly covers more than a hundred or so years. Visitors to the town savour the nautical influence as soon as they approach the airport in their incoming aircraft. The approach on both sides affords a wide view of the vast naval dockyards full of all kinds of vessels from submarines and other surface vessels through to several massive aircraft carriers. It is probably just as well that the view from the cabin is so interesting as otherwise most incoming travellers might very well experience more than just some slight discomfort. Before the aircraft even flies over the perimeter fence around the airport with its undercarriage fully deployed and locked down the wheels almost brush the top of a roof on a bright yellow warehouse building on a small hill on the landward end of the runway. While the plane is still in the air or at the very latest, as the wheels first touch the runway the pilots who have to be specially certified to land there, slam the engines into reverse thrust and bang down on the short strip as if they were landing on one of the carriers. It is the sort of landing where you feel that an arrester hook on the plane would really be entirely appropriate. It always reminded me of the BEA Tridents approach into the old Edinburgh airport at RAF Turnhouse, where the plane just cleared the railway line before touching down. If it ever looked as if the plane was not slowing fast enough, ground control would very quickly activate a wire net at the other end of the runway to protect traffic on what at that time was the main A9 Road which is currently no more at that location. San Diego had no wire net but they did have a large Marina which fortuitously is the home of the San Diego fire and rescue service who could intervene if planes were still burning rubber when the end of the tarmac was reached. If a plane had overshot it might have skipped right over the marina like ducks and drakes and landed into the Seaworld Oceanarium among the killer whales, although admittedly it would have needed to be quite a skite of just more than a mile. Once outside of the airport it seems that everyone that you bump into is either an admiral or a retired admiral with the emphasis perhaps on the latter. If you were in the shopping mall and shouted out "admiral you have dropped your wallet" you might easily be killed in the convergence of old guys wearing sun glasses and baseball caps covered in gold braid. If the brass as the guys with the gold braid are often referred to, used to prefer Pearl Harbour in Hawaii as a base then this is no longer the case and they are now all firmly entrenched in southern California. Perhaps Pearl Harbour may have lost all or most of its former gloss in late 1941. Around San Diego too some of the best houses in some of the best areas have little flags or pennants on the neat lawn outside announcing their occupants rank and status. Being an admiral in the US Navy is quite obviously one of the better paying jobs on the West Coast and very probably on all the other coasts as well. Many Mexicans used to transit through San Diego on their way north to a better life as there was a major border crossing where US Highways 5 and 505 converge at Tijuana. For some of them it was where they pick up their first real money and for a few it is where they pick up their first ever words of "English". It is told of two boys who were only seeking their fortune in the land of the free and the home of the brave that they first stopped off at one of the palatial residences and asked if there was any work that they could do to earn some money. The lady of the house decided that she did have a job for them and led them over to the enormous double garage at the side of the main building. She pointed out some cans of paint in the garage and then loudly instructed them to paint the porch before retiring back inside for her daily siesta. Sometime later she was awoken by the doorbell. The boys had finished the job and had come for their money. She was puzzled however that standing at the door she did not smell any fresh paint, as she would have expected to. It was only when she glanced over to the double garage where the door was still open that the full horror hit her. The boys had painted her Porsche 911 a bright shade of pink. These two may very well now be back over the border in hiding but there has been no shortage of replacements and many of these are from much further south in central or southern America than Mexico. Some will no doubt get jobs in the tourist industry in San Diego but many will head north. As they get off the Tijuana trolley in downtown San Diego they can walk across the street and board the Pacific Surfliner at the Santa Fe depot to take the train up the coast to Los Angeles. From there many disappear into the black economy unless and until Donald catches up with them and trains them as brickies back in the south again.

A Lovely Pair of Melons

Bert was a big bluff hail fellow well met type and regarded food as fuel. He certainly managed to get through a few Kilos every day just to stop him fainting from hunger.

We were at a very formal technical institute dinner and the first course of melon and port was already on the table as we were ushered to our assigned seats by the Maitre D'. There were twelve seats at each table but as we started the meal there were only ten diners as one couple had not turned up. Bert demolished his melon in no time and smacked his lips as he scooped up the last of the port. Before his wife or anyone else could say anything, he swapped his empty melon skin for the full melon which was still sitting at the empty place next to him. On finishing this he did the same with the other spare melon. No sooner was this third piece of melon polished off however when my eye caught a movement at the door. There was the Maitre d' Hotel scurrying towards us closely followed by the two latecomers who were still to share our table. Even before sitting down, they realised that their melons with Port were not like any melon with Port that they had ever had before or that they could ever have anticipated. There were the empty skins with spoons still stuck upright in them. These two tardy latecomers were speechless with amazement and possibly embarrassment but Bert was completely unfazed. Adding considerably to their discomfort Bert loudly shouted for the waiter to return to the table. When he did so then Bert loudly informed him that "some swine" had obviously "ett thae folks' melons" and instructed the waiter to make sure that they got an extra ladle of soup which was the next course on the menu. It was no real surprise that Bert and his wife were not invited back to any of the local institutes future dining functions since the committee were obviously concerned by the potential cost for extra melons and port held on standby or even god forbid caviar.

One of Bert's hobbies was causing serious obstruction and delays on the roads and he contrived to do this by almost never driving anywhere in his car without his caravan in tow. On a wet Thursday he was heading down a steep hill when a wooden pallet which was not properly secured on a lorry in front of him was dislodged and fell into the roadway. To give him his due he reacted very quickly by both braking and also swerving to miss the obstacle and took great satisfaction form avoiding near disaster. He was less amused to find that as he braked, he was overtaken by his own caravan which had broken free of the towing hook and passed him at high speed only to be smashed to pieces on hitting a banking at the side of the road further on. He was even less amused to find that it was one of the company's lorries that the pallet had fallen from. Bert was good for my career however as by necessity and choice he prioritised his responsibilities in the company's mines rather than in managing the factory which he was in charge of and which was integral with one of them on their Castlecary site. As a result of this aided no doubt because of my qualifications and experience paying off as the plant and technical manger I was also appointed in addition to be the works manager. Since I was only twenty-six years old at that time, I was mildly surprised but mightily pleased although some of the minutiae like reading everything before I signed it was a pain in the gluteus maximus. It had its excitements as well such as the time I came across several gypsies one weekend loading scrap metal from material stored outside of our engineering department. Some of the scrap was tungsten carbide steel plates which we used on our hydraulic brick presses and was normally recycled for machining and reuse because it was so expensive. Rather than physically confront the whole gang on my own I noted the descriptions of the perpetrators as well as the type and number of their truck and phoned the police. Even my lone presence had however seemed to deter them as they quickly left before the police could arrive from their nearest station which was some miles away. After discussing everything with the works engineer, I filled in a detailed report including what we thought was missing from our stock. I must admit that I was not totally convinced that we would get a result even although the police assured me that they were certain they knew who the villains had been. Three days later however the police turned up with the truck and the driver and asked me to identify any items on the truck which had been stolen from us. The engineer and I were able to identify some tungsten carbide steel plates as similar to the ones we used on a daily basis in the plant to make thousands of special bricks.

I took the detective sergeant aside however and told him that in all honesty I could not positively identify the plates as having been stolen from us as many very similar steel plates were used by several other local brick plants for the same application and any competent defence lawyer could easily have claimed they were legitimately obtained elsewhere if the accused had gone to court. The very large detective sergeant put this arm around my shoulders and told me that this was an eventuality that would never materialise as the plates were definitely from our stock. When I asked him how he could be so sure of this when I could not be totally certain of ownership, he explained that it was because he himself had put the plates amongst all the stuff on the truck when neither the driver nor I had been looking. The drivers goose was well cooked.

Going Clubbing

Bill, John and Tony flew in from London and I made sure that I was at the airport in good time to pick them up. I decided not to use the company's fluorescent lime green Cortina. Peter had only managed to get it in the first place because he convinced my boss that Ford did not do drab standard colours in Mediterranean markets and if we did not take what was offered from stock there would be at least a six month waiting list during which he would have to hire some exotic alternative. It was the first visit to Greece for all three and John and Tony were looking forward to it. Bill who was the new MD never really looked forward to anything or if he did it was only in the sense that he was certain not to enjoy it whatever it was. They were all senior people in the company from Head office and we had some important meetings lined up over several days to launch our new Greek branch office as well as discuss some projects including the possible acquisition of a local company. I had made a little extra effort in the form of some meticulous planning to make sure things went as well as they possibly could. After meeting them as they exited from the arrival's hall, I ushered them across the road outside the terminal and into the car park where the Mercedes was parked. As I helped put the luggage into the boot, I could see that John and Tony were impressed but equally I could see that Bill was not. Never a shy man he quickly let me know that he thought that the car was over the top. I pointed out to him that the car was not for my benefit since he as a very senior executive of a prestigious British company who was visiting important Greek clients with his senior managers, we could hardly bowl up to their offices in Del Boys Reliant Robin. I also assured him that I had got it from Hertz at virtually the same price as a Cortina. I thought that it was entirely diplomatic however, not to mention that it was the same price for a Mercedes for a day as it was for the Cortina for a week. Bill appeared to be mollified by my explanation especially as it cast him in the role of visiting royalty. I encouraged them all to settle back and relax during the drive into town. with the aircon keeping us all comfortably cool while the occupants of lesser marques had to dangle their extremities out of their open car windows as they tried to create what draught they could by getting the airflow up their sleeves if possible. On the way in to our five-star, central Athens hovel (sorry Hotel,) I kept up a running commentary on all of the places that we passed and all of the famous landmarks that we could see further afield. I thought that this might head off any more awkward questions about the car like how many miles to the gallon did it not do or more accurately how many litres per km we might or might not achieve. I also genuinely thought that they would be interested as John and Tony certainly were. As we got into the city centre and passed the old Olympic stadium. I explained that we were passing close to the old part of town, which was built on the steep slopes of the Acropolis and was called the Plaka. I told them that it was the part of town where there were many restaurants and nightclubs and that most roads in that area of town led to the summit where the famous Parthenon was located. I added that although theirs was only a short visit I was sure that we could find time to go up there briefly one evening to see the floodlit ancient monument at close quarters. John and Tony thought that this was an excellent idea. Bill however said "Oh no you don't, we are here to work and we are not going to any tavernas, nightclubs or any other tourist attractions". How wrong he was on several counts as he would very soon discover.

Dicks Last Stand

The flashing illuminated sign announced it to be an establishment by the name of "Dicks Last Stand". Something told me that it was the kind of place that if anyone had an accident in the kitchen it would probably end up being eaten but not necessarily after having been well done. It was some American's idea of what a typical Australian restaurant would most probably resemble but it was in fact six thousand miles from Australia in Honolulu Hawaii. The staff however, were trained to the very highest standards. They were trained to be highly slow, highly sloppy and highly rude led by a few expats. They not only achieved their objectives but they surpassed themselves by far. It was a restaurant designed for masochists where greed triumphed over taste. It relied heavily on the fact that most clients would be in transit through a city that they did not know well and that most would never return. The only miscalculation, which they made, was in assuming that I would automatically leave them a tip at the end of my incredible dining experience. It was fairly easy for me to demonstrate that not tipping was an obvious riposte to their underwhelming offering and one, which Scots like me had honed to the highest art form over very many years of constant practice. It was also easy for me to demonstrate that being badgered by them for the tip that I did not give stood not the slightest chance of success. I had after all served part of my own early apprenticeship in Oz where I had learned that it was fatal to falter slightly in any matter. In the Antipodes I can confirm that it is a serious error of judgement to venture even an observation that perhaps it might rain later on in the day as this bring down heaps of scorn and epithets such as whinging Pommie bastard. It is far better when one is commenting on the weather in such circumstances to opine that it is certain to piss like a stallion shortly and that the bloody weather in Australia is about as reliable as a Melbourne tram in a power cut. Comments along these lines always earned immediate and full approval along the lines of "Struth, too right mate, it will defo be as wet as the inside of a goon bag by the early affo or I'm a drongo".

Not that I have anything against Australian restaurants their food or their staffs. I have been to several excellent establishments in Hong Kong, Singapore, Athens, Bahrain, Aachen and Earls Court. I have even been to a number of excellent establishments not only in and around Sydney Harbour but further out in Double Bay, Wooloomooloo, and other locations in New South Wales as well as Perth and Fremantle in Western Australia. In Wolfies, at the harbour front one memorable starter was of crocodile although I should hasten to add not a whole crocodile followed by a main course of Kangaroo tail although again not the entire tail. In Double Bay it was seafood and even in a barbecue style restaurant close to the airport there was a wide choice of meats and shell fish done to perfection since you were required to do them yourself. The Wooloomooloo restaurant did fish and chips to equal Harry Ramsdens although I would seriously council against a Vegemite sandwich in main street Kurri Kurri or indeed any other location. In Hong Kong the Chinese Australian waiters provided a high level of service while in Germany the theme was interpreted extremely literally. In Singapore Barry introduced me to a Bullshot. At first, I thought that it was perhaps a misprint but they proved that it was not when they brought a large steaming mug of Bouillon laced with strong Vodka for the soup and come to think of it the only course.

In Earls Court they struggled only slightly but if pushed admitted a problem with their "Barbie", as the urban area has tended to become somewhat deforested over the years. Fortunately, Calor gas came galloping to their rescue with a weekly cylinder delivery. In Bahrain they solved the potential food problem arising from not having too many edible Artiodactyla or beef cattle by concentrating on their highest priority which was to provide alcohol to transiting Quantas crews. The crews reciprocated by making sure that the restaurant was never short of fresh steak, which only forty-eight hours before had been mooing in the outback. It seemed like the ideal "Quid pro Cow" all round especially to westerners on a Friday lunch hour when most of the rest of the country was heavily engaged in their religious observance of Friday prayers.

A Rum Do

It was my first of very many visits to the Caribbean and there was a lot of ambience to soak up not to mention copious quantities and the ready availability of the strong local Rum. I dined on the terrace with the sun sinking fast in the west and dusk falling with a speed that surprised someone like me coming as I did from a far northern latitude where dusk always lasted a lot longer. The Caribbean Sea lapped gently under the decking of the veranda on which I dined and the surf broke gently on the white sand of the steeply shelving beach stretching on both sides of the house. Luckily it was not September, as I imagine that with a hurricane coming howling in from the south east the veranda would have been a different place and might well have been very heavily storm shuttered. To my left was the old fort still adorned with a few Carronades made in a large foundry just a very few miles from where I lived in Scotland and used, so I was told, by the pirate crew led by Bluebeard whose mansion was in the hills nearby. To my right the beach curved away under the palm trees in to the gloom lit only by the phosphorescence of the surf as it broke on the shore. The surf was quite clearly visible and no doubt kept may drunks on the beach safe from stumbling into the sea. We all know of course that since there is no phosphorous in the sea itself the glow comes from when enzymes trigger chemical reactions in bioluminescent bacteria.

After dinner I went for a stroll back towards town along an avenue lit only by a few flickering gas lamps which were intended to make the place look more picturesque. If anything, it actually made the place somewhat more menacing for those with only the slightest of nervous dispositions. It also made it more likely that you would trip over something like a rope, empty fish box or even someone lying fast asleep on the grass. At the end of the avenue was a little shop, which sold everything for the tourist. Most of this it seemed was stuff which had washed up on the beach like large shells and the floats which had broken free from fishing nets. Part of the shop however was given over to selling the extensive local assortment of Bajan rums. The thing which caught my eye, immediately was a bottle, which in fact just happened to contain wine. It was a bottle of Napa Valley red wine as it turned out but had quite a dramatic look about it. It featured a black label on a black bottle. The label depicted an enormous old steam locomotive, rushing through the coniferous forest in the Rockies at dead of night. The wine was imaginatively called Night Express and I decided to try it and hoped that it might possibly prove to be an interesting oenological experience in my young life. Some weeks later I was striding through Columbus Park in downtown San Francisco and noticed an old hobo lying on a park bench asleep but snoring like a locomotive. Still clutched by the neck in his vice like grip was the now empty bottle that he had been drinking from. Yes! you have guessed it. A quick glance confirmed that indeed it had been Night Express that had been tucked into the large brown paper bag he was holding. Obviously, this guy was a very sophisticated and discerning wine drinker just like myself but he appeared to prefer his pleasure in a bracing open air environment with a touch of early morning dew glistening in the first rays of weak

sunshine. Some of the rest of the vast range of rums of the Caribbean in all their rich
variety of colours and flavours were slowly sampled and enjoyed over the years even
although a few of them had a dash of some local fruit juice or spice added to lower or
heighten the taste. Most islands make a range of rums based all on distillations from
the local sugar cane crop. The cane is cut, crushed, digested and distilled leaving a
residue of crushed cane called bagasse which is the fuel for the process and large
quantities of sweet molasses, which can be used to produce cane sugar. The process
also creates the most fantastic smell which you pick up some distance away from the
distillery if you are downwind. All rums are thus colourless to start but range from a
clear liquid to an almost black liquid after blending with spices and colourings for sale
and consumption. Bacardi Rum from Cuba may be the best known and can be drunk
with many mixers. I have been known to sample the odd Cuba Libre or three but the
name confuses me even before I drink it. It means free Cuba and was originated in
Havana in1900 after the Cuban American war of independence. How adulterating
Bacardi with Coca Cola signifies Cuban freedom from American rule and influence I
can't even start to guess. I find that not even thinking about this puzzle while drinking
it enhances the flavour. Bacardi also do many other brands such as the gold coloured
Anejo which means "old or mature" but may be a marketeers cunning ruse to bump
the price up "mucho" which means that they saw you coming in your hordes.

Jamaica naturally enough have their marketeers too and one of their many tactics is to
make some of their rum like Appleton's Estate almost colourless and some of them
like Captain Morgan, black and spicy with additives. No doubt this helps some people
imagine that they are Blackbeard or more likely maybe Johnny Depp in his heroic role
as Captain Jack in Pirates of the Caribbean, rather than of course as in Sweeney Todd
or Charlie and the Chocolate Factory. Barbados too which claims to be the genuine
original source of Caribbean rum first distilled there almost four hundred years ago
has a wide range including Mount Gay. This like many others is rum to be savoured
and in my brief flirtation seemed not to leave an incapacitating hangover next day.
The local tour company which run Jolly Roger pirate ship cruises from Bridgetown
harbour every day probably don't serve this. I imagine that they use something more
economical to ply their unsuspecting clients with. Few seem to get outside the harbour
before succumbing to the heat and hilarity and when returning from their pirate cruise
in mid-afternoon after their liquid lunch many seem to need to be oxtered down the
gangplank into waiting taxis and ambulances to convey them back to local Hotels for
a further snifter or even to the Bayview Hospital for a session with a stomach pump.
There are about 30 significant islands in the Caribbean of which I have been on more
than a dozen more than once and between them well over a hundred varieties of rum
and that doesn't even cover the manager's welcome party fruit rum punch in St Lucia.
Basically, it is still pretty much a work in progress but I guess somebody has to do it.

Going Down on Kansas

They say that the older a man gets the further it was that he had to walk to school
although in my case this is not true. I only lived about fifty yards from the school.
Well, all right then it was probably nearer to twenty-five yards but I walked very
slowly as indeed it is said Shakespeare was alleged to have done in his day. Kids

these days have almost never walked to school as they are all driven there in 4x4 Chelsea tractors usually by adoring mothers or their often pissed off partners.

After my early triumphs in pedestrianism I have managed to travel a bit myself by many other different and varied modes of transport. I reckon that I have flown at least a million miles or more and it doesn't half make your arms ache. No, of course not from flapping them, but more from resting them on the rock-hard narrow armrests on plane seats as I stared out the window from thirty-five thousand feet or from twelve thousand metres if you were over Europe. It was not always as sophisticated as this however as in the early days it was more usually nearer to ten thousand feet or less in propeller aircraft, before I moved onwards and upwards and progressed in the world. One memorable lower level flight was the one I made over the prairies in the USA. The flight was from Kansas City which is the third largest city in Kansas and also the largest city in Missouri at the same time because they managed to build it on both sides of the state line. They even managed to get Kansas City International airport located in the wrong state which sometimes gets people into a right state and so often even causes utter confusion for anyone trying to figure out their actual flight itinerary. We took off late into the southwest in mid-afternoon with the dusk slowly gathering behind us and very soon the pilot started to look a little nervous. He pushed the only throttle full open as he tried to keep up with the setting sun but he failed because the plane was doing about one hundred miles per hour and the earth was rotating in the opposite direction at thirty six thousand miles per hour which made it a very uneven contest. I asked him what his problem was and he confided to me that he was not certificated for night flying and he had to try to reach Topeka by six-o clock to stay within the letter of the law. As we sped on, I reckoned that we stood a fairly excellent chance of making it until that is the engine faltered slightly. A few minutes later it did it again and soon it was spluttering on and off. More off than on and this caused the plane to lose some height as it moved down as if on a gentle roller coaster. Some wit once said that the propeller was to keep the pilot cool and if it stopped you could then look at the pilot and see him sweating. It did, so I did and he most definitely did.

It did not take long however for the engine to cut out completely and the plane went into a long shallow glide picking up speed as it went. As we got lower, I could see that the Kansas countryside was not really as flat as it looked from higher up with lots of little hillocks and a few isolated farmsteads. Even the flatter bits had the odd tree and boulder distributed randomly around. The pilot meantime was muttering a lot to himself and so I just assumed that he was a Catholic doing a bit of lobbying, or from his lips to Gods ear, as some say. He told me later that he was running through his flight checks but who knows. After what seemed to be an eternity if you will pardon the pun, the pilot slapped himself in the middle of the forehead with the palm of his hand before leaping to throw over a toggle switch on the dash. I thought at first that maybe it was his ejector seat or something but it turned out to be the switch which activated the auxiliary fuel tank. He admitted sheepishly that his preoccupation with pressing on had made him forget to switch over to the auxiliary fuel tank as per the standard operating procedures as he should have done earlier before the main tank was fully exhausted. Luckily the engine restarted and the corn in Kansas would be cut that year by a combine harvester as usual and not by a low flying Cessna with a part qualified pilot and a completely terrified front seat passenger. In circumstances like that you might be forgiven for consuming a stiff drink when once again on Terra Firma, but not in Emporia Kansas which was in a semi restricted dry County. The system was that you could only get a drink in a private club such as a golf club and only if it was ordered and charged to a member when it was poured from his own dedicated bottle behind the bar. As a Scotsman I was delighted that someone else would always be picking up the tab but not so delighted that I would have to find a private club and a generous member to sign me in and assuage my raging thirst. It's seems ironic to me to think that not being able to get a drink even in moderation just makes the desire to drink even stronger and the likelihood of overindulging greater. It's very likely why prohibition never caught on but Kansas didn't seem up to speed.

Boing, Boing

Most countries are fine while you are there in them. Most are different, but fine just the same. If you take people as you find them and try to fit in, then they too are fine. Different, but fine. It can be an entirely different thing struggling with officialdom however as they are trained not to relate to people but only to their own procedures.

It was things like this that made transiting through Mehrahabad airport in Teheran such a chore. The situation was that the airport was usually crowded and could be very disorganised especially if you neither spoke nor read Farsi. It took patience, which I was short of, and persistence, which I had in plenty, to achieve my objective.

It got to the stage that if the Iran Air staff insisted that there was no round the world Pan Am flight coming through that day when the time table said that it would, I just agreed with them and asked them to put me on any imminent west bound flight to almost anywhere. It was in this way that I first met Garuda International Airlines.

When I got onto the plane, I realised that it was an old stretched DC8 but I did not realise quite how stretched it was. When I looked up the aisle however, I could see for miles. Why Garuda put such a huge aircraft like that on a sparsely travelled route I would never know but it meant that the four other passengers and myself had a choice of about four hundred different seats. There was no need to squabble over whether it should be a window middle or an aisle seat when it could be all of them. The crew outnumbered us about three to one and there was no shortage of food so long as you liked spicy samosas and other exotic eastern delicacies. We spent most of the flight to Athens huddled in the middle of the plane playing cards in at least three languages. As we came in on our final approach from the East over the sea none of us noticed that the plane was a little bit higher than it should have been on the flightpath. This meant that when the plane crossed the perimeter at Vouliagmeni the pilot had to lose some additional height quickly and this caused him to flare out and make an extremely hard landing half way down the runway. As the pilot slammed on full reverse thrust, the airbrakes and the wheel brakes, caused the plane to decelerate violently and there was the noise of a galley cupboard door bursting open in the rear galley. As the plane then quickly slowed to a halt a large empty metal coffee pot came hurtling down the whole length of the plane bouncing every few feet until it finally crashed against the back of the cockpit door. Fortunately, when landing even in those days the regulations were that they kept the cockpit door shut and locked otherwise the coffeepot might have gone on right out through the cockpit window and kept on going till it hit Piraeus.

Hubble Bubble Toil and Trouble

I have never knowingly taken drugs although different countries have very different ideas as to what substances are allowed, tolerated or encouraged in each jurisdiction. In Saudi Arabia for instance alcohol can sometimes result in death because they tend to cut offenders heads off on a Friday night. If someone had been unfortunate enough to drink even a small quantity of the illicit home distilled alcoholic drinks sometimes found in the Kingdom, I imagine that being decapitated might actually be considered a relief and to result in considerably less pain to be endured throughout the next days.

In the USA they often tend to separate smokers off from society rather than from their heads which is perhaps odd when you consider that Virginia seemed to be the centre of the whole worldwide tobacco industry originally. For all I know it probably still is and for me there is strong smell of raw tobacco when you drive out of town into the more rural areas which still have big plantations. This is handy for all Scotsmen as they don't even need to buy fags and can inhale a whole lungful of nicotine laden air completely free. It also completely amazed me that a large multinational company in Pittsburgh gave a lot of their employees high quality padded jackets so that they could leave the warmth of the building in winter and stand in the street smoking at minus forty degrees and golf umbrellas so that they could brave the pouring rain to have a drag in spring and fall. The alternative employee gift was a heavy-duty canvas and leather travel bag which I chose so that I could exercise the option to leave the city and go somewhere warmer. In California hotels used to have a disclaimer on the documents given to you when you checked in on arrival that if at any time in future you contracted lung cancer it had absolutely nothing whatsoever to do with them as they had always disapproved of smoking. Nearly all of them however gave guests, multiple packs of book matches advertising their establishments and not everyone it seems regarded these as being solely collector's items although I confess, I did.

I firmly believe that when travelling far from home it is usually wise to watch out for psychoactive Mickey Finns, which come in all shapes, forms sizes and occasions too. Most Micky Finns are very unpleasant and have extremely undesirable consequences. The first time I saw a Hookah or Hubble Bubble as I called it, I thought that it was quite funny. The waiter almost had a hernia bringing it to the table after the meal as it was about the same size that he was. The base consisted of an enormous glass carboy of cold water. A small plug of brown fibrous material sat or was soon fitted into what looked like a small candelabra at the very top. When the plug was lit you could suck on a mouthpiece at the end of a long rubber hose and inhale the smoke, which was first bubbled through the water to cool it. After watching various people have a go, I was persuaded to give it a try. I could smoke or not smoke and was not much bothered but decided to have a couple of puffs just for the novelty of it. Whether I was doing it all wrong or whether somebody knew something that I did not, I am not sure but my attempts with the pipe seemed to cause some merriment throughout the restaurant. It would have been easier it seemed to play a set of bagpipes although not when on fire.

The smouldering plug that had been inserted in the equipment especially for me could have been heroin or pipe tobacco or it could have been a blend of dry camel dung and used bus tickets. All that I do I know is that it tasted a bit acrid and I decided then not to risk my vocal cords even although I had no intention whatsoever of singing on that evening or indeed any other. I have to report that I did not become addicted even to the extent that I turned down a subsequent offer of a Hookah in the far east of London in Ilford and that I have been able to go through the rest of my life since that first long ago occasion managing to resist the urge to even consider repeating the experience.

Bammie Barbecue

Long before CB radio became legalised in the UK due in a very small way to efforts from me to influence the government by lobbying for CB in meetings in some rallies in Scotland and in a demonstration in Trafalgar Square, other countries operated it as part of the legal radio spectrum. Even in Jamaica all of the lads had transceivers fitted into their white Fiat 124's. The trading company that they all pretended to work for not only encouraged this but also paid for the units to be bought and fitted. The theory was that no matter where any of the sales reps were anywhere within the island of Jamaica the company switchboard could contact them and give them a message or more likely another new assignment. This assumed of course that the sales guys were always within earshot of their vehicles with the ignition on, as none of them had hand held transceivers. Most of the time they were within the greater Kingston area and the system worked fairly well but occasionally if one of the guys would go further up into Mandeville or Ewarton, in the Blue Mountains where some of the mines and the other processing plants were located, it did not. In those cases, reception was difficult and sometimes the message broke up or did not get through at all. At other time the guys would just all decide collectively to give themselves the afternoon off. They would change channels and privately arrange a rendezvous, which was usually on a secluded beach while their regular channel was unanswered for an hour or two. In no time flat when they all hit the beach someone would collect some driftwood and scrub and start a small fire going not because it was cold but because they wanted to cook something on their impromptu barbecue. They all brought something to the party and between them cooked fresh fish, fruit and Bammies, which were washed down with cool Red Stripe beer from bottles in their vehicle cooler boxes. Sometimes there would even be a bottle of the local rum passed round. In fact, it was so local that one of them might have distilled it on an illegal still. The recipe for Bammies was so simple that even I could make them. Flour, water and salt well mixed and thoroughly kneaded so that they could be wrapped around a stick without dropping off and then cooked slowly over the glowing embers of a bonfire. Years before I used to make items similar to these when in the boy scouts only then we called them Twists and burnt our fingers as we ate them to a rousing chorus of Ging Gang Gooly Gooly Wotcher Ging Gang Goo.

None of the guys as far as I knew were in any of the two hundred or more gangs which apparently operated in the Kingston area but they still liked to add some little extra seasoning to spice up their Bammies. While no one would admit to it and indeed no one ever enquired about it I would not have been in the least surprised if one of them had added a pinch or three of Ganja. The Bammies never seemed to affect me in any way or at least that is my story and I am sticking to it but the Red Stripe lager and the fierce heat used to wreak havoc with my complexion and sense of balance. On one occasion I even took my socks and shoes off and waded into the shallow sea to gain some respite from the blazing sun which was turning me the colour of boiled lobster. Unfortunately for me someone had used the beach for a barbecue before and while in the water I managed to tread on some old fish spines, which snapped off and stuck into the sole of my foot. Although I removed them immediately as best I could one foot became very swollen and tender so that I was unable to get my shoe on over my sock. For the rest of that week it gave a whole new meaning to the old term of "island hopping" and I may have looked a bit Long John Silverish but without hat and parrot.

Discount Card

Fred had been banging on all week about it. On the flight from Singapore to Kuala Lumpur and on the connecting flight from KL up to Penang he had felt obliged to mention it again. He must have told me about his new international traveller discount card at least ten times. The card had cost him a bundle of Singapore dollars but he assured me that with up to 15% discount on hotels and car hire he would soon recover this and be in pocket many times over. I am not completely certain why it was such a big thing since Fred was a director and minor shareholder albeit in a family company. This effectively meant that while he could not go mad no one was scrutinising every cent of his expenses. Maybe it was just about winning or maybe he was proving to his boss what good value for money he was but neither was really necessary since it was obvious what he did. The card did not work in the taxi from the airport to the hotel either however and I had to mention to him that it appeared not to be the answer to everything. This was a mistake and when we got to the hotel Fred was in a defensive mood. He strode up to reception desk and dinged the bell for service. The receptionist was there in a flash to process our reservations and allocate our rooms to us. Fred flashed out his gleaming new card and handed it to the receptionist. He demanded that we both be given the maximum discount of 15% on our bills when we checked out. The receptionist started to explain that this would not be possible when Fred ignored her again demanding his discount. She again started to say no but Fred immediately asked to see the manager whom he was sure would be much more amenable to giving him what he believed was his due. The Duty manager was summoned and before he could say anything Fred again launched into his routine. The manager eventually managed to get a word in edgewise and explained to Fred that the receptionist had been trying to tell him for the last five minutes that she could not give Fred a 15 per cent discount since in the hot summer season the hotel gave all its guests a twenty per cent discount to boost business which was always a bit slow in that hot humid season. Fred's face was a picture and I still have it. I am not sure whether he still has the card.

I was back in northern Malaysia on my own on the island of Langkawi in October 1987 staying in the Sheraton which was a five-star luxury hotel on a beach in the west of the island and now apparently renamed as the Century Resort. The rooms then were mainly in chalet type buildings scattered throughout the grounds and on the beachfront. When I arose early in the morning to be first "down for breakfast" I had to go along the wooden walkway which ran along the shoreline and which connected the chalets to the main hotel building with its reception areas bars and restaurants. As I walked to the restaurant, I was astonished to see quite a few little monkeys leaping around on the handrails of the pathway as well as the adjacent trees. Suddenly it made sense of the notice that I had read in the room which strongly advised guests to keep their sliding patio doors firmly closed when not in the room. I came to the conclusion that it would be an equally good idea to keep them closed even when I was, as the air conditioning worked better anyway. There was also a notice on the walkway rail itself which advised caution as the monkeys were apparently incapable of distinguishing between food and human fingers so I nonchalantly put my hands deep in the pockets of my chinos as I sidled past them. The dining room itself was remarkably monkey free and as the first guest of the day I enjoyed the best pick of the breakfast buffet which suited me just fine and dandy. The hearty cooked meal and a couple of cups of coffee set me up nicely for the day's business of several meetings in the islands large cement plant. When I had reached the main building itself however on my way to breakfast, I had noticed a separate doorway in the main building with a large sign announcing that it was a nightclub and would be open for business that night and presumably every other night as well. I thought that in the evening I might have a quick drink there before heading for bed. This plan however was thwarted by an announcement on radio and television that the King had died and the country would, as one would expect, be observing a period of deep mourning. As I was due to leave Malaysia for Singapore early next morning the kings unfortunate demise had minimal direct effect on me as the closing down of many of the national institutions had not really had time to fully take effect. If I had waited any longer however for any reason it could have been very different as I could have been stuck in Langkawi or even KL for a few more days because of all the regulations imposed and the ceremonial that the country was observing. Getting home on schedule was a small price to pay for missing out on what might in any case just have been an expensive beer in a small almost empty night club .Sharing the bowl of mixed nuts on the table with a troop of frolicking music loving monkeys cavorting around me might not have been much fun.

Ambush in Athens

If you are under twenty-one then you have never been in Athens Hellenikon airport because they shut it in 2001 to make way for the newer Eleftherios Venizelos airport in time for the Olympics in 2004. The original airport which opened in1938 was soon commandeered by the Nazis and used as a Luftwaffe base until the end of the war when the Americans took it over. It had two terminals, the old western terminal which was used by Olympic Airways for all their domestic and international flights and the newer glass and concrete Finnish architect designed eastern terminal which all of the other international airlines used. Actually, there was a third terminal between the two which few ever saw, or were even aware of, but was used by the US Airforce as part of the NATO agreement right up until the end of 1991. The east terminal was often busy but never crowded. All of the arriving and departing international passengers were bussed in and out between the aircraft and the adjacent arrivals departure doors in the main terminal because it had no piers. On entering the building airside, you first walked through the lounge which served both for transit and departing passengers, to the escalators in order to reach the main ground level with immigration controls and the baggage collection area. This meant that any arriving and departing passengers could actually socialise if they knew each other or even if they didn't but just wanted to try their chat up lines. This is something which was pretty unique and would never be allowed to happen now in any airport because of stricter security considerations.

It had been another good visit for me. Business had been brisk and everything had gone absolutely to plan for once. Ian and I were in good spirits some of which were seventy proof. We had decided that we could afford the luxury of a good meal in a decent restaurant to finish the day off. There was no real hurry so we lingered over desert and coffee. We did not have to check into the East Terminal at Athens Airport until almost midnight. If everything went according to plan the QUANTAS 747 from London Heathrow en route to Sydney would touch down just after midnight and we would be off to Bahrain about an hour later on an overnight flight sector. When we reached the airport neither of us wanted to buy any postcards or souvenirs so we went straight through security and immigration to the departure lounge which was fairly empty at that time of night. Security had barely detained us at all so we reckoned that this gave us a few more minutes in the bar before the flight departure was scheduled. When the jumbo did arrive, it was quickly processed. Deplaning passengers from the UK disembarked with their luggage and the plane was refuelled and revictualled for the next leg of its journey. Just before the flight was called for boarding another flight arrived and parked nearby on the apron. It was a Libyan Arab Airlines flight from Tripoli and some of the passengers came into the transit lounge just to stretch their legs. Some were wearing western clothes and some flowing Arab robes and head dresses. We barely noticed them as we went through some perfunctory last-minute checks on our boarding cards in the short queue of passengers before catching the bus out to the plane for the flight to Manama. Some two weeks later the lounge that we had been sitting in having our after-dinner drinks, before boarding the plane, was bombed and machine gunned by a group of terrorists. There were four in all, two men and two women dressed in gaudy western clothes as if they were on their way to visit Venice Beach in greater Los Angeles. They arrived in from Libya intending to hijack an EL Al flight to Tel Aviv but it had already departed. In those days each airline printed its timetables in little booklets but maybe they could not read in Hebrew or in English. In spite of their target having gone they still produced automatic weapons and grenades from their hand baggage before shooting indiscriminately into those who were in the lounge that night. The brunt of the attack was borne by passengers waiting to board a flight to New York. Before airport security men could react three victims were killed and fifty-five others injured in the attack. The two gunmen were convicted and sentenced to death but the two women were released as it was claimed that the two Black September terrorists were just using both of them as cover. Today the whole airport is a vast refugee camp for over three thousand people who have landed in Greece or one of their many islands by boat as refugees mainly from Africa. Although a "leisure complex" is planned this is one of these projects which will have to be seen to be believed and only time will tell if the proposals by a large Sino Greek financial consortium are really serious or not but the prospects do not seem good.

A less traumatic ambush resulted from my meeting with Kiri Lagos a jovial gent with thinning fair hair at his foundry north of route 56 in north east Piraeus. Jovial ginger giants are not ten a penny in Greece especially ones which own and operate ancient establishments which would make even Steptoe's yard appear to look excessively tidy. His head office was a large shed which had obviously undergone several earth tremors which are not entirely unknown in the region. It was air conditioned by the light onshore breeze which ruffled the reed thatched roof of his large veranda. We sat in an assortment of chairs in its shade chewing his homemade Greek coffee. He spoke as much English as I spoke Greek but the conversation between us was relayed by a classical Greek scholar and an Australian. We seemed to hit it off enormously well to the extent that we even received a modest order for some Touvla, (furnace firebricks). On taking my leave I was presented with a large rough old glass flagon of at least two litres capacity. The glass had a number of small bubbles indicating that it must have been handmade although by whom, where and when remained a total mystery to me. It contained a colourless liquid retained firmly in place by a large cork held in place by some rough twine around the neck. I enquired through my intermediaries what in hell it might be and was told with enormous smiles all round that it was most certainly Greek Whisky. I in turn enquired if Mr Lagos realised that he still had to pay for the order. I was told that the payment would indeed be made from a big wad of Drachma. I was also quietly informed that Mr Lagos would be most deeply offended if I did not appear to be totally delighted with this impressive unsolicited gift. "Efcharistó para polý" was my beaming response to my benefactor as we extricated ourselves and then made our way through all the debris strewn in the scrapyard back to the car which was parked in the cool shade under nearby trees. Now I was ambushed, bushwhacked and tangoed. I was well and truly lumbered with this gift and lugged it all the way back to London Heathrow. I passed easily through immigration now called border controls but I am sure that the duty officer pressed the emergency bell on the underside of his desk to prewarn the lurking customs officers who were no doubt enjoying a coffee of their own, that there was a right one heading for them. In the customs hall I swerved rapidly towards the red channel for goods to declare, plonked my overloaded bag down on the low counter and announced that her majesty's customs and excise had a big problem. I explained that I had no idea what was in the flagon and whether my genial giant had given me a big bottle of strong drinkable spirits or whether he had filled it with water for a joke on St Boris's day. The officer called for backup and told me that if it was alcohol it would cost a lot of money. I told him that I was not paying a fortune for what might well be only a misshapen unlabelled bottle of warm water. After much more dialogue he suggested that we call it ten Bob. I immediately named the carboy ten Bob before exchanging a small crinkly brown note worth 50 pence in today's money for a customs and excise receipt and scarpered very quickly out into the main terminal to catch the shuttle to Edinburgh. Can anyone possibly envisage the reaction today if someone pitched up in a major European international airport with a large glass container of clear viscous liquid with a wick sticking out of the cork in the neck. I admit that it is sheer conjecture but my best guess is that within seconds you would have the entire building more or less completely to yourself. Within a few minutes more you might have an entire SWAT team with long barrelled sniper rifles trying to shoot you from behind their armoured cars at a range of eight hundred yards.

Don't you just yearn for the good old days of foreign travel when life at least usually appeared superficially to be very much less complex than the global dog and pony show with all its fiendish, dreary, time consuming new rituals that travel involves today in this enlightened modern age. Me too, but dream on because it is never ever coming back.

Simply Simon

Simon believed that Singapore was the Garden of Eden. He liked the people, he liked the ambience, and he liked the food although some of it could be just a touch spicy at times. He liked the shops on Orchard Road and the surrounding areas where countless bargains in cameras, radios, TVs, watches and all sorts of other things abounded.

The weather was not bad either considering its proximity to the Equator. It had been a steady temperature and humidity for the entire time since he had arrived and he had acclimatised well and been able to get on with a lot of work in reasonable comfort. It was indeed a tropical paradise until it rained. Actually, rain is an entirely inadequate description of what it did. It sheeted down as if a waterfall was emptying onto the town. When we came out of the exhibition hall, we could not believe what we saw. The roads were awash and the storm drains were working overtime to dispose of the millions of gallons of rainwater, which swirled down them. It was only about 50 metres from the building to the waiting taxis but we were loath to make a run for it since we knew that we would be wet when we got there. On the other hand, we did not know whether the storm would last one minute or one hour. The Singaporeans are however world renowned for their business acumen. Even as we hesitated, several hawkers appeared in the foyer of the building selling transparent plastic ponchos and black umbrellas. Enormously relieved at their appearance Simon decided that he would take charge. He rushed over and demanded to know how much the umbrellas were. The hawker offered him the choice of any one from his substantial stock for 5 Singapore dollars. What if I buy three? asked Simon in full bartering mode looking forward to getting a substantial quantity discount off the list price. "Three umbrellas for twenty dollars" responded the hawker in a flash of inspiration since he was very considerably more accomplished in bartering than our young Simon was. "Done!" shouted Simon and fished out his wallet to consummate the deal. You know, come to think of it, the hawker did look just a little bit like Del Boy. With a clean shirt and tie instead of a coloured tee shirt he might even have featured on the trader's floor of the Hang Seng or other oriental Stock exchange battling it out with Nick Leeson. This seemed to be quite an amusing incident I thought, but then I remembered that back in the UK Simon was an officer in the Territorial Army. It was alleged that he personally commanded a reconnaissance squadron of light tanks which I always presumed were not the inflatable models used to mislead observers in enemy aircraft. It is only to be hoped that if the Russians ever crossed the Elbe, Major Simon and his men would know exactly which steps to take to halt their rapid advance on the town of Morpeth. Billy Connolly tells of when he was a Terri on exercise in the Troodos Mountains in central Cyprus. His platoon captured the enemy infiltrators that they were sent out to find including someone who worked in the same shipyard in Glasgow as Billy did himself. He pointed out with absolute logic that he could have saved a lot of time effort and money if he had just crept up behind him in the canteen before going on manoeuvres. When Simon was much younger and working as the sales manager for a small company in Morpeth in Northumberland, Simon was first introduced to the T.A.

by his then boss. Peter was a country gentleman who lived in a large house set among trees in its own extensive grounds a few miles south of Morpeth. He was too young to have served in the second world but might have been in the Korean conflict or even been conscripted as a national serviceman for all I know. Because of his standing in the community he was probably at the very least a colonel in the Northumberland TA. He was concurrently a major shareholder in a small local manufacturing company which fortunately as far as I was concerned had a professional manager and a long serving experienced workforce so that you may gather that Peter and I were never "besties." At one point I mistakenly agreed under pressure to subcontract an order to Peter's company for some products needed as part of a package for a large project but outside the manufacturing range of my own company's normal supply. As the day of shipment approached, I contacted Peter to advise him that I had been designated to carry out a technical inspection of the goods before they were assembled in our own packaging and shipped out abroad. Peter seemed slightly reluctant when I spoke to him on the phone but did not make a big issue of it partly because neither of us knew the other very well. When I arrived on site the order seemed to be in good shape and almost ready to pass my inspection. Before I finished and signed the order off, I realised that there were a few standard items that were not yet assembled. When I questioned the plant personnel it transpired that Peter had sent a couple of his men to the reject pile to retrieve a few of the better ones to make up the total quantity needed for the order. I did not take this well and neither it appeared did Peter as in the three hours it took me to drive home Peter had been on to my boss complaining about the young whippersnapper who found it necessary to inspect what he had produced and especially since they were only for a bloody foreigner. When it was "Buggins turn", Peter was duly elected to serve for one year as President of the long gone and soon forgotten Refractories Association of Great Britain. Here at the annual President's inauguration dinner and dance it was customary for the assembled throng to be addressed by the incoming incumbent on the state of the economy, the woes of the industry and the apocalyptic outlook for the future. Peter holds the record for the shortest speech in the history of the association. With seven words delivered in three seconds he announced "Ladies and gentlemen let the dancing commence".

To Hell and Back

Scandinavia can be heaven or hell depending on where you are and what time of year it is. Anywhere where tankards of beer are virtually impossible to come by and cost about eight quid each if you find one inevitably leans more towards the latter than the former in my humble opinion. In fact, one winter night I actually briefly encountered Scandinavian Hell almost quite by chance and have no desire to repeat the experience. We started on a floating restaurant in Oslo harbour which I understand is no longer there. I regret that this particular ship has sailed as they say or may perhaps even sunk. It was on this boat moored by the quay serving mainly sea food ranging from fresh lobster bisque through whale meat to exotic Scandinavian cheeses and deserts.I had a memorable meal. Being below zero in the dead of winter we were totally enclosed in a large warm comfortable dining area and extremely snug. After the hearty meal and drink or three including the inevitable toasts in Linie Aquavit which is distilled like vodka from potatoes and then flavoured with caraway, dill, coriander, anise and various other ingredients no one was feeling any pain, the extreme cold or indeed very much else at all. Afterwards we made our way to the Centraal station and boarded our night sleeper train for a fifteen-hour, journey north to Moirana which was located just on the Arctic Circle. Sleep came easily in the warm train as it gently rocked and rolled north but I woke when the train stopped in the middle of the night in what appeared to also be the middle of nowhere but was actually in the middle of Norway. I sleepily peered out of the window and saw that there was a sign saying "Welcome to Hell" which I admit initially caused some slight concern until I realised that it was indeed the name of the little community near Trondheim where the train had stopped to change crews or perform some other mundane operational activity. I also noticed that the snow was about two meters deep alongside the single line track but was slightly reassured when I recalled that the train had at least one snowplough at the front and maybe had one at the rear as well for all I knew. When we reached Moirana on a cold dark overcast morning with a stiff breeze blowing I alighted from the train. I found on reaching ground level that I was standing on a sheet of ice. It was dark and overcast perhaps not so much because it was early but mainly because it was midwinter and thus for dark twenty-four seven. I took a first small tentative step forward and found myself being propelled across the open ground to the main station building by a stiff freezing breeze which fortunately was going the same way that I wanted to travel. A late full Norwegian breakfast set me up for the rest of the sub-zero day and we flew back to Oslo that night after a full day's meetings in the Iron and Steel plant. On the way to the airport John commented that the big signs at the side of the road with the black figure 80 inside a red circle meant that we should not be driving at more than 80 km/hr. "What are tungsten carbide studded tyres fitted on all four wheels at enormous expense, for then?" I asked somewhat perplexed at his naïve comment. To be fair he was Norwegian but had spent the last 15 years in Brasil and so was not good on ice.

There must be music somewhere in Norway but the only example of it that I ever remember is of an Oompah brass band marching along a main street in Oslo one summer giving it large. Sweden on the other hand gave us Abba whether we wanted them or not and every Thursday night goes crackers on music and dance. Thursday in fact appears to be national grab a granny night in every town in Sweden from Kristianstad in the south to Kiruna in the north and virtually everywhere in between that has a hall that is big enough for at least a couple of grannies to be musically grabbed. Even worse was to be grabbed by a granny which was why inevitably for me Thursday was a night for watching satellite tv in a variety of languages. If you have never seen Taggart dubbed in Swedish German or Italian then you have never truly lived the dream. One Saturday afternoon in Stockholm I also saw a drug addict who had been shoplifting run out of the NK department store hotly pursued by a security guard. He was weaving in and out of the many pedestrians in Hamngatan but the fit guard finally grabbed him. It was at this point that a Swedish granny who thought that a scrawny little guy was being mugged by a big tough guy started to hit the guard over the head and shoulders with her umbrella allowing the junkie to break free and vanish into the crowds. To me this confirms you do not mess with a Swedish granny as they can be incredibly confused and literally anything can happen and usually does. One of my other escapes from Sweden was from Helsingborg in a big noisy Sikorsky helicopter direct to Kastrupp airport outside Copenhagen. This bone shaking almost deafening experience took a little under an hour to complete although it seemed longer perhaps because it was all over water. It could have been worse if some of it had been underwater but at least there was clear view of Copenhagen for the last ten minutes. Copenhagen truly is as wonderful as the song has it and was a favourite destination as well as a transit point within Scandinavia all year round. The Tivoli is unmissable but there are dozens of other delights throughout and around the city. A visitor can always round the day off with a tour of the Carlsberg brewery which they very modestly claim has probably the best lager in the world and who am I to dispute that humble claim without perhaps at least one more tasting. As well as the food and agriculture which abounds, Danes also make iron, steel, aluminium, petrochemicals and liquorice aplenty. Their vast municipal incinerator which burns their waste and generates lots of electricity is very cunningly disguised as an artificial ski slope used by thousands as they have almost no hills. Tony introduced me to Erik but who knows if that was his real name because all Vikings are called Erik aren't, they and this one was larger than life and living in Naestved which is a pleasant little town in southern Denmark. He didn't have a hat with horns on top when we had dinner but for all I know he had a spiky tail and a pitchfork to go with his devilish grin. We were sitting in the bar of a restaurant which I recall may have been the wooden pine panelled Ilden having a pre-prandial drink to settle the dust of the day before sampling the fine local cuisine. In mid swallow I was mildly surprised to see an enormous hairy biker with full leathers but hornless helmet come into the bar and head over towards us followed by some equally hirsute clones. I was equally surprised when Erik and he exchanged greetings and Erik then introduced us to the giant as the president of Denmark's Hells Angels chapter. Erik offered to buy him a drink but he said that he had just stopped by to say hello and had to be off somewhere else to take care off some business. Since the Danish Hells Angels and the numerous other big motorcycle gangs in the country were in a permanent state of war with each other over drugs and god knows what else I was delighted to hear his visit was to be so brief and that if a murder was about to be committed that it would probably be in some other location that evening. While sitting with us he was joined by his moll who was wearing an enormous loose tee shirt under her leather jacket. During a lull in the conversation he lifted up her tee shirt put his head under it and shook it violently from side to side making odd blubbering noises. She seemed barely to notice this and I felt it was not really my place to comment on every day Danish folk customs. As they left shortly afterwards, I could not but help noticing the message inscribed on the back of his leather biker jacket which stated "If you can read this then the bitch fell off." I took Tony aside later and suggested that he not introduce me to any more of is Danish friends as I felt that I had sufficient of my own who normally trod the paths of righteousness. Danish hells angels have probably descended from the early Viking raiders but have lost much of their innate charm and bonhomie over time as they slowly evolved giving up their long ships and acquiring Honda's and Harley Davidsons instead even although these are less seaworthy.

The Abominable Snowman

"If you don't care, fly Quebecair", went the local saying, although that seemed a little harsh. I thought that they tried hard under sometimes difficult circumstances. Still this was one of the shortest flights in their schedule from Haute Riviere to Rimouski so as long as they made it across the St, Lawrence I thought there was little to worry about. Mind you it was in a DC3 and it must have been at least forty years old if it was a day.

The Douglas Dakota was sitting just outside the building. One very slight problem however was that it was at least 40 below zero. Another was that there was a stiff breeze blowing up the river which took the wind chill factor down much further yet. A third problem was that it was snowing hard as well as horizontally. However, the pilot weighed up the odds in favour and against and then decided to go in any case. His warm home and cosy bed after all were on the Eastern shore so he had every incentive to make it quickly and safely across the St Lawrence river in one piece.

We ran crouching over into the wind driven snow, which was felt like sharp needles. It was advisable also not to breathe during the short journey, as the cold air would have been like being stabbed in the throat. I climbed up the steel ladder and clambered up the steeply sloping plane to my seat at the centre of gravity. A large box girder ran across the cabin floor from side to side. I consoled myself however that it helped to hold the wings on as I arranged myself in the bucket seat and fixed the seat belt. The Stewardess pulled the ladder in and slammed the hatch shut before going to her seat at the front. Both engines fired with a tremendous roar and the pilot ran them up against the brakes to warm them while short blue flames stabbed out of the twin exhausts on either engine. We taxied out onto the holding position at the end of the only runway when the radio crackled into life and the pilot was asked to give precedence to another aircraft for takeoff. The other plane was the Quebecair BAC 111, which was running late going back to Montreal because of the time they had taken to de-ice it. Suddenly as we sat in the holding area there was a muffled crash and the door hatch fell open allowing snow and freezing air to blow in. As the stewardess got up to close the hatch again a bag came hurtling into the plane closely followed by what looked like the abominable snowman who then lay on the floor gasping for breath." Bon Soir" said the snowman as the stewardess helped him into a seat and slammed the hatch again. The pilot shrugged, shook his head, released the brakes and turned the plane onto the main runway. He gunned the engines and we shot off down the runway a few minutes after the BAC 111. For some reason I could not help thinking that it must be the local equivalent of running to catch the last bus home from Stirling every Saturday night.

Polar Beer

 Although I was bit jet lagged and not at my sharpest when I turned around, I was as near to having thermonuclear diarrhoea as I have ever been in my entire life. The first thing that I saw was a enormous off -white polar bear which was at least eight feet tall standing on its hind legs with its front paws outstretched. Each of its two huge hairy front paws was adorned with several razor-sharp claws all of which were it seemed reaching out to grasp me while it presumably bit my head off in one bite. It took me a few shocked seconds before I realised that the bear was stuffed as had it not been, I most certainly would have been. It served admirably however to bring me back fully awake after the tedious eleven-hour long flight from London to Anchorage Alaska on BOAC that I had just de-planed from in transit to Tokyo. After a few seconds more to regain what passed for the rest of my composure I decided that I badly needed a drink after that traumatic experience and sought out the airport bar wherever it might be located in the terminal. I knew that we would have a stopover of about an hour to refuel the plane plus whatever time it took to unload and load any transit passengers and their luggage. This was not long enough to go into town but long enough I hoped to be able to stretch my legs by strolling around inside of the rest of the fairly small terminal in what I sincerely hoped was a polar bear and wolf free zone. Following the signs for sustenance I walked upstairs to the lounge bar which overlooked the apron in front of the terminal where the BOAC Boeing 707 was parked and where it was now being quickly serviced for the remaining final leg of the flight across the bleak snowy wastes of the North Pole to Tokyo's new Narita Airport. The Tokyo airport was in fact so new that even a few days before local Japanese farmers had still been trying to abandon their tractors on the runway to discourage incoming flights. Fortunately for everyone the Tokyo police had been immediately mobilised to change the farmer's informal parking arrangements and drag them back to the other side of the perimeter fence. In the meantime, I achieved my immediate objective by locating the upstairs lounge and slipped gratefully onto a stool at the bar. I admired the panoramic views out over Alaska all the way to the distant mountains in the cold crystal-clear weather with only a few scattered cirrus clouds in a bright blue sky. Someone once said there are two seasons in Alaska winter and next winter. There was a light covering of fresh snow and the whole scene could have been taken from a Christmas card or indeed put onto one by anyone with a good camera. My first priority however was to quench my high-altitude induced thirst resulting from too many hours in a low pressure, aircraft cabin. When the barman came over and asked "What can I get ya" neither of us really had any doubt whatever as to what I would like and in fact the sole reason for my visit to his domain was definitely to have a cool drink. I was almost hallucinating about the imminent arrival in front of me of a large cold lager type beer in a tall frosted glass. As is always the way in America however ordering something is only the first step in what can often be a rather lengthy process of interrogation. The barman insisted that he wanted to know exactly which brand of beer along with numerous other irrelevant details such as the shape of glass and the type of nuts to go with it. Since I had never been to Alaska before and had not studied the availability of their alcoholic drinks, I had no idea what the local poison was so that was exactly what I ordered - a local brew, just to make it easy for him I thought. This still seemed to flummox the barman slightly but after he had expertly poured some of the amber nectar straight from the tin retrieved from the big fridge behind the bar into the glass, I took a big swig before idly looking at the can. This had been left half full of the remaining beer for me to top up my glass when I was ready for it as service only went so far and it was deemed more satisfying all round to pour the dregs yourself. Frankly I was confused when I saw that it was a Budweiser beer claiming on the tin that it had been brewed in the

Anneheuser Busch main plant in Milwaukee Wisconsin rather than even under licence locally in Alaska. Even in my befuddled state I realised that Milwaukee was some three and a half thousand miles away to the south east of my then current location. This was about the same distance that it was from Glasgow to New York and I had never heard of Tennant's Lager being served in Manhattan as a local beer. I thought that it was perhaps worth just mentioning to the barman that I had really been hoping to experience the joys of a new untried local draught beer to add to my list of global travel experiences rather than a tin of imported American lager. "Buddy" he replied "that is as local and as draughty as it gets around here in winter". "In that case you had better set another one up right away" I replied "I usually only drink pints". I did manage two followed with a trip to test the plumbing before they called the flight for Tokyo to re-board one more. I made my way downstairs to the boarding gate again keeping a sharp look out for giant polar bears or anything else for that matter that may have posed a danger to my life and limb before I once more regained the discomfort of my hard seat on the next leg of my trip across the pole to the land of the rising sun.

Grivas Bodily Harm

The Ledra Palace was a large luxury hotel built in the traditional Mediterranean style. Unfortunately, it was built in Cyprus which is currently an area of the world where all and sundry seem to regard prominent buildings as targets since no matter how terrible your aim is, it is it is statistically impossible to miss them all of the time when at close range. For some years it managed to survive relatively unscathed. Quiet and refined it sat in its own manicured grounds between Shakespeare Avenue and Drakos Avenue to the west of the old walled city of Nicosia. it long gave the impression when inside the building that it was an oasis of peace where you could sit in the afternoon and have tea served on the terrace overlooking the lawns. Lunch or dinner in the dining room also provided a view out of the French windows with a similar peaceful outlook.

Outside the hotel grounds however it was hell. The so-called green line was nearby and bisected the city and the island into two warring camps. In the north the island was more or less under Turkish Cypriot control and in the south, it was under Greek Cypriot control. Perhaps control is too strong a description of the situation which most of the time was at best loosely administered by the United Nations. It was possible to drive around the hotel or indeed the town, but not always advisable to do so especially at night when one of the least of the problems was being stopped at a roadblock and asked for identification. In one company that I visited in Nicosia the street that it sat in as well as the building itself seemed perfectly normal for a small-town business. In the manager's office however the large window at the back opened onto the totally uninspiring view of a grey breeze bock wall only a mere couple of feet away. When I expressed some surprise that local building rules and regulations would allow such an aberration, I was told that this was a wall hurriedly built to indicate the position of the green line which was the demarcation between the two squabbling local communities. It was really just one way of many ways in which the majority of the Greek majority population hassled the minority Turkish population in every way that they could think of. In my humble opinion it was bigotry exacerbated by greed cloaked in nationalism.

In the south of the city the security procedures were if anything more prevalent. Blue helmeted troops drawn from Denmark, Canada, or Ireland used to assemble the many motorists who wanted to drive down to Larnaca into a convoy. They would then take them under armed escort to their destination. The main road passed a low lengthy escarpment, which was especially dangerous, as it was frequently to be found to be the haunt of snipers. Whose side the snipers were on was never clear perhaps the protagonists took it in turns to ambush travellers just for the target practice. It was quite likely that they were mostly just bandits trying to make a living from a little light highway robbery. Britain had large sovereign bases in the south of the island housing both Army and Airforce personnel but they left the convoy duty to the UN troops as the opposing factions and rag tag and bobtail in the mountains seemed all to be equally unenthusiastic about the presence of any British nationals on their island. The UK had tight security on the bases even although the bad old days of EOKA terrorism were supposed to be long gone and over and done with. I had no doubt however that there was a George Grivas lurking behind quite a few of the rocks and maybe even an archbishop Makarios lurking behind the taller ones so that he did not need to remove his hat. The ordure really hit the rotating object in midsummer 1974. The Turkish government finally got fed up with all the pussyfooting around on the island and launched a full-scale military invasion. Within a month of their landing they had partitioned the island, but this time there was no doubt where the borders lay.

The next time I saw the Ledra Palace was on the TV news. When I returned home to the UK. A camera looked over the shoulder of a Greek Cypriot Bren gun team. The gunners were lying on the luxury carpet on the drawing room floor in the hotel and shooting out through the French windows at advancing Turkish troops who were coming across the lawn dodging behind Rhododendron bushes and the odd palm tree. Unlike the British who tried to keep on talking the Turkish Government had tired of diplomacy, which they believed was getting them nowhere slowly. Within a short time, a ring of steel had been thrown across the island and the republic of Northern Cyprus unilaterally proclaimed. Suddenly EOKA evaporated since instead of a stern talking to and a cool look from the British, they were getting hot lead from the Turks. Turkey then encouraged mass immigration from Turkey to Cyprus so that today there are about 330 thousand "Turks" in the north and 660 thousand "Greeks" in the south. The island is now claimed to be in the EU except of course that it isn't because the northern third is still administered separately by Turkey which is not a member of the EU. Turkey is unlikely ever to give up the north and seems equally unlikely at present to ever be a member of the EU. If I was a cynic which of course I not I am sure that I could draw some similarities with Ireland except of course obviously for the weather.

Cuba Libre

Things are seldom what they seem. The Cuban language is a lot like Spanish but with many fewer words for luxury items which have been in short supply or non-existent for the general population for many years. Cuba has had a very large mining industry from which they derived most of their foreign exchange since in those days there were not really all that many tourists. Nickel is very much more valuable than the tobacco exports which the USA banned and the tourists were a bit wary after the Americans under John F Kennedy threatened to incinerate the island if the Russian freighters carrying missile did not turn back. The nickel smelters consumed vast quantities of raw energy and materials to produce the little shiny grey pellets, which were exported round the world to make stainless steel and other strategic items. The Americans made it difficult for the Cubans to do business with anyone and the Cubans it seemed to me made it almost as difficult for anyone else to do business with them either.

So here I was flying in for a meeting which had been arranged only with very great difficulty and was to be held in Vienna rather than Havana. It did occur to me that it had been a mistake over the poor phone line but it was also true that Vienna was a place where capitalism and communism often did meet up on neutral territory. My meeting was with three Cubans who were not keen for me to go to their embassy. Perhaps they thought that if I did, I might see or hear something that I should not. Nether was it in one of the main hotels as presumably they thought that it was too public and we might be overheard. The meeting was arranged to take place in a small restaurant in the early evening. There may have been a perfectly simple explanation such as they just enjoyed a meal and a drink at someone else's expense but it was like something out of The Third Man. It was an overcast winter's day with snow clouds gathering all adding to the general gloom. The dimly lit and smoky restaurant was in a cellar with a stone floor and stone pillars supporting a vaulted ceiling. We sat behind a pillar at a small table that had a piece of material like a carpet as the table cloth. There were three of them and at least one was the security officer, looking after the technical expert and the commercial man. With a candle sputtering in a holder in the middle of the table and the sound of zither music echoing around the room it was indeed very Third Man as depicted by Graham Greene in his 1949 novel and black and white film. At one stage a small group of Gypsies came round the room playing at each table and it did cross my mind that they were from MI6 trying to overhear the conversations. I expected Harry Lime to leap out from behind the pillar at any time. Maybe the whole thing was a figment of my overwrought imagination but I decided to enjoy it to the fullest because it was a bit different to the usual wet Monday night in Bonnybridge.

The meeting appeared to go well from both a business and a personal point of view. We all parted on very good terms with me receiving an invitation to make a follow up visit to Cuba. Apart from the business, one of the many attractions held out to me were miles and miles of empty tropical beaches on the north coast of the island. I found out later that the main reason most of the beaches were deserted was because the Americans at Guantanamo naval base regularly used them for gunnery practice.

PA 103

The first news flash came in about half past seven and said that there was a major incident and large fire. It was spot on, on both counts. The second report suggested that perhaps a garage had somehow exploded and that the underground fuel storage was on fire. This one only got two out of three assertions correct since there was an explosion and the fuel was on fire but it did not originate in or under any garage.

Eventually all the facts became only all too clear. A bomb had blown Pan Am Clipper flight 103 "Spirit of the Seas" out of the sky. It happened at three minutes past seven

on the evening of December the twenty first 1988 at thirty-one thousand feet over
Lockerbie in Dumfriesshire. The 747 had come in from Frankfurt to London and had
been delayed in Heathrow before setting out again for New York. Whether the bomb
was on a timer or was barometrically operated when the aircraft reached a defined
altitude, it was probably planned to not to explode until the aircraft had tracked out
over deep water in the Atlantic Ocean. Instead it detonated when the aircraft was still
climbing to its Trans-Atlantic cruising height when it was fifteen miles north of the
English border in Scottish air space and jurisdiction. The resulting explosion killed
eleven local people as well as all two hundred and fifty-nine souls on board the plane.

Forty-eight hours later while driving north for Christmas we found ourselves stuck in
a long slow-moving single line queue of traffic on the A74. The reason was that all of
traffic in both directions had to use the two north bound lanes since the two lanes of
the southbound carriageway had been totally obliterated. Instead of a road there was
now only a deep crater almost one hundred yards long running from the crash barrier
on the central reservation in a south easterly direction towards the adjacent town. The
crater itself seemed empty but considerable debris still littered the side of the road.

Drivers were forced to slow down considerably because of all the traffic restrictions.
Equally however they slowed because of the scene of utter devastation. Several badly
damaged houses overlooked the road and other gaps could be seen where houses once
stood. Diesel generators powered emergency lighting which cast an eerie white glare
over the entire scene and many civilian and military personnel were still deployed and
working hard in the clear frosty night to find casualties still trapped in any wreckage
on the ground. This search was eventually extended in the new year over a distance of
almost 100 miles stretching as far east as Newcastle since the prevailing wind that
night as with most other nights had been from the west. Smaller debris and even some
casualties were eventually mostly recovered after an arduous long and difficult search.

This was an evil deed made even worse if that were possible by the fact that it was
just before Christmas when goodwill to all men was supposed to be the order of the
day, not indiscriminate acts of international terrorism to people who were in the main
heading home to their families for one of the main holidays of the year. In an attempt
to solve the mystery of how and why it happened and to apprehend the perpetrators
Scottish Police and others followed a long and tortuous international trail. It led back
through London to Germany, Malta, Libya with alleged involvement by others also.
The case took a very long time to come to trial and it is not even certain that everyone
involved was ever brought to account with only one person charged, convicted, jailed
and then released early on compassionate grounds. This compassion was all that was
ever visible in this saga as other parties sought to justify the act by reference to other
unconnected acts by various different groups in far flung locations. Scotland was only
the bare stage that others chose completely by accident for the tragedy to unfurl on.
The terrorist bomb did not only blow flight PA 103 out of the sky but also hastened
the final demise of the entire Pan American Airlines company only three years later.
A few jumbo jets still survive in operation thirty years later but are in steep decline.

The French Connection.

The middle seat of five, in a row of ten, in the centre of the rear cabin, of a Jumbo jet, was not my favourite place to be. Fortunately for me however, it was not somewhere that I found myself very often. This particular TWA flight from London Heathrow to New York JFK was jam packed full to capacity and the seat choice was pretty much take it or leave it. To the check in staff and the cabin crew I was only just another of the four hundred or so bums on seats that they had to contend with every day in life. The travel adverts in glossy magazines especially their own inflight magazines would have you believe that it was all so special and different but there was no glamour in the trip that I could easily discern. I usually got off at the other end bent double with legs that I had difficulty in controlling properly and with a long scar down one or both of my forearms where I had been leaning on the hard, arm rests while dozing fitfully.

After stowing my coat and hand luggage in the bin above my head I settled down into my seat and pulled the seat belt on tight so that I could relax for the rest of the six and a half-hour flight. If you did plan on dozing and were lucky enough to grab a flimsy blanket to ward off the cold stream of aircon during the flight it was wise to put the belt on over the blanket so that they did not poke you awake to check the belts status. The trolley dollies did their usual rounds with drinks and snacks about forty minutes after take-off when we were just clearing out over the west coast of Scotland to track across the great circle route to Gander and New York The actual track varied widely every day depending on the position and strength of the jet stream as the pilots did their best within reason to avoid strong headwinds, turbulence and other weather but sometimes unsuccessfully. TWA and other American carriers always charged fixed prices for all alcoholic drinks unlike BOAC which would let you have the drinks free even in tourist class. They did sometimes try hard to avoid your frantic hand signals however if you wanted more than two which I suppose was not entirely unreasonable. Following the drinks service, they then trundled their little aluminium trolleys out for the main event of the day which was lunch service. If your seat was more than fifteen rows from the front however it was a waste of time to peruse the menu and ask for anything to eat other than pasta, as steak, chicken or any other choice was long gone. I have several menus from TWA indicating the fine dining gourmet dishes that I could have had if things had been different and the management had not been so stingy.

Shortly after the meal had been partaken and the dishes cleared, they again made their rounds with duty free sales and at the same time pulled down all the window blinds and activated the large screen at the front of each of the cabins so that the film could commence. This was in the days before each seat had its own video with about fifty channels of entertainment. The cabin staff did another round of the passengers selling headphones without which you could not hear the soundtrack of the film. You would find out before landing however that they wanted all the earphones back and so it was a rental rather than sales transaction. This was in the days when flying was very much more about actually travelling than seeing movie premieres and recent releases as they were rolled out. The film on this occasion was "The French Connection" with tough hard bitten, French criminals and tough hard bitten, New York cops so the sparks were sure to fly and the adrenaline course round your arteries as the plot unfolded. No matter what film they showed however I seldom rented the headphones not because I was tight but because with the cabin darkened it was usually a time for me to dose off.

I always found this part of the journey quite soporific and usually managed to snooze if not actually have a deep sleep during most of the flight. This habit meant that I must have missed lots of good films in my time and there are others that I have only seen snatches of without the sound track since I almost never wore the earphones provided. This induced rest never did me any harm on all my travels and must have lowered any stress involved in travel especially across multiple time zones. At one particular point in this film however I awoke from my slumbers and glanced blearily at the screen to see the New York metro train that I was meant to be travelling in as part of the plot hurtling along the elevated track through the city. The bad guy Alain Charnier, was being hotly pursued up the train by the good guy Popeye Doyle, but in the midst of all this lather the train driver got himself shot which I find is never an ideal situation. The driver being shot caused the emergency brake to be applied although the train still continued to thunder on towards the next station on the line where another stationary train sat at the platform on the same track. Just at the very last moment and at exactly the same instant that the driverless train struck the back of the stationary train only a glancing blow, the plane itself hit some localised area of very severe turbulence and bucked wildly for three or four seconds before resuming its normal straight and level flight. This caused most of the passengers who had been absorbed in the drama to have a fit and some screamed or cried out in panic thinking that they were in a crash.

It did not have quite so dramatic effect on me as I was still semi-comatose, and for a few seconds I was still trying to figure out how I had got from a TWA Jumbo heading west in mid Atlantic to a Lexington Avenue local subway train heading north to the Bronx without passing go and picking up two hundred pounds or even going through the usual endless JFK airport immigration, baggage collection and customs routines.

Tora, Tora, Tora.

The Japanese bombed Pearl Harbour early one Sunday morning in November 1941 but they did not actually invade the islands until many years later. Initially they had sent in several waves of kamikaze bombers and then much later they sent in even more waves of kamikaze honeymoon couples. For the penultimate stage of their new cultural invasion they then dug in by constructing Japanese restaurants like Benihana of Tokyo at strategic locations each with a clear field of fire across WaiKiki beach. The inevitable third wave which followed on eventually came in and developed and built new hotels and condominiums so that many thousands more tourists could then colonise the islands for periods of up to fifteen days. Still more could leap ashore from cruise ships for a full day's happy selfie taking. Apparently, the thinking was that if Japanese people were going to spend mega dollars in Hawaii then they might as well spend it with Japanese companies as with American ones. The invaders treated the local population quite well however and continually threw fistfuls of money at them in tips or had tips swiftly extracted from them if there was any sign of hesitation or reluctance. This resulted in very few complaints from locals in current times about the invading hordes of mainly young people from the land of the rising sun with not a

Zero dive bomber between them and barely even a gaudy headband this time round. On the occasion when my wife and I visited Hawaii together a deux it was not in fact for a second honeymoon but was just because it was there and she had not been, up until that time. When asked where she would like to have dinner on the first evening, I got the stock reply from my wife along the lines "I don't mind, anywhere you prefer". When I suggested the old Hibachi hot cuisine at Benihana of Tokyo however I could immediately see that maybe I had the beginnings of a small potential problem on my hands. Sheena had never been to Tokyo or to any of Benihana's fine gourmet dining establishments. Eventually her curiosity overcame her reluctance to see what was actually on the other side of the bamboo curtain stretched across the restaurant front entrance and the not unpleasant smell of slow cooked steak. Once inside and seated on stools with little wooden arms on them set around the big rectangular hot stainless steel, topped metal table I got the distinct impression that things could only improve. We did go through the usual slight setback however when as was customary we both introduced ourselves to the other diners seated around the rest of the communal table They were almost exclusively Americans with a Canadian couple from Vancouver thrown in for good measure. It took the normal few minutes opening introduction to assure everyone that we were not Australian, that Scotland was indeed a country and set them right as to its approximate position on the Earth's surface with relation to England and Europe as well as its achievements in steam, radio and TV along with golf, whisky rubber tyres and shipbuilding, bagpipes, kilts and haggis. It was at this point that the chef appeared and immediately took charge of the whole proceedings. He was a rotund Japanese gentleman about the same height as the rest of us but only because he had his tall white chef's hat on. I decided not to comment on his stature however as he was juggling with some razor-sharp knives at the time. I did not want to interrupt his concentration during his kendo display and I had long ago in life been taught never to catch a falling knife. When he started to slice shrimps and vegetables, I knew I had made the right decision as his twin blades were moving so fast, they were almost a blur. We all just smiled and nodded a lot and assured him that the table top fried shrimp were cooked just the way we liked them. The hot Sake helped too. Although it tasted like a cross between hot Tio Pepe and rice pudding it slipped down a treat. A few more of these I thought and I may forgive some of the Americans for not knowing that Scotland existed in real life. Obviously not golfers and possibly not widely travelled or possessing passports either because Hawaii was after all still an American state albeit one slightly more distant compared to the other forty-nine.

Later in the week after the Sake hangover had dissipated, we decide to go back to one of the more expensive Japanese owned hotels and try a different style of cuisine. As we entered the marble floored foyer which was circular in shape, we could see that it was built in the shape of a wide balcony overlooking the dining room which was two floors below. A great spiral staircase swept down to the dining area. One entire half of the circular wall, which was nearly twenty feet high, was made of thick glass. Behind the glass were millions of gallons of seawater and in the water swam sharks, sting rays, barracuda, electric eels, turtles and many other types of fish. Only tuna and dolphins were missing presumably because they had already been eaten by the hungry Japanese guests. This was a fascinating and unusual backdrop to a meal and there were a couple of occasions when I was following the movement of a particularly interesting denizen of the deep that I stuck my soup spoon in my ear or my fork in my nose. Seated at a table against the curved glass wall was an American family of four. Father, Mother and two kids, one of whom was obviously celebrating a birthday. Apart from a few gifts, which changed hands, the waiters brought a birthday cake with a live sparkler in the top. Then to my complete amazement we saw a mermaid swim down through the fish in the tank to a point just on the other side of the glass from the table where the family sat. She then unfurls a little banner which said "Happy Birthday Chuck" so I just hope that Chuck whoever he was, was suitably impressed. "Forget it said my wife you will get the usual tie or socks from Marks and Spencer's for your birthday and like it". We did head back to the hotel through a shopping mall however and stumbled into a genuine Hawaiian Bavarian Beirkeller and since it was Octoberfest in Munich at the time felt obliged to observe the festival by partaking of a stein of cold beer although I drew the line at the Wurst as we had already dined. When it came to flying back to Los Angeles it was Halloween and the check in staff at the Daniel K Inouye international airport felt compelled it seemed to be in full witches and warlocks mode and had obviously gone to some trouble and expense with their costumes and makeup to do so. I just sighed and hoped that it was not going to be a Tam O' Shanter flight back across the pacific with the devil chasing us all the way. and us landing in LA with a tailless plane as this would probably be slightly more inconvenient than a tailless horse. What is it with these Americans that they celebrate everybody else's festivals? Don't they have enough of their own to be going on with? They have Columbus Day, Groundhog Day and who knows what else.

Mabuhay.

Tagalo is not heard much around here since it is a dialect restricted mainly to the Philippine archipelago. The first time I heard it I could not figure out what kind of language it was nor understand what was said but it was not unique in that regard.

Mind you I was not at my best having flown from Jakarta in Indonesia up through Brunei and on to Manila which is in the north of the Philippine Republic. As I came out through immigration and cleared customs in the old Manila airport, I was struck by a wall of sound comprising hundreds of conversations from thousands of people meeting and greeting arriving and departing friends and relatives. The heat and the humidity also struck me. As dusk fell a few lights glimmered into life and I went in search of a taxi through the crowds to the road outside. The trip into town was a bit different from the usual airport taxi. It was in a Jeepney, which so far as I know is peculiar to the Philippines. Most of them started life as US military jeeps from which the spartan bodywork had been removed and replaced by something much more exotic. Aluminium superstructures were fitted onto the original chassis and painted in garish colours and designs. Custom seating was also fitted along with all sorts of other adornments from religious artefacts to bamboo curtains. Most of them also are fitted with musical horns which make La Cucaracha or Colonel Bogy sound really demure. Another indispensable fitted extra was combined reversing lights and warning devices which sound like demented cuckoos. Mine was probably the only one in Scotland.

The air of carnival was slightly dampened however by the fact that the entire country was under martial law according to the edict of President Ferdinand Marcos. This was something of an exaggeration since there were large areas in the south where the populations of whole islands did not acknowledge this fact. Around Manila however there was quite a strong military and police presence although strangely this seemed disconcerting rather than re assuring. There also seemed to be heavily armed civilians everywhere but I could not quite work out how this fitted into the scheme of things. It all seemed to smack of the "Wild East" and I just hoped that they had a good sheriff. When the cab pulled up in the dim yellow light that spilled from the foyer of my hotel the bellhop came out to my taxi to pick up my case. As he showed me in to the reception I noticed that he was wearing a revolver in a leather holster. His gun made Dirty Harry's look like a toy. The desk clerk did not appear to be armed but no doubt could lay his hand on a weapon quickly under the counter if the need arose. As I was shown to my room, I could not help noticing that there was an armed guard with a rifle sitting on a rattan chair on each floor. This was obviously not the kind of hotel where you forgot to tip the staff or tried to sneak out without paying your bill. Apart from me most of the other guests appeared to be Japanese. I could not help thinking that they must have felt a bit like the Filipinos did during the war except that nobody seemed to be forcing them to build railway bridges over rivers with funny names.

What's your Poison?

Radio Interviewer – "I suppose that must have been one of the low points in your life" Interviewee – "Yes it was at a time when I had to leave Rawalpindi after the servants tried to poison me". In my case it was never the servants since I never had any but it was usually the chef. Once or twice they succeeded in coming perilously close if that was even their unintentional objective or just their sheer ignorance of food hygiene. I was introduced to the island's national vegetable on a visit to the Caribbean. It was not served with cod as is normally the case but with a salad in the posh Blue Ridge restaurant in the Blue Mountains behind Kinston in Jamaica. I had gone into the hills there for lunch to escape some of the heat down in the densely populated town. The chef who came personally to the table with the menu informed me that for about ten months of the year it was poisonous and for the other two it was not only edible but absolutely delicious when eaten either cooked or raw. The Ackee fruit apparently is for those who like to live dangerously. It was introduced into Jamaica in 1778 and is now the country's national fruit. Unripe Ackee fruit contains a strong poison called Hypoglycin, and so it is very important that it is fully ripe before it is eaten. Even when ripe the fruit's protective pods turn red, prior to opening naturally but the only edible portion is the yellow Arilli, which surround its black seeds and which are still always very toxic. The chef seemed sober to me at the time so he must have been right about the two months or wrong about the other ten. Maybe he was even winding me up but this is not something chefs usually do about their own cooking - only other peoples. It always concerns me however in situation like that when the management ask for payment in advance as it is indicative that they are definitely concerned about the outcome. To be honest I had the Ackee salad after a plate of Callalloo soup which was quite spicy and so the taste of the vegetable was not that memorable and I could easily omit it from all of my dietary requirements both now and in the future if I had to do so.

It was in Tokyo on another occasion where the master chef again presented himself personally with the menu before he served me with a small portion of Fugu fish. He was an ugly specimen, the fish I mean, not the chef. The fish was like a globe from which the chef had removed with a razor-sharp knife the small gland filled with deadly poison allegedly rendering the rest safe to eat. This was a still a fairly risky procedure, which sometimes resulted in the paralysis of the central nervous system followed rapidly by death. The diner's death I mean of course and not the fish. I was assured that the chef was fully trained and certified not only in rendering the fish safe but also in committing seppuku if he got it wrong and a client died. Looking at the wild look in his eye I was almost convinced that he probably was indeed certified.

After I had eaten a small portion of fish, I thought that I too should be certified as I could feel my lips starting to go numb which was usually the first sign of impending paralysis. After a few minutes I could feel the numbness spreading and was quite seriously concerned until I realised that what I was feeling was the effect of the very large ice-cold Vodka that had drunk before ordering the fish in the first place. The thing, which really caused a rush of panic, however was when I saw the price.

The fish in China by comparison appeared to be incredibly cheap compared to Japan. In Beijing a group of us sat around a table with a revolving centre piece which was laden with a large number of dishes of different types of Chinese food. As the table was slowly turned, I made wild stabs with my chopsticks at a few of the dishes some of which I thought I recognised like the boiled rice which tends to be an easy one. Others were totally unrecognisable to me and became even more so when various people pulled lumps out of the dish and scoffed them. I tended to get the larger lumps of food especially if it was a bit sticky and didn't fall off the chopsticks onto the table.

I was helped with one dish which I had a stab at because I was convinced that it was white fish but was advised to be very careful when eating this with chopsticks in case there were still any small bones in the flesh. I duly reported that there were no bones either large or small and that it fact it was actually very bland and not at all fishy in texture whereupon I was advised that in this case the food was most definitely snake.

It was very nearly what should have been a simple safe Club Sandwich in a good hotel in Cairo that did the most damage. It could have been the chicken or it could have been the mayonnaise or it could have been the water they washed the lettuce in. It might even have been something entirely different. Either way the effect was devastating and gave me an insight into how mummies felt while being embalmed. After three days in a darkened room surviving on duty free scotch, I started to feel almost subhuman again and resolved to have the waistband of my trousers taken in a couple of inches leaving the dimensions on the bottom large enough to fit a nappy.

Through all of this I never faltered even once and I just kept on selling. That's one of the good things about five-star hotels. Most of them have phones in the bathroom.

Mortar this than meets the Eye.

It was fairly rowdy in the hotel. There were not all that many restaurants in town even although there was a substantial population most of whom worked in the local steel mills or associated industries. The locals tended not to frequent the restaurant on the top floor where guests normally dined. They tended to prefer the coffee shop, bar and disco in the basement, where prices were cheaper and the heat, noise and discomfort were possibly more like the steel mills that most of them toiled in for a living.

It was John's first visit to Hamilton and indeed to Canada but partly because he was a director and had travelled a long way to meet them for negotiations there was always a good turnout at the meetings which I had set up. We were not the only bidders but it certainly helped us that we came from a very long way out of town. To be more precise he was more than three and a half thousand miles out of town since he was based like me in Scotland. They may even have mistaken as both as being Scottish although in Johns case only after a few drinks. John was very pleased by the progress that our discussions seemed to be making and was even more delighted when the plant manager and the senior purchasing manager accepted his invitation to dinner.

We met down in the Hotel's basement bar early in the evening and had a swift aperitif for at that time of the day it was still deserted before all the regulars arrived en masse. After laying the day's dust we then proceeded in the lift up to the top floor restaurant for a simple yet satisfying meal of local specialities. These dishes had included stuffed cabbage for starters, stuffed turkey as a main course and stuffed baked apple as desert. By the time we were finished it was me that felt stuffed. A few glasses of the local red Niagara escarpment wine then helped wash it all down to assist the digestive process. We decided after a black coffee that we could make it back down to the basement bar for a post prandial libation. This however was not the smartest decision that we could have collectively arrived at. By this time local throng had definitely arrived and the disco bar was lashing with strobe lights and throbbing with sound at over 100 decibels as the music pounded out and reverberated off the concrete basement walls and roof. We managed to find and occupy a table for four and under the flash of the fluorescent strobe which I think had been borrowed from off the top of the steel plant chimney we signalled to the waitress in international sign language to bring us four large brandies.

All through the cacophony of the Son et Lumiere John had mistakenly attempted to continue the sensible conversation he had started over dinner about the plant's annual supply contract. He went on at great length to enumerate the undoubted virtues of our special high quality ready to use wet mortar which he believed was the envy of the industrial world. Our two guests were doing their absolute level best to be polite and would in fact commit to a substantial contract with us. It was obvious that they were having the greatest difficulty in hearing what was being said to them in the unusual surroundings for a business discussion. John had to repeat himself getting ever louder each time. One of the guests had just politely enquired how the mortar was normally delivered to our many satisfied clients when the music suddenly stopped and John was caught completely by surprise as he shouted almost at the top of his voice in the relatively hushed room "it's wet and sticky and comes in buckets". I conjecture that there may still be some surviving senior Canadian citizens who still occasionally yet wake up in a sweat in the middle of night of fitful sleep at the very thought of it.

Tia Maria.

Patrick's nickname was Tia Maria, which I would have taken offence at had anyone applied it to me. He revelled in it however and no matter where we went, he was met with smiles and shouts of "hey, Tia Maria my man, how you doing"? Even the sight of my pink or latterly more reddish sunburnt face only caused a momentary hesitation, as he was obviously a very popular guy. I could never figure out how he got stuck with this name as he wasn't gay and he wasn't Spanish. I would have thought that Tio Pepe would have been more appropriate in the circumstances. Maybe that moniker was already taken. When I eventually asked him how it came about, he explained that it was really very simple. His family owned the distillery in which Tia Maria liqueur was made on the island of Jamaica. This and the fact that he was well off made him even more popular than his sunny disposition would have made him in any case. He is probably much richer now as his family have since sold out many years ago to a major global brand with a stable of other alcoholic beverages

I waited for Patrick on the veranda in the cool of the evening and idly flicked peanuts at the little green geckos, which ran up and down the wall. When Patrick arrived, we got into his car and drove off to find somewhere to have dinner. I always liked to get a flavour of the place that I was visiting and Patrick excelled himself that night with its ethnic authenticity. The restaurant was little more than a very large shack in the midst of the jungle. It appeared to have no glass in the windows just large rattan blinds, which stirred idly in the slight breeze, as it rippled through the forest of palm fronds. It turned out that the attraction for all the clientele was not the gourmet food although there was basically nothing wrong with the curried goat stew which a little earlier in the day may have been roadkill. Apparently, the main attraction was the video which played quietly on the 8-track attached to the TV set on the shelf in the corner of the room. It was probably made in Amsterdam or Hamburg but it did not appear to me to be not a travelogue without dialogue and it had a reddish cast to the whole film.

I didn't really think that the locals were very comfortable with my presence even although I was with Patrick and we decided not to linger after the meal was finished. We moved onto a club in Kingston town where after an enthusiastic welcome at the door we were plied with several free Red Stripe beers. I was tired however and told Patrick that I was going to call it a day so he offered to run me back to the hotel.

We had just pulled out of the car park onto the road when the engine of his car coughed and died. He tried several times to start it but when that failed, he insisted on stopping a passing taxi which got me home in less than twenty minutes and I hit the sack. Next morning, he was late and when he finally pitched up about an hour late, I asked him what had happened. He explained that he had sat cross-legged on the bonnet of the car all night laughing and waving at all the drunks staggering by so that they knew that it was his car. He explained that if he had left the car before the breakdown truck had arrived in the morning, he would probably have been short of one car at dawn's early light. If he had ever got it back it would probably have been one piece at a time in the market and on several different stalls all of which sold spare parts for popular models like Patrick's. It was a case of possession being ten tenths of the law except there were times when there was very little law around Kingston and so maintaining possession was entirely down to one careful owner.

Five o clock Shadow

Peters fluorescent bright green Cortina was a pleasure to drive. It was supposed to be built specially for Greek roads and it should have been special for something because it cost about fifty per cent more than it would have done if it had been bought in the UK because of taxes and the law of supply and demand. I suppose about a tenner of the extra cost was absorbed in moving the steering wheel and pedals over to the left-hand side of the car and adjusting the rear-view mirror about 30 degrees. Peter was always happy to let me drive because with Milto navigating he could retire to the back seat and doze off to sleep. It seemed that we were heading to Kerkyra that particular day. It was a Friday afternoon and the boys had decided that I should have a relaxing weekend on the island and that they would escort me to ensure my absolute security. It seemed that they also felt in need of rest and recuperation although from what I am not sure as I had no evidence to indicate that they had been exerting themselves in any way, During the drive without he advantage of satnav or smart phone I had carefully calculated in my head that we had loads of time in hand. I planned to drive to the port of Igoumenitsa and have a leisurely cup of coffee at a taberna on the quayside before catching the five-o clock ferry for the short twenty kilometres sail to the island. As we neared our immediate destination the road ran down through the mountains into the small town on the Ionian Sea. It twisted and turned its way through the pine trees down to the fertile coastal plane. The pines eventually gave way to olive groves and eventually the road ran flat and straight as a die to the now not quite so distant port which was still invisible in the light afternoon heat haze which shimmered up from the road. Peter was fast asleep in the back seat and light snores could occasionally be heard as we drove smoothly along at about eighty kilometres an hour. There were very few road junctions and we did not have to deviate which was just as well for me. Milto who was nominally the navigator but who was not good with maps had the disconcerting habit when we did approach junctions of saying "that way" in Greek at the very last minute. He of course thought that he knew which way he meant but I never shared his confidence so he was really of neither use nor ornament in his self-appointed role. His other speciality was to advise me to go right while sticking out his left hand or occasionally go left while sticking out his right hand so I tended neither to look or listen to him while he was engaged in making his extravagant guesses. It was for this reason also that I usually had closely studied a decent map and attempted to memorise the route as much as possible before we set out on any journey.

As we whizzed along, I spotted an old shepherd up ahead sitting in the shade of a large olive tree by the side of the road. Since road signs were few and far between in rural Greece, I thought that it was probably worthwhile just checking that we were indeed on the right road and how far it still was before we reached the port and our ferry. I smoothly pulled and since he was sitting the verge on my side of the road up I asked him in my very basic Greek if we were OK for Igoumenitsa. He must have understood me for he beamed a toothless smile and answered immediately. I did not fully understand his complete response but just caught the words "ine ora" (one hour) and "Igoumenitsa" which of course was the name of our intended immediate destination. I immediately panicked on the hearing the suggestion that we were still an hour away. I waved my thanks, threw the car into gear and rocketed off down the road leaving a cloud of exhaust smoke and burnt rubber hanging in the still air. If he was right my plan for a leisurely cup of coffee and even the five-o clock ferry sailing were now seriously jeopardised. I rightly guessed that it was the last sailing of the day and did not particularly want to spend the night in town as I reckoned that I was not really in need of all the relaxation it might provide. In less than five minutes however we hurtled into the small town and screeched to a halt on the quayside to find ourselves first in line for the ferry which had not even arrived into the harbour at this time. It was about then after I let out a great sigh of relief and relaxed that I realised that the old shepherd had given me his estimate of the journey time on the basis of him slowly strolling into town perhaps even with a small flock of sheep or bleating goats. This I thought was a useful reminder that we all live our life or lives at a very different pace. I also pondered that I might have a couple of goats fluent in Greek with me in the car.

Christmas Day

Although he had lived in Australia for over eighteen years Bill still had more than just a trace of his original Yorkshire accent. He was well integrated into the local community. He lived in his own house in a distant suburb of Sydney surrounded by Gum and Eucalyptus trees. He even had his own possum, which came and drummed on his roof most mornings. Bill would have preferred an alarm clock like most other people but he was not allowed to shoot the possum because it was protected. He was also a member of the local volunteer fire brigade as most of the men in the area were. He took the drills seriously and turned out whenever he was not away on business since he well knew the extent of the damage a bush fire could do to life and limb. Business for Bill was normally in a city skyscraper near the bridge, which he referred to as the biggest coathanger in the world. It followed a reasonably predictable nine till five routine with the five at least being observed religiously. At about five minutes to five every day desks were tidied, jackets thrown on and everyone headed for the lift. As they poured out of the lift at ground level it was almost exactly five and the pub on the ground floor threw its doors open. As everyone crammed inside it was obvious that the barman had been hard at it pouring scores of schooners of lager and setting them out on the bar to be grabbed by the crowds rushing in and throwing their money at the till. As the first hundred or so disappeared they were replaced by midis and at six o clock everyone weaved out of the door to try and find their way home by car, train or ferry boat as best they could. It's not for me to criticise the licensing laws which were in force at the time as other countries like Canada, Scotland and many others also had their own special take on how alcohol should be responsibly managed.

Sometimes however Bill had to travel all over the continent often accompanied by colleagues from the UK. On one such trip he was doing the grand tour with an English colleague. After a few hard days they ended up in a small copper mining town in Northern Queensland. The hot sticky drive into town from the airport over dusty roads left them coated in fine dust and with a raging thirst. On arrival at the clapboard two storey hotel the porter reluctantly came out from the shade of the porch to the taxi and watched as they stomped up the steps with their luggage. Forcing through the bat wing doors they stumbled over to the deserted reception desk and rang the small brass bell. At his point the porter transformed into the receptionist. After checking them in he became the bellboy and walked on ahead with their keys as they struggled up the rickety wooden stairs with their bags. After a shower in tepid water and a change of clothes they met back down stairs for a cold beer. Bill thought at this point that the barman had an incredible resemblance to the bellboy, receptionist and porter but decided to say nothing. Two beers later they made their way through to the dining room to be greeted with a familiar looking head waiter who showed them to their table in an otherwise almost empty room. When finally sat at the table with their elbows firmly on the green and white chequered wax tablecloth, as local etiquette demanded they ordered. Steak and chips followed fish soup. After clearing the soup plates, the waiter returned with the main course, banged the plates down and turned to go back into the kitchen. Before he got two steps away Bill shouted after him and politely enquired if it might be possible to have some tomato ketchup with the meal. The owner for indeed it was he who played all these multiple roles stopped in his tracks and turned to look at Bill. A heavy since hung in the air broken only by the quiet whirr of the overhead fan and the desultory buzzing of an Aussie mossie. The boss turned walked to the kitchen door and pushed it partly open with his boot. "Hey Mary" he shouted to his wife who was clattering utensils in the kitchen "there are a pair of Pommie bastards here think it's Christmas. They want ketchup with their steak and chips".

Blue Uniform

Ray was a hard worker but had the smallest of chips on his shoulder about not receiving recognition for his true worth. He was not averse therefore to taking all the perks that the job offered. Many would have thought him well off for his beat was the whole seaboard of the United States and Canada west of the Rockies.

Ray was American but his boss was an archetypal English gentleman who had one day found himself the opportunity of promotion to a senior job in the United States. Geoff was somewhat puzzled one day to receive a phone call from Ray which eventually got round to the subject of whether or not the company could stretch to Ray getting a new blazer. Geoff was all in favour of the sales and marketing personnel being well turned out and thought it was a good idea if Ray turned out to visit clients in Blazer and flannels. He immediately agreed as long as the blazer was dark blue. Some weeks later Geoff was on a routine call on the West Coast region and flew into Portland Oregon where Ray was based. Ray met him at the Northwest Airlines gate and escorted him to the baggage claim to pick up his bag and on out into the short-term car park. When they got to Rays car was somewhat taken aback to be ushered into a 3.5 litre turbo charged V8 four-wheel drive Chevrolet Blazer with only a few thousand miles on the clock. "What on earth is this?" asked Geoff. "It's the blazer you told me I could lease said Ray. I thought you would be pleased as it's even in the exact colour you suggested to me". At least the Portland Police were delighted that Ray had his Blazer even if Geoff was not. A few days later we were driving in the dunes at Seaside Oregon when we came across a police car stuck in the sand. It was a fairly conventional Chevrolet which was souped up for patrol work but was totally unsuitable to be on sand dunes. Apparently in their enthusiasm the crew had followed a speeding dune buggy from the road into the rolling dunes and quickly became stuck. Ray hitched a wire tow rope onto his winch and pulled them out of the deep sand then using the Blazers normal tow bar back onto the road where they should have stayed. There was no charge but Ray probably dodged a few speeding tickets as a result.

It is possible that Ray was a petrol head because on another occasion we drove up the nearby Mount St Helens which is an active Volcano. On this occasion we were in his private bright yellow E type Jaguar which could probably have outrun any lava flow. It proved unnecessary however and in fact it was more likely that we might have had to try and outrun an avalanche because there was deep snow drifting on the upper slopes. Fortunately, this also proved unnecessary as it would have been much more difficult and dangerous than dodging a lava flow which would have given much more warning and in fact did before it blew its top about six years later years later in 1980. We did stop at a hotel for coffee where there were hundreds of tons of snow backed up against thick plate glass reinforced by large steel girders on the uphill side of the mountain slope. Much later and in a different state he also took me for spin in his de Tomaso Pantera two-seater sports car. This was in Des Plaines Illinois on a short trip to Elk Grove to sample the heights of academe with a visit to the campus of the Big D Hamburger U. The University was a serious commercial establishment training MacDonald's franchisee from all over the world in all of the mysteries of the Big Mac and Apple Turnover. I did wonder about the herd of Bison which were grazing nearby and tried to guess if any of them ever ended up in any of the aforesaid Big Macs.

Happiness Costs Such a Lot

I liked working in the Pacific Northwest almost as much as I liked working in the Pacific Southwest. The people were by and large friendly or at least most of the ones I met in business were friendly. There were of course a lot of Fruitcakes, Hippies, Flower Children, Flakes, Revolutionaries, Sex Maniacs, Illegals, Starlets and Entrepreneurs. Still you can't have everything. Business was good and it was an incredibly interesting part of the world. In the North were the towering snow-capped mountains and dense pine and redwood forests while in the south were the arid deserts of the Sonora and New Mexico.

In between of course was Northern California, which for me was dominated by San Francisco with its famous bay and bridges. I tended not to think that it was also dominated by the threat of earthquake and devastation. Nobody spoke of the ever-present threat but many people seemed to live their lives to the full in the expectation that there might not be a tomorrow for them. North beach was a madhouse twentyfour hours a day seven days a week while the Royal Bank of Scotland on the top floor of the Transamerica Pyramid observed the time honoured custom of offering visitors tea and biscuits at the appointed hours every morning at eleven and later at three. You had to work just as hard for business in this area as elsewhere in the world but the clients were generous when they could plainly see a genuine effort being made on their behalf. After one such large contract was concluded we decided to have a celebratory dinner. We walked round from the St Francis on Union Square where cable cars clanged up and down the hill between Market Street at the bottom and the Fairmont hotel at the top. After crossing a dimly lit and almost empty car park we came to a secluded doorway over which flashed a neon sign announcing that it was the entrance to Phil Lehrs Steakery. This was verging on Indian territory and was technically on the wrong side of the tracks because it was south of market street where the badlands started. In fact, it was not then literally on the wrong side of the tracks because it was only years later that the city dug up all of market street and installed the city subway. A smaller sign in a glass case at the doorway promised prime steak by the ounce to be cooked just as you like it. Downstairs in the reception area we sank up to our ankles in a plush carpet in the middle of which stood a large refrigerated glass topped cabinet. Inside this were several large pieces of prime steak of every imaginable type. Before showing us to our table the Maitre D summoned the butcher and asked us to choose the type and size of steak we required. I was not well qualified in butchery although a butcher had once inadvertently sliced into my finger when I had innocently put my hand on his counter at about age six. One of us should have gone to Specsavers while the other went to the doctors. The steaks were all exotically named with references to New York as well as Kansas and Omaha. Some were claimed to be from corn fed animals which everyone knows makes them vastly superior to those which just ruminate on green, green grass. This surprised me considerably however since in another American restaurant in another location when I had asked for corn on the cob as a starter, course I had been informed that they only fed that shit to their hogs. If the cobs were all served soft boiled and dripping with butter, I could understand why the hogs and the Americans both had extensive flanks but shared with my hosts the thought that this was pretty half baked. Since I had no idea of the pros and cons of each cut of meat in this case so I just pointed to the smallest T bone that I could see and said how about that one there although as a Scotsman I was a bit uncomfortable about none of the steaks being priced. I have no doubt that this was purely intentional on the basis that no American would be brave enough to ask as the staff in such establishments were all specially trained to sneer at such customers and belittle them in front of everyone in earshot. The piece of meat chosen was then whisked off to the kitchen to be cooked exactly as requested as we were shown to a small table in the dimly lit windowless underground bunker. I was amazed that no quibbled with my choice of the steak being well done as this is always another opportunity for staff to sneer any clients who don't eat it raw. The exception to this obviously is an American barbecue where the steak is raw in the middle but incinerated to have a carbonaceous residue on the outside. In this case of course there are no Maitre D's or waiters but only incompetent untrained amateur chefs convinced that they were God's gift to the culinary arts. At the table Ray was in high good spirits even before he was high of good spirits. When the wine waiter approached with the list Ray glanced at it but did not get much beyond the first on the list. He imperiously ordered a bottle of vintage Chateau Mouton Rothschild. The Sommelier nodded his approval, bowed, turned and started to scurry off to retrieve it from the cellars. After some half dozen steps however, he stopped, turned and came back to the table. He hesitantly coughed and asked us if we had seen the price in the subdued lighting of the restaurant. "It is forty dollars a bottle sir" he said. "Never mind my good man," said Ray in his best faux English accent "just be a good chap and toddle off and get it. Let us worry about drinking it and paying for it" he added brandishing his company gold Amex card.

Volos was a sleepy little seaside town mid-way between Athens and Thessaloniki on the Aegean coast of Greece. It may in fact not always have been sleepy but I always seemed to arrive in mid-afternoon when all of the inhabitants were having their siestas It reminded me that when I asked Milto what the Greek word for tomorrow was he told me it was abrio. When I asked if that were similar to the Spanish word manana he agreed except that it did not convey the same sense of urgency as the original Spanish.

On the few occasions that we stayed in this place we normally checked into the hotel Xenia, which was a small two-star establishment on the edge of town. This afternoon There was not a breath of air stirring in the heat of the afternoon and the only sound was the rustle of cicadas in the grass under the pine trees. On arrival Milto usually went to his room to rest and since no one in business was available to see at that time of day for meetings I rested in my own room reading information or making notes. On this particular day however, he must have been feeling a bit peckish since he normally had his meagre breakfast which usually consisted of little more than a cup of Earl Grey about 5 am and we had been on the road since early morning. After checking into the almost deserted hotel we took the car down to the harbour and parked in the shade of a large tree near to where we found a modern style café restaurant still open. We sat there in the shade of the canopy over the front of the establishment with a very slight onshore breeze providing some slight relief from the heat of the day. We had decided on partaking of some strawberries and ice cream and washed down in my case by a Nescafe or American coffee as the Greeks usually referred to it no doubt as it allowed them to charge a few drachmas more. The esplanade on the sea front was almost deserted at that time of day and the waiter only made occasional appearances to see if we were happy or needed to order anything more. The only other movement which caught my eye apart from a slight movement of the canopy in the breeze came from the flickering black and white pictures on the TV screen high up on the shelf in the corner of the room. After sitting there digesting my light snack for a short time I was starting to doze off when I was brought back awake as Milto shot bolt upright, struggled up out of his wicker chair and went into the restaurant to get a better look at the TV. The waiter, who was probably also the owner and maybe the chef had also made his way over to the set to turn the sound up a little as they both stood there, silently, staring up at the screen for a few minutes. When Milto came back to the table he looked a bit shaken. The waiter brought both of us a strong black Greek "Metrio" coffee which Milto sipped thoughtfully while I asked the waiter if he could stretch to a Metaxa brandy which indeed quickly appeared on the table. Eventually Milto told me that there had just been an announcement on national TV that a Junta of Greek military Colonels had deposed the King, dissolved Parliament and declared martial Law. There seemed to have been some doubt at the time as to whether all units of the Greek navy would fall in with the arrangements but so far as I could see there were no battleships offshore with their guns trained on the town. Neither were there any fighter jets screaming overhead nor even a truckload of steel helmeted soldiers disgorging out on to the pavement. It was obviously a bit warm for full combat gear. Milto was of a generation which had lived through a lot of turmoil in Greece and was obviously thinking that the last thing they needed was another Civil War. It rapidly became clear however that although there was great consternation and serious concern expressed throughout the country no one was going to challenge the Junta militarily. We decided however that it might be advisable if we made our way back to Athens to see what was really happening so we paid up and wandered back to the car. The first thing I did was to fill the fuel tank right up to the lip with petrol. We decided to take the scenic route back to town because it was a more pleasant coastal drive but also because the Greek air force were in the habit of appropriating a flat level stretch of the A1 national road just south of Lamia to use as a makeshift runway for their jets. This had been designed with no trees or telegraph poles to be their forward base to support dogfights with Turkish jets if Greece had been invaded. This had never happened but it was maybe ironic that it was the invasion of Cyprus by Turkey seven years later that actually helped to end the coup and return Greece to parliamentary democracy and then eventually join the EU which most Greeks think is worse than the military junta. The coup itself on that day of Friday the 21st April 1967 was completely bloodless with the King going into exile the parliament dissolving itself just a few weeks before the next elections were due and the TV and other media quickly joining the winning side. This was obviously the side that had a few brown tanks trundling around and maybe parked in Syntagma (Constitution) Square where the parliament building was located   I have to say that as we drove into Athens from the north I did not see any military presence and to be honest the traffic was quite a lot quieter than usual which for me was an immediate attraction.

But life in Greece under the colonels turned out to be pretty controversial for most Greeks. Leila a well-known socialite and her pals in the upper echelons of Athenian society were turfed out of nightspots regularly as midnight chimed and all the lights were turned off. Georgio the music lover could shout "Whoppa" all he wanted but couldn't break plates. Costas the civil servant was forced to actually show up in the office rather than at his other two activities testing hammocks and evaluating sun screens by his villa's pool. Worst of all some Greeks actually had to pay most of the taxes which they were due but had regarded as purely optional since byzantine times. This was a pretty brutal departure to what people had been used to. Eventually the Junta set the country back on its feet economically and eventually most Greeks seemed to admit albeit grudgingly in some cases, that the net effect was good for the country and thus ultimately for all of them. It couldn't last of course as shortly after democracy was one again introduced Greece joined the EU and the Euro and had their legs kicked from underneath them to land on their arses with a thud one more time. If only the Greeks had had a few more colonels and maybe a couple of tanks to spare to send up to Brussels then things could have been very different for all concerned.

North by Northwest

I stood where the Roman Legionnaire Decimo Brutus had once stood more than two thousand years before. Well maybe not in his precise footprints but very close to the point where he watched the sun sink into the sea. As it slowly disappeared from view under the distant horizon, he was seized with terror especially as he was convinced that he heard a loud sizzling noise which he associated with the light fading quickly into darkness. This may however have just been the brochetas de ternera (kebabs) on someone's parillada (barbecue). He had journeyed for many weeks to reach Finis Terrae the end of the earth or at least so far as he and his contemporaries knew at that time. I had got there a lot quicker by three flights from Manchester first to London then onwards to Galicia via Bilbao in Vizcaya. The final fourth stage of the journey was to be completed by Avis hired car because the EC which was what preceded the EU had invested a millions of euros in the roads in and around Galicia and even up to Cape Finisterre which was just north of Vigo in the most north westerly point of the Iberian peninsula. The three of us had flown into La Coruna airport by Iberia Boeing 727on the third leg of our journey from Bilbao where we had all met up together. It was already dusk when we landed and even darker by the time that we collected our luggage from the baggage carousel. The last leg of our journey that day was to a small hotel on the Atlantic coast at Cabo Prior which was due north of El Ferrol. Pedro who was Spanish but from Valencia in south eastern Spain refused to drive on the wild unknown roads of the north western highlands since it was dark. He was not going to be budged even when I took him round to the front of the car and pointed out the two devices called headlight that our rental car was fitted with as standard and assured him that they were both in good working order. John who was an Englishman living in Germany agreed to navigate on our journey. After I threw my travel bag in the boot I climbed into the car and sat in the left-hand front seat to begin to familiarise myself with the controls. John went to pay for the parking so that we could exit the airport while Pedro was advised to load the rest of the luggage before getting into the back seat and trying to make himself invisible. I set off at a fair speed picking up the new toll road just outside the airport. Even on the lower grades of road between Betanzos and Cabo Prior I sped along at a fair rate since there was very little traffic late at night with all the good burghers in bed. We arrived at the hotel just before midnight and quickly parked to unload the luggage. It was then that we found out that at La Coruna airport Pedro had not loaded the rest of the bags in the boot as suggested - only his bags. Johns suitcase he had left lying at the back of the car for some reason. John not unreasonably cast doubt on both Pedro's mental capacity and his parentage but this achieved little except to make John feel marginally better. He even did a Basil Fawlty and asked Pedro if he was sure that he was not originally from Barcelona. No doubt this question went right over Pedro's head partly because he was not a very tall Pedro. John was then struck by a sudden thought and rushed into the hotel reception where he startled the sleepy night porter by demanding access to a telephone since this was in the days would you believe where no one had mobile phones far less smart phones. He dialled into directory enquiries and was soon put through to the Guardia Civil duty officer at the airport. "When the sun comes up and dawn breaks your car park Amigo" he informed him "you will find a large silver Samsonite suitcase sitting in the middle of it in one of the many vacant spaces". Even I could hear the furore at the other end of the line as the officer became convinced that a Basque terrorist with a funny German accent was warning him in English of an imminent intended bomb outrage. Eventually after some shouting back and forth in Spanglais John managed to convince him that the suitcase had been left there totally by accident by an idiot rather than by an international terrorist. He pleaded with the officer and eventually received his assurance that the case would not be detonated by a controlled explosion but that it would be rescued and kept safely in security until we all returned ensemble to La

Corunna airport late the following afternoon for our onwards flight south to Valencia after our business meeting in San Ciprian. The meeting itself was highly successful partly because we encouraged Pedro not to contribute to the discussion but mainly because we could provide the specialist goods and services need to quickly repair their large alumina flash calciner furnace lining. When we got back to Valencia which was Pedro's home patch, we agreed with him that if we were treated to a sumptuous Paella Valenciana and a large bottle of Cava followed by a couple of Carlos Primero cognacs we would discuss the possibility that we might eventually start to forgive him. On my return to the UK however I emphasised to all my crew that they should make their own travel arrangements especially with regard to their luggage and hand tools and not to take up any offers of local assistance from our man from Barcelona.

Social Intercourse.

One thing about taking an instant dislike to someone is that it saves a great deal of time. When Terry turned on the charm it was usually a prelude to him setting out to be obnoxious. When he did this, he could be world class obnoxious without really trying.

All the way up from Atlanta he had been witttering on at me to cancel my hotel reservation and to spend the weekend at home with him and his wife. I was reluctant to do this since I felt that I preferred the freedom that living in a hotel gave you rather than the obligations that being a houseguest conferred on you. Eventually he prevailed however by the simple expedient of not stopping at the hotel on the way from the airport to his house. I must say that I was made very welcome and Terry's wife rustled up a mean spaghetti bolognaise and a very drinkable red wine for dinner before we retired for the night. Next morning when I went downstairs it was obvious that Terry and his wife were into round two or even three of a ding dong argument. It eventually became apparent that this was because Terry wanted to charge me twenty-five dollars for bed and breakfast. Terry's wife was adamant that they were not going to charge houseguests for accommodation and when it became evident that Terry was losing the argument he stomped off in the huff. Terry's wife tried her best to make amends and offered to show me some of the surrounding Pennsylvania countryside. This included part of Pennsylvania Dutch countryside in which many Amish communities were situated. We drove out through rolling farmlands on a beautiful sunny Saturday morning. The Amish farmers were going about their normal business dressed in their traditional black garb. No one appeared to have heard the one about the Amish man and his son who had to travel in a bank in a skyscraper in the nearby city. While in the lobby they saw an old lady press a button whereupon two steel doors slid open and she passed through before they slid shut again. A little light above the doors showed numbers rapidly rising then falling back to zero again. When the doors again opened for a second time a beautiful young lady got out and walked right past them. The Amish farmer and his son looked at each other in amazement for a few moments and them the farmer said to his son Jeb why don't you go fetch your mother.

We passed across several of the typical roofed bridges, which were a feature of the area and gave the impression that you were driving in the front and out of the back of an old wooden barn. Just as well really that they were ridges and not barns as some local might have left some bales of hay in it or even shut the back door.

The route took in many small villages with odd sounding names such as Blue Ball, Inspiration, Ecstasy, and Intercourse. At Intercourse we stopped and looked into some of the local craft shops. After browsing for some time, we went to a local café and we had a cup of coffee and one of the local cookies which were freshly baked in the back before returning via Hershey famous for its chocolate products. In the afternoon it was off again on business for Terry and I as we had a long journey before meeting up with a local sales executive on the Sunday night and starting work once again on Monday morning. Another day another Dollar.

At the end of the trip when I was sorting out my expenses, I came across a receipt which caught my attention. It said "Intercourse, Pennsylvania, five dollars with thanks. Now you all come back now you hear". This could take a bit of explaining I thought as I wondered how I could bury this somewhere in my monthly expenses.

One Careful Owner

I like cars as much as the next auto maniac. I passed my driving test first time at eighteen to the utter amazement of my instructor and in a driving career spanning over sixty years have driven well over sixty different marques and models of automobiles around the entire world. Perhaps twenty of these were owned by me while the rest were leased, rented or borrowed. My first car was an Austin Mini which was as basic a car as it was possible to buy but very reliable. On a good day it could reach sixty miles per hour going downhill with a following wind not that it was often asked to. While driving this I came across a Simca, Matra Baghera which was launched in France and lusted after it from the day I saw it. It was an incredible two door, three seat, mid engined, family sports car which preceded the launch of the Lotus Europa and was also a forerunner of the Porsche 924 all of which looked quite similar to one another. It had a 1300 cc Matra engine and incredibly was very modestly priced. I got so far as going into the Simca Showroom in central Paris but the sales manager was so impressed by my appearance that he would not even discuss the car with me. In pique I decided to buy British and ordered a Lotus twin cam Cortina from Ford in Stirling. The speedo went up to 150, the car went up to 118 but I never went above 104 all the time I had it which was only about a year as it was not cheap to insure maintain or operate. It actually reached 104 in mid-air as it negotiated a hump in the road whereupon it resorted to low flying only for me to notice a T junction about 200 yards in front. I can confirm that four-wheel disc brakes do not slow any car when it is already airborne. I ran it once at Ingliston racetrack in Edinburgh under an RAC beginner's competition Licence. I was refused insurance for driving the car while it was on the track but had to pay insurance for the track itself and everything else on it and surrounding it and so drove it most incredibly carefully being lapped by MG midgets and even pushbikes if there had been any on the track. From here I graduated to a couple of 1100's one of which was an MG and then a company Cortina XL no less in fluorescent custard yellow so that when I was flying into Glasgow and Edinburgh airports I could see it in the carpark and save time trying to remember where I had left it. It should be noted that this strategy does not work at all in

Montreal where the cars are covered in a foot of snow for 6 months every year and was often even a bit dubious in a wintry Scotland. I had to wait 40 years to move to England to have car stolen and a further year to have the same car stolen twice in three days. The first time it was from the obviously unsecure car park of the five-star George Washington Hotel and then the second time a couple of days later was from the Sunderland Police car pound. The car finally turned up on the beach in Whitley Bay twenty miles north on the other side of the River Tyne. The fuzz dropped me off on the esplanade and when they saw the doors were open and the battery flat wished me every success it getting home again 200 miles to the south in Chester. The AA proved to be the equivalent of the 7th cavalry and started the car on jump leads. Since the car had also had the ignition lock barrel removed, they also made certain that the ignition was properly hotwired so that I could tip toe home over a period of about five hours driving. I think that driving my Rover 800 SDI gave me one of my very few tickets for speeding in my many miles behind the wheel. I was driving north through Glencoe on the A82 on a fine Sunday evening in dry conditions with no other vehicles on the road. As I approached the shore of Loch Leven to turn west to South Ballachulish the speed limit dropped from 60 to 50 and I slowed down. Just before the road turned to run along the southern shore of the loch, I noticed a police car parked behind a building and thought that they must be having a fallow spell if they were out looking for wrongdoers. After proceeding for a further few miles within the limit I noticed blue flashing lights in the distance behind me and slowed even further. The police land rover came right up behind me with flashing headlights so I pulled immediately over and stopped. Two enormous bobbies invited me to join them in the back of their vehicle. The car had an English registration and my licence showed my current English address so I got a lecture on rich English tourists in huge powerful motor cars putting the life and limb of the honest god-fearing local Scots population in jeopardy. I carefully weighed up the situation and decided to say absolutely nada as I had obviously woken two sleeping SNP dragons from their slumber. Two weeks later I got a summons from the procurator fiscal in Fort William. The envelope was addressed to me but inside they had managed to put the documents for a local highland tinker who had been drunk and disorderly in a local shebeen. What infuriated me was that they were fining the tinker less than they were fining me for my alleged offence. The fastest that I have ever travelled in a car was at about 150 mph in a new BMW 7 series on the unrestricted Autobahn between Dusseldorf and Cologne but on this occasion I was an apprehensive passenger being driven by a portly German who had just go the car that day and couldn't it seems figure out where all the controls were as he appeared not to be able to find the brakes. One of the slowest drives was for a few kilometres on an Autobahn running from Germany into France near Saarbrucken. When we eventually got to the dual customs posts on the actual border it seemed that the officials on the French side were working to rule or at least their interpretation of their rule which was to stop every single vehicle and to gaze at it for a short while. This seemed to affect cars with non-French registration marks more than any with French registration. As we rolled up to the barrier as two furious Brits in a German registered Mercedes with a German in the back the official mistook us all for Germans and held his hand up imperiously for us to stop and be overawed by him. I guess that he spoke English because of the look on his face when

I wound down the window and told him loudly and clearly that it was great pity that the French had not stopped the Germans so efficiently in 1940. As we drove on, I noticed in the mirror that Wolfgang sitting in the back was looking very puzzled. I asked him what the problem was and after some thought he told me that they had not actually used that road as Germany invaded France through Benelux which was much shorter. Who said that the Erics had no sense of humour? This guy was comedy gold standard although possibly he just had no sense of what was lost in translation.

Turkish Delight.

The stench of defeat was in the air but at least it was British stench not tainted by any foreign influence and was entirely of our own making.

I had just travelled from Glasgow to London and on to Istanbul where the Orient meets the Occident and Europe and Asia regard each other with tension and suspicion across the Bosphorous. The last leg of the flight with Turk Hava Yollari Turkey's national airline had conditioned me only slightly for what was to come. The taxi journey from the airport into Istanbul's central bus station completed most of the transformation. Normally I would have flown on to Ankara to be met by a chauffeur driven car to take me to the hotel but this visit was destined to be different. We had over early two years protracted negotiations mainly in the United States landed a very substantial order, which was eventually destined for Eregli. During this time John had progressively reduced our agents healthy commission to zero because of the fierce bargaining which had taken place and the price reductions, which it was necessary to give.

After delivery however it was apparent that there was a problem, which required an urgent visit. It was at this point that the agent shrugged his shoulders and said, "well nothing personal David Bey but I really can't afford to service this business on zero per cent". It was for this reason that I found myself in Istanbul central bus station looking for the bus I needed to take me to my distant destination. It was a life experience on the bus and the journey itself seemed to take almost a lifetime. The rest of the passengers seemed fascinated by me just as much as I was by them. It was not an everyday experience for them to have a passenger wearing a suit, shirt and tie and clutching a brief case on his lap throughout the journey. Neither did I normally share a bus with men wearing upside down red flowerpots with tassels on their heads, and with women wearing black veils. There were also an incredible variety of household goods including big brass samovars and assorted livestock competing for space. Although the journey involved passing through some interesting places the way the driver drove the bus discouraged looking out of the window especially looking at the road ahead as he played chicken with oncoming truck drivers. The road from Istanbul to Ankara must have been one of the most dangerous in the known world and I was actually relieved when he turned onto a secondary road and set off into the mountains.

To while away the journey, I read the Sunday Times and it did not take long for one of the other passengers to pluck up courage and indicate that we would appreciate seeing a section that I had finished reading.

In no time at all there were individual pages of the paper all over the bus. The only person that seemed not to be reading it was the driver but I have no doubt he was doing his best to see it in the mirror. If the Sunday Times circulation in Turkey increased during 1975, I think that I can justifiably claim a large part of the credit.

When we eventually reached Eregli I found myself in a minus three-star hotel. By the look of it I was fortunate that the restaurant was closed and I had a large glass of Raki and a plate of salted almonds for supper. I did not get a great deal of sleep that night as I sat on top of the bed so that I could throw my boots at scurrying cockroaches and other things that made rustling noises in the darkness.

Next day the job itself was everything that I feared that it might be. I made detailed notes and measurements as well as taking lots of photographs. Later I then headed back to Istanbul by hitching a lift in a battered Land Rover and made my way to Yesilikoy to catch an Air France Caravelle to Athens and a BEA Trident to London.

I had telexed ahead from Athens with some of the details but in spite of this when I got back to the office I was met by a chorus of "I don't beleeeive it!" by a bunch of demented Victor Meldrews in an echo chamber. Neither would I had I not had the unused return portion of my bus ticket to prove it. Unfortunately the magnitude of the problem involved the works manager getting the sack for the enormous cost to replace all of the many thousands of cracked bricks but it should have been the MD for electing to make the bricks by a new untried process to start with "to save money."

Rumble in the Jungle

Have you ever noticed that the smaller a country is then the more elaborate its own official's uniforms are? When you arrive in the UK through places such as Ringway or MIA as its now better known to the younger generation the immigration staff are almost casually although always smartly dressed and the customs officers seldom wear jackets far less any imposing headgear. In some African states its very different with some pretty fancy outfits on show including some with so many medals that the wearers are lopsided. These numpties are inevitably backed up by others in different military style combat uniforms that look like they have come from Oxfam, This is before you get to the gophers who tend to wear whatever they can find on the floor in the dark when they get out of bed in the morning but almost always have a pair of very dark sunglasses. The effect seems to be solely intended to intimidate visitors to soften them up so that they can be relieved more easily of cameras and other personal effects.

This is not racist it is absolute fact as personally experienced by me in the 80's so if there was any bigotry it was directed by the locals at me and most other visitors and not by us at them. I don't think that it was even colour that was the issue as I believe it was solely based on the fact that visitors were perceived to have material possessions which most local didn't and could never ever even aspire to. The socialist ethos was that these material possessions should be much more evenly if not necessarily actually equitably distributed. It was par for the course in any number of underdeveloped countries at the time and something that you could either anticipate or if a first-time visitor maybe even be taken aback or shocked. At least while one was in the airport it was extremely rare for possessions to be physically torn from you while in the country at large this was not necessarily the case. It was not so much crime for many of the unfortunate locals as it was survival for some. Arriving in one equatorial African country at dusk from somewhere in western Europe like Brussels Zaventem on Sabena was definitely an interesting if somewhat testing experience. Its actually such a bloody experience never again for anyone who is into acronyms and equally if you are not. You are confronted by all of the aforementioned layers of bureaucracy and much more. Even although it is almost pitch dark with at best a few feeble flickering lights to see what you are falling over most of the officials wore their ubiquitous sunglasses. You then have to fill in questionnaires on several pieces of recycled toilet paper in near darkness. The main aim appears to be to establish how much money you may have. Once outside the building the full heat, humidity and cacophony hit you even although the sun has long set. I believe that there are people in the world who make an unofficial and precarious living just from being outside airport buildings while others pass through "their territory". These include the locals who vie to carry your luggage usually removing the handle in the process. Even when met, by colleagues or business associates, the onward journey is not a bed of roses. Alec and I were VIP's and were being conveyed to out distant destination by company car with an experienced local driver. The car was a large old Peugeot estate car as the parent company was French and it was one of the few marques in the country anyway. We were not alone in the car as the front passenger seat was occupied by a large gentleman who may have been our security detail. In the back Alec and I shared the bench seat with an ample lady and I voted that Alec sat in the middle. Our fellow passengers might perhaps have been nothing to do with the company and just getting a (free?) ride from a friendly driver. He also managed to load the back of the car with an incredible array of goods. Our companions in travel were no trouble but Alec was unenthusiastic about the fact that every time the driver braked to avoid an obstacle a large metal cooking pot in the back rolled forward and hit him on the back of the head. Reloading part of the hardware quickly resolved that issue. The journey up country over unmade roads in a crowded car is a bone jolting experience. When in the dry season there is a cloud of dust, which never settles, and this gives an incentive to drive fast enough that the dust never catches up with you. In the rainy season the cars are axle deep in mud most all of the time and this gives an incentive to drive fast enough so that the mud never oozes in through the door, The change from dry season to wet season can also be a shock since it is often as sudden as having a bucket of warm water thrown over you.

On this particular occasion the driver of the battered Peugeot swerved from side to side to miss the worst of the potholes. I worked out that he seemed to have a theory that he was supposed to drive on the right but actually if he drove in the centre and frequently swerved to the left that this would avoid the worst of the potholes. Since he did the same on the return journey however, I can confirm that this technique is almost entirely ineffective. At one point in the journey just outside a tiny isolated jungle village with a few thatched huts and where the track was in total darkness the driver slammed on his brakes causing the large cooking pot in the back of the car to roll forward again and hit me between the shoulder blades. This was getting boring.

As they dust settled around us, I could see by the weak light from the dusty headlights that there was in fact a chain stretched across the road. It was fixed firmly to trees on either side of the road and dangled down to about eighteen inches above the ground at the centre. This could have ruined the mood if I had been driving rather than by our local expert. It is about this time in such episodes that you wonder if your company will pay the ransom demand when they eventually get the request relayed to them via the British Embassy several days later. Below one of the trees in almost total darkness squatted some kind of local militiaman dressed in a motley diversity of camouflage clothes, which passed for his uniform. There was nothing funny however about the automatic weapon which he clutched in his right hand with the butt resting against the ground and the muzzle in the air. In such scenarios there is always a better than fifty fifty chance that the weapon actually works and that he also has a few rounds of live ammunition in it. It did not take long to establish that he was not only the local village security presence but that he was also the local tax collector. It occurred to me that had we been in a hire car instead of a company vehicle he would have collected more in his chain than he had bargained for and that the value of his catch would far have exceeded the small sum of money which changed hands between the driver and him to have him lower the chain to the ground to ensure further passage was unhindered.

Fort Apache

The Americans referred to it as Fort Apache but then everything tended to be themed around cowboys and Indians with them anyway. It was not however some little old wooden stockade down in the badlands that they were referring to though, but in fact it was a twenty-seven acre site in the middle of Teheran, in which some two thousand people lived and worked. The Iranians had a less amusing name for it. They called it the nest of the great Satan. Like the Germans perhaps the Iranians have never really been noted for their sense of humour in spite of Omid Djalili and Shappi Khorsandi.

The Americans had made one of their many mistakes when they ousted Mossadeq and his government in 1953 in favour of the Shah and his imperial family. They not only installed the ruler of the peacock throne into his exalted position but they poured lots of money into the economy to bolster the Shahs regime in an unstable environment. Their rationale behind this was to create a bulwark against communism and to stop the Russians from rampaging south all the way to the shores of the then Persian Gulf. In doing so Iran became America's biggest customer for the sale of arms and built up a huge arsenal of modern weapons. Many of the people of Iran were increasingly very unhappy with the situation as they saw much of the new found wealth being funnelled through or to the Shah his family and friends and being used for amongst other things to build up a huge, well resourced, state security apparatus. The SAVAK as it was known ultimately became one of the most efficient and feared security services in the world and intruded into everyday Iranian life to help keep the Shah in power. These tensions ebbed and flowed for more than twenty-five years and divided society into an us and a them. They peaked in 1975 when the Shah threw one of the world's biggest parties to celebrate two thousand years of the peacock throne. The throne itself was only pinched from India in the mid seventeen hundred's but it was the modern-day representation of the dynasty founded by Cyrus the Great in 550 BC. I have no idea if

Shah Reza Pahlavi was entitled run the country but he and the Americans decided that he was. People came from all over the world for his second millennium bash which was held on a remote site in the desert south of Teheran called Persepolis which was near to the city of Isfahan. Somehow my invitation must have got lost in the post, as did the invitations to most of the Iranian people who might have expected a day off work and a few buns at the very least to share the unbounded joy of the Emperor and the imperial family. Although I went to down to Persepolis the cordon sanitaire which SAVAK set up around the site meant that I could see it only in the distance but could not gain admittance to the site itself as the roads were all blocked off by surly security forces. A bit like the millennium dome at Greenwich you might think except there is no desert and fewer peacocks. After being turned away by a bunch of tough looking troops in full combat gear at the roadblock in the desert the irony did not escape me.

Here was the USA subsidising a celebration of two thousand years of the Aryan race while thirty years previously they had been bombing hell out of another Aryan race based in Berlin. This was a double millennium celebration that I mostly missed but perhaps I could still get tickets for Hogmanay in Edinburgh in 1999/ 2000 I thought.

I certainly didn't want to miss two millenniums in one century as that would have been careless. When I thought that the Iranian one would have to have been washed down with Raki, I must admit that it lost a lot of its appeal. I knew that the Shah would have few decent Jeroboams of champers on ice down in his marquee for his official guests but the local town was officially dry which if you have ever tasted Raki is a veritable blessing in disguise as a side effect seems to be the muppets playing drums loudly inside your head the following morning providing of course you managed to survive the night. At least up town you could usually rely on a few decent cold beers to settle the dry desert dust in your throat. On one occasion at least however my mate Tel must have unearthed a bottle of dubious Scotch when he was being entertained by one of the Shahs myrmidons who wanted to be appointed as general agent for one of the forerunners of British Steel. This position was at that time characterised of course by the British company taking all the risk and doing all the work while the local agent allowed himself the consolation of collecting all of the very considerable commission. On the way back to the hotel in the agents Rolls Royce he was offering blandishments to Tony like his wife or his daughter or both if he were appointed to be the distributor. After a glass or three of the Scotch Tony told him that if he were allowed to drive the Rolls Royce that might be enough to swing the deal. The car stopped immediately and he was thrust into the driver's seat. It was at this point that he realised that he did not know which side of the road the traffic drove on in Iran but since nobody else seemed to know either it did not seem an insurmountable problem. What did prove to be more of an issue was that when he swung the car through the gates into the hotel grounds there was another vehicle coming down the drive. Tony swerved the Rolls Royce and missed the other vehicle but ran headlong into one of the pam trees lining the drive. The promise of the contract being initiated however solved all of the issues of driving while under the influence and a myriad of other minor things like panel beating the left wing back into the original contours bodywork scratches and partial resprays. Isn't life just fine and dandy at least for some anointed folks when greed, corruption peacocks and quick thinking ruled the roost. I guess it just proves the old adage that Money talks. Too bad mine usually says goodbye

Blue Seas, Blue Booze and Blue Pelicans

I am consistently better with my A's, B's and C's then I am with my 1's, 2's and 3's but I can still undertip when I need to especially in establishments that start with about 15% on the bill and then try to shake you for even more for the good service that you very probably didn't get because there wasn't any. You know the type of places that I mean where you have to ask for the "William" instead of the bill. They say that the Scots are mean but my old friend Milto in Athens taught me Greek starting with the phrase "To logarismo parakalo" which is of course asking for the bill. Trouble is he never mentioned what it meant for at least the first month.

If you look at the Caribbean as a geologist might then you can see that the sea bed is a more or less a plateau surrounded by a circle of land formed around continental central and south America and the rest a chain of about thirty islands. It is as if the land and the islands are mountains surrounding three separate volcanic caldera or areas of ancient meteor impacts which they probably are. The Venezuelan Basin lies in the east the Colombian Basin in the centre and the Yucatan Basin in the west. Outside of the chain of islands the seabed falls away rapidly for example just north of Puerto Rico it plummets to a depth of about twenty-five thousand feet so we could regard that as the deep end and not for beginners especially as it is at one apex of the Bermuda Triangle and probably best avoided whenever possible.

Some of my most favourite Caribbean island ABC's have to be Aruba, Bonaire and Curacao which are located from west to east in the Dutch Antilles with Aruba being less than about fifteen miles north of Venezuela. The capital Oranjestad with its Queen Beatrix international airport is only a short boat ride on the Punto Fijas ferry to the small Venezuelan seaport of Piedras Negras. In the extreme north of the island is the oddly named California Lighthouse which must have one hell of a bright light since it is at the very least two thousand miles south east from San Diego on the Mexican Californian Border and separated by densely forested mountain ranges in central America. Like my crazy professor it might be bright but useless. The locals say that there are some iconic views available but either you like seeing waves all the way to the horizon or you must have remarkable eyesight and obviously in no need of Specsavers. Curacao is even more Dutch with its colourful numerous windmills and its sprawling capital Willimstad. I Stayed in the Willemstad Hilton which no longer exists in its original location overlooking the Queen Emma Swing Bridge which also no longer looks anything like it used to. The new bridge in the original location spans St Anna bay which I would have called a wide canal or a narrow river linking the sea to Schottgat which I would describe as a small bay with dozens of coves and inlets. The bridge had to open to allow ocean going vessels access to the bay from the Caribbean Sea. Some of the traffic would be cruise ships but many others were tankers as the underground oil deposits in Venezuela also lie under the island which had its own refinery in the Schottgat on Refinery Isla which is a peninsula and not an island. This is what's known as progress although there was nothing wrong with the setup when I was there as far as I could see. I have to admit that a lot of what I did see was a load of Bols from the top floor bar in the Hilton over a couple of cool Blue Curacaos in a tall glass. Two options were Blue Lagoon which was Curacao and Vodka or Blue Hawaiian which was Curacao and rum. I stopped a long way short of Sex on the Beach which is Curacao and peach schnapps partly to ponder how such a bright blue drink could have such a bitter orange taste and partly to note that I had not seen any beaches on my visit. B might be between A and C but Bonaire is east of Curacao and the smallest of the group of three Dutch islands off the Venezuelan coast. Slightly further east again is about as far as it is possible to travel alphabetically as you end up in Trinidad or in the nearby Tobago which is famous for its hummingbirds. Trinidad looks very much as if it has been chopped off the east coast of Venezuela which is less than five miles away at its nearest point. The Hilton in Port of Spain where I stayed is the "upside down Hilton" since it is built into a steep hillside with the reception at the top of the wooded hill and the ground floor six or nine floors below this level depending entirely on whether your room is south facing or west facing. In one fierce tropical storm I was mildly surprised to see water cascading down the side of a nearby hill with all sorts of debris in it including a nest of local snakes one of which might have been a small green anaconda although I readily confess that I did not approach them with any slight curiosity whatsoever as there were multiple varieties in the torrent and many were venomous. Conventional wisdom is that snakes are scared of larger mammals like humans. Well I know that and you know that but did anyone think to tell the snakes. Best not to confirm the theory. The neighbouring island of Tobago is said to have no snakes so maybe St Patrick was there.

In the top floor dining room, I sampled the spicy local cuisine while to reduce the high risk of spontaneous combustion, I sank a couple of Carib Brewery's Mackesson Triple X stouts. The dining room at dinner was plagued by a small wandering Spanish or Mexican type minstrel complete with sombrero and guitar. He was circulating around all the tables and embarrassing the diners by serenading them for mucho dinero. He stopped at my table and asked if I had a request. I must have enjoyed the stout as instead of telling him what I really wanted him to do I suggested that he play Celito Lindo. Although this was probably the best known Mexican nationalist anthem ever, it appeared to be outside of his repertoire. My request was therefore along the lines that he go forth and never come back until he was proficient in every respect.

It was also in Trinidad that I broke my lifelong golden rule never to buy a T shirt with a logo. I was enjoying a cool Guinness or three in the Pelican Inn but the heat and humidity must have finally got to my brain and I invested in an expensive cheap vest with a pale blue logo. I suppose the logo faded before the shirt wore out so I was able to wear it under even a white shirt so all was not lost. The pub was originally opened in the early sixties by local couple Beetle and Harry Ross but was later run by the new owners Sean and Suzie in the eighties. It may be one of the most missed watering holes in Port of Spain especially by the Caribs and other Rugby teams some of whom it is claimed trained there. After more than sixty years dispensing cheer the pub has since gone out of business. I have a watertight alibi but am at a loss to understand how a pub with a clientele drawn from the more than four thousand six hundred rugby players in Trinidad along with their WAG's can possibly have closed. After leaving the hallowed premises with my colleague ex squadron leader Jim Leighton, or was it his brother Alastair? or were we all three there? as that would help explain the three pints of Guinness; we wandered across the large well- kept green sward at the front. It seemed that this would often resound to the sharp whack of leather on willow from the pub team. It also reverberated every carnival to the deafening cacophony of twenty-gallon oil drums and lids and the pounding of many dancing feet. Leighton Rice are based in the southern suburb of San Juan just off the Churchill Roosevelt Highway and unlike the pub are still very much in business so apparently, I did them no fatal damage during our brief happy mutual association.

Arms Akimbo

There was a large old low definition TV mounted on an unpolished antique mahogany dresser at one end of the large rectangular dining room on the top floor penthouse of the ten-story concrete tower block. We had tried to switch it on earlier in the day but there was no picture although there appeared to an external aerial connected and to be an adequate supply of electricity. We concluded therefore that there were no TV transmissions in the afternoon in this mountainous jungle covered area more than fifty miles from the capital on the coast of west Africa. Since some of the population were Muslim, we did not know whether this was for religious or other reasons since we knew that the local branch of Al Shabab was not much into light entertainment. We were just glad really that there was no power failure because it meant that when we came back from the plant in the oppressive heat and humidity of the afternoon, we could enjoy a cold beer from the fridge. We sat on a cane settee in the dining room looking out through the large unwashed windows over the rolling jungle. From our vantage point on the tenth floor of the block of flats incongruously stuck on top of a hill we could see for a very long distance although there was a light heat and humidity haze which caused little wisps of fog to hang like smoke below in the trees. It seemed pretty weird to me that we were in the guest suite of the mining company flats while ten storeys below we were surrounded by hundreds of little wooden huts and small one storey buildings with either grass or corrugated tin roofs which comprised the mining town of Kimbo.

In the evening as dusk gathered about a dozen of us expats drawn from at least five different nationalities assembled in the dining room for a meal at one large communal table. The engineer who had been there longest claimed seniority and sat at the top of the table and held court. The lingua franca was mainly French with a smattering of English but both he and his wife were keen for news of what was happening in back in Europe and we two new boys provided the bulk of the topics of conversation so that the meal passed quickly and pleasantly enough. At about eight someone rose from the table went over to the dresser and switched the TV on so that it flickered into life but still without a picture. After a few minutes however we heard some martial music and an announcer appeared on the screen to introduce the president no less who was to do yet another one-party political broadcast. The president stood there in his best immaculate white uniform which was unsurprisingly adorned with many honours and decorations all over his ample garment. He was standing on a first-floor balcony of the presidential palace or other impressive stone-built government building in the capital we assumed although he could have been in Disneyland Paris on a custom-built movie set. His people or at least a specially chosen enthusiastic few stared up at him in awe and rapture as he addressed them from his podium in one of the many local dialects. They obviously adored him and hung on his every word or else were well rewarded extras from equity. As he spoke, they gently waved palm fronds although whether this was a sign of respect or to keep cool or both I was not sure, as I was totally unfamiliar with the local protocol. About fifteen minutes later the same speech appeared to start all over again which rather perplexed me until I figured that he was delivering the same message in another dialect. A further twice the message was relayed again in other dialects until at about nine o clock the TV flickered and abruptly went off. That it appeared was that for the evening so we reinvented the art of conversation for a short time before everyone called it a night and retired to bed. Bed was a thin palliasse on a polished tile stone floor was surrounded by a circle of rough rope. There were nets over the bed which was treated with anti mosquito spray to keep most of what flew or crawled at bay we hoped during the hours of darkness. That combined with vigorously shaking our clothes and boots before we dressed in order to shift any small spiders, tarantulas or snakes more or less started each day.

Next day in the capital Conakry as we made our way through the city to the small international airport were able to see and experience the full extent of the people's awe and adoration of their leader and his government. A large crowd of angry people were complaining loudly about some newly imposed tax and were besieging an army truck full of soldiers which was trying to clear the way for an official car to drive past. Since the large black Mercedes limousine car had matching smoked black armoured glass windows, which were closed tight I could not see the occupants but the people seemed to recognise the car and its occupant. They crowded in on the vehicle and beat at the car and the windows with their fists and pieces of wood or anything else that they could lay hands on. The soldiers who were well outnumbered very sensibly had no intention of getting down from their truck to mix it with the local populace. They either fired indiscriminately into the air or beat the nearest citizens over the head with the butts of their rifles. To me it gave a whole new meaning to the term head banger.

You Bet Your LIfe

I always thought that it was a very friendly little airline with little aircraft and no pretensions. It only operated around the islands but the planes were frequent and the service was like service should be, unobtrusive. Punctuality was never an issue because if a plane was delayed because of weather or mechanical problems there would always be another along shortly. Most of the time the weather was not all that bad except in the hurricane season September to December. The rest of the time the only excitement came from clear air turbulence. This usually happened because the sun heated the land more than it heated the sea so that in the late afternoon the currents of air were drawn across the surface of the water until they reached land when they rose sharply as a thermal. This could make things ever so slightly bumpy and so it was best to fly in the morning. But not too early in the morning because the sea held its temperature overnight better than the land and so the air currents were drawn across the land until they reached the sea when they rose as thermals. The best time therefore was mid-morning to mid-afternoon and this provided a great excuse to rise late and take a leisurely breakfast before setting off. To do otherwise would have meant spilling your coffee in the morning or your Pina Colada in the afternoon. The dry cleaners around the Bermuda Triangle must do pretty well I always thought. On one early flight out of Miami an American tourist enquired of the stewardess as to which islands they would be flying over. Ever eager to please the paying customers the stewardess asked the captain to give a running commentary en route. The pilot however had a better idea and sent back a detailed map of the flight plan all marked up. Just before coming in to the final approach in Antigua however the captain came on the PA system. He announced that we would be landing in less than ten minutes and asked politely if he could have his map back so that he could find the airport. I laughed like everyone else on the plane because I was sure he was joking. When he asked the second time however, I was not quite so sure and certainly would not have put any money on it had someone offered me a wager.

Guy Fawkes

It is not everybody that can say that they have had a pint of bitter and a game of snooker with Guy Fawkes on the 5th of November. Well to be strictly accurate it was not Guy himself but his great, great, great, great grandson. Neither were we in the cellars of the houses of Parliament although armed guards surrounded us. The meeting took place in the British Embassy in Bucharest Romania. It was the eve of the first democratic elections since the fall of Ceausescu and there were a lot of nervous people around since no one knew what the elections would bring. Nobody suggested that anyone was going to blow up the parliament building or even the British Embassy but there was plenty of talk of blowing up the old political system which was supposed to be communist but which operated largely on nepotism. The power was supposed to have lain with the people but in fact it resided in the President, his family and his cronies. Now that they were largely no longer around there was something of a vacuum which created much uncertainty.

It was not possible to predict accurately what was going to happen or what effect it would have on people's lives. It was almost possible to cut the atmosphere with a knife and both the police guards and the embassy security men were a little tenser than usual. Out in the city currency speculation was rife and Romanians were offering a handsome premium to anyone who wanted to change Pounds, Dollars Pesetas or Deutschemarks for their money. The Romanian currency was not the strongest at the best of times but people were hedging their bets that a new democratic government would put the country and its economy back on its feet and attract inward investment from the west. Everything was on a knife-edge however and if it went the wrong way it would have made Transylvania look attractive by comparison.

The new British Ambassador Mr Crabbe was quite optimistic and talked up the prospects for business after the election but then he would, wouldn't he. Some of the other snooker players were a bit more cynical but were going to make every effort to make it work anyway since it takes a pretty committed person to do business in Eastern Europe anyway. Not only do you have to be fairly tough minded but you also need your own supply of toilet paper and a dense rubber ball to act as a universal bath plug. A pair of rubber gloves is also useful in case you plan to plug or unplug any electrical equipment on the off-chance that it may be live although not necessarily operational.

The irony is that looking back on the bad old days there was a corrupt system that everybody understood perfectly. With the onset of democracy everything was thrown into turmoil and nobody could understand what was happening. Now buyers could be heard asking for lower prices where before they always insisted on higher prices.

I blame the Americans myself. It was not like that before they opened a McDonalds in Bucharest.

Super Mario

Flying across six time zones from Manchester to Chicago could take over 9 hrs depending on the strength of the headwinds in the Jetstream and a shedload of European flights used to all struggle in around two o clock in the afternoon each day. I cleared through immigration and customs and was back in the air in less than two hours for a further 4-hour flight to Phoenix in Arizona. I was joined on this leg by Tony who had booked us first class for this flight and the large cabin was pretty empty with only about 6 passengers. Tony constantly laboured under the misapprehension that he had been born to enable as many women as possible to swoon at his feet. Some of the passengers were moving around the cabin and Tony ambled down to the galley. I knew that any stewardess unlucky enough to be on duty there was about to be regaled with Shakespeare's 18th sonnet comparing her to a summer's day and then with Del Boy's chat up line that her name whatever it happened to be was his most favouristist name in the entire universe. I have no doubt that flight attendant training school has a module on how to combat this and similar approaches even although they are flying first class. I made a mental note that if a couple of stews handcuffed him in a seat with plastic ties, I would assist them by happily inserting the gag and then putting a large canvas bag over his head.

One of the other passengers who had been stretching his legs and who looked like a smaller and more handsome version of Bill Clinton with curly dark hair was just returning to his own seat across the aisle, smiled and nodded to me as he sat down. I nodded back and we got into conversation as you do with bronzed celebrities. He quietly introduced himself as Mario Andretti whom even at that time I knew was an Italian-born American racing car driver. He was actually only nine months older than me and while already famous he ultimately became one of the most successful Americans in the history of the sport being one of only two drivers to have won races in Formula One, IndyCar, World Sportscar Championship, and NASCAR in the USA and around the world. He asked if I had any interest in fast cars and I shyly confessed that he was talking to the driver of a Lotus Cortina who had been newly awarded an RAC provisional racing licence for all UK circuits. I don't think that this still exists today but at the time it entitled me to a sign with a large white diagonal cross on a black background on the back of my car. This warned other racing drivers as they lapped me that I was rookie and thus totally unpredictable so that they should keep well clear in case I decided on a 360-degree spin or flipping the car over onto its roof just for a laugh. I felt a bit daft explaining to one of the best drivers in the world about RAC licences but he laughed and said that he had not been aware of that situation although he had raced in England. I told him not to fret too much as Edinburgh Ingliston circuit where I scared myself to death was not actually located in England and that it was also beyond belief that anyone who drove like me would ever be seen on the same starting grid as him in any case. During this conversation another American passenger sidled over and insisted repeatedly that he knew who my new friend was and that no one should help him because it was on the tip of his tongue. After a couple of minutes of this Mario tired of the bore and told him that he was Mario Andretti and that this was his Scottish pal Dave putting the bores gas on a peep and allowing him to slink back to his seat and contemplate having been in the presence of the gods of speed. It turns out that Mario was also staying at the same hotel the Arizona Biltmore in Scottsdale that I was booked in.

To be honest I did not see much of him in the bar or in any other part of the hotel or grounds because I don't imagine he went near the bar when racing and in any case we both had heavy but very different schedules. His was in qualifying for the front row of the grid at the Phoenix International Raceway in Avondale for the NASCAR race that Saturday while mine was more mundane. I must honestly say however that I really did not envy him driving endlessly round a huge banked oval track at high speeds of up to 200 mph followed by a pack of other cars in temperatures of up to 40 degrees centigrade. I toasted him in cold lager served at 4 degrees centigrade in an iced cold glass when he finally triumphed and won the race. I did not see him leave as he later boarded his flight for Daytona in Florida where the conditions were roughly comparable but with the faint chance of a light breeze and maybe the odd alligator scurrying across the track at as night drew in. I have since had my name added to the tailfin of the Bloodhound jet car trying for the world lands speed record of 1000 mph in salt flats in the Kalahari South Africa by way of a modest donation. At the time of writing the Rolls Royce powered car had not reached 1000 mph in trials on land and I certainly never intend to approach anything like this speed on land unless I get caught up in a large explosion which at this particular time, I have no firm plans to do. Incidentally did you see the report last week that an old Boeing 707 at the Davis Monthan air force base boneyard near Tucson Arizona had been found with a wizened little old skeleton with a wide lunatic grin on its face firmly manacled to a first-class seat with plastic restraints.

Soused Herren

Kevin suggested that I go to visit him in Finspång, Sweden even although it was mid-summer and most Swedes had headed south to the beaches of the Mediterranean or the Balearic Islands for their annual break. I flew into Finspång, and rented a car for the drive to Finspang which took me about an hour and a half since in these days there was no satnav, I did not know the way and the "Polis" were very active with their radar detector outfits. During what was the main Swedish holiday exodus period they presumably reckoned that they would mainly nick tourists rather than their friends and relations. On arrival I found the hotel very easily as the town was not large and the traffic was very light to almost non-existent. There was even parking right at the door. When I climbed the steps however, I found that the front door of the hotel was locked. My first reaction was that I had misunderstood Kevin's suggestions and gone to the wrong place. I thought however that I had better ring the bell in case there was anyone inside and the hotel was not shut for the summer. After a few minutes Kevin himself came to the door and unlocked it to let me in. He confirmed that the management and staff were all on holiday but that since he was a long-term guest and was employed as a senior manager at the biggest company in town, they had left him in sole residence. Since among the keys that they had left him with was one for the bar I was sure that everything was going to work out just fine and dandy. We chose our poison poured them into tall glasses and took our beer out onto the terrace. We actually discussed some business before I checked myself in to the second-best room in the house. After coming back down to the bar for the other half he told me that we were going to go to dinner later at the company guesthouse which was nearby and which thus was only a short walking distance away. This would have been quite an honour for any visitor in any case but I was especially impressed that the Housekeeper had come back from holiday to open up and to prepare and serve dinner for five managers and myself. It made perfect sense to walk the short distance over to the guesthouse since no one in their right mind would ever go to a formal Swedish function such as this was and then attempt to drive themselves home afterwards. The meal was a set menu with all the local specialities such as gravadlax and forty kinds of pickled herring. The only local specialities which we missed out were the meatballs and the non-alcoholic beer. The drinks too were to a set to a strict pattern and accompanied by formal toasts, which required me to throw the Akavit as far back down my throat as was possible without having it touch lips, teeth or tonsils on the way. As the evening wore on the toasts became "musical" and more of a challenge and it was then that I realised that I was in trouble. Even after all the strong drink I had consumed I could not sing in Swedish but I consoled myself that I could not sing even in English either so that it would not have made much difference. I resolved this problem by bribing Kevin with extra drinks to sing for me when it was my turn and he amazed our hosts and me by his renditions of such well known hits as "I belong to Glasgow" albeit with his heavy west midlands accent. If I had been forced to participate I would have given them a very slurred version of the "English" version of the old Swedish classic "Hej Johann var är din häst" which very roughly translates as "Hi Jock where's yur cuddy" which I am certain would have cut short any further requests for any more musical interventions. We made our way back to the hotel by taxi because although it was only a short distance, we were not feeling very athletic and because the only sober taxi driver in town had been pre-booked to do the rounds. I knew that the hotel bar was quite secure in our hands that night since neither of us could have faced another nightcap. On reflection afterwards I reckoned that the cost of the drinks at dinner had we paid for them would have been over £1000 for the six of us. I convinced myself however that this was because most alcoholic drinks in Sweden were difficult to come by as well as very expensive and not because we drank a lot. With very weak beer at about three pounds for a small bottle and spirits at five pounds per glass you really do need to be very rich or very thirsty to have a serious drink in Sweden, Norway, Iceland, Finland or indeed anywhere else in the Nordic area in general. No one is going to admit to it readily but there is a definite market for the large-scale production and consumption of illicit ethyl alcohol under the generic name of Schnapps and it is barely allowed to cool rather than to mature before it is drunk. It sure as hell shortens the supply chain. Maybe only in Scandinavia is it possible to meet people who are so incredibly uptight and formal in business dealings and then prone to being so totally wasted after a drink or three with a meal. So please don't get me started on being basted in a blistering hot sauna and then chased naked through the snow while being beaten with big bunches of birch twigs and all for fun they tell me. I will give it a bye whether drunk or sober.

Finnish Fun

Tony always said that his idea of heaven was to fly to Bangkok on Finnair or was It to Helsinki on Thai airlines. I never could remember. By the time I got around to asking him why he was always off in a world of his own he always had such a beatific smile on his face and I did not like to intrude. To me Finnair was just another Scandinavian airline, which meant that the pilots were first class even, when your ticket was not and that they could take anything that the weather could throw at them. My first flight to Helsinki was not on Finnair however it was in an old de Haviland Comet of BEA as it then was. The flight from London was uneventful and I reflected that it was a lovely plane but only after they solved the mystery of why several of the earlier models had mysteriously crashed. My only gripe was the very small windows, which was the very price that passengers had to pay for safety in flight. I suppose that not being able to see much was indeed a much better outcome than decompressing at 30 thousand feet. Once we left the English coast near Felixstowe our next landfall was not for nearly two hours later over Bremmerhaven in north western Germany. We then tracked over Jutland to Lubeck and subsequently out over the Baltic Sea to approach Helsinki from the southwest. The approach into Helsinki Vantaa airport itself was over lots of small islands although the airport itself was located to the north east of the city. As the old Comet was on its final approach on the flare path it flared out imperceptibly with its wheels down and flaps fully extended and ready to touchdown in a text book landing. At that moment however a flock of very large white birds decided to fly in front of the aircraft. They may have been geese or swans or storks although they might as well have been albatrosses. There were several perceptible thuds as a number of them smashed into the plane striking mainly on the front edge of the wings and the engine air intakes. The plane dropped the last few feet and landed a little more heavily than planned. Or goose was cooked you might say but at least we were able to walk away safely after the engines were finally switched off. The fowl had no such luck. Walking away alive is to me the ultimate acid test of the "good flight" which everyone usually enquires if you have just had when you are met at your destination. The bus trip into town was fairly tame by comparison. The driver only skidded a couple of times on the ice and but we were not hit by any moose. We were dropped at the central bus station in the middle of the city. It was when I tried to get a taxi however that I realised that the rest of the trip was going to more challenging. During a long conversation where neither the taxi driver nor I understood a single word the other said I grasped that a knowledge of French, German and some Spanish was not going to be of much help.

I asked him if he could take me to the hotel Vakuna and eventually he understood but still obstinately shook his head when it came to transportation. As night fell and the temperature dropped even lower, he loudly said Hotel Vaaaaaakuna and pointed to a large brightly light building about 100 metres across the cobbled square. I wished him a merry Christmas also and then set out walking across the square dragging my own luggage towards the warm and inviting lights of the hotel which I was totally certain would be licensed to sell the local antifreeze at extortionate prices.

Michelin Man

The car journey back down from mining site in the mountains through the equatorial jungle was like a scene from the classic old TV car commercial. If you are old enough you may just remember the one where the Peugeot races on a narrow track through the dense bush which is fiercely ablaze on both sides of the road. This scene is being accompanied by an orchestra and a choir while the vocalists belt out "Take my breath away". I have never ceased to wonder how they got the full orchestra and choir in the back of a Peugeot 206. Send answers on a post card please directly to the Guinness book of records. I no longer wonder however why the car was being driven flat out since I can assure you that it is not a good idea to linger in such circumstances. At one point in our journey we too were forced to drive through an area of burning jungle on either side of the road while at the same time trying to shield our faces from the heat of the flames in addition to the high ambient temperature. Perhaps though the really unnerving part of this episode was to emerge from the flames and acrid smoke to be immediately confronted by a steel grey river running between steep muddy banks and crossed by a makeshift bridge. The bridge mainly consisted of two of the original longitudinal support girders, which ran all the way across. Most of the bridges original wooden decking had however rotted away or had been stolen for firewood but in any case, had long since gone. The driver lined up the car so that the wheels were in direct line with the two large I beams spanning the river. Without slackening pace very much it seemed we shot over the remains of the bridge to the other side of the river accompanied by the cheers of some small children who were playing down at the water's edge thirty feet below. If we had gone into the water it would probably have been the most interesting thing that they had seen all year and we might even have got an even bigger cheer. I am convinced that my central nervous system went into suspended animation but I confess to feeling some pain in my sphincter from it being tightly clenched until we reached the road again on the other bank. The driver just seemed to be grinning from ear to ear but they tell me that some skeletons have grins and seldom have much to smile about so it may well have been a rictus of fear.

When he finally dropped me off outside the airport terminal with my hand baggage I was streaked with sweat mixed with red dust and must have looked like an absolute apparition. The plan was that I would go into the airport check in area and sit there waiting while the director of protocol of the company who were sponsoring me came to meet me with my passport exit visa and tickets. Incredibly security let me into the building without any of the aforesaid documents so they must have been just a little bit overwhelmed by my appearance and maybe even more so by my foul demeanour. I must admit that I thought that the odds of anyone actually turning up at all with any documents must have been close to fifty, fifty. To my amazement and delight he did actually appear after less than a couple of hours which for that part of the world is really pretty prompt. Not only did he have the documents I needed to allow me to leave the country but he had also managed to manipulate the local black market so that both of us ended up with a profit from some blatant currency speculation. I had given him exactly 10 pounds sterling to pay for the exit paperwork. He had changed the sterling at incredible rates, got his profit in local currency and I got mine in French francs which although very grubby were at the least still hard currency. Due to my early arrival at the airport I found myself almost the first passenger to be processed for embarkation on the UTA flight to Paris. Security, customs and immigration took the form of some stocky men in paratroop's camouflage fatigues of the type, which had pockets everywhere. When challenged by one in very bad French I replied in kind and could see his eyes start to glaze over as he considered my reply as he looked at me standing there streaked in red dust. After a perfunctory riffle through my luggage to ensure that I had no camera or electrical equipment which he would have been duty bound to confiscate he seemed to lose interest slightly. He did have one last almost obligatory question to ask me however and that was whether I had any of the local currency, which it was deemed illegal to take out of the country although why anyone would even want to totally defies any logic as it would be worthless. The script called for me to say "Sacre bleu! I have a couple of leftover banknotes, which will be utterly worthless should I remove them from your wonderful country". "I know I have just had a the most wonderful idea". "Why don't I give them to you to dispose of for me". He even managed a tired little smile since he understood that I understood the system. He stuffed both notes which in total were worth about four pounds sterling into one of his many battledress pockets and I passed through into the departure lounge. While sitting awaiting boarding I noticed three Dutch people keen to board a KLM flight to Holland but unwilling to pay the departure tax. They were totally messed about for some time until the steps were about to be removed from the Jumbo. At this point they realised that they had the choice of throwing down a few grubby notes before legging it up the steps at a high rate of knots before the door closed or possibly even spending a further spell in this sun-kissed tropical idyll. It was a no brainer even for Dutch people who are reputed to be even more financially prudent than we Sots are. Later as I myself was one of the first up the stairs into my waiting Jumbo I caught a brief glimpse of the paratroop look alike again but this time he seemed to bear a close resemblance to Michelin man with banknotes stuffed in all of his many pockets of his one piece uniform. As I entered the plane the stewardess smiled brightly and after she checked the name on my boarding card indicated that I should turn left and showed me to a window seat near the front of the almost empty first-class cabin. When she brought the first of several glasses of chilled vintage champagne to help settle the dust in my throat, I contemplated that it must have been one hell of an attractive exchange rate that got me an unexpected upgrade as well as all the champagne I could drink. About ten minutes after take-off and before I fell into a deep slumber the captain came onto the PA system to welcome us escapees aboard and then to announce that the next scheduled stop was Ouagadougou in Burkino Faso. This was met by all aboard with total indifference but when he announced that no one onboard wanted to deplane there and there were no passengers to pick up there he had decided to overfly straight on to Paris CDG. This caused a further run on the bar at the back of the plane. During my slumbers the plane apparently also over flew Timbuktu in Mali but at 10 thousand metres above low rainclouds on a moonless night I gave not a jot at all and my next recollection was of the view of misty fields in France as we came into land.

Peanuts

When President Jimmy Carter launched his ill -fated bid to rescue the American embassy hostages in Teheran in 1980 the student activists holding the 55 diplomats dispersed them all to the four corners of the country in small groups to foil further rescue attempts. The captors were both furious and scared and decided to make themselves and the hostages very hard to locate by changing locations regularly. One small group of four was sent in an unmarked van to a village in the extreme north east of the country near the border with the USSR and Afghanistan. My own journey there some short time before had been in a four wheel drive off road vehicle but was probably not a great deal more comfortable because the roads were somewhat bumpy.

The other passengers were the managing director of a big Iranian joint venture glass company and a Japanese technical manager from the partners head office in Tokyo. The driver was a huge Iranian who was not only the chauffeur but also the managing director's bodyguard. Just outside the city the roads were dual carriageway and well surfaced but as we headed further out the road quality deteriorated substantially. On the main roads the driver merely seemed to be enthusiastic or occasionally slightly aggressive. When we got onto the unsurfaced mountain roads however, he drove like a lunatic. He seemed to be convinced that the charm that he wore round his neck and which we could see from his unbuttoned shirt would ward off all evil. Unfortunately, all the truck drivers coming the other way must have had similar charms and beliefs so the journey was like a continuous game of chicken. They evidence from crashed and burned out vehicles along the side of the road every few kilometres seemed to indicate that there were some flaws in the system. When he got into his stride, he was hurtling along gravel surfaced roads which often overhung swiftly flowing torrents of white water in the ravines below. Finally, I snapped and asked the MD to tell his driver to stop acting like an idiot. The Japanese who had lost some of his inscrutability agreed. The MD nervously refused saying that the driver was an ex member of the Iranian special forces and was trained in driving. He also added that in any case the driver might get really upset and kill him with his bare hands. It was at this point that I solemnly assured the MD that if he did not tell the driver to slow down then I guaranteed that I would kill both of them with my bare hands. This seemed to do the trick although sine the MD spoke in Farsi to the driver, I do not know exactly what passed between them. When we finally reached our destination, we went straight to the factory before checking into the hotel. As we alighted at the plant the MD asked the Japanese and myself to stand against the factory wall and it did cross my mind that this was where the body guard got his own back by shooting us. As it turned out he did - but with his boss's camera so my next thought was that this was probably for a wanted poster. It turned out however that they got so few international visitors that taking their photo during these rare visits had become something of a ritual. I expect that it is still in Revolutionary guard files somewhere.

Public Relations

I was half way through my Cornflakes when the phone rang. It took me a few seconds to realise that it was Tony and that he was gibbering incoherently. Quick as a flash I just knew that he had a problem and he figured that maybe I had a solution to it.

We had been working on the major in-house seminar and exhibition for weeks. Hundreds of hours and thousands of pounds had gone into the brochures, technical data sheets, point of sale display material, copies of technical papers, samples and the myriad of other things, which go to make up a successful event.

The previous evening Norman and Willie had loaded up the rental van and set off south after fuelling the van and no doubt their selves to sustain them on the long journey. The whole thing had gone pear shaped in the early hours of the morning when the van had developed some kind of trouble on the Preston bypass. Norman had pulled over onto the hard shoulder and had got out with Willie which was just as well since they noticed after a few seconds that wisps of smoke were coming out from underneath it. As they watched it burst into flames and within a very short period of time had burnt out to a charred smoking skeleton. The only recognisable part of it were the keys which Norman had thoughtfully removed from the ignition and dropped into his trouser pocket before he got out. They had then flagged down a passing truck, which took them to the nearest police station where they spent the rest of the night helping the incredulous police with their enquiries into spontaneous combustion. The police were so impressed that they offered them the hospitality of one of their bunk bedded rooms until morning. The likely lads had been offered the chance to make a phone call but had decided to wait until daybreak since as they put it they did not want to cause anyone any distress or unnecessary suffering. The upset to Tony however was no less in the cold harsh light of dawn.

When I understood his predicament, I agreed to pitch in and help. We went into the office early and collected every piece of relevant information and literature, which we could find. We added a few photocopies and tied everything with string into twenty-five kilo bundles, which we loaded into the back of my car. We then headed for Abbottsinch Airport Glasgow where we checked ourselves in as passengers and the literature in as baggage for the flight to London. At Heathrow we sprinted from the gate to the baggage carousel in terminal one and grabbed a trolley so that we could get all this paper across to Tony's car in the short stay car park. Perhaps due to turbulence on the flight or due to our lack of skill with bowlines, sheepshanks and two half hitches or even a baggage handler's sharp knife blade we were in for a further surprise. As they klaxon sounded and the carousel sprang into life all of the literature came up the belt but in single sheets scattered among all the other baggage on the flight. It took us the best part of an hour to retrieve all of it and reassemble it in some sort of order. We also planned to give the delegates so much to drink before the event that none of them would care much what they were given to read and might even be forgiving of the presentations as well.

From R&D to A&E

John knew his stuff. He had come up through the ranks in a conventional way with a good grammar school and then Sheffield University where he ultimately gained his PhD. Now as director of Research and Development he had not only some excellent qualifications but also substantial experience in the area of assorted high temperature materials. At times his expertise was almost a draw back. When expounding on his subject he could all too easily lose his audience not all of whom were like him into microscopy, tertiary phase diagrams and the Precambrian movement of tectonic plates during continental drift. The fact that he was six foot six and his audience in this case were an average of five foot six did not help much either as a lot of them gave up when their necks got stiff. At a previous presentation he and his staff had obviously bamboozled most of the audience who had been press ganged into attending and who were in any case either mechanical or production engineers. When they became plainly restless John suggested that if he was taxing their intellect then perhaps, they would be better suited to go out and wash all the company cars with water and chamois.

On this occasion however he was convinced that he was talking to people on the same technological wavelength as himself. He was waxing lyrical on the relevant merits of Periclase, Spinel and Dolomite. What he did not realise however was that the sales and marketing staff had anaesthetised the audience to such an extent that if questioned most of them would have sworn that Periclase and Dolomite were the two Turkish wrestlers who were top of the bill at the town hall on Saturday night backed up by no doubt by Sophocles, Damocles and Testicles   A steady stream, if you will pardon the expression of punters going to the toilets and a few sonorous snores soon alerted him to the fact that he had a problem. Some of them had short attention spans and some limited bladder control. John however ploughed on determined that no one would leave knowing less than when they arrived. About half way through one of the audiences crumpled slightly and with a quiet moan slid slowly to the floor between the rows of chairs. This caused irritation to wrinkle his youthful features and he hissed out of the side of his mouth to his two helpers Ron and Lex to "get the bugger back up into his seat". After a short struggle while they tried to adopt a shield of invisibility from the rest of us, they were forced to admit defeat. They hesitantly passed the word back to John that in fact the casualty might I fact have suffered a heart attack. This caused momentary disruption to John's flow on the topic of Dicalcium silicate while Ron and Lex dragged the unfortunate member of the audience out of the room and summoned an ambulance. The ambulance was on the scene within minutes and had the heart attack victim in the local A&E facility before John had got to direct bonded Magnesite. After a couple of days care and attention the victim was released from hospital and fortunately for the company could not remember the circumstances of his attack and could not understand why we were all so solicitous of his wellbeing.

Plaka

To me the best part of visiting the Plaka was its ambience. It had grown from a tiny cluster of ancient buildings three thousand years ago more or less on the north eastern slopes of the Acropolis to the tourist mecca that it still clings onto emulating today. During the day the old two and three storey tall buildings and narrow winding streets protected the few slow-moving pedestrians from the worst of the direct heat from the sun's rays even when in mid-summer the temperature touched 50 degrees centigrade.

At night it was different. It was transformed from a silent fairly deserted area to a hub of activity. As the sun set and dusk gathered lights would twinkle on all over the area casting pools of coloured light in the darkness. In summertime most of the restaurant business was transacted on their many open roof terraces where there was the faint chance of a very slight breeze to cool the diners at their tables and shield them from the worst of the heat retained in the stone structures. Nearly every one of the many establishments had live Bouzouki or Sirtaki music and even the smallest bars would have tapes or records of their favourite artists. Strolling through the streets at this time was a pleasant mix of sights sounds and smells. People in every imaginable attire, the cacophony of music and the smell of Moussaka, Keftides, Dolmades and even some Barbouni, wafting through the still air. For the tourists who did not feel adventurous enough to go Greek there were always Pizzas and maybe Gyros. For fans like myself I could even pick up and distinguish the whiff of the aniseed flavoured Ouzo aperitif and the resinous smell of Retsina wine in among the other olfactory pleasures. The chilled Fix Hellas lager beer had no smell but tasted great as a favourite way to kick off the evening's dining experience with a bowl full of pistachio nuts. Oh, what fun it was to argue whether the Fix was better than the Amstel knowing that it was the same beer from the same brewery with different labels on the bottles made in the very same Youlia Glass Plant. Most evenings started late and finished even later by northern European standards. As the evening wore on the few taxis or the occasional private car would glide away and the area would become pedestrianised by mutual consent. By midnight each night the streets would be thronged by people enjoying themselves by just strolling through the area, listening to the competing sources of music soaking up the atmosphere and relaxing.

That Friday evening a faint distant popping could be heard above the sounds of the music and conversation. It quickly grew in volume as a small engine capacity motor bike came roaring up the cobbled street scattering pedestrians who threw themselves out of harm's way. The bike was not going particularly fast but it was making a lot of noise and causing massive annoyance. The bike clattered past followed by outraged cries in half a dozen different languages. Through all the background noise we could hear a faint squeal of tyres as the rider slammed on the brakes and threw the bike into a 180 degree turn to come screaming back down the street. There is something about the mix used in car tyres in Greece and the mix used to surface the streets that makes any kind of manoeuvre sound more dramatic than it really is. While the bike was still some distance away with the rider revving its tiny engine two waiters emerged from one of the outdoors restaurants grabbed some bottles of olive oil from the nearest tables and quickly emptied them onto the cobbles in the middle of the street. Too late the rider saw the dark area on the street as he hit it at about thirty kilometres an hour. It was enough for the rider to lose control especially as he tried to apply the brakes. The bike tipped over and the brake pedal caught the ground. The bike and the rider both slithered along the street separately for a few metres before ending up against the wall of one of the buildings. As the rider got back to his feet and limped off pushing his somewhat battered looking bike there was a burst of loud applause along with a few shouts of "encore!" from the tourists and "Whopa!" from the locals. When I tired of the meat balls and kebabs, I sometimes went a couple of miles further east to the next hill along which was called Lycavvettus or "the place of the wolves" in English. What is now the Horizon café restaurant was an upmarket eatery next to St Georges Church with a walled terrace from which you could look back over the Parthenon as far as Piraeus and a lot more besides including the red tiled roofs of the Plaka area. The height above sea level and the inevitable cool breeze made it a pleasant spot to drink ice cold imported beer and eat international food without Bouzouki in your ears.

Viva Zapata

One of the tallest buildings in the city of San Diego was the local jailhouse or the metropolitan correction centre in downtown on State Street as it is referred to locally. It was a new light brown coloured stone building, which differed from most other high-rise construction in the city, in that it appeared to have no windows. Much closer inspection revealed that it did in fact have windows but that these were exceptionally narrow enfilades like the ones seen on medieval castles which were supposed to let the defender's arrows out but keep attacker's arrows from getting in to do any damage to the inmates. Not that there are many bows and arrows to be seen now in greater San Diego. Any remaining Indian tribes are now widely dispersed onto small reservations around the state although there are still a large number of remaining inmates from every ethnic group and most social classes in the facility banged up in the building.

In this particular case however, only light was expected to pass through the armoured glass of this building located almost in the middle of the historic gas light tourist area.

If the inmates could have seen out then those on the upper floors on the western side of the building at least would have had a magnificent view of the harbour with the old sailing ship Star of India moored at the quay. Further out across the harbour was the Coronado Island with its legendary red turreted grand hotel Coronado which is now a national monument It has been visited by me and also frequented by Marilyn Monroe although not at the same time and I suspect that she had an even better room than me. The Star of India was actually built on the river Clyde and had sailed around the entire world before then becoming a permanent display for tourists on the San Diego sea front. If neither the prisoners nor the Star of India could currently go anywhere, plenty of other smaller craft could and did. These smaller vessels took visitors around the harbour and vast naval dockyards full of every imaginable type of warship from vast aircraft carriers down to smaller submarines. The more adventurous tourists went past the naval dockyards, out under the Coronado Bridge and further out to sea to observe the huge annual migration south down the Baja California coast of thousands of grey whales. These whales made the annual journey from Alaska to breed in the very much warmer waters of the pacific gulf stream. Jurgen decided to charter a small vessel and take some of our more important customers and their wives who were attending the annual Materials Society congress out whale watching as it could be quite a spectacle. There was seemingly quite a bit of competition to accompany them more to see the whales than the customers. I freely admit to being totally ambivalent about being on a small boat out in the Pacific Ocean to look at whales so I was not really even slightly disappointed when some others present successfully claimed precedence over me. Instead I took out my trusty old Russian Praktika camera with my expensive Japanese assortment of lenses and went to photograph as many entrants for the Americas Cup race as I could find in and around the marina. Most of the national racing yachts were in practice or in preliminary heats that day so I managed to bag almost all of the boats.

Later in the evening in the bar I came across Jurgen on his own not looking his usual cheery self. On enquiring why this might be I was informed that a stiff old breeze had created difficult sailing conditions for the landlubbers aboard most of whom were very seasick. I honestly think that I got the best deal on offer that day for with my 200 mm telephoto lenses got shots of grey whales a large blue whale and dozens of local dolphins as well as the Americas Cup boats including the favourite to win it which was the New Zealand entry KZ1 crewed by the Mercury Bay Boating Club team. I was slightly surprised to see that when any of the boats came back into harbour and were lifted out of the water a tarpaulin skirt was draped from the deck to prevent any sight of the design of the hull or keel being seen by any of the competitors around.

 Less adventurous types could keep their feet firmly on dry land and catch the Tijuana tram. This travelled the short distance from downtown to the Mexican border and was then met by various forms of transport to take tourists further into Mexico. I could hardly believe it but large numbers of American and presumably other foreign tourists would cross the border each day to visit Mexitalan. This was an incredible place. The Mexicans had built a town along the lines of what foreign tourists expected a Mexican town to look like because few of the towns in the region came anywhere close to any visitor's expectations. It was effectively a Mexican theme park where the main theme was to help as many tourists as possible get as many dollars as possible out of their current accounts and into the hands of local entrepreneurs. Zapata would have been justifiably proud of so much money being separated from so many gringos without a threat being issued or indeed a single shot being fired into the air as encouragement.

Bermuda Triangle

There I was in La Guardia; New York's second airport and it was still not yet eight-o clock in the morning. I had checked out of the Hilton on the Avenue of the Americas at about six thirty and had taken a yellow cab to the airport. On arrival I checked in with American Airlines for my flight to Port au Prince in Haiti. After check in I relaxed, yawned and stretched a little, as I drank a coffee and caught up with the business news in the Wall Street Journal.

As I sat there not properly awake, I heard many announcements over the PA system in the background. There were announcements on arrivals, departures, Skycaps, ground transportation and people generally meeting, greeting and parting from each other. Through my half-awake state it suddenly occurred to me that the last announcement had been for me. I was certain that this could not be the case because no one knew precisely where I was at that exact moment. Several people knew approximately where I might be at any given time but I was sure the call was really for someone with a similar name. There it was again however more urgent this time. "Would Mr David Jarvis, a passenger on American Airlines flight AA 987 to Haiti please go to the nearest white courtesy telephone to pick up a message". "Gosh" I thought perhaps I had better see what is afoot". I walked over to the American Airlines service desk and announced myself to the young lady on duty. She smiled and passed me the telephone receiver. As I put it to my ear, I did not have time to say hello before I was subjected to a torrent of words in a mixture of what seemed to be American English and Modern Greek. This continued to perplex me for some seconds as I tried to work out what on earth could be going on. Eventually I realised that it was my friend or more accurately my ex friend Costas phoning me from the offices of a large Greek cement plant situated to the west of Athens. When he eventually calmed down slightly the story began to emerge little by little. The good news was that apparently the quarter of a million-pound order that he had placed with my company some months before was ready on time and sitting on the quayside at Liverpool ready to be loaded onto a waiting freighter. The bad news was that he had received a telex message from my boss informing him that due to rampant inflation in the UK economy the price of the goods had to be increased by ten percent. The even worse news was that my boss had informed him that we would be unable to load the vessel until confirmation of the new price was agreed in writing. "There goes another Christmas card," I thought. "OK Costas" I said "it is eight o clock in the morning in New York, one o clock in the afternoon in the UK and four o clock with you in Athens." "Thanks for the short history of time," said Costas" but I had hoped for more from you." I understood that he was not a happy chappy and promised to get back to him by the following morning with what I hoped might be a helpful solution to the problem. As I put down the phone, I wondered how on earth he had tracked me down in New York. Maybe he was a friend or relation of fellow Greek Lieutenant Kojak. I went over to the US Post Office in the terminal and placed a call back to the office. I argued the pros and cons with my boss until it was time to board the plane but he stuck to his guns and I knew then that it was the end of another beautiful friendship with my customer.

As we winged south just off the eastern seaboard of the United States, we passed into the dreaded Bermuda Triangle. At one point the plane appeared to have flown into a brick wall and was thrown around before dropping about twenty feet like a lift. Was this a punishment? I thought to myself. And for what, as I didn't really think that I had sinned in any substantial way as far as I could recall. The oxygen masks deployed but I had a theory that this was not so much to provide oxygen when you fitted them but to muffle the screams. I was in seat 8F which was the right-hand window seat in the first row of economy immediately behind the bulkhead of the first-class section. There was a substantial Haitian lady in seat 8 D on the aisle and an empty seat between us. In the midst of all this fun she instinctively reached over and grabbed my

wrist and hand which was tightly clutching the arm rest of the empty seat. This is
serious I thought and asked the lady to unhand me on the grounds that I wished to
count the money in the several currencies that I had in my wallet. They say that you
can't take it with you but in this case, it looked as if they were to be proved wrong and
me and my money were both destined for a closer acquaintanceship with the rocky
seabed of the Atlantic Ocean around 5000 feet under the surface of the waves. If this
was to be the case, I just wanted to have some idea of what my final residual worth
actually was. It was a situation which I think was designed by psychologists to
establish people's true attitude to Atheism and seemed to work. With passengers wild
eyed and screaming and everyone hanging on to the arms of their seats it may not
have lasted long but I guarantee no one was on their smart phones mainly because
they had not been at that time been invented. Even if they had no one possessed
enough arms to hang on and take selfies. Miraculously no one including flight
attendants who managed to buckle up were injured and we did finally manage to
touch down in Port Au Prince airport. But that is another story.

Kelly's Mountain

We sat in the lounge at Dorval, which was Montreal's airport but of course has been
renamed Montréal-Pierre Elliott Trudeau International Airport to give it a bit more
cachet as befits a nation that launched Ms Markle into her meteoric new acting career

We sat and waited and we waited it seemed for ever. I had already flown the Atlantic
from Prestwick to Montreal in a BOAC 707. This was a six-and-a-half-hour flight
more or less keeping pace with the sun which meant that when we landed at three o
clock local time it was already eight o clock in the evening. It took a further hour to
go through customs and immigration and to transfer from the international to the
domestic terminal This made it four o clock local time and the Air Canada flight to
Sydney was not until five o clock. Sydney I should explain was Sydney Nova Scotia
not Sydney new South Wales. For years Sydney could only be reached by a three and
a half-hour flight due east on an ageing four engined Britannia propjet. With the flight
time and the one-and-a-half-hour time change between Quebec and the Maritimes I
used to arrive at my final destination not knowing whether I was coming or going. On
this visit however I was pleased to see that Air Canada were now operating one of
their DC9 jets and this I calculated would knock at least forty-five minutes off the
journey. This meant forty-five minutes earlier to bed when I eventually arrived and I
looked forward to that. This was not to be the case today however as severe
snowstorms had closed the airport down at Sydney and our jet still sat at the gate
empty. Normally Sydney was easy to find from the air. A plume of orange red iron
oxide dust, which emitted from the steel plant stack and spread eastwards on the
prevailing winds, would streak the crisp white covering of snow. At twenty-four
thousand feet you could see this from nearly fifty miles away on a clear day. This was
not a clear day however. Dusk was falling rapidly and a blizzard was raging across a
wide area on the eastern seaboard. Suddenly the flight was called and the plane
rapidly departed. The weather forecasters were predicting a window where the gale
would abate and the snow stop for a few short hours sufficient for the plane to reach

its destination safely. About two hours into the flight the captain informed us however that the forecasters had been too optimistic and that the snow was again blanketing Sydney. Rather than return all the way to Montreal the captain proposed to divert to Halifax to refuel and to reconsider his next move. It was not snowing in Halifax but the temperature was well below zero and there was a stiff breeze blowing. When we alighted from the plane, we had been warned about the conditions but I was unprepared for the events of the next few minutes. I found myself with knees slightly bent and with arms outstretched to keep my balance being blown across the ice from the plane to the terminal building. Fortunately, someone opened the glass doors when I reached them and I sailed right into a bright warm lounge. By ten-o clock the captain had made up his mind to terminate the flight at Halifax for the night and to continue the next day if possible. He advised us all to find a bed for the night and to check again in the morning. After some discussion our party decided that instead of finding a hotel or motel, we would rent a car and drive the rest of the way. By midnight we had enjoyed a hot meal, rented a car and were heading out of the airport on our hundred- and fifty-mile drive to Sydney. In the UK this might have taken us three or four hours but not in this case. Years later I am still not sure whether we made the right decision. Much of the road we travelled was in bright moonlight and with the car heater at full blast we were not fully aware of how cold it was outside. When we got higher up into the mountains it was starkly beautiful but on reflection, we must have been stark staring mad. At some points we ran into small snowstorms where the wind drove the snow horizontal and made the driving even more hazardous. Not that we were driving fast even with chains on our tyres because the several inches of fresh snow on the road covered sheet ice. We crossed Kelly's mountain in the early hours of the morning and by six were coming down into the outskirts of Sydney just as it got light. In Sydney there was about nine inches of new snow and not even the snowploughs had been out to disturb it. As we made it to the motel, we were not surprised to find that our rooms were still available but the staff in the hotel were amazed to see us. After a few hours' sleep and a good breakfast, we were off to the steel plant to keep our appointment. The personnel there were no less amazed than the staff at the hotel and after a short discussion to clarify a few important points rewarded us with a very large contract.

Sushi

Albert met me at the reception desk in the hotel. I had just spent the last twenty-four hours travelling half way around the world with virtually no sleep and he had spent the last half hour travelling across Tokyo so he was slightly fresher than I was.

I don't know how he got a name like Albert. I suspect that it was something to do with his parents' admiration of Queen Victoria and her husband the Prince Consort but it was certainly a unique name for a Japanese. Being thoroughly Japanese it was one of his most solemn duties to be hospitable and being knackered it was one of my solemn duties to be irritable. He insisted that we should go to lunch when I would much rather have gone to bed. Since he was so remorselessly polite, I eventually gave in and agreed to have lunch with him even although I felt like a zombie.

He led the way to the Sushi bar in the New Otani Hotel. It always amazed me how the Japanese idea of an internal door was some strips of fabric with ideographs hanging half way down the doorway from the lintel. I have to admit that it irritated me a little because it meant that I could never see through the doorway but on reflection maybe it was meant to give some privacy while still offering visitors a welcome.

The seating arrangement inside was quite conventional with stools at along bar rather than the Floor seating on Tatami which I always found excruciating after the first ten minutes. I sat on one of the barstools and Albert perched precariously on the one next to me because even as Japanese go Albert could never have been described as tall. When we were both seated the chef served up the first offering without seemingly masking any reference to a menu. Not that it would have made any difference since I would not have known the difference between one dish and the next in Japanese. The Sushi was visually stunning and looked far too good to actually eat. It was also although I did not know it exorbitantly expensive. It was a great pity therefore to my uneducated palate it was also revolting. When asked how I was enjoying it I lied stoically and diplomatically but was chagrined to realise that this was a mistake as Albert encouraged the chef to give me more. Each one he brought looked better and tasted worse than the one before. I was extremely embarrassed because I was obviously receiving the five-star treatment and I was detesting every minute of it. Neither did I realise at the time that every time I ate one of the chef's morsels, he was obliged to put another one on my plate.

The only way that I got through the meal was by drinking copious quantities of strong Sapporo beer to wash away the taste of the raw fish and seaweed. Neither did I know at that time that protocol demanded that Albert drank along with me. The meal was mercifully brought to an end when Albert threw back his head to consume another morsel of sushi on the end of his chopsticks and fell off his stool onto the parquet floor. The only injury was to his pride and he kept apologising profusely. I in turn kept telling him that it was not a problem and that had he not thrown himself off of his stool would have thrown myself off mine.

Feigning exhaustion was easy since I was indeed exhausted and after much mutual bowing and thanking each other we decided to retire to rest before round two which Albert solemnly assured me was scheduled to commence that evening at seven o clock sharp. I assured Albert that indeed I would be fighting fit and ready to go to dinner on two conditions. The first was that whatever we ate had to have been dead for several hours and also that it was well cooked. It was by this token that Albert came to realise that it was indeed true that foreigners were "Ainu" or barbarians.

Boothill.

Tombstone Arizona like all good American cities was laid out more or less in a grid. It lies midway between Benson which sits on Interstate 10 and Bisbee which doesn't lie much of anywhere except that it is about 15 miles north of the US Mexican border. According to the local tourist guide Tombstone is about 26 miles from both or from either which I suppose goes back to the days of the Pony Express. This was probably as far as a Wells Fargo rider would travel in the desert without an ice cool Sarsparilla drink. The main east west street is "Historic Old Allen Street" with Freemont Street to the north and the aptly named Toughnut Street to the south where the original old firehouse is situated. The north south streets are numbered from one to seven. In my opinion it is a wild exaggeration of course to call Tombstone a city in any case as it has a permanent population of perhaps a couple of hundred within the town limits and another couple of dozen in Boothill Cemetery which lies atop a small hill to the north west corner of town on Highway 80 to Benson. It seems perhaps that if you survived you maybe made it out of town as fast as you could all the way to what passes for civilisation and if you didn't you stopped over at Boothill for the long sleepover.

I drove in from Benson, which lies some twenty-six miles north west of Tombstone. The route took me past Tombstone International Airport, which consisted of a small, black and white sign in a more or less flat field about two miles west of town. It is designated an "International" airport because a small plane from Mexico once strayed the few miles over the border when the pilot became disorientated with mezcal juice before touching down to a hard landing between the Saguaros or one of the other 127 cactus varieties in the region or maybe because of someone's weird sense of humour.

When Wyatt Earp who was the sheriff but who's second income derived from a cut of the gambling profits in the oriental steak house had his little spot of bother with the Clantons, it is possible to imagine their route and follow for most of the way in their footsteps. Maybe Wyatt was also brooding about the shooting of his younger brother Virgil over a glass of Sarsaparilla in the Bird Cage on the eastern edge of the town.

At the time this was a theatre, saloon, casino and bawdyhouse and was probably the best-known establishment of its kind at this time outside of San Francisco. It is said to be the establishment, which originated the old song "Only a Bird in a Gilded Cage." Wyatt and his deputies might have walked west along Allen Street past the Wells Fargo office and the two storey Oriental saloon which still has one of the old original Pianolas which operates by turning a handle to rotate a drum inside the instrument. This is especially useful for people who cannot read music and has been electrified for people who can't turn handles. After the boys reached Fourth Street they would have turned north and headed across a large paddock to the OK Corral where the Clantons already lay in wait. After the bullets stopped flying and the smoke cleared it was only a short climb up the road to Boot Hill. It was this last journey that Billy Clanton, Frank McLaury and Tom McLaury made feet first on the morning of October 26th 1881. The fate of Ike Clanton who started the whole fracas was weird because he survived and sued the sheriff for killing his brother and for trying to kill his brother first. It took them all of six years but he did eventually get well ventilated for cattle rustling.   Today the Mclaurys share their resting place with at least two dozen other colourful characters. There is Red Sample and Red River Tom. There is Dutch Annie, who was probably German, Bronco Charlie, Indian Bill and Three Fingers Jack Dunlap known as Lucky. There is also Black Jake and the unfortunate Mr George Johnson who it is recorded was "hung by mistake". So far however nobody has yet owned up to the sad mistake. It's probably just as well as there was certain to have been a crooked lawyer from out of town who would have sued and maybe also a crooked judge who was just passing through and would have awarded hefty damages on a no win no fee basis after the deduction of hefty legal fees.

Down South

Downtown Invercargill in the South Island is a neatly laid out city with broad streets. Most of these are named after rivers, many of which are in the UK. There is Forth Street, Tay Street, Don Street, Dee Street and a dozen others. Unless you travel by train the main approach to the town is by the road which comes in from the Airport which lies a few miles to the west of the city. As you reach the city limits this road becomes beach road which crossed the Waihopai river into downtown at the busy intersection of Tweed Street which runs east west and Clyde Street which runs north south. The town has a frontier look about it and indeed it is very isolated place. Some of the sidewalks have been made from wood and roofed over to provide some form of protection for pedestrians from the worst of the weather The most notable feature of downtown is the huge wooden water tower but the most interesting feature for me was the fact that the single track Lyttleton, Invercargill, Bluff railway ran for part of its length along one of the main streets. We decided to take lunch in the Clyde Tavern on the corner of Tyne Street near St Catherine's College. This was wholesome food, which was much influenced by the fact that the Chef was Italian. It was piping hot Spaghetti Bolognese and went down a treat followed by some local dry white wine. Yes, I do know that you are supposed to drink red wine with spag bol but a bottle of the white sauvignon Blanc, Haymaker from the Glengarry winery seemed to fit the bill and the budget. I could have stretched to a bottle of the Duck Hunter, or the Mudhouse, the Russian Jack or even the Nga Waka although more sophisticated palates like your own might have opted for the Brancott Estate. "Chacun a son goute" as they say.

After lunch we turned south and set off down Bluff Road for the short journey to the world's most southerly Aluminium smelter at Waitai Point. I would not be surprised in fact if it were the world's most southerly industrial location. The smelter buildings were constructed from multiple layers of wood, fibreglass and aluminium cladding and were bright and warm inside with a mouth-watering aroma of coffee percolating. Outside however the sky was overcast with dark clouds scudding across it at high speed from the stiff breeze which blew in off the South Atlantic into the Fouveau Straight between Waitai and the bird sanctuary at Stewart Island. Billy Connolly went to Stewart Island on one occasion but I think he misunderstood the situation when told by someone that it was an outstanding place to see lots of birds. Give him his due however since he stayed to crack a few meandering anecdotes with all the natives. Standing there leaning into the wind and looking due south I was only too aware that the next landfall was Antarctica. Judging by the chill bite to the wind I did not think that it was all that far away. I was glad that it was November and midsummer but somehow was reminded of the Glasgow Fair holidays back home where hot weather would have been unsettling as it would have required hiring a couple of deckchairs.

All In

Saturdays in the northern suburbs of Newcastle New South Wales were different to my usual routine and to be honest a little slow to get started. When the manager of the Sunset Motel had said that the room rate was twenty-five dollars with breakfast thrown in, I did not realise she meant that it would be more or less thrown into the room on a tin tray at about nine-o clock by the maid. Thinking back though the term maid was also itself a bit of a misnomer, as she looked like an eastern European light heavyweight all in wrestler. After we had consumed our gourmet cornflakes in the privacy of our rooms Arthur and I got together and decided to go into town. Although it was already mid-morning by the time we got there, we could see that there was not much happening and we knew that most shops closed at lunchtime so the prospect of another stimulating afternoon was receding fast. After looking round a few shops we decided to buy the biggest bottle of wine we could find which actually to our absolute joy turned out to be two litres and take it back to the motel so that after our lunch we could polish it off while watching "footie" or whatever sport was on the local state television. In our enthusiasm we had made one vital error however. We knew that we had tumblers in our rooms but we forgot that neither of us had a corkscrew about our persons as we did not normally travel with swiss army knives or tool sets. Not willing to admit defeat we decided that the motel must have such a critically important device on the premises and decided that we would borrow it for a few minutes to extricate the cork and solve our main problem The manager however had other ideas it seemed and refused to part with her favourite tool either by allowing us to borrow or even buy it. We begged and pleaded on the erroneous basis that she could not possibly object to us drinking in the privacy of our own rooms. Apparently however it turned out that this was not the actual nub of the problem. Arthur being an extremely perceptive gent quickly established that the problem was that we had not invited her to share the wine. We soon reached a good old British compromise by the expedient of us and the wine joining her and the corkscrew in the sparsely furnished motel reception area which did however at least have a working television set. It did not take the entire afternoon to empty the bottle and when we had drained the last drop of this the manager decided that she still had a raging thirst and went back into the office where she had a fridge where she rummaged around in it until she found a half empty bottle of a different wine. After this too had rapidly been put to good use, she went back to the fridge yet again and reappeared with a few assorted "tinnies". Even after these the manager was still quite obviously suffering from a debilitating thirst and delegated Arthur and I as acting assistant managers to look after the motel while she drove down the road in search of an off licence. Looking out of the reception window we could see her get into her battered old tan coloured Holden which I had thought had been abandoned by someone in the car park and after some difficulty started it up. The car then shot backwards at high speed out of the carpark down a slight ramp and out onto the main coast road where it was struck by a large slow-moving bus heading south to Newcastle city centre. The manager and the driver both got out and exchanged a string of oaths which we could hear about a hundred feet away with her scoring about double that of the astonished bus driver. Eventually it was decided that the large reinforced bus front bumper was virtually unmarked and the Holden did not look any more battered than it did before. This allowed the bus driver to resume his leisurely journey and the manager to concentrate on more important matters such as where to buy more of the amber nectar. At this point I promoted Arthur to the role of assistant manager appointed in sole charge while I retired to bed with a pounding headache.

Big D

It looked to be very peaceful with what little traffic there was moving serenely down Commerce Street and the counter flow back up Elm Street. These were one- way streets running from east to west on either side of Main Street where traffic flowed both ways. Half a mile away to the east was downtown Dallas "Big D". The skyscrapers of the First National Bank, Dallas Federal Savings Bank and the LTV Tower reflected the light of the early morning sun. Behind them the twin towers of the Southland Centre and the Sheraton Hotel dominated the skyline between downtown and the Central Expressway Interstate 75.

Immediately in front of me was the Records Building and the Old Courthouse while between them along Main Street I could just see the Dallas Historical Plaza with its replica log cabin from the early settlers' days in Texas.

It was the triple underpass at Deeley Plaza on which I stood that concentrated most of my attention however. It was here some thirty years before that shots had rung out from the tenth floor of the Texas School Book Depository Building behind me to my left. These bullets had claimed the life of the young Democratic President of the United States John F Kennedy as his motorcade slowed to turn onto Stemmons Freeway to head for the airport. Now everything was quiet with relatively few sightseers. The ones that there were present mostly stood silently with their own thoughts on that momentous occasion which altered history. Every one over a certain age remembers where they were when JFK was shot. It was only Lee Harvey Oswald that did not seem to have a good alibi for that particular moment and as a result was shot himself by Jack Ruby who had appointed himself judge jury and executioner. I felt that I wanted something to mark the visit but not any cheap old souvenir. I walked down Main Street for a short distance and found Nieman Marcus the city's flagship store, which is as well known around the world as Harrods. Entering the store was like entering another world. Until I was actually inside, I was not sure that they would let me through the door. The shop is so exclusive that you have to be a multimillionaire to qualify to be on their Christmas catalogue mailing list. I wandered around inside for a bit trying to find something suitable in my price range. This was not easy. At one point I saw a little silver brush which attracted my attention. I thought at first that it was for brushing a moustache and considered growing a moustache and taking out a second mortgage on the brush. It turned out however that it was designed for removing lint from navels and at this point it lost a lot of its attraction for me. This I thought was the two-hundred-dollar accessory that I could probably live without. In the end I settled for a tie. Not any old tie but one costing more than I normally paid for a shirt. It was blue and white striped with little thistle motifs. Nothing flash. Nothing obvious. Just understated elegance. That's me folks.

Visit to Hiroshima

Although it was some years ago now my visit to Hiroshima provided one of the most profound experiences of my life.

The bright diffuse light of the early morning sun illuminated the city, which lay in a bowl surrounded on three sides by mountains and on the south by the Inland Sea.

As we flew over the city at about twenty thousand feet one of the most notable landmarks to be seen was the "T" shaped Aoki bridge at the confluence of the Motoyasu and the Ota rivers just to the south of the modern baseball stadium. It was the bridge that the bomb aimer of Enola Gay lined up his sights on more than fifty years ago before releasing the first atomic bomb over Hiroshima. "Fat Boy" as it was known exploded high in the air over the bridge early one morning as the city was waking up.

Directly below the airburst was a substantial concrete and steel building occupied by the Ministry of Industry. It stood on the eastern shore of the river only a few yards from the bridge. The shock wave when it hit the building stripped it to its shell, which has been preserved today as a monument to that terrible maelstrom. The steel girders of the domed roof stood out against the sunlight in silhouette making a stark statement to all but the most insensitive. Much of the rest of the city was flattened as the shock wave raced out from the epicentre at the speed of one of Japans now famous bullet trains. This was closely followed by a fire, which raged through the city consuming most of the damaged buildings, many of which were made of wood. The fire eventually burned itself out and was finally extinguished by the black rain, which fell as darkness came.

Today the area between the Atomic Bomb Dome and the Hiroshima TV station is totally reconstructed and laid out as the Peace Memorial Park. Amid the noise of a large bustling industrial city the Peace Memorial Park is a haven of quiet it has a catenary commemorative arch and an eternal flame which burns as a tribute to the victims. Scattered throughout the well-kept gardens with their tidy flower beds are what appear to be more personal tributes to individual victims or families. Although many thousands died in the explosion itself or from its aftermath the Peace Memorial Park is a place for quiet reflection on the past, to give thanks for the present and to contemplate hope for an even better future.

As we approach the new millennium fifty-five years after the terrible event which destroyed this provincial Japanese capital, I would like to revisit the dome and the new city which has grown up around it and which to me symbolises triumph over adversity and progress over time.

Dewitt Iowa

Steve was a big lad even for a Liverpool bricklayer. He had a very slight squint so that even when he smiled which he did a lot he could still look pretty evil to the casual observer. He was the sort of bloke that you would always prefer to have on your side rather than to be ranged up against.

The work that he did was very arduous. It was hot it was heavy and it was exacting. The type of work which took a physical toll even if you were match fit. To make it worse the weather had been thundery and there had been torrential rain even although the ambient temperature was very high. This made the conditions both hot and humid. After work the two teams on the contract travelled back to their hotel, showered, changed and had an evening meal. They were unused to the American system in the mid-west of serving enormous steaks along with French fries and large mixed salads. Although the crews were hungry it was a lot for them to digest after a hard day and they often got the hotel to put the steak that they could not eat into a doggy bag so the they could have a steak sandwich for lunch the next day at work. After the meal they would unwind in the hotel lounge with a very large jug of chilled beer. Normally they would retire early for they had an early start next day to try to avoid the worst of the heat. On the evening before their day off however they would occasionally sit a little longer and chat. It was on one such night after a few glasses of beer that Steve realised that he had again developed a slight hunger pang and asked at reception if he could have a sandwich. Unfortunately, the kitchen was closed. Steve however was not in the least put out as he had noticed a "Jack and Jill Drivethru" hamburger joint across the road from the hotel and decided he had to have one of these delicacies. Since he had partaken of a few beers and since the two crews only had a large van and since it was only fifty yards away Steve set out to walk. On arrival he went up to the service window and asked for a hamburger. The young lady with the radio mike was a bit nonplussed. She pointed out to Steve that it was a drive-through and that there were one or two cars in line. Not to be out done Steve left the window and unknown to the girl serving, joined on at the rear of the line of cars, walking forward behind them as they moved up to the window. As he went other cars came in and followed up behind him. Some good-humoured badinage ebbed and flowed between Steve and the other drivers. When he reached the window again, he again politely requested a hamburger. The young lady had just started to explain to him that in America when they said an establishment was a drive through, they expected clients to have at the very least a motorcycle. Steve was very patient but fuelled by his hunger he explained to her in his clearest Scouse that his transport was parked at the hotel across the road and since it was him that was going to pay for and eat the hamburger, he could not really see her problem. She looked Steve up and down, considered her dilemma very carefully, looked him up and down again and smiling a sweet forced smile, served him with his late evening supper which he consumed before he was half way back across the highway.

The Gay Hussar.

Tony was a city slicker and I was a country boy. Even worse in Tony's book was that the country was Scotland. He knew that I was going to be a problem and that he was going to have to look after me every step of the way in case I got lost or was just bewildered by the throbbing metropolis. Tony met me at the ticket barrier in Euston and was plainly surprised that I had made it all the way along the platform. This was in the good old days when stations had ticket collectors and barriers for them to man. When we met up, he ushered me quickly to where he was illegally parked in the days before the Denver boot when drivers in London seemed to be constantly competing to see the most awkward place to leave your car where it would cause the greatest inconvenience to other road users. He must have been of the more successful exponents of this art since his Mini Cooper had a small boot stuffed with parking tickets in polythene envelopes so that there was not a lot of room for luggage. Fortunately, I travelled light in those days. The Mini cooper was not his official company car. This was a Granada but he preferred the Mini cooper in the city for many reasons some of them quite sensible. It was a much more suitable form of transport to break the speed limit in and to accelerate away from traffic lights in and to cut up other drivers at junctions. Give him his due however he could probably have passed his black cab drivers exam if he had sat it. He certainly had the knowledge when it came to the streets in greater London. He knew all the short cuts in traffic and some in life in general. He certainly looked after me exceptionally well. During the day we would get round a few clients whom I particularly wanted to see. At night he always found me suitable accommodation even if sometimes it was in his own home where I apparently was always a welcome guest. For lunch we usually found a cheap and cheerful snack bar while at night it was more usually something with an ethnic ambience. One night we dined in the Gay Hussar when gay still meant happy. It was in Soho and was a little expensive although not as expensive as it would have been if he had not been there. Tony was in a good mood and he decided that while we were in Soho we might as well see the inside of a club. The nearest one was reached through a dingy doorway with a neon sign flickering above it. There was then a steep stairway down into a basement area where we could just see the bulk of two large bouncers in the dim light from a forty-watt bulb. Tony had warned me that these places were admitted members only and had asked me to say nothing and to leave all the talking to him. This I was more than happy to do especially if the doormen were going to need their palms greasing for us to gain entry. As he reached the door, he launched into a well-rehearsed routine but it became obvious after a few minutes that he was getting nowhere fast and we were barred entry. As we turned to leave eventually one of the enormous bouncers caught sight of me properly for the first time. Squinting through bushy eyebrows and over a well broken nose he said "Aw hi Dave Wait till ah get rid o' this bampot and you can get in" he growled. It was big Jim McQuade Third Dan and chief instructor of the Osaka Judokwai in Albion Street in Glasgow. "Well actually Jim the bampot is with me and I am trying to keep him out of trouble" I laughed. "Well ok then as long as you can vouch for him, he can come in with you" said "Jim but if he gets too obnoxious, we can have a bit of fun throwing him back up the stairs." Och Aye the noo", these were the days to surprise people with your hidden depths.

Chilli, Chilli Sauce.

With Mexican food it does not really matter what you order since it all seems to taste the same. It is just that they fold it so many different ways to confuse the uninitiated gringo diners. The secret in my opinion is to have enough chilled beer that no matter what you have eaten it extinguishes the fire, which is raging in your mouth and throat. Without copious quantities of Corona or Dos Equis there would almost certainly be spontaneous combustion of the trachea and tonsils. To a Mexican chef there are only two types of chilli, Red and Green but both of them come only in industrial strength and are capable of reaching the same temperature as the surface of the sun if eaten in any more than microscopic quantities. In Douglas Arizona we cautiously went into a little restaurant in search of lunch. Since it was less than a mile from the US Mexican border at Agua Prieta it could be said to have had a chef influenced by the way they did things south of the border. "Make mine extra hot" said Jim with much bravado and incredible stupidity when we found out that we had a choice of chilli con carne or chilli sin carne. Make mine extra cool I told the waiter who after he had written down our orders stayed on at the table for several minutes to try to dissuade Jim from his almost suicidal choice and moronic course of action. It was foolhardier than barricading oneself in the Alamo when faced with Santa Ana and his six thousand infantry we told Jim but to no avail. His view was that to have less than the hottest of the hottest chilli was to exhibit a character flaw which cast doubt on one's manhood. Give him his due however when it was served his lunch, he munched his way stoically through the entire bowl assisted only by having several glasses of iced water. By the time we paid and returned to the office however he certainly did not look so cool calm collected or comfortable. His complexion was purple and beads of sweat had come out on his forehead. The perspiration was so heavy that some ran down and dripped off the end of his nose while some of it rose as clouds of steam from the top of his head. After only a few minutes he clutched his throat which was obviously constricted and made pitiful noises. We shook our heads. It was hard not to feel sorry for him even though his problem was entirely self-inflicted but he had been a complete berk. No one in his or her right mind would have thrown down the gauntlet to a Mexican chef like that. Especially not someone who came from so far north he was almost an Eskimo or at least a Canadian. After we threw a few pails of water over him and he retired to the toilet for some considerable period of time he came back looking much chastened but still very far from being fully recovered.

"How do I look?" said Jim. "Well Jim to tell you the truth you could look almost like a million dollars" I said. "Your face is now turning green all over and very wrinkled". With that he retched and rushed back to the toilet where he spent some further time in slow recuperation. Before we left, we made sure that he was OK but to his annoyance since that time he has got very flushed every time we referred to him as Jalapeno Jim. It was actually a source of some puzzlement to me as to why every time we had the prospect of some decent business in the copper belt in the southwest Jim who was located firmly in the rust belt in the north of the midwest was designated by our agents to be our chaperone. To be kind to Jim his knowledge of the nonferrous industry could only be described as sparse to say the very least so whether someone hoped that he would pick something up from travelling with me and others or whether they just wanted him somewhere else or anywhere else I just don't know. He was a pleasant enough guy but dangerously susceptible it appeared to chilis and indeed any kind of "sauce". On one trip with John he had to be locked in his Houston Texas hotel room for his own safety until he came back to join the rest of the population here on planet earth. In Tucson we also found ourselves with me time during a slow Sunday and drove from our downtown hotel out to the Skyline Country and Golf Club on Skyline drive close to the popular scenic route 80 to Phoenix. I may perhaps be the only Scotsman in the world who has actually played golf at such venues as Glen Eagles and Glenbervie. I have putted at St Andrews but the ball got stuck in the little windmill and so don't play golf from choice. To me every country club in the USA does always have a few golf nuts but also inevitably always has hundreds of others who are there for the social standing that they imagine it confers. I have had a US Senator in one of them in Missouri lobby me for my vote until I finally managed to convince him that Larbert was not actually within his constituency. Without exception however they all seem to have large well stocked bars which on this occasion proved yet again to be Jim's Achilles heel. It would have been fine if the Maitre D' had not done his usual crap act and announced that a table would be made available in twenty minutes. Notwithstanding the fact that the dining room was not at all busy and a decent carpenter could have knocked a table up from wood in less time. Twenty minutes was actually almost 30 minutes by the clock and amounted to five large Bloody Mary's on Jim's score card after which he slid gently off the bar stool with a soft thud to land spread-eagled on the thick woollen Navajo rug on the floor. Given the choice between lunch with a zombie slumped across the dining room table from me or a taxi back to the hotel was a no brainer and the club doorman rustled up a taxi in seconds and helped me pitch Jim into the back seat and the hotel doorman helped drag him out at the other end. I don't know what Jim dreamt about if anything but I had an interesting trip around "Old Tucson" which has been refurbished in shabby chic as a busy film set. Believe me when I tell you that if you have ever seen any old cowboy film it was either filmed in Old Tucson or Italy and Old Tucson has fewer jets flying overhead and is about as authentic as a western film set can possibly ever get.

Moscow FM

Almost everyone will have seen television documentaries, news or adverts on the manufacture of cars. The cars move slowly along tracks with robots zipping in and out spot welding, bolting, riveting and screwing like mad while trying to keep up with the passage of the vehicles along the production line.

It was not like that in the old Moscovitch car factory in Moscow in its heady heyday. The skeleton of each vehicle which consisted mainly of the floor pan and lower part of the car, minus the engine and wheels did indeed move slowly along a track but the robots in this case were Russian workers. The roofs of the cars which had been pressed separately would be lifted up at the corners by four operators and laid on top of the protruding windscreen, door and rear pillars. Welders, some of them women who could well have doubled for the Russian Olympic shot putt team would then go inside the shell and manually weld the roof in place on top of each of the six pillars. Since this was done manually or womanually and very quickly the welds were less than perfect to the eye of a critical and experienced metallurgist such as myself. After the welds were buffed almost smooth to remove excess metal by hand held angle grinders it could be clearly seen that they often had significant holes through which daylight could easily be seen especially on the very wide rear pillars horizontal joints. When the front and door pillars were spray painted it was difficult to tell the quality but even after painting the back could look decidedly dodgy. The answer here was to fit a little chrome flashing on the outside of the bodywork of the rear pillar over the weld as a small embellishment to the car even although this hid a multitude of sins. My thought was that this was one car that I would never want to see in an accident where it was rolled over as I had the impression that the car and its roof could be soon parted. This however meant that the rescue services would never need to cut the roof off with hydraulic shears to free trapped occupants. This was a stroke of genius as I did not see any evidence of the use of hydraulic shears nor of any AA or RAC patrols far less of the existence of any emergency services although I am sure that the whole situation is greatly improved today. At the very end of the production line after all of the accoutrements such as an engine, battery steering wheel and seats had been fitted a worker would jump into the driving seat turn the key and with a bit of luck the car could be driven off to storage area before being shipped out to a customer. Probably because I was watching one of the cars was driven off the driver gunned the engine with special vigour to make it sound extra dramatic. The whole desired effect was ruined however when the front offside wheel, which had not been properly secured, fell off and it was obvious the car was going nowhere until two guys rushed forward and rapidly pushed it off the end of the production line and out of sight of the visitors.

From time to time throughout the entire visit we had been given the long version of the introductory speech extolling all the virtues of the Russian manufacturing system. This car model had apparently originally come about due to negotiations between the Russian authorities and the Italian communist party to persuade Fiat to licence their 124 cars in exchange for supplies of Russian steel to the Fiat company for their own production needs in Italy. It was originally designated the VAZ 2010 in 1939 then the Moskovitch 412 which had one of the worst safety records of any car in the world until it was improved upgraded and marketed as a Fiat 124 lookalike the Lada 1200. All of the way around the factory to the end of the production line our group had been dogged by a shady character that I had just assumed was someone attached to the state security and had ignored. It transpired however that he claimed to be a reporter from Radio Moscow. He produced a large tape recorder, from under his raincoat which looked as if it had been made in the Lenin shipyard and tractor collective enterprises. He slung this over one shoulder and an oversize battery pack which had also appeared from under his coat over the other shoulder. In his hand he had a microphone which he elected to thrust towards my face as he asked for responses to several questions.

"Is the Lada a popular car in the UK?" he asked. "It certainly is" I assured him. He beamed widely and asked if I would explain why this might be to all of his listeners. "Because it is subsidised by the Russian Government and thus available immediately at half the price of the next most expensive British car which is of course the mini". This was not what he really wanted his listeners to hear as Russians at that time could wait for several years for delivery of one of these cars. This was probably just as well since they cost them several years' salary to acquire one unlike the mini in the UK. "What is the cars most attractive feature to UK buyers" he persisted. "It's definitely its comprehensive tool kit" I responded. His face darkened a bit at that as the entire broadcast was potentially going out to millions all over the world on Radio Moscow English language service. He was not sure if I was taking the piss and so I decided that I would not tell him how a Lada could be doubled in value by filling its petrol tank with fuel. No mention of the heated rear windscreen to warm the hands of those pushing a broken-down Lada passed my lips. Neither did I tell him that in Glasgow the name for a Lada convertible was a skip. Had the Lada convertible been fitted with twin exhausts it would of course have been reclassified as a wheelbarrow and if any version of the car had ever been encountered at the top of a hill it would have been renamed as the Lada Miracle. I could sense that I was pressing the wrong buttons entirely and decided that since I was no Jeremy Clarkson and discretion was definitely the better part of valour in soviet Russia and since I did not want a transfer from the Hotel Ukraina where I was staying to the Hotel Lubyanka which I had no wish to see the inside of I quickly decided to shut up and melt back into the thin crowd around us.

Irish Coffee

The Pan Am Boeing B314 Yankee clipper luxury flying boats would regularly swoop gracefully down and gently skim along the top of the waves in the Shannon estuary as they headed west into the prevailing winds for a gentle landing. These huge flying boat planes provided the first commercial passenger flights to take the so-called direct great circle route between the United States and Europe. Previously the normal route was Cherbourg, Southampton, Shannon and then onwards to New York. They did however always still make a refuelling stop in Gander Newfoundland as a precaution against almost certain bad weather en route as they traversed the skies above southern Greenland.

The first flight landed at Foynes on the 9th of July 1939 to a rapturous welcome before refuelling again and flying on to Poole in Dorset. Although enthusiastically welcomed by rich travellers the service was terminated again only a few months later because of the onset of the Second World War. During the war however many flights were still made flying military and diplomatic personnel across the Atlantic by this route. It was on one of these missions that Charles Blair chief pilot of American Export Airlines made a totally nonstop crossing direct into New York harbour in a Vought Sikorsky VS44 Flying boat. This entire journey had a flying time of twenty-five hours and forty minutes at an overall average speed of about one hundred and twenty-five miles an hour. When he eventually landed, he was down to the last few gallons of fuel in the plane's tanks but the jet stream had been kind as he was flying at fairly low altitudes.

Another wartime service, which operated out of Shannon estuary was the Short S25 Sunderland and Short S30 class flying boats between the UK and Africa. The planes took off from Poole and headed to the Shannon before tracking down past Lisbon in Portugal to Lagos in Nigeria so that their route would keep them west of the enemy.

It was during this time in the winter of 1943 that the chef at Foynes, Joe Sheridan is credited with inventing Irish coffee to restore the spirits of exhausted passengers. It is an invention still celebrated today at the John Powers Irish Coffee World Festival, which takes place every August in the nearby Adare Manor Hotel close to Limerick.

Today little remains of the infrastructure of the service other than a small museum built into the old control tower opposite the pier where the flying boats tied up. In a little internal walled garden is the burnt out remains of one of the flying boat engines. Hopefully it was not there when the service was still briefly operating commercially.

The major site of civil aviation has now moved to the northern shore of the Shannon estuary where a major international airport has grown up. Apart from the Aer Lingus Jumbos daily flights from Dublin which stop over before crossing the Atlantic there are other more exotic carriers such as Aeroflot's wide-bodied heavy jets which also frequently stopover on their journeys back and forth between Moscow and Havana.

It is an impressive sight to see a full Aeroflot crew in fur hats, ankle length coats and shiny black leather boots march stiffly into the dining room of a Limerick hotel for breakfast before taking over from the incoming crew who march stiffly off to bed. While the crews are swopping over and the aircraft are being serviced the passengers are turned loose in the enormous duty-free shop at Shannon. Sadly, for most of the many passengers the duty-free shop was like the Berioska back in Moscow and was only available to those with hard currency but it did not stop the passengers staring longingly. I know the feeling well as I can remember being upset that the duty-free shop in Moscow would not accept my Scottish money for a set of Russian Dolls. This was even after they had admired the money which I proffered and which at that time had the portrait of Robert Burns who they appeared to know, on the five-pound note. It was some slight consolation however that the cold war passengers between Moscow and Havana were never let out of the KGB's sight in the airport and could never run amok with a pint of Guinness in Durty Nelly's Pub on the banks of the Ratty river next to Bunratty castle and its upmarket although still alcoholic mediaeval banquet.

It should be slightly easier for the Russkies today however as I see that entrepreneurs have opened up Durty Nelly's in lots of other world locations inside and outside Eire.

Kamikaze Karaoke

He was not a fully qualified kamikaze pilot because we all walked away from the aircraft in one piece. He had brought the big DC8 down so hard on the runway that it was more of a controlled crash than a landing. The diminutive little All Nippon Airways stewardess in her fluorescent orange uniform contrived to smile inscrutably as she made the landing announcement. "Radies and Gentremen we wish you a big wercome to Hiroshima and we hope you enjoyed your fright with us". Not really.

It was in Hiroshima that I was introduced to Karaoke. I thought that I was going to be taught to split planks of wood with my bare hands of piles of roof tiles with my head but apparently this karate. It was actually much worse than this at least for them as they insisted that I sing. After dinner we walked through what appeared to be an old railway station which had been converted into a market. The market was full of stalls and small shops, which sold everything from jewellery to electronic equipment to fruit and vegetables and sushi. On the other side of the market was a warren of smaller darker streets. Yoshi stopped at a recessed doorway in the side of one building and rang the buzzer. He was hen interrogated over the intercom and after a few seconds we were admitted to the bar. The bar was about five metres long and quite narrow. In front of the bar counter were about half a dozen stools fixed firmly to the floor. Since there were only three of us, we had a choice of seats. Behind the bar the solitary barmaid was quickly joined by two others who appeared through a bead curtain in the gloom at the back of the room. There was obviously not going to be any delays in serving the drinks in this bar. The barmaids busied themselves taking the order and serving it up. The whisky was Suntory but the water was in a separate individual jug and each of us had an individual silver bowl with ice cubes and little tongs to serve them. The barmaids made a big thing about adding the right amount of water and the correct number of ice cubes according to each of our preferences. They then scurried back and forth putting little wooden bowls of nuts on the counter. When all of this had been accomplished, they reached under the counter and came out with some large thick A4 books. These had each page in a polythene cover so that even if someone tipped their drink over the books would not get wet. Each book was fixed to a stanchion under the bar by a thin chain and so could not be removed from the bar. These books apparently contained hundreds of songs but of course the words were in Japanese ideographs and so might as well have been in Klingon as far as I was concerned. I also pointed out to the assembled throng that even if the words had been in English it would not have helped me since I could not sing anyway. There are two types of people who should never go into a karaoke bar those who should not drink and those people who should not sing. I was firmly in the second category. They politely assumed that I was being modest and insisted that I join in. When a song had been chosen one of the barmaids made a telephone call and after a few seconds a television set on a shelf behind the bar burst into life. Apart from pictures the words of the song appeared in Japanese but in roman script like subtitles at the bottom of the screen.

As the TV set played the appropriate tune a little ball bounced along the words at the bottom of the screen so that no one could get too far from the script. At the same time a microphone appeared from nowhere and was passed back and forth between us so that one voice was superimposed more loudly on the rendition.

As I learned later this apparently this was one of many such bars in the area all linked to a central master jukebox type machine. This machine not only played the requested tunes but also rung up a bill on each account which would be added to the cost of the drinks at the end of the evening. If we had enjoyed ourselves too much a couple of bouncers would also have been despatched from a nearby Pachinko parlour to sling us out on the street but fortunately, we were able to hold ourselves in check and it never came to that. These bars were franchised by the local Yakusa or gangsters who took their cut from the proceeds of the singing and drinking in the area. Come to think of it in Japan there is really not much difference between kamikaze pilots and gangsters as they all have a penchant for cutting off their little finger before they go into battle.

East Berlin

From the hotel in Bismarck Strasse we took the U Bahn past the Deutsche OperaHaus to the Zoo Station and changed there, onto the S Bahn which would take us into the eastern sector of Berlin in the Deutsche Demokratik Republik. The U Bahn took us up past the Tiergarten and the unfortunately named Bellevue station with its view of the wall and the cleared area on the eastern side.

A short distance further along the track past the Lehrter Stadt Bahnof and we were into the Freiderichstrasse U Bahn station. This was a main access point into East Berlin for pedestrians and was virtually beside Checkpoint Charlie who was used by vehicles crossing from West to east and vice versa. Looking back to the Lehrter Stadt station we could see where the land had been cleared about fifty feet from the wall and mines planted. Sand had been loosely spread over the mines so that no grass or weeds would grow but any footprints in this area would show clearly when the guards with dogs made their regular patrols. This was in stark contrast to the western side where stone tenement buildings came within a few feet of the wall.

The border guards at the Friederichstrasse station took their usual firm grip on all of the proceedings. Much time was spent standing in several different queues which gave them a chance to strut around and exert psychological pressure on any one who was in the least impressionable and on some who were not. A token amount of west marks had to be changed and some of them used to buy a visa. Passports had to be scrutinised, questions asked and travellers generally left in no doubt as to who was in charge. There was a feeling of being watched the whole time and most of the time the feeling was thoroughly justified.

When John and Brian and I went through I began to notice pattern developing each time we changed queues. John went first because he spoke German best and was closely followed by Brian while I was left to bring up the rear. It was obvious that Brian was not going to be separated from us and frankly it was not hard to share his obvious concern.

The STASI had a saying that "we will never leave you and you will never forget us" and I bet that there are a lot of Germans today who still wake up in a cold sweat thinking just that.

East Berlin of course was an enigma and no I don't mean a big mechanical decoding machine which helped us win the war because we figured out the wheels went round. Even the once impressive bid stone-built buildings had an air of gloomy foreboding in the weak sunshine, which almost failed to illuminate them and show how rundown and dilapidated they really had become and the Trabants outside just made it worse.

The Ministry building which was our destination was in Marx Engels Strasse which was only a short walk from the station. This was just as well as there were no taxis in evidence. We did pass some Trabants parked by the side of the road on our short walk but frankly I would have had some doubts about travelling in one, as they seemed to be made of recycled papier-mâché. Inside the high-ceilinged office, the walls were painted a drab colour and the rooms were heated by brown painted large bore steel hot water pipes similar to those that I remembered from my school days. The negotiations took some time and effort but surprisingly the atmosphere thawed out towards us as they proceeded. Eventually and much to my astonishment they accepted an invitation to join us for lunch and the party walked back along the street to the Intercontinental Hotel whose modern façade looked totally out of place. It was about then that it occurred to me that between the three of us we did not have enough east marks to buy a round of drinks far less a meal for six people. The hotel however obligingly agreed to relieve me of a large sum of money via my American Express card which was the only American thing welcome in the eastern sector and then only in a few locations.

The menu had little which had been imported and much that had been either home grown or hunted locally outside the city. We started with Bortsch which was watery beetroot soup well spiced with black pepper. To accompany this, the waiter brought some slices of hard bread. Brian called back the waiter and asked him to bring some butter to the table. Our guest's faces remained impassive while the waiter did not appear to understand so we asked him again in the four European languages, which we could muster between us. It turned out however that it was us who did not understand. We did not understand that there was no butter in the hotel or perhaps in the city. The waiter walked away shaking silently with laughter. He soon returned however with a small dish which looked as if it had melted candle grease with some unidentified black specks in it. John and I silently cursed Brian, as we now felt obliged to spread it on our bread and eat it. The fish course was trout from one of the local lakes with a potato and the main course was wild boar from the local forest with the other potato.

Leaving Berlin again by the S Bahn we saw the train pull in from the west driven by an East German driver in an immaculate uniform. The train was then thoroughly searched inside by police with dogs and outside by police with mirrors on long poles so that they could look underneath and on the carriage roofs. A West German driver who was so casually dressed that it looked as if he shopped at Oxfam then took out the train. We however cared nothing for his sartorial elegance or lack of it as we headed back to the west and bread with butter.

The Good Old Days

Back in the good old days there was a lot less automation and mechanisation and much larger numbers of people in employment. Companies recruited mainly from the local area and often had several generations and branches of the same family working for them at any one time. Companies tended to have an avuncular or even dare I say a paternalistic outlook and took an interest in the welfare of their employees to the extent of providing tied housing, sports facilities and social clubs. This situation often extended to retired employees and pensioners who were able to use the facilities such as bowling greens and welfare halls for their social functions at no cost to themselves. One company Cape Industries even jokingly referred to their pensioners as Excapists

At one such soiree but with a different company Harley Marshall was both master of ceremonies and entertainer in his role as solo accordionist an example of multitasking.

Being MC allowed him to feature himself prominently in the programme but in any case, the audience seemed to appreciate all his rousing renditions on the squeezebox. In his capacity as MC he was supposed to warm up the audience for the following performers and in this, he perhaps had aspirations to emulate Bruce Forsyth on Sunday Night at the London palladium. Unfortunately, he did not have the same calibre of scriptwriters as Bruce nor the ability to tap dance while wearing his heavy accordion.

As part of one introduction he solemnly informed the audience whose average was probably sixty-five years old that he had just received a message. He then went on to say that regrettably the young lady who was to have performed the striptease would be unable to be with them that evening. He brightened their day at that point by announcing that the next contribution would therefore be made by a large local lady soprano who would entertain them with her rendition of Annie Laurie. The lady then launched herself quickly into verse one accompanied on the piano by the village church organist. The token and very junior member of management who was present and who just happened to be a relative of the chairman buttonholed the MC in the wings. "I am very sorry to hear of the stripper's plight" he said, "I do hope that it is not a serious problem which she has encountered". "I am not exactly certain," said Harley "but I understand it may have something to do with a large Boa Constrictor".

Walter worked with Harley and was also a character in his own right in that his days may have been pretty mundane but his weekends were punctuated by golf where he had a single figure handicap and this probably showed where his main interest lay. As a youngster he had developed a limp but this did not affect his swing in any way nor the way he could drop most drives close to the green and at a pound a hole he surely augmented his salary significantly. In spite of is prowess on the golf course he was really quite shy and unassuming and was never mistaken for a lady killer at social functions. That night he had consumed enough drink to make it impossible to hit a golf ball in one swipe never mind score a hole in one. He spotted a young lady who attracted his attention but hesitated to bound over to her when the band struck up. His friends however were determined that he would ask her up to dance and gave him a hearty shove in the back as encouragement. Walter stumbled forward and losing his footing tripped and did a complete forward summersault. His impetus was such that he came back to his feet just in front of the girl and calmly asked her to dance with him. She probably wondered where the hell he had come from but readily agreed.

New Joisey

The only thing I wanted for my birthday was not to be reminded of it and being in a motel on Route 22 the Garden City Parkway near Newark New Jersey there was no one to remind me. Not like back at home where I always knew that my wife's birthday was the day after she reminded me of that fact. In any case the last time that I had a birthday cake and lit the candles the heat had driven me back so I would not have known whether to be more depressed at being reminded or not being reminded. The Motel did nothing to cheer me up. There was nothing specifically wrong with it except its location but it had little to commend it. It was a functional establishment for people passing through and stopping overnight. The staff were equally depressing in that they made it patently obvious that they were only there for the money and until the unlikely event that they were hired for something better somewhere else. It was the sort of place where if you had rung down to the porter's desk and asked for a pack of cards you would have been given them. You were left with the impression however that they would have been delivered to you one at a time and a separate tip would have been expected for each delivery made. In the evening I decided that I was not driving out to seek a gourmet restaurant which in that locality would have been quite a feat in any case. I simply went down to the dining room, which had the same cheerful décor as the rest of the establishment. Dark plum coloured flock wallpaper, as I recall which would not have been out of place in a funeral parlour. The menu had a limited choice but of course by the time that the waitress had finished her interrogation it seemed much more extensive than it really was. Did I want the soup with grated cheese, croutons, bread rolls, bread sticks or crackers? Did I want the salad with house, Caesars, oil and vinegar, blue cheese, ranch or Thousand Island dressing? Did I want baked potatoes, boiled potatoes, French-fries, hash browns or mash? with the steak which itself was offered several different ways. I have a theory that the chef did things pretty much as he thought that they should be done in any case and few of the diners were discerning enough to notice or even to care if they did. To accompany the meal, I had a bottle of their delectable house red which I am sure was trucked in from the Niagara Falls escarpment some miles to the north and bottled locally.

After dinner I was feeling mellower and went into the bar, which was lit so as not to make too many demands on the local electricity generating company. Over a period of an hour or so I had a few drinks and put them on my tab. When I eventually decided that I could take no more excitement even although it was my birthday, I asked the surly swarthy barman for the bill. On receipt I glanced at it and asked him to charge it to room 232. Because I knew that this authorisation would be unlikely to satisfy him, I also gave him my room key as confirmation. He glanced at this and then peered more closely. "Hey buddy whadda ya tink youse playing at? This is the key to room 323" he growled. Holding it up so that a stray shaft of light caught it I could see that he scored ten out of ten for observation and about two out of ten for diplomacy and charm.

I apologised and signed the bill with the correct room number. He snatched it from me and again scrutinised it closely. "Hey buddy whadda ya tink youse playing at. Youse has not added a tip". Again, he got ten out of ten for observation but zero out of ten for the service which was totally lacking and which I had always regarded as being recognised proportionally to its existence and to the skill with which it was delivered.

How could I follow on from these previous highlights in the Garden State I thought to make my birthday and the night complete.

I decided that the answer was to go to bed, which I duly did. To help get to sleep I put a quarter in the slot of a small black control box by the bed. This was to make the bed vibrate gently for five minutes to relax guests and promote sleep. It worked for me and I fell asleep almost instantly. I woke early and tried to figure out what was happening. It took a few seconds to realise that the control had jammed and that the bed had been vibrating gently all night. Thin wisps of blue smoke lazily emitted from the electric motor which drove the cam so I decided that the best thing to do was to pull the plug out of the wall. I quickly dressed and checked out of my underwhelming urban motel room before somebody got the idea of checking up on why their meter was spinning up their electricity bill and adding the cost of this on to the room rate.

Don't Go Down the Mine Daddy.

Nestling securely in the Avon Gorge less than three miles from the centre of Bo'ness lies Birkhill one of Scotland's best kept secrets from the industrial past of almost one hundred years ago.

In 1835 John Hurll left his native Ireland to seek work and eventually found his way to Garnkirk in Lanarkshire where he obtained a position in a brick works making refractory bricks for Scotland's nascent Steel Industry. In less than fifteen years John had progressed to the position of manager and ten years later in 1861 he formed a partnership with John Young and James Dunnachic to found their own company which eventually became the famous Glenboig Union Fireclay Company.

In the meantime, John Hurlls two sons Peter and Mark had entered the business working first for their father and his partners but soon seeing the enormous potential the boys struck out and formed their own company just a few miles away from their fathers works. Not only did they make such mundane items as roof ridge tiles, chimney pots, domestic firebacks, drain pipes and even flower pots but Scotland's growing industrial appetite consumed all that the brothers could make and more. Every locomotive hauling iron ore and coal had boilers lined with firebrick as did every steam ship plying the Clyde and further afield. Gas works and Coke Ovens consumed hundreds of tons of refractory firebricks per annum as did Iron Blast Furnaces and Steel mills which were burgeoning in the west of Scotland. The quality of Scotland's firebricks were soon recognised and sought after worldwide and consumed voraciously by sugar plants in the Caribbean and fledgling industries in Africa, India and other far flung Commonwealth countries.

So great was the demand that Mark Hurll was forced to set out and explore the possibilities that other premium grade fireclay deposits existed in central Scotland. He soon identified that such materials were available relatively close to the surface in the Avon Gorge. As soon as he was convinced of the quality and quantity of these deposits, he laid ambitious plans to exploit these to the full. To handle the quantities of clay necessary to supply the enormous demand required building a new railway line from the centre of Bo'ness along the shores of the Forth and then south through the Avon Gorge to Birkhill where sidings and a station were constructed. The line then continued further south to Manuel near Linlithgow before heading Southwest across the moors to Glenboig. Although the line from Birkhill to Glenboig no longer exists the line from Bo'ness to Birkhill is not only still in existence but carries passengers. The Bo'ness and Kinneil Railway has been refurbished and steam trains take eager travellers on the fifteen-minute trip from the Victorian station in the middle of Bo'ness to Birkhill where passengers may alight for a mine tour. The service is operated by the Scottish Railway Preservation Society who run six return trips per day in Summer and charge adults less than £3 per head for passengers to recreate the golden days of steam travel. The service is operated by volunteer staff as are the mine tours which are run by the Bo'ness Heritage Trust and financially supported by a large number of organisations and individuals who are keen to preserve this living monument to the industrial revolution and Scotland's role in it.

Work is currently progressing in the restoration of the derelict mine Buildings and Mills. This includes the fitting out of the boilerhouse with boilers and a steam engine similar to the original units first commissioned in 1916. These not only powered the mine haulage but also were part of a complex of five mills, which ground grain for local breweries, flint for local potteries and sawdust for a small factory making linoleum.

Mine tours underground take visitors more than one hundred feet below the surface under the watchful supervision of Tam, Sammy and Geordie to see the rich clay seams which also contain the fossilised remains of sea creatures, ferns and trees some of which are more than three hundred million years old.

For those who do not want to venture underground there are ample opportunities for walks in the surrounding picturesque glen and meadows and facilities for picnicking near the mine itself before the return trip to Bo'ness by a later train. The woodland and meadows around the mine abound with an abundance of wild flowers and fauna in their natural habitat and irrespective of the weather can provide hours of interest

For those adventurers who wish to reach the Birkhill Mine by car it is necessary to proceed East from Grangemouth on the B904 road alongside the remains of Antonines Wall to nether Kinneil then south on a C road to Upper Kinneil where a private road leads down to the Station and Mine. Exit can be made by continuing South on the same C road, which emerges onto the A803 about one mile west of Linlithgow Bridge

Shy and Retiring

Dear John,

1 have heard on the grapevine that you are retiring - 1 must say that 1 do not believe this, as I know that you are not a shy person! Neither can you be leaving for health reasons, as no one could ever become sick of refractories. In any case, there is no reason for you to go, as I understand that the cleaning lady has hung your sales graph back upside down when she dusted it last month.

The company are, however, advertising for your replacement. They are looking for someone with initiative, drive, enthusiasm, determination and leadership. Someone they believe who can inspire others. In short - someone who can pull the company darts team up from the bottom of the league. Successful applicants must be married men, as they are less likely to become upset if someone shouts at them. I have been told that the ideal candidate should be between twenty and thirty years of age, with at least forty years' experience.

If it is true that you are going John, then 1 would like to wish you every success and happiness, especially if you are going to become associated with another non-profit making organisation although in truth this enterprise was never planned at any time to be non-profit making. Perhaps sales expenses have contributed to this undesirable situation. I can recommend an excellent book to you, telling you how to manage in retirement, especially if you can recommend a good book to me telling me how to manage in the meantime!

Retirement is wonderful, 1 am told, if you have enough to live on and enough to live for. 1 am sure that the new interest and challenges that you are embarking on will provide plenty of both. Putnam, Attenborough and Spielberg obviously think so too, as they are giving up the film industry and going into refractories! They obviously can't stand the heat and are getting out of the kitchen.

Sincere good wishes to you, Brunni and the family in your new life in Spain. I am sure you will enjoy it and Sheena and I hope to hear from you occasionally, or even regularly.

Kindest regards.

Allo Allo

Brussels might now be in the heart of the European Union but it was not always so . There was a time before it became the sophisticated place that it is now. These were the days when if asked to name three famous Belgians one might have been forgiven for answering Rin Tin and Tin.

You have to wonder about the culture of a capital city of any country which has as its most famous statue a naked dwarf having a piss. The statue itself is well hidden away in a quiet corner in an old part of town near the hotel Bristol which is supposed to have been the Gestapo headquarters at one time.

Soon after the war the Hotel Astoria in Rue Royale was still running on an electricity supply consisting of ninety volts DC. It was in this hotel that when I tried to use my electric razor it pulled out each hair individually and painfully before making a peculiar noise and quietly going on fire. Half shaven and with spots of blood all over one side of my face I decided that I was no more bizarre looking than most other people around and went down to the bar to meet Jimmy and Mel. After we got a drink and settled at a table Jimmy remarked on how impressed he was with the beautiful girls sitting at the bar on every second stool. As he eventually got up to order his round, he stopped at the bar to chat to one of them. When he came back to the table with the drinks, he had a big smile on his face and confided in us that although the girl did not speak much English, he was certain that she was mildly infatuated with him. "Jimmy you berk I said she is mildly infatuated with any bloke who looks like he might have 2500 Belgian francs. It took him some time to work this one out.

After our preprandial drinks we trooped out to the Maison Ardennoise for dinner since they did not appear to have a Harry Ramsdens. Belgians of course are big on chips if you will pardon the expression but they have not quite mastered the fish. Normally they think in terms of mussels which are steamed or eels which are smoked and both of which can be vile. They don't really do cod but if you are very lucky, they may offer a flounder from Flanders.

Belgians are also big on beers if you will again pardon the expression and have an enormous selection to choose from. It no doubt helps make up for the fact that they have neither wine nor spirits indigenously. If they have a spirit, I cannot think what it might be and, in any case, would tend not to drink it as alcohol in Belgium is very expensive especially when drunk in one of their hotels or private clubs such as the Royal Aeronautical club in the Grande Place. It also pays to keep your wits about you in any case when heading home as so many older Belgians had no requirement to sit a driving test and it shows in the standard of driving. It is not only Belgian hedgehogs, which need to look out for Belgian road hogs when crossing the road.

Have You Come Far

It was a pity really that Her Majesty was not able to meet me although I turned up quite early at Heathrow at about 09:00 hrs off the BEA Shuttle from Edinburgh. The truth was really that neither of us knew that the other would almost cross paths on that day in April 1969. You could say in fact that we did cross paths but just not at the same time. Queen Elizabeth obviously knew that she would be there because she cut the ribbon and officially opened the new Terminal 1 building which was named after her and which at that time was the biggest single airline terminal in the world. My arrival had been along some newly decorated corridors down the escalator and into the underground station situated centrally in the airport complex before spending the day in London on business. Coming back was more chaotic even although I was given a lift to the terminal which in those days was approached up a broad sweeping concrete ramp without any restrictions or security checks whatsoever. When I entered the huge new building however to board the last Edinburgh Shuttle I nearly panicked since the new terminal was virtually deserted and I had no idea where the boarding gate was as I had never used it before on any previous flight. I rushed up to a lone BEA lady standing forlornly in the middle of the empty concourse and asked for directions. She quickly pointed me in the right direction and just before I turned to jog off, she thrust a large brown envelope into my hands and said congratulations. Fortunately, the shuttle in those days did not even require reservations as you turned up took off and could pay on the plane so there were no holdups before boarding as there was no queue. When I reached the gate, I was given a little sticker indicating my seat number and went straight on board. The plane was almost empty and to even out the passenger load I had been allocated a seat in the small rear cabin of the Vickers Vanguard. Shuttles were one class services but the rear cabin on a Vanguard was fitted out as first class. The Shuttle service also served up a complimentary meal appropriate to the time of day which is something that is long gone. I don't know anyone who ever flew for the food but it was nice touch especially on the Edinburgh route which being operated by propjets took a few minutes longer than the Glasgow service which was served by Trident jets. This was because Edinburgh airport at the time was still using the military side of Turnhouse which had a shorter runway. Even at that the Vanguards use to come in very low almost touching the railway line on the embankment at the end of the runway and go into reverse thrust as soon as the wheels touched the end of the tarmac. On the few occasions that jets did operate into Turnhouse the fire service manned a large steel net at the other end of the runway in case one overshot onto the main A9 road. Another incentive for commuters to use the Glasgow shuttle was that from time to time and completely unannounced BEA would use a Concorde as the backup aircraft but still at shuttle prices which were about £40 each way so whichever route you used there was always the chance of an unexpected thrill. When I did settle down into my seat, I opened the envelope and out popped a big certificate informing all and sundry that I was one of the first passengers to use the magnificent new terminal building. I bet her Majesty never got one of these and probably even had to hand the back scissors that she cut the ribbon with or maybe she has her own scissors that she carries in her handbag anyway.

Oucha!

In the distant past when I did Judo eight days a week, I was retained by the local education authority to teach a class at a small provincial school in Scotland. During that period I was approached one day by the convenor and told that the Duke of Edinburgh who was then in his early forties would be visiting in the near future to promote his award scheme and that they wanted to put on demonstrations of several sports to show the breadth of activities that they sponsored for the young people of the county. I was happy enough to agree to put on a short session at a large new Academy on the outskirts of town especially as it meant that we would get some new tatami mats which we could continue to use for regular training. We set about working up some short routines and tried to feature as many of the regular class as possible to demonstrate the sport which although on the education curriculum was not yet at that time featured in the Olympics. On the appointed day we all turned up with gleaming white Judogi sporting range of coloured belts from red to black. Prince Philip seemed genuinely interested and stopped for a few minutes to watch during which time I demonstrated a "seoi nage" shoulder throw which as a major technique always looks good to spectators. My partner added to the theatre by demonstrating a very loud slap as part of his breakfall. The Duke winced slightly and asked me if that had been painfull but looked kind of taken aback when I said "not to me". I just hope that it wasn't me that started him off making his many offbeat comments in his later life.

A short distance away from this Scottish high school is a high security prison for young offenders up to about the age of eighteen where they lock them up and try to dissuade them from graduating to solitary in the "Bar L" or death row somewhere.

It was with some amazement therefore that I heard myself agree to assist my friend and colleague Tommy when he asked me to help him run "self-defence" classes there.

These had been requested by some wit and the authorities had apparently thought that this would be a brilliant idea although I am not sure the enthusiasm spread as far as the prison officers who worked there and probably envisioned even more grief. When we turned up in the gym on a Sunday afternoon as arranged, we were confronted by about twenty inmates. Tommy had a big advantage over me in that his nose had been broken more than once and he probably appeared to fit in better than I ever would unless of course I was about to have my nose broken too for the sake of authenticity.

Tommy had the situation well in hand however as he explained to the assembled scholars that the course would involve lots of boring stuff like exercising to warm up the relevant muscle groups and several sessions on how to break the fall if thrown.

He claimed that in view of that he felt that he had to demonstrate something a little more interesting to maintain their flagging interest. He chose the biggest ugliest youth and grabbing him by the lapels demonstrated a shoulder throw involving lifting him in the air and crashing him down flat on his back on a not very substantial exercise mat knocking all the air out of his lungs. Oddly enough we never had any hint of any trouble from anyone after that and in fact Lurch seemed to be on our side so rest of the rabble picked up the vibes from him and more or less fell into line and behaved like ordinary members of the human race which most of them were in any case.

Choo Choo Train

My younger brother Robin was "handed the controls" of the late tram to Slateford in Edinburgh one Sunday night when he was probably only about ten but we managed to survive the journey with me in the relative safety at the front of the passenger cabin with my nose against the window. This was probably because his main contribution was to keep stamping on the button situated on the floor which rang the warning bell. I have been on a few metros around the world as well from the tiny clockwork orange underground in Glasgow which runs round in a small circle to the massive Shanghai Metro with a few in between like Athens, Atlanta, Beijing, Bilbao, Brussels, the Chicago El and Detroit People Mover, both of which are part subways, Dusseldorf, Hong Kong, London Underground and the DLR, New York, Madrid, Moscow, Paris San Francisco Bay Area Rapid Transit and Tokyo to name but few of the ones that I can remember.

Which was or is the best - well it's not for me to tell you but I will say that Glasgow

Underground often refers to one of its routes as the Inner Circle has a special ticket called the "sub crawl" which for a mere £3.80 allows you to dismount and remount again if you are able at fifteen underground stops adjacent to well-known city pubs and licensed premises where liquid refreshment may be purchased with Scottish money. Maybe that's why when a well-known actor was appearing in pantomime as the evil Abanazar at the Kings Theatre and was posing in full costume for publicity shots at nearby Charing Cross station a local staggered up and asked him if his magic carpet had broken down.

In total I have been on the footplate of a few well-known trains however and most recently these have included "The Flying Scotsman" and "Thomas the Tank Engine" both of them in Llangollen Wales although it has to be said not at the same time.

Thomas actually took me up the Berwyn valley at a fair old lick while the "Flying Scotsman" which was designed and built by Sir Thomas Gresley in 1923 did not. Although it is a bit like Triggers broom in Only Fools and Horses in that it had just completed a £5 million pound rebuild and has actually had at least eighteen new boilers since it was first built. While so much of it has been renewed over the years it retains its original soul and is best known for being the first steam train to reach 100 mph in commercial service in 1936. It did it again in 1983 for 48 seconds going down a slight slope just outside York which is not too shabby for a sixty-year-old veteran.

Diesels and electric trains in the UK are currently limited to 125 mph and I have been in many of these some of which like Pendolinos lean into the corners at high speed.

The world record for a train is held at the time of writing by the French TGV which reached 356 mph in 2007 between Paris and Strasbourg but this was with a short 3 coach train with two electric locomotives which had larger diameter wheels fitted. The fastest TGV I have ever travelled in was the commercial service between Lyon Part Dieu station and Paris CDG at 190 mph which at half the speed was fine for me. I have also travelled in the Japanese Shinkansen Bullet Train from Tokyo to Nigata and it doodled along at 200 mph. The Chinese equivalent train from Tianjin to Beijing did the 70 mile journey in 30 minutes and also touched 205 mph according to the digital speedo reading at the end of each coach It was very safe and smooth because it was running on rail lines and signalling systems specially built fairly recently modern for high speed transportation and the trains themselves are lightweight aluminium alloy. The ultimate for me however has so far been the Maglev from Pudong Airport to Shanghai. It completed the 34-mile journey in less than eight minutes and although it has been operated at over 315 mph the train that I travelled on touched 265 mph but only briefly as the journey is so short. About 30% of the energy in a train is dissipated in friction between the wheels and the rails so Maglev is massively more efficient. The train levitates to a height of less than half an inch above the concrete track base. Electromagnets in a very short length of track immediately in front of the train pull it forward and electromagnets in a very short length of track behind the train push it forward at the same time creating the propulsive force and you hope also the stopping force when you reach your destination. The journey is incredibly smooth and silent as well since the train is heavily insulated and as long as you look directly out of the window you do not get the impression of speed. When two trains pass at a closing speed of around 500 mph it is the only time that you do get an impression of speed. Apparently, TESLA are working at trains to operate at 540 mph but to be honest I think that I will pass on that one as I have no desire to get from London to Glasgow or from Glasgow to London in 45 minutes and Euston station might need bigger buffers.

The Russian Ballet

Big Dougie was general manger steelmaking at Scotland's biggest integrated iron and steel plant in Motherwell and as one of the white helmets was hardly ever seen except occasionally striding through the melting shop with his white mac flapping in his wake. Wee John was the steel plant manager and as far as I could see spent most of his time in managerial pursuits in his first-floor corner office except when he was seen in pursuit of Big Dougie. Big Ian was the assistant to Wee John and seemed to be on site 24/7 and constantly engaged in trying to extricate himself from a succession of crisis situations. Big Jimmy was responsible for the multimillion-pound maintenance in the plant. Pat was the senior sample passer and Tex so called because he had once been to America was one of the shift sample passers who controlled the production of metal in the five big two-hundred-and-fifty-ton steel melting furnaces.

Dougie was in London at a conference with some of the other management but he and they tended to move in different circles because his interests were generally a little more refined than most of theirs. They were all in the hotel lobby after the business session discussing how to while away the rest of the evening when someone came up with a the suggestion of a visit to the Brush and Pallette which was alleged to be a club where drinks could be consumed while young ladies posed naked but motionless on a small stage at one end or so I was informed by big Ian. The assembled managers were somewhat taken aback when Dougie who was in the lobby expressed a very keen interest in accompanying the rest of them for the evening excursion. When they arrived there however, he was a bit put out and immediately left them too it as he claimed that he thought that he had overheard them planning a visit to the Russian Ballet.

John was the only person authorised to take his car onto the melting shop deck and park it immediately outside the office block so that it was immediately available to him at all times and in all weathers if he was called to a senior management meeting.

A salesman who thought that because he imagined that he was a close friend of John decided that the parking embargo would not apply to him drove his car onto the outside deck and parked it neatly facing the wall close to the rail track that was used to bring molten iron into the furnaces. While he was in the office impressing the management, a locomotive brought a torpedo ladle filled with 250 tons of molten iron to pour into the hot metal mixer and when the crane was engaged on other duties the ladle was left parked for twenty minutes next to the car. The radiated heat was enough to blister the paint on the car all down one side but not enough to crack the windows and it was only on returning home that the ace salesman saw the damage to the passenger side of the vehicle which cost him several times as much as a parking fine.

At Christmas all the sales reps contrived to call early or the middle of December with a bottle each for the mangers and one between all the shift supervisors such as myself. Pat volunteered to handle this onerous chore so as not to distract any of us from our duties but somehow or other accidentally forgot to take the dozen or so bottles out of the boot of his car and took them all home by mistake and was so mortified by his mistake that he had to drink them all himself. This reminds me of two Motherwell men sitting in a bar after consuming a substantial quantity of whisky and one saying to his pal "look at those two drunks over there and consider that we could be like that in ten years". His pal upset him though saying "ya eejit you'r looking in the mirror"

Sky High

On one visit to Tokyo I decided kill some time to visit the Tokyo tower which at 333 metres tall and painted in alternate bands of brilliant white and bright red is hard to miss. I spent a few hours in the museum the restaurant and of course the souvenir shop although I resisted the temptation to buy a model tower. Apparently, the Japanese decided more recently that it could not broadcast TV programmes far enough to cover the whole of the growing city and so have constructed the Skytree which at almost twice the height at 634 metres fills the requirements better. Since it weighs in at about sixty-seven thousand tons it is quite an achievement but it sits on massive piles that not only support it normally but also serve to make it as earthquake proof as possible. Everyone thinks that the higher the towers are the better the view but if there is low cloud or even heavy smog which is not entirely unknown in Tokyo then it does not work and spending a lot of money to go to the top to see clouds is against my religion. One of the selling points for tourists is that if they go up to the free observation deck about half way up the Skytree then they can see the other tower but you can see both from the ground so this seems to me to be a non-starter even for the keenest tourists. Being high up on any structure in fact can be a disadvantage in cities like Tokyo which can suffer extreme weather conditions as I know from my personal experience.

I had landed in Tokyo during the Typhoon season which actually lasts from January to December with an average of about twenty-five a year of which perhaps three would be very severe making landfall and the very worst of which with winds up to 150 miles an hour would peak around September. Japanese storms are not named but usually numbered in series like Taifu 1. They are fairly well predicted because they approach over the sea and so are no great surprise although are none the less fierce for that.

I made it safely to the hotel under the darkening skies and rising wind by airport bus and taxi and checked into the New Otani about lunchtime on Saturday. Following a leisurely lunch, I thought that I would go back to my room kick my shoes off and lie on top of the bed reading and did not consider that having a room on the upper floors of the garden tower would be at all relevant to my situation. The Otani was originally built in 1932 for the Tokyo Olympics but had been refurbished a few times. The Garden Tower was built in the shape of three spokes of a wheel emanating from a central core to give as many guest rooms the best view of the city as was possible. It also meant that whichever way the wind blew at least one of the spokes would be taking the full force. This became apparent as the strengths of the wind rose and the spokes actually flexed as they were no doubt designed to do but the thing that unnerved me slightly was the creaking noise which the structure made as it moved.

I figured two things however the first being that I was very tired with jet lag from the journey and the second being that the hotel had withstood the weather for over fifty years with no obvious damage or sign of panic from the management and other guests so I did fall asleep and got a decent rest overnight unlike some arriving travellers. On Sunday morning the TV featured the graphic story of a Philippine Airlines DC8 aircraft which had attempted to land at Narita international airport and had been caught by a strong gust and turned over by the wind to land upside down on the main runway. The totally amazing and good news was that there had only been one serious casualty in this crash and that was from a passenger having a heart attack when the plane flipped over but that they were rushed straight to hospital and survived the experience. I expect that the aircraft needed a good steam clean after that though.

Idle Rich

If you have just come back from New York then maybe you won't recognise my description of their main international airport but that could be because what I am describing relates to a time more than forty-five years ago. It's in South Jamaica which makes it seem that New York is quite a lot bigger than in fact it really is but as the crow flies the airport is only ten miles from downtown Manhattan. The airport was constructed in 1948 on Idlewild golf course and beach resort so named because it was constructed it is said to serve the Idle Rich. After they filled in a few bunkers, threw the flags away and made it a slightly more level it grew to be one of the main airports in not only New York but in the entire United States currently serving up to sixty million passengers each year of which I used to be one on a regular basis. Not as frequently as David Frost but frequently enough for me I can assure you.

 I admit that I never flew to or from it while it was called Idlewild and that I waited until after late November 1963 when it was renamed JFK after the assassination in Dallas Texas of President John F Kennedy. The terminals are built more or less in a circle but since Americans insist on driving on the right-hand side of the road the terminal numbering is anticlockwise so travelling from Terminal Seven on foot to Terminal Six took five minutes walking or 45 minutes by the official shuttle bus. Today it would take a lot longer as Terminal Six no longer exists perhaps because it was the TWA terminal and TWA no longer exists. Terminal Seven was an architect designed concrete and glass shed built and operated by BOAC and Air Canada and was the only foreign owned terminal in the airport. Its front and back walls were full glass panels from floor to ceiling which was good for views airside to La Guardia airport about ten miles to the north but much more interestingly Manhattan which was about ten miles to the North west. The roof had a gentle slope from front to back and made me wonder if at some time of year this ever contributed to dumping tons of snow onto the service road in front of the boarding gates. While Terminal Seven had no curves Terminal Six had no straight lines with the roof being domed and the walkways also being hemispherical.

The currently unused "TWA Flight Centre" may at some point be re commissioned. I gently mock Terminal Seven but on one occasion I got from Aircraft to Taxi in twelve minutes which today is unheard of in any International Airport due to the formalities. I have also been in west side Manhattan near Wall Street thirty minutes after landing using the New York Airways helicopter service which was withdrawn in 1979 after a helicopter toppled over on top of the Pan Am Building causing very serious accident. The irritation for me was that I watched the ground crew leave my suitcase on the luggage trolley as the helicopter lurched into the air. I decided however not to pull the communication cord. After the landing at the West Side terminal (which was actually smoother than the take-off) I leapt up and down effing and blinding and demanded that they put my bag on the following flight which arrived about 45 minutes later.

Terminal Three is also missing mainly because it was originally the Pan Am World Port and Pan Am did not survive the fallout and repercussions arising from the Libyan sponsored Lockerbie bombing over Scotland in the week before Christmas in 1988. The terminal continued to be used by other airlines until it was demolished in 2103. The Pan Am Worldport terminal was also architect designed and looked like an alien flying saucer so architects have a lot to answer for as far as I am concerned. The dome was originally dived into twelve sections each adorned underneath by a sign of the zodiac. This was not popular although it probably helped sell a lot of travel insurance from the Kiosk in the middle of the departures area on the top floor of the building.

It was both hot and overcast and slightly humid so the heat seemed to rise back off the roads and pavements making it tiring to walk very far on that Sunday in May in Beijing. I had spent some time at the Birds Nest Olympic stadium which is set in the middle of a wide concrete slabbed pedestrianised open square. The stadium itself is huge and took some time to go around. Outside some distance away there seemed to be an episode of a TV show like China's Got Talent or The Chinese X Factor being made although I confess that I have never even seen the UK versions and so cannot comment. A large stage had been set up in the middle of the square surrounded by temporary low barriers enclosing it and the enthusiastic audience who seemed to appreciate whatever talent was on display on the stage and was noisily joining in. Some of the participants were dressed in traditional Chinese costumes and some in cool teenage gear of T shirts and tight jeans. The backdrop on the stage featured The Asian Games in Guangzhou 2010 while across the square on a 35-storey skyscraper with a top curved like the Olympic flame a five-storey high TV screen was featuring the Beijing Olympics 2008. Confusing or what, or was the heat getting through to me.

To ameliorate the heat, I had a bottle of water and took a Taxi out to the old Summer Palace where at least a cool breeze wafted across the Kunming lake from the palace on a small hill to the eastern shore near the Shiqkong Bridge south of which the name of the lake changes to Nanhu lake. Confusing or what, or was the heat still getting to me. Another taxi took me back to Tianamen Square and the Forbidden City which seemed to offer the advantage of quite a few cool shady temples and other buildings. The Forbidden City has the distinction of having many major palaces and about nine thousand individual rooms which for centuries have been inhabited by at least twenty-four different Chinese emperors and their retinue. since completion in 1420. I entered like most people over the bridge from Tiananmen Square ceremonially guarded by numerous members of China's armed forces and through the impressive Meridian Gate

 It seemed that on that day at least, the complex closed officially at half past five and security started urging everyone to leave about 45 minutes before that presumably because it is so vast so I saw relatively little of the city except around the main gate onto the Square. A subsequent visit showed just how vast the whole place really was when I was able to explore the entire area within the walls. It took almost a million labourers more than four years to build around six hundred years ago during the Ming Dynasty. Raw materials like wood and stone were transported from forests and quarries more than two hundred miles on sledges on ice roads during the bitter winters in central China.

Ten thousand Phoebe Zhennan wood pillars each created from individual tree trunks were brought in and set on individual stone bases so that they could move independently of each other during an earthquake of up to 11 on the Richter scale.

One of the large temples has about 68 pillars supporting a heavy tiled roof which sits on complex wooden cradles which slot together and lock in place without a single nail being used which highlights the complexity of the design created six hundred years ago and the sophisticated level of construction used by the builders.

Outside the rear wall of the Forbidden City a moderately high hill rises up and for anyone who climbs the steep path all the way to the top of Jingshan Hill there is a panoramic view of the whole complex from the north which provides an ideal location from which to take photographs. What really amazed me however was to learn that the hill itself is man made using earth excavated from the Forbidden City.

Press Button A

No one under the age of sixty will remember the good old days when there were no mobile phones in the whole of the UK and some under the age of fifty will scarcely believe that that was the case or care even if they do believe that t was probably true. If you were out and about and wanted to contact home or office or other third party you searched for a big red phone box with no one in it or at worst only a short queue.

You lifted the receiver put in your initial money which was two two penny pieces equivalent to one third of a new penny and input the number on the big rotary dial on the box. If your party answered you pressed button A and spoke until the phone beeped when you either hung up the receiver to end the call or put in more money. If no one at all answered you pressed button B and got your money back unless you were very unlucky. Most people called others at predetermined times if they could. For someone to contact you was more complicated as they had to know where you were to the nearest building and have a number which would be answered by an operator or someone who would summon you to the phone or who would pass on a message. On one business visit to London I attended a two-day meeting in the offices of a professional institute and left a note of the organisation's phone number with both my wife and my secretary in Scotland. It was a relaxed agenda with coffee, smoke, lunch and comfort breaks so it was no problem for me to break off and find a phone if I needed to. The first morning's session was interrupted however by a secretary who apologised and announced that there was "a call from Berlin for Mr Jarvis" and that since it was from overseas, she thought that it might be important enough to bring to my attention right away. To say that I was surprised was an understatement as I was not aware that I knew anyone in Berlin far less anyone who would spend money phoning me. When she handed me the note with the number however I immediately figured out the solution in that the dialling code was for Stirling in Scotland and not for Berlin in Germany. It was a call from home on some domestic arrangement but I decided not to enlighten the secretary or the rest of the meeting of the caller or of the content. Next morning at the beginning of the session the same secretary again sought my attention and informed everyone that there was a call from Bangkok for Mr Jarvis which really elevated my street cred even higher than it had done on the previous day. Once more I was a bit bewildered until I analysed the number on the note and realised that it was for a small Scottish exchange called Banknock, rather than the capital of Thailand. This was from my company head office as my secretary wanted to update me on some information and get instructions on how to draft a reply in my absence. Again, I did not enlighten anyone on the source of the call but wondered what might have been announced to the meeting if there had been a call from a man in Dunoon.

Even in today's digital age of communications with smart phones which are often more intelligent than the users there is still an infinite capacity for misunderstanding.

My friend Dougie had cause to phone a company to complain about a car insurance premium and that call was forwarded to a large UK call centre kitted out with the latest electronic gear to log calls by number and physical locations by post code. Just after the call had commenced Dougie heard the call handler gasp in amazement and say to her supervisor "My god I have Buckingham Palace on the line what do I do?

At this point Dougie helpfully interrupted her to say "excuse me dear but if you look at your screen again you will see that the post code is for Buckingham Place and not for Buckingham Palace and if you have a google map on your screen as well you will see that it is in Brighton quite near to the station car park.".

Eric who was fellow director phoned me late one Friday afternoon. I had not asked him to and he did not really require to but he did of his own volition. He told me that he had had a good business meeting which had just finished and that he had stooped at the first red phone box just to update me. He also advised that he was near Shap on the M6 in Cumbria and would be fighting the rush hour traffic for the next two hours or more to get home for dinner. I think that he was a bit taken aback when I asked him if he was phoning from a phone box or from the Tardis which of course is well known for being much bigger on the inside than it appears that it could be from the outside. To remove any confusion that he might have been suffering I explained to him that I could hear a TV set in his lounge playing Countdown and also a small dog barking in the hall perhaps because someone was at the front door of his bungalow in Cheshire. My theory was that since I was then commuting between Cheshire and Scotland, he decided to phone me late on Friday afternoon to see if I was still in the office. If he had been as bright as he obviously thought that he was he could have worked out that if I stayed in the office a bit later until after the worst of rush hour I could still have a much faster and more comfortable run home and get in at roughly the same time than if I had set out mid-afternoon. Since I was his boss, I can only imagine that he was hoping for some leverage to use on me at some future point but he did not remain with the company long enough to even try due to other issues which came to light.

Perhaps though the more technology the more capacity there is for misunderstandings, which is why I have survived for so long without an Apple Iphone X and all the apps.

I Kent His Faither

I never knew my father. No wait a minute that's giving you entirely the wrong sort of impression because what I mean is that I never knew my father as well as I might have done during most of his 89 years. When he left school, he immediately became an apothecary's apprentice and while as far as I know he never transmuted lead into gold he certainly whipped up a few potions. Oh! the fun we had with many of his pills and powders. After working in the shop for a few years while also studying Chemistry and Latin at night school he no doubt concocted a few efficacious remedies unknown to the NHS mainly because it did not exist at the time but also because of his skills.

There would have been acetylsalicylic acid or aspirin to you and me and Seidlitz powder which was in fact two powders for the price of one. The powders were often packaged in a small envelope containing two coloured paper wraps, one white and one blue. The white packets contained tartaric acid, and the blue packets contained a mixture of 75% potassium sodium tartrate and 25% sodium bicarbonate. When taken with water the first would clear your head and the second your bowels. Externally things got a lot more colourful with purple potassium permanganate, brown iodine pink calamine or blue $C_{25}N_3H_{30}Cl$ which everybody knows as gentian violet so a class full of kids at school could really be quite striking on a bad day. He eventually went off to seek his fortune in London and did a stint at Boots in Piccadilly Circus which must have survived the worst that a Scottish pharmacist could do since it is still there. After that he exchanged Boots in Piccadilly for boots in the British army when he signed on for the Royal Army Medical Corps which the recruiting sergeant said was varied and challenging, and provided the opportunity to work in exciting locations. The first location was apparently Fort George which not even the Roman army managed to reach and may have been the incentive for him to ship out abroad soon after in the search for somewhere drier and warmer. The boat he was embarked on sailed right past Gibraltar to his great disappointment stopping only very briefly in Alexandria for coal before finally docking in Haifa. Most people probably recall that the UK set up the British Protectorate of Palestine in 1917 as a homeland for Jewish people so long as this did not inconvenience the Arabic population and everybody certainly knows how well that worked out. In the thirties both the Arab and Jewish populations of Palestine hated each other only slightly less than they hated the British. One day dad and his mate Nobby stopped their ambulance at the side of a road on Mount Herzl overlooking Jerusalem to get a bird's eye view of the city spread before them. After a few minutes a couple of shots rang out and bullets ricocheted on the rocks behind them. Dad leaped into the ambulance shouting to Nobby to do the same and he drove like hell further up the road and round a few bends. It was only then that Nobby pointed out that he was the driver and that dad did not even have licence to which dad's reply was along the lines that he had saved Nobby's life and he might at least pretend to be grateful. After such a tumultuous welcome from the locals in the Holy Land the old man decided that they all deserved each other and transferred back to Edinburgh worked in the castle and eventually met my mother. At least when my parents had differences of opinion there were fireworks but seldom firearms involved.

Just Deserts.

For me the ideal desert is not too big, not too small, not too hot during the day and not too cold at night with a nice oasis or two and some decent blacktop roads through it. On this basis I prefer the Somoma desert to the Sahara and Tucson city to Timbuctu. Tucson is about 100 miles due south of Phoenix on Interstate 10 and about 100 miles north of Nogales just over the Mexican border on Interstate 19 which as far as I know is the only road in America with distances designated in kilometres rather than miles. Maybe this means that Tucson is only 62.5 miles due North of Nogales but who cares. Tucson also has a suburb called South Tucson which is actually almost in the dead centre of the city but since it is a Hispanic area maybe somebody wanted the people to feel closer to Mexico.

When I visited for the first time it was for a metallurgical convention as it is a big copper mining and smelting area. After deplaning I was walking through the terminal to the baggage claim and passing one departure gate, I was astonished to see there was a Luftwaffe plane. It was gleaming polished aluminium coloured Boeing 707 jet not with swasticas but with big black iron crosses painted on the body, wings and tail fin. I checked and apparently it was not Hitler or Himmler on his way to South American exile with his entourage and a load stolen loot but in fact the German Airforce taking advantage of the consistently good weather to get in circuits and bumps for some of their rookie pilots. When I looked outside, I could also see a Lufthansa 747 constantly circling the airport on a similar training schedule so a generation of German pilots were being spared the frustration of foggy Frankfurt at least while they were training. The relatively light traffic density of other aircraft helped a lot too although I was mildly surprised that the Luftwaffe jet was operating out of Tucson International rather than Davis-Monthan air force base, a few miles to the north east. It seems that Tucson International Airport seems to be both a civil and a military facility partly because Davis –Monthan is the site of the largest "Airplane Boneyard" in the world. The Boneyard has maybe a thousand military and civil aircraft in various conditions of storage from "just arrived" to "completely falling to bits through extreme old age". To be honest the suffix "International" appended to Tucson Airport puzzled me a bit too as I could only find six airlines flying to eighteen different destinations none of them outside of the USA but the name was certainly more justified than Tombstone International Airport which was grass strip with no scheduled flights to anywhere. In spite of TIA's claim also to be the second busiest airport in Arizona it proved to be only a short two-minute walk to the rental car in a relatively deserted parking area. My recollection was that I stayed in the Congress Hotel which was about as central as it was possible to get in what was a not very big city area at that time particular time. I did at one-point drive out to a country club which was basically a bar and restaurant and might even have had a golf course somewhere out at the back. The most stunning thing was that behind the bar was a large curved plate glass window through which it was possible to see two apparently all black panthers pacing around. Whether or not this had some connection with the Arizona Wildcats basketball team I never asked. Also visited was Old Tucson which used to be a movie set in the days when people made and watched cowboy films and is now a theme park because no one makes or watches cowboy films any more. The stuntmen bursting out through the saloon's bat wing doors fighting each other seemed a bit jaded like they knew that the sheriff was going to win again anyway but it was better than being a cowpuncher whatever that is. The cows were probably relieved not to be constantly being punched as well.

Emporia

If I had had any sense, I would surely have taken a Greyhound bus from Kansas City Missouri to Emporia Kansas which is a small community about 100 miles south west as the crow flies but about 150 miles as the little commuter plane flew as it transited via Topeka. Today Emporia is just another midwest town which happens to be half way between Topeka and Wichita but just off the Kansas Turnpike near the junction of US route 50. Ironically although I believe that it is still possible to take a chartered air taxi to and from Emporia, there are sadly no longer any scheduled flights. Topeka which is located about 60 miles from Emporia is even now listed as the local airport in spite of the fact that Ryanair and Easyjet don't even serve any of these destinations. The first leg of my flight was fraught with concern due to an inexperienced pilot who could not find the switch for the reserve fuel suppl. To compound the problem, he had to land before it got dark because he was not certificated to fly after lighting up time which in his case was 18:00 hours central time USA. I was flying as a passenger in the front left-hand seat of the small Cessna and I suspect that at that time I had flown many more hours than the "Captain" had although in my case mainly with a glass in my hand rather than the control column. I should hasten to add that I had not flown over Kansas at low altitude with a glass in my hand however as much of the states was dry at that time. This meant that the rules for serving alcoholic drinks on internal commercial commuter flights was often extremely confusing. If a plane was flying between multiple destinations then it was theoretically possible to buy and be served one alcoholic drink between take-off and landing on each leg of the flight. If the plane flew over a dry area however the stewardess was supposed to retrieve what was left of the drink. This inevitably resulted in one last big gulp as she approached down the aisle. These rules were irrelevant in this case however as the plane only had four seats with no stewardess and no bar so nobody was serving drinks or indeed anything else to anybody To make matters worse on this particular small plane there was a drunk salesman and a young woman sat in the two seats immediately just behind.

It was pretty obvious that the middle-aged overweight man was proving to be more than a slight nuisance to the woman sitting next to him who was a total stranger he had never met before while she was becoming increasingly agitated. I envisaged a fullscale struggle developing in the back and I reasoned that the pilot might not be able to handle three emergencies on the same flight even if they were consecutive rather than simultaneous. I had already checked that there were neither life jackets nor parachutes under the seats so some innovative thinking and inspired action was very urgently needed. The short duration of the flight and the pilots lack of certification gave him the ideal excuse for the short diversion to Topeka so he descended straight down onto the runway and taxied quickly onto the apron in front of the small building which served as the terminal. As soon as he switched the engine off, he popped the door open and announced that there would be very short refuelling stop and that we would all have to deplane while this procedure took place. The salesman's eyes lit up and he asked the pilot if there was bar in the airport. When assured that indeed there was, he happily staggered off towards the terminal. When the young woman and I went to follow him however, the Pilot advised us to get back in to the aircraft as he was proceeding immediately to our destination. While we climbed back into our seats, the pilot opened the luggage hatch, removed the salesman's suitcase and slung it to one side away from the plane. He then fired up the engine, called the ATC for formal permission to take off and taxied towards the end of the runway. As we quickly took off for the short final leg of the journey, I looked down expecting to see the salesman leaping up and down in fury but there was no sign of him at all outside the terminal building. Either he had found the bar if there was one and was restoring the alcohol level in his blood stream or he was still searching for a drink but in either case it appeared that he had lost the urge to force himself on the young woman or indeed it seemed reach his intended destination. I imagine that he probably fell asleep and eventually woke up in a corner wondering where he was or maybe even who he was.

I was pretty certain that no complaint would be lodged with the FCCA regarding the incident and I was even more certain to insist that the return flight the following day did not transit Topeka. There is nothing worse than your plane running over luggage.

Great Wall of China

Tony and I travelled up to the great wall with Yong's car and driver. To be even more precise it was a well-preserved part of the second great wall as earlier there had been a wall which was not so high or as well constructed as the one which can be seen today. I have only ever reached up onto the wall itself by cable car at Badaling which is at a distance of about 70 kilometres from downtown Beijing and is probably the nearest access point to the city. To be honest the cable car looked about the same age as the wall but inspired less confidence that it was not on the verge of imminent collapse. I had just had a meal before we got onto the cable car and was delighted that there was not enough wind to cause it to sway. The Great Wall is probably one of the largest constructions projects the world has ever seen or ever will again. As someone interested in this type of construction it is fascinating to think that it has about one billion bricks each of them weighing about 10.5 kilos. The bricks were fired in about 200 kilns spread along the length of the wall and transported to the actual construction site on wheelbarrows which the Chinese had invented many years before when the first barrows had been regarded as a secret military weapon. The builders also used about 6.25 million tons of mortar which at that time consisted of sand, lime and three percent by weight of sticky boiled rice which was another military secret. This starch additive accelerated developed and retained the strength of the binder to hold the wall together over the last hundreds of years. Anyone who has seen the wall can attest that the cement in the joints is very white compared to the blocks themselves. At 8 metres high and 6 metres wide in parts and over 5500 kilometres long it is like an ancient motorway. It was manned by about 750000 men based in forts and guard towers along its length when it was completed. A further length of 5500 kilometres has now collapsed or is in disrepair. Traveling along the wall for any distance is extremely hard work as the rise and fall of the wall follows the terrain and can be exceptionally steep while the stones underfoot are slippery whether the weather is hot and dry or wet or snowing.

It has been described as the longest cemetery in the world with over a million deaths and some of the fatalities probably occurred much more recently than when it was first built between 1368 and 1644 during the Ming dynasty. With so much time, hard work and human lives invested it is debatable as to whether it was the success it is claimed to be. For many years it did prevent the Mongols under Genghis Khan from entering China but eventually there was a civil war at the same time as the Manchu were trying to invade from the north east. The commander of one section of wall seemed to prefer the Manchu over and above the rebels and opened the gates to let the invaders pour in.

Like castles all over the rest of the world China was finally invaded through the gift shop at the main gate which instantly meant that it doubled the size of the country overnight. There was now about the same amount of China on each side of the wall which was now almost in the middle of the country and more of an obstacle than before which possibly explains why a lot of it has been allowed to deteriorate today.

Three Doors Up

When we were teenagers George lived three doors up the Crescent from me at number thirty-five. I really must credit him for having introduced me to what at that time in my life were some unique experiences. On separate occasions it must be stressed there was homemade Rhubarb wine and there was Jazz a la Satchmo aka Louis Armstrong. Neither George nor I persisted for more than 24 hours with either especially the wine. He also introduced me to ice skating and to Judo which were activities that he did not pursue for more than a couple of weeks but which I became heavily involved in over a long period especially the mistitled gentle art of Judo which was actually fairly brutal. It was a Saturday when George and I first took a half hour bus trip and a walk of a mile or so to reach Falkirk Ice Rink on Grangemouth road in the town's eastern burbs. After paying our admission we each hired a pair of well used boots fitted with figure skating blades which had sharp serrations at the front capable of bringing skaters to an abrupt stop. George fell on his front and I fell on my front before George fell on his back and I fell on my back. When George fell on his head however, he gave up skating or life while when I fell on my head, I vowed that no such activity was ever going to defeat me. After a few weeks I saved up every penny that I earned as tips from a part time job delivering milk and just before Christmas bought a pair of new Canadian CCM hockey skates at a sports emporium in Glasgow. I also managed to acquire a light blue zipped cotton wind cheater which I adorned with the cloth badges of most of the leading north American ice hockey teams sourced from a friend in Canada whom I had previously met through the Boy scouts. My outfit was completed by a pair of yellow leather motorcycle gauntlets bought from an ad in the Daily Express. With my long trousers tucked into my socks this ensemble might have seemed very slightly bizarre had it not been for the fact that I had become one of the fastest skaters in the public sessions. Although very competent on the ice the gauntlets proved to be extremely useful on the very rare occasions that I still went arse over tip. Leather gloves can reduce your velocity considerably as you hurtle towards the chest high wooden barrier surrounding the ice. I also had an ice hockey stick but decided that if I really wanted to get into a brawl which I never really aspired to do then it was totally unnecessary to buy expensive gear as there were ample opportunities most weekends in many locations in the neighbourhood for people dressed in a variety of apparel. It was on another wet Sunday afternoon perhaps almost a year later that George then decided that we should both first sample the dubious delights of the gentle art Judo at the Azami (Thistle) Judokwai.

This required two bus journeys totalling almost an hour and then a short walk to the Grangemouth Boxing Club located in the Sealock Hall. This was apparently so called because the building in which it was located sat adjacent to the first sea lock which separated part of the actual docks in Grangemouth from the eastern end of the Forth and Clyde canal itself. The whole area had been bombed during the war and the next nearest building which was on the other side of the lock was the old Queens Hotel. Its clientele may well have included the odd old queen and certainly also a few sailors but since I was not eighteen and drinking was restricted on Sundays I wouldn't know. At the back of the sparse first floor gymnasium contained a full size boxing ring for both boxing and wrestling while at the front was judo mat which at the time was a complete travesty of health and safety requirements to the point where it was almost of neither use nor ornament but marginally better than the bare hard wooden floor. George once more soon landed on his head and decided that Judo in Scotland would have to do the best that it could with no further assistance or involvement from him. I landed on my right shoulder and later on being informed by the doctor that my clavicle was not broken vowed revenge on the moron who had used me as a beginner for his cannon fodder. It took a while and a lot of sweat although thankfully involved virtually no blood or tears at least not on my part. Whoever named judo as the way of gentleness was either smoking banned substances or it had lost much in translation or the interpretation of the original moves changed significantly as many more people got involved or possibly a combination of all three. It could also of course have just gone back in a full circle and reverted to the original Budo the way of the warrior.

Camel Back Mountain

Most of my approaches to Phoenix by air have been from the North coming in from Chicago or from the east of the city if arriving from the other huge east coast transit hub in Atlanta. As you approach that corner of southern Arizona there is a huge urban area laid out in a grid format in the desert which at night is ablaze with the light from millions of homes, businesses, hotels and street lighting. Outside at least one Hotel the Kon Tiki the street lighting was from natural gas flares which was both expensive and potentially dangerous but certainly eye catching from quite a distance away as indeed it was intended to be. Immediately to the east of the city centre however there is one dark patch at night that aircraft are well advised to stay clear of because it is the site of Camelback Mountain which reaches a height of 840 metres at its peak. Fortunately, it is far enough away from the airport which lies to the south of the city and its regular east west approaches that it does not constitute any real danger to commercial flights. It really just sets off the brightly lit urban areas which comprise the conjoined tourist meccas of Scottsdale, Phoenix and Tempe. The only camel in Phoenix was in the zoo so I suppose it's called Camelback because of its shape. However, it certainly requires a significant amount of imagination or a few glasses of Mezcal to identify the profile of the mountain as that of any type of camel. It must be poetic licence but it seems to work at a marketing level as others have jumped onto the supposed hump bandwagon. The airport itself is also a bit oddly named as Sky Harbour because like every other airport that I have been in around the entire world it is located firmly on the ground. There always seems to be a corny marketing angle to everything in America. People would transit there by plane whatever the name of the actual facility as it is the main commercial airport in the entire Phoenix area and the name is probably immaterial.

I always found the area to be very relaxing as generally the pace of life seemed to be slower in the desert than it was further north due no doubt to the fact that most of the year it was pretty hot except sometimes just before dawn although my experience in that area was limited to a couple of times that I flew in from the east and still had jetlag. When driving through the desert scrub up to Palm Springs however I noticed that there was a sign by the side of the road which stated "No Hunting" but with two neat rifle bullet holes through it that someone had fired to show their disagreement.

Even the hundreds of windmills in the desert near Palm Springs seemed to turn very slowly and unhurriedly as if they could hardly be bothered to generate electricity. There were occasional wind storms from time to time one of which I encountered that turned into a dust storm that blocked out the sun but only for a very short period of time. Almost immediately rain started hammering down and then the sun reappeared as did lots of little flowers in the ground and on cactuses as the desert steamed dry again. It did explain why at a few places in the desert where the road appeared to dip slightly there were warnings of flash floods which could appear and then disappear again just as suddenly but had the power to overturn a vehicle if caught side on. "Danger Flash Flood" was easily understood even by me but another sign "Wet When Raining" was both a statement of the bleeding obvious and not so very informative. I had more problems with the heat than the night chills or very occasional rain storms. I had a plastic covered Francis Chichester guide which melted on to the dash sufficient to adhere firmly and need careful removal. Getting into the car was a performance where you leapt in, started the engine and leapt out again until the air conditioning made it cool enough to actually sit on the seat and grasp the steering wheel or gears. Only once had I unwisely chosen a US Ford Capri which looked good but with the aircon on full blast did not even have enough grunt to get above forty miles an hour. Believe me however in the desert slow and cool is much better than fast and on fire.

Iran

Iran has a much higher number of inhabitants than the UK but also has a much greater land area so that except than in a few urban areas the population in the large deserts and high rocky mountain areas can be very sparse to non-existent. I am told that the number of road accidents per capita in Iran is one of the highest in the world and although I have never actually seen one in all the times that I have been there I have been close a few times and can well believe the statistics without any shadow of doubt whatsoever.

Traffic in Tehran seems to move almost randomly with frequent changes of direction and speed but more or less in the same general direction on the same side of the road although a few do get into the centre of the road or even the opposing lane from time to time. This could be due to other vehicles, pedestrians, animals or maybe lack of concentration and results in frequent loud horn blowing which seems to cause little or no offence to anyone. Easily distinguishable by being bright yellow in colour taxis seem to make up a large proportion of the traffic but this does not necessarily make them easier to get even if you are a local and know the system. In the morning it was easy for me to get the doorman at the Teheran Hilton to whistle up a taxi from a nearby parking lot. He would then take some trouble to explain to the driver exactly where it was, I wanted to go to ensure that there were no language difficulties and that he profited from a small tip. Coming back however was a very different story and hard work. The system seemed to be that taxis were all shared and they would weave in and out of the traffic quite slowly so that you could shout your destination at the driver as he went past. If he heard you and if he understood you and if there was a seat free and he was going in that general direction a door would pop open. You would then have to run out between the other cars and motorbikes and throw yourself into the vehicle which never really stopped moving during this manoeuvre. With a bit of luck, you would eventually arrive at or near the destination that you hoped to reach and give the driver the quite small fare that you thought he requested as you exited. Tony did not use a taxi at all on his visit as he was working for a UK steel company which was interviewing candidates to be their Iranian agent. Since there was an enormous amount of construction going on at that time the agency could well be a potential gold mine with no heavy digging necessary. The potential agent that he had short listed took him out for dinner and managed to ply him with a copious amount of alcohol before during and after the meal. When they left the restaurant, the chauffeur brought the agents Rolls Royce to the door and they all stumbled in for the journey back to Tony's Hotel. Tony had never owned or even been in a Rolls Royce before and commented that he wondered what they were like to drive. The agent did not take him up on this but Tony persisted and when they reached the hotel gates the agent suggested that he would let him take the car up the long curving driveway to the door. Unfortunately, Tony was distracted by a young Iranian lady whose skirt barely reached her knees never mind her ankles. At this point one of the trees in the driveway seemed to veer over and smack the rolls on the end of its bumper causing anguish all round. It was rapidly agreed however that agency appointment was a done deal and the slight scuff could be polished out without any further slight upset or fuss being necessary. Randy was in Iran because he was the plant manager of the joint venture Reynolds Iralco aluminium plant built at Arak in Central Iran in 1972. Even as an American he liked the job but was not enthusiastic about being supplied with both a company car and a company driver although he accepted that the standards of Driving in Iran were totally different to those in Virginia USA. He claimed that the driver made him very nervous and randy actually took over the wheel on odd occasions although he had no Iranian driving licence. While in Teheran to see me, he went out for a meal and a drink and unfortunately insisted on driving the car from the restaurant back to the hotel himself. While swerving to avoid a dog he managed to get the car into what was quite a deep drainage ditch beside two trees on what was a steeply sloping suburban street. The driver rightly pointed out that it was his job to swerve to avoid dogs and that if any of the local police happened by, he could have some awkward explaining to do. Compromise prevailed and Randy got a taxi back to the hotel while the driver extricated the car from the ditch and Randy from his slightly embarrassing situation.

If you look at the Johannesburg skyline by day or by night it could look like almost any other large city and photographs of course are always framed to show the best perspective of any subject. This perspective may show downtown Joburg, Germiston or Sandton but rarely shows many of the large yellow slag heaps in some parts of the city. It is the biggest city in Africa with about 8 million people living in the greater Joburg area which of course includes townships such as Soweto. Many of the older buildings are now demolished and replaced by new skyscrapers owned by huge global businesses. The city does not have any significant bodies of water in it or even around it or even very much water under it but it does sit on a reef. The gold reef was discovered over one hundred and twenty years ago where it came to the surface on a farm and this started the gold rush which established the city in its present position. The reef today runs more or less due east west just south of the city centre and there is no longer the activity that there once was to recover gold. On one occasion when I visited the city there was the opportunity to see a working mine and foundry run by Simmers and Jack. They allowed visits to the refinery so that it was possible to see the whole process from the ore through to the finished gold ingots. Approaching the site, I drove through an area which had a few old South African Railways steam trains and rolling stock as well as some other heavy industrial equipment. This was all redundant but kept spic and span for the visitors. The mine itself was similar to several that I had been in before in other locations. We had our own footwear but were kitted out in new overalls helmets and lamps and taken down the shaft itself in a large safety lift cage. The tunnels ran out in a grid pattern which was all quite brightly lit with good electric lighting and their height was sufficient to allow me to walk upright unlike most coal mines. The remaining gold itself was mainly in very fine veins running through a very hard quartzite rock. Gold in quartzite deposits like this is rarely found in nuggets and its concentration in veins can be as low as 7.5 parts per billion so there is a lot of rock to be mined to retrieve relatively little gold metal. Every afternoon the rock face was drilled and several sticks of explosive tamped in place. The explosives would be fired and next morning when the dust had settled the miners would come in and transport the broken rocks to the surface in small trolleys. The rocks would be crushed and then the gold separated physically or chemically for smelting. The rocks would be dumped in a pile on the surface and these mine dumps rose to a great height and still blight the landscape in some local areas of the city such as near Soweto. The crushed ore was melted in a crucible at over a thousand degrees Celsius and the gold separated from a thin layer of slag which was skimmed off. The gold was then cast into ingots. Security in the mine was restricted to a hard hat and the advice to watch your feet. In the new foundry however where the smelting took place it mainly consisted of a very large coloured gentleman with a shotgun who locked the doors and stood guard while the melting and casting operations took place. Nobody seemed in the least surprised by this except me who was more used to floor to ceiling turnstiles and CCTV as when I had previously visited at the Royal Mint in Wales and a platinum refinery in Scotland. Come to think of it the Hulletts Aluminium plant near Durban had their own slant on security too since as you passed through the turnstiles, they offered everyone a free condom but only on the way out so as not to distract workers from their paid duties. In Africa it appears they just see things and do things differently including leaving most of the mine dumps many of which were alleged to contain some nasty toxic materials largely untouched until quite recently when there have been some attempts to clean things up after a virtual myriad of complaints from the locals. A local company has now apparently also turned part of this area into Gold Reef City which has become a theme park and entertainment destination with hotel accommodation and a working casino to try to get gold flowing back in to the country again for the benefit of locals.

I did not acquire any nuggets while there and wouldn't buy a Krugerrand because the premium in cost over the value of the metal is too exorbitant for me but I did obtain a facsimile of a Simmers and Jack shares certificate which unfortunately has not yet fooled my bank or broker but it looks impressive in its illuminated frame on the wall.

Ice Maiden

Did I mention that I had drink and a meal with Miss Iceland - no? Well to be honest I don't suppose she confided this fact to too many people either as I am certain it did not really register much on the scale of the most memorable thing to have happened to her in the early seventies. George Best is supposed to have said that it was not true that he slept with seven Miss Worlds. He insisted that it was only four because he did not turn up for the other three. In my case it wasn't exactly a candlelit dinner with soft music either since it cold more accurately be described as Breakfast. It comprised mainly of a plastic tumbler of BEA orange juice to complement a small plastic tray of sausage with scrambled egg served on the shuttle flight from Glasgow to London. I was sitting in the window seat and she was in the middle seat in the row. The guy sitting on the aisle optimistically asked her for her number at one point and she told him that it was in the telephone directory. He must have pondered that and then told her that he did not know her name either but she replied that it was in the telephone directory too. As someone who has spent some considerable time wrestling with Icelandic telephone directories, I can confirm that the odds of him ever getting this information from that source were infinitesimal. She was going to Heathrow to change onto Philippine Airlines bound for Manila to take part in the Miss Universe contest. Have you ever noticed how many Miss Universe winners come from earth rather than anywhere else in the multiple galaxies which the title seemed to indicate were eligible to take part? To be honest I was surprised that it was still such a popular contest since it seemed to have more than its fair share of knockers but on the other hand that might have been a large part of the attraction. I was going to Heathrow to change onto the Piccadilly line bound for Marble Arch to take part in a selling contest in the Bulgarian embassy. The young lady was headed to Manila in the Philippines. I consoled myself with the thought that she might come first in the competition but that even lacking in good looks I would surely arrive first in life. I have since noted that the Miss Iceland contest made a definite point of stating that it has nothing whatever to do at all with the Miss Universe contest but that it is affiliated to the Miss World competition. I suppose that this increases the chances of some young woman from Iceland winning at least one of the several beauty competitions although with a total population of less than Chelsea the odds must have been pretty well stacked already. God knows what Miss Iceland made of Manila with her undoubted vast array of thick woolly sweaters and pixie hats with a pompom on the top in her catwalk wardrobe. Maybe she had a woolly bikini as well although I am told that they tend to sag when wet and Manila in the typhoon season does tend to geta little bit humid occasionally.

All of this banter was going on in the middle of the three Cod Wars that Britain had with Iceland between 1952 and 1976 when Iceland repeatedly expanded its territorial waters to exclude foreign fishing boats. Sadly, there was one fatality on the Icelandic side during that period but they also managed to bend a couple of their patrol boats ramming them into UK navy fishing protection vessels. Iceland eventually won the third and final war because they threatened to withdraw from NATO and America piled into the argument behind closed doors because they wanted to keep their huge air base at Keflavik as a front line defense against Russian nuclear cold war bombers. The Icelandic government were communist and were aware that the Americans based a shed load of their own strategic B52 nuclear bombers there for first strike capability. Iceland bought all their oil supplies from Russia. and I suppose paid the Russians in US dollars earned as rent for the base. As an American base it also had its own colour TV station with all the Hollywood films and cartoons which Iceland itself did not. A few Icelanders tried to patch their black and white TV sets into the American services although the local communist government severely discouraged this in case it seduced any of the locals away from the path of pure living and righteousness. The base also had a PX where copious volumes of beers and spirits were freely available at subsidised military prices. In the island itself the government banned the sale of alcohol after 12 noon on Wednesdays when a very few people on the base went into town. The chances of the visitors finding or even being remotely interested in trying to buy local hooch were infinitesimal but made the locals feel that they were helping prevent any excessive behaviour from their visitors. This achieved absolutely nothing for the sobriety of the local population some of whom would have a few jars before noon and again after midnight or just keep drinking their own moonshine anyway.

That was then and this is now as Icelanders discovered sex and the population grew exponentially. Many became Kronur billionaires, some bought UK businesses and a few started banks. The economy was a saga based on a myth wrapped in a legend and we all know how well that turned out for everyone concerned. Still if you are stressed you can always sit in a geothermal hot spa like the blue lagoon and try to forget it all.

Oh, Lucky Jim How I Envy Him

At lunch time we went to the company dining room appropriate to our rank and dined very well on a varied and well-prepared menu cooked by chef and served by waitress. The management dining room was also a source of networking because no one rushed lunch as there were very few places to go afterwards other than back to our various offices or laboratories. After lunch there would be a leisurely stroll back to the office block to help digest the meal especially if the weather was good. Junior staff usually had to make their own arrangement which could include the canteen or their lunches. On one such fine day Donald had got a new motorbike and Jim was desperate to see it so after they finished their sandwiches, they took the bike up onto the road between the plant and the mine and inevitably Jim had to have a go. The mine road was not paved and had a surface consisting of some rocks well compacted into gravel and hard dry dusty earth. Even more inevitably Jim had a minor spill but one which involved him being dragged along the road for a few yards. This ensured that his trousers were ripped, one his knees and leg were bleeding and that he was covered in fine brown dust. Donald was mainly concerned for his transport home but Jim limped off to the cloakroom where he at least hoped to be able to have wash and brush up and maybe not go to the ambulance room. On his way he passed one of the senior directors who was either entirely preoccupied or managed to exhibit a really incredible degree of self-control and merely muttered "Afternoon" as the two passed in the office corridor. Jim shared a very small office with Lawrence. It had two desks two chairs one filing cabinet, one computer screen and one phone. Jim had one desk chair and the phone because Lawrence only had one eye and was extremely hard of hearing so would not have been able to hear the phone or see it even if he had heard it ringing in any case.

Lawrence was in charge of keeping track of all stocks and so spent most of his time in peering at his computer screen. Jim was something in marketing and so spent most of his time peering out of the window. On one memorable occasion Jim had come across a golf ball and a penknife when idly raking through the contents of his desk drawer. His natural curiosity led to surgery on the golf ball which went reasonably well until he neared the centre of it. When he bent over the ball concentrating in penetrating the centre with the blade of his knife some evil smelling sticky substances squirted right up into his face. He was partly blinded as well as choking and slid under the desk gasping for breath. Lawrence missed the entire episode while engrossed in the stocks. Jim managed to crawl next door to the cloakroom to wash most of the mess away unaided and on his return found Lawrence still hunched over his computer terminal. Jim turned up for work one day driving a British racing green Mark 1 Jaguar which had over a hundred thousand miles on the clock but still looked moderately impressive.

Not unnaturally this had raised quite a bit of speculation as to how he had acquired it on his modest official salary but he certainly did not attempt to hide the car in any way. In fact, he offered to show all the girls in the typing pool how comfortable it really was in the front and also in the back seats though he had few if any takers. While parking it in reverse against the office building, he grazed the side of the car on a low wall protecting the doorway and not unnaturally was pretty devastated at the damage. His mate Bobby the transport manager however told him that he had a drinking buddy who owned a local garage and the two of them both set off to get an estimate to repair the damage. The quote for the respray was incredibly cheap and everyone assumed that it was "mates' rates" but the go ahead was immediately given. After a week a few of us piled into several cars to go and see Jim collect his car which seemed to be as good as new. To prove how happy, he was he drove the Jag round the garage forecourt several time at which point we noticed the respray was only on one side of the car and was almost a good match with the original paint on the other side. Perhaps Jim's true feelings were reflected more accurately by the fact that he took almost two months and some threats from Tommy to scratch the side of the car again before he could bring himself to pay up even the bargain price that had been agreed.

Bananarama

You may or may not know how many British airlines have gone out of business over a period of the last fifty years or so. The answer by the way if you want to know is very close to one hundred different companies. The largest of these to go under was probably Laker Airways which went bankrupt in the early eighties for the equivalent of what in today's money would be about one billion pounds. Many of the others were taken over some by what is now currently known as BA so there must have been a lot of respraying going on. Danair was a charter and short haul company to be taken over by BEA but British Caledonian before its demise served destination around the globe. I remember being surprised in a sports stadium in Jakarta at a Highland games which was sponsored by the Japan Gas Company which had a BCal pipe band marching all over the arena. I don't think that I was quite as surprised as the Indonesians however.

One of the original airlines from the fifties was Britannia Airways which eventually became absorbed in Thomson which is now TUI. My first long haul flight ever was in a Bristol Britannia prop jet from Prestwick to Tenerife Los Rodeos airport which is at a height of over 2000 feet above sea level which with low cloud could be problematic.

This low cloud was blamed as one of the primary causes for what was the world's worst aviation disaster in March 1977 when two jumbo jets collided and killed almost 600 people. Both had been diverted from Gran Canaria earlier due to Canary Island separatists exploding bomb in the flower shop at Las Palmas airport. When he the all clear was finally given for both charter jets to resume their journeys the KLM plane attempted to take of while the Pan Am jumbo was still sitting on the runway. The Pan Am Jumbo N736PA Clipper Victor was the same plane which had made the inaugural commercial jumbo flight from JFK to Heathrow in January 1970 and the plane still had a slight dent on the nose from the champagne bottle that they hit it with before its first departure. I don't know if I flew on that plane very soon after its inaugural flight but I believe that I probably did fly on it from London Heathrow to New York JFK.

The taxi or bus journey down the winding mountain road to Puerto De La Cruz the island's capital which was at sea level on the northwest coast could be hair raising but you certainly saw a lot of bananas on the way if your eyes were not shut tight on the way down through Oratava. There were so many bananas that they even distilled them into Liqueur Crema Banana which I had every night after dinner while on the island in an attempt to keep the stocks at reasonable levels. In spite of this they never ever ran out unlike the stocks of Bells Scotch at the Hotel Monopol which Harry managed to reduce to critical levels. As I reminded him however no-one makes whisky from bananas at least yet. I don't remember much about the six-hour long flight from Glasgow to Tenerife but I certainly remember just a little more about the flight back. We had all gone out for a farewell dinner the night before our return journey and all I will say is that I have not and will never drink Sangria ever again. I did not sleep as I had a gremlin pounding on my temples but at the appointed time went down to reception to checkout only to be advised that the plane was delayed in Scotland due to storms. The delay was in fact thankfully 24 hours long and gave me time to recover slightly as I could not possibly have made the flight back without having had a few rainbow fountains on the journey. Possibly more than a few because when we approached Glasgow it was clear that the storm was still raging. Most passengers on the plane flew a return journey on holiday once each year but I had made enough flights that the Britannia was not under normal conditions supposed to approach the airport in a steep side slip while rising and falling like a roller coaster ride. Michael O'Leary of Ryanair says that pilots are not needed because modern planes can fly themselves but he has never been in an aircraft which was attempting to land on a north westerly runway in a high gusting cross wind from a very strong westerly Atlantic gale. Michael might think or at least say that he thinks that he does not need them but we did and they both earned their money that night. Unlike nowadays especially in America the landing was not greeted by a round of applause just the sound of more than one hundred sphincters slowly relaxing back to the default position.

Silver Bird in Sky

I have long ago made it a new year's resolution not to revisit countries where people stop and point at aircraft in the sky. There is usually a good reason and in my limited experience it is very rarely a good reason. Following the so called Six Day War between Israel and Egypt in 1967 there was sporadic fighting all around the whole middle eastern area right up until the Yom Kippur War in 1973 again featuring Israel versus Egypt and several other Arab nations. When the BOAC 707 landed me in Cairo in 1972 I had little idea of what to expect other than a grilling at immigration on the way in. If my passport had contained an Israeli stamp in it, I would probably have landed in jail and they did not seem any more enamoured of a couple of South African entries and exit stamps either for reasons that were not immediately clear to me. The problems started before that however since the Egyptians did not seem to follow the normal pattern with baggage trucks, cleaning vehicles and refuelling tankers rolling up to the plane more or less in that order. On this occasion two Egyptian armoured cars turned up first ostensibly to protect the disembarking passengers but spoiled the effect by pointing their machine guns at the passengers coming down the steps before walking across the tarmac to the arrivals building. What a great start and welcome to Egypt I thought. Cairo airport even in this state of uncertainty was besieged by many civilians outside as usual. Some were fighting to carry your luggage, some to guide you to a taxi of their choice and some even to introduce you to their fragrant sister. I managed to get my case back from two fighting porters before they managed to tear the handle off it chose a taxi for myself from the many parked haphazardly at the kerb. Since it was effectively wartime the taxis headlights were dimmed by taping over them and since it was dusk and there were few street lights the taxi started to make is way very slowly out of the airport. Just passed the first roundabout two men stepped out from under a palm tree where they had been waiting and the driver pulled over. The men were dressed in police uniforms and they started chatting to the driver in Arabic. It was apparently a prearranged stop as the policemen were going off duty and the taxi driver was giving them a lift into the city. He asked me in English of it was OK with me which I thought was quite funny as my opinion counted for little. The driver and the two other passengers were quite chatty however with the driver translating some of the nuances as they tried to persuade me to exchange dollars for Egyptian pounds at good exchange rates which we all knew was black market, illegal and not to be recommended not least because the local money could not be changed back into any hard currency without an official receipt. The two police soon alighted with cheery waves and shouts of thank you and made off homewards into the gloom. The Cairo Hilton on arrival was almost in darkness but this turned out to be because it had heavy black out curtains and inside was normal although the lighting in public areas was subdued in any case as was the case with many hotels around the world. After dinner I went up onto the roof for a drink in the terrace bar where there was a small cool breeze which made things slightly more comfortable. At one point however between beers there was a pulsing noise which grew louder and had clients running for the exits. It turned out to be three air force helicopters flying on patrol at low level over the darkened city but the rest of the clientele had obviously decided not to chance that they were Israeli air force helicopters rather than the Egyptian air force. At the steel plant there was the usual army contingent with assorted weaponry beefing up company security at the gates and around the plant itself. I decided to invite two of the managers away from their dingy office in the plant and out for lunch with me at the Mahdi sporting club some miles away. We sat at a table in the garden under some palm trees by the pool and enjoyed a preprandial Macdonald's ice-cold bottled beer in the shade. Unfortunately, contrails were spotted in the clear blue sky from two aircraft flying overhead at high fairly altitude. To say that I was surprised was very definitely an understatement when my two companions knocked their chairs over and dived below the table. The table was a heavy cast iron model with an open lattice work design on top so we looked at one another through the lattice for a few seconds before they got back to their feet and sat back down again. I thought it best not to mention the war or indeed the fact that not only had blood not been spilled on this occasion but that the beer was unharmed. It is possible their reaction was more sensible than mine.

Roll On, Roll Off

When the wheels smacked down on the concrete and the long taxi into the terminal began the stewardess cam on the intercom with her message of welcome to Keflavik. This worried me a lot because I was travelling to Reykjavik but apparently Iceland pioneered having their main airport 50 kilometres from the city many years before it even occurred to Ryanair to make this dodge universally unpopular. In fact, I think that I only landed at Reykjavik once and it was what you might call an unscheduled stop. The Iceland air Boeing was capable of different seat configurations and on one flight there was a partition closing off the front half of the cabin with all the fairly few passengers sitting in the rear half. Naturally I could not help myself from asking what kind of freight was being carried from the UK to Iceland and immediately wished that I had not done so. Apparently in the front of the plane was a spare Pratt and Whitney jet engine for the aircraft that I was flying on which was going to be swapped over at the maintenance base at Reykjavik airport because the engine on the plane had done the specified mileage before replacement became due. I was fascinated to consider how the engine on one wing could wear out before the engine on the other wing did. Maybe the plane had been going around in circles a lot. I was also puzzled as to how they got the complete engine into and out of the plane as the door was not big enough. Perhaps they had a guy who specialised in putting ships in bottles as a hobby. My third thought before I turned to drink was that it was steep narrow approach into the city airport taking the planes wheels within a few feet of green painted corrugated roofs of local houses before the plane had to decelerate rather rapidly on the relatively short runway to avoid becoming a seaplane with no floats. I suppose that the upside was that I did not need to take a 50 km bus ride into town from Keflavik as my Hotel Loftleider was actually about 50 metres from the runway and a very short hop from the terminal in a taxi if it was snowing. It was absolutely no surprise that it was indeed snowing.

I had booked a rental car but decided to pick it up at the hotel as I intended to take a taxi from the airport into town to get the lie of the land.

There were a few taxis outside the terminal but fortunately for me there were also several buses which were much cheaper and indeed essential for many of my fellow passengers some of whom had consumed prodigious quantities of duty free. When the flight departed originally from Copenhagen most passengers had their full duty free allowance which they drank on the plane. When it stopped over in Glasgow they all got out and restocked with sufficient duty free alcohol to get them to Iceland and when it landed in Iceland they restocked for the third time from the local duty free shop the Horn of Plenty which was not only open on the way into the country but almost an obligatory stop for locals. When I saw Reykjavik in winter and realised the prices and lack of availability of local drinks, I then understood exactly the incentive. At the hotel I had a choice of rental cars a beige VW beetle or an olive VW beetle although most locals seemed to favour Land Rovers with five metre radio antennas. I quickly gathered that VW beetles were not the ideal mode of transport if you wanted to go much beyond the city limits. The roads outside town were surfaced with crushed lava and marked from the surrounding tundra by poles marking the safe area to drive. Ice lander all tended to drive in the centre of these roads but to give them their due most passed on the left. The surface was generally sufficient to keep switching the car radio off but to be honest there was not much on it any except Icelandic folk music. I drove down to the harbour to get the ferry to Akranes and could not help noticing an Icelandic gun boat with a huge bash on its bow and so decided not to mention the war. In the port I looked in vain for the roll-on roll of ferry but could not see it and thus I wrongly imagined that I was early and it had not arrived. I was directed to park on the quay next to a small freighter and invited to board after which I was amazed to see the car swung over the rail on a derrick and plonked in the middle of the deck and lashed down. The crossing to Akranes was not far but it was far enough for me with a rough choppy sea running and a freezing wind gusting hard against the boat the whole trip. It was about forty miles there as the crow flies and a hundred and fifty miles back by road but guess which route I took on my return. I decided then that I would ask my next client and his wife to travel to me instead and invited them to join me for dinner in the hotel. Since we did not know each other at all I was hesitant to ask them if they wanted a pre- dinner drink but thankfully it turns out that they did as well as wine with the meal and brandy to follow. They realised that in a country with very little alcohol on sale and all at enormous prices I had pushed the boat out so they invited me home for a nightcap. It turned out that when they checked they had no well-known major brands but had a supply of Aquavit which they had distilled themselves. After two of these they were just able to phone for taxi and I was just able to get into it. When I awoke, I was in bed fully clothed but the only part of my body I could move were my eyeballs. Sometime later I was able to roll over and fell out of bed and much later still I went down to the restaurant for a breakfast of strong black coffee. It was quite few hours after that when I was sober but nauseous that I drove myself out to the office at his plant. Fortunately, this was close by on a straight road with no other traffic and the weather was unusually bright and sunny. I was consoled that he did not seem in any better shape than I was but we were both able to conclude the business in hand.

Big Olive and Wee Tam

Olive was 1,775 millimetres tall in her Doc Martens. She may possibly have had hollow legs as this was the only explanation that I could think of as to how she managed to drink so much lager without going to the toilet or falling over. Tommy was about 55 kilos soaking wet and he may have been hollow from the soles of his feet right up to the top of the inside of his skull as he could match her consumption. Both were regular attendees at the thirst-quenching sessions that we seemed to have every Friday night in Alastair's when everyone appeared to materialise after work. Tom was a clerk in the company shipping department and sent goods all over the world or at least as far as Grangemouth docks which were probably about fifteen miles down the road. I recalled that his previous situation was that he lived in a third floor flat in the town centre and worked in the butcher's shop on the ground floor of the same building. After a few pints of Tenants lager, it was sometimes possible to get a few words out of Tommy and often the same words. His greatest revelation came when we were all discussing holidays and Tom happened to mention that he was unable to enjoy holidays every year in exotic foreign destinations such as Majorca like the rest of us. I imagined that this may have been because of the expense but apparently this was not the case. Tom confided very confidentially to the small group around him that the reason was that he risked being snatched by KGB operatives who were keen to pick his brains on his time and his exploits with her majesty's secret service over a number of years. Even after a couple of drinks this came as some surprise to the group as we had been unaware that we had been able to socialise with someone with a double zero code classification after his name. Perhaps it should not have been such a surprise to me as I had often passed him walking the four miles or every day to and from work. I had even stopped to offer him a lift but he always declined and so must have been very fit or short of his bus fare or perhaps both. I had also seen him in action with his hacksaw, cleaver and deboning knife in the butchers and wondered where he had been weapons trained to hone his skills as a perpetrator of" wet affairs". Sean Connery who was also "Tam" to his friends in the early days had done his basic training delivering milk to my mother's house in Gorgie in Edinburgh with a bit of weight training in the evening. Perhaps Embra's St Cuthbert's Cooperative as well as Munro the butchers were actually running undercover training of Britain's secret services. One Russian had actually turned up at the company as an Inspector for an export order but this was probably an innocent coincidence as it was before Tommy's time. In fact, it might even have been before Tommy was even born. On that occasion the inspector had arrived in Glasgow by boat and had set out to walk the thirty miles or so to the company's heads office which was the only address that he had. Presumably he had no Scottish money or maybe he had no money at all. When he arrived at the head office, he was well received but he was not a happy bunny when he discovered that the plant making the order was about a further twenty-five miles east. The company obviously arranged transport for him but when he arrived on site it transpired that he planned to sleep on site until the conclusion of the inspection. The company also arranged for some better sleeping accommodation nearby which they would have been more than happy to do in any case as it was a large important prestigious order. I was certain in my own mind that The USSR as it was at that time was not planning to wreak revenge on Tommy for some slight misunderstanding that had happened years before. To make doubly sure that his resolve did not weaken and in a moment of weakness might lead to him succumbing to a few days abroad with its risk of kidnap it transpired that Tom did not actually have a passport nor a black silk parachute or a helicopter at his disposal and had not even delivered a box of Cadbury's Milk Tray. To set his mind further at rest Olive clasped him to her ample bosom and assured him that if any foreign agents ever came looking for him, they would have to get past her first. My money was definitely on Olive.

George

George was what was known locally as a "Bawheid", a "Blawhard" or a "Bampot" none of which were in the least complimentary descriptions but all of which he still seemed to revel in. Even his best pal told him that if he swallowed a nail, he would shit a corkscrew. He was ecstatic that he had exercised his substantial low cunning guile and managed to out manoeuvre several colleagues to win an invitation from one of, if not the biggest, of our major contracting clients to the monthly Saint Andrews Sporting Club evening at the Holiday Inn, as it was at the time in Glasgow. Dressed in his evening dress and suitably refreshed at the interval he stumbled to the gents to run a quality control on the plumbing facilities. Unfortunately for him he jostled another patron standing at the urinal and patent leather shoes were lightly sprinkled with said patron's urine. George thought that this was hilarious but the gentlemen concerned was alleged to be someone in whom the police had a strong interest in interviewing in connection with a number of violent crimes and murders in the city over quite some time. His perspective was somewhat different to George's and George was informed that his life expectancy was minimal when the gentleman had finished his ablutions. This seemed to sober George up so that he turned pale, turned tail and headed home immediately by taxi leaving a spare seat at one of the ringside tables. It was surely coincidence that George was due to fly out to Australia just a few days later for about a month which he reckoned would provide a cooling down period in which his death sentence might be revoked or maybe even if he was lucky just forgotten about. The Australian trip was one which he had also elbowed some colleagues aside to get. He appeared not to realise however that the focal point of the trip was not the Sydney harbour bridge or even the black swans on the Swan River in Perth although his journey did take him through Perth airport. He then took a lengthy commuter flight to Dampier and then a further small company aircraft to a construction site near Pilbarra between Mount Sheila and Mount Tom Price in the north western Australian desert. I can imagine that George had mixed emotions about this since there was a distinct lack of swimming pools surrounded by bikini clad ladies but there was also a very large distance between him and possible retribution in Glasgow.

On his sunburnt but jetlagged return he quickly realised that he could not find his car in the car park at Glasgow airport and started phoning, the police, the AA and for all I know the Samaritans. It appeared that during his long sojourn in Australia it had been stolen but no one knew when or who might possibly have been involved because of his length of absence. Again, I am certain it had nothing to do with the underworld but was merely an opportunistic theft. Back in the office the company secretary quickly sorted out the insurance claim on the car but George insisted that he needed a separate substantial claim for the contents. He took the claims form up to the drawing office and sat down with all the lads to complete the details for submission. There were the new his and hers sets of Golf clubs, his record collection, a tumble drier, a piano, his snowmobile and of course his new Dunhill gold cigarette lighter. A meeting between George, his boss, the company secretary and an insurance loss adjuster reached the conclusion that the insurance would not pay out but that George was free to go to court and table his list of contents along with the receipts. Apparently, the insurance company had concluded that large though George's company Granada was, the boot was not capable of holding all that had been listed as having been lost in the robbery. There was also a question of how the theft could have been carried out. One of the suggestions being that George had been in such a hurry to get the shuttle to London that he had left the keys in the car and the parking ticket on the dash. This suggestion was strenuously denied although he could produce neither the car keys nor even the parking receipt both of which he would normally have retained in his possession during his trip and subsequent return. The good news if there were such a thing was that nobody had to pay for a month's parking in the open-air car park at Abbottsinch.

Leith Walk

To me Leith Walk in Edinburgh was just another three-mile-long busy thoroughfare with tram cars going tanking up and down clanging their bells and squealing as they took the few bends or braked to a halt at each stop. I always thought the street a bit odd however as it was at a much higher elevation at the southern Princess Street end than it was at the northern end around Leith docks and most people in conversation tend to refer to up north and down south. I personally did not spend much time on the street itself in those days but rather at each end of the thoroughfare where there was a major Judo club to be found if you were sufficiently well informed of the location. In spite of their status in the martial arts communities of the day neither was a landmark.

The Tora Scotia was the oldest judo club in Scotland having been founded in 1944 and was located in a long low one-story building in a back lane between Arthur Street and Balfour Street. It was a bit run down as far as the premises were concerned but it was the home to Rab Smith the senior Judo teacher in Scotland who at that time had a third-degree Black Belt. Before him and before my time there one of the coaches had been George Kerr before who had won a sports scholarship before he set off to train in Tokyo. He eventually returned to Edinburgh via London after dabbling in private coaching and some years later was awarded 10th Dan status after some time as a professional. A contemporary of Georges's had been Sean Connery who worked for St Cuthberts Coop and delivered milk in cans to my granny before heading west to Hollywood as George was heading east. Obviously, a forerunner of Luther Hobdyke who as we all know was the hitman for primrose dairies in Last of the Summer Wine. Well you pay your money and make your choice as they say.

While I was at the club the coach Rab Smith it was only a part timer and he earned his main living as a painter and decorator. He had spent a lot of his time finishing his judo training in Tokyo during which time he did not decorate any of their paper walls or ceilings. He was aided and abetted in the club by Solly Scott who was a cooper and was as broad as one of his own whisky barrels. I normally visited the Leith club on a Sunday when Bob Hyslop would come up from Galashiels to hold one of the three monthly promotion exams for the east of Scotland. These could be pretty rough affairs and it was there that I won my first promotions. Later I visited the Edinburgh Judo Academy which was in Greenside Place at the north end of Leith walk adjacent to the Playhouse theatre. It was coached by Andy Bull who was then a second-degree black belt but eventually was promoted to third Dan and to Scottish National Coach for his sins. This club was reached by a rickety wooden walkway running from Leith Walk round the back of the building and which at that point was about forty feet above the roadway and absolutely nothing like it is today as the whole area has been redeveloped and completely modernised. It was a fact that you took your life in your hands especially if it was raining or dark or both even before you went through the door into the Academy which in fact was more like Borstal. I was also surprised to read recently in the Rough Guide to Scotland that this area of Edinburgh was referred to as being the Pink Triangle since in my day when I was there it was red in tooth and claw. One night three of us came out of the club to be intercepted by a local lady who advised us that she would do anything for any of us for twenty quid. Joe suggested that she could paper and paint his front room. I still thought this offer a bit expensive but I admit it depended on whether the paper and the paint were included. Come to think of it there was another occasion when visiting the Edinburgh Festival and staying overnight in the now long-gone St James Hotel across from the club at the top of Leith Walk when I saw a tall heavily bearded figure in a very glamourous frock get into a taxi. It turned out however that this was Artemios "Demis" Venturos –Roussos, the self-proclaimed revolutionary and Greece's greatest love machine who was off to perform Forever and Ever and his other hits at his show.

Diplomatic Service

At one point I quite fancied a career in the diplomatic service as it seemed to mainly consist of being sent abroad at someone else's expense to exotic locations around the world to eat and drink for your country with occasional exposure to Ferrero Rocher. I even thought about trying for a job as a Queens Messenger as I occasionally came across one of these gentlemen usually with the front row to himself in first class on a BEA European or BOAC intercontinental flight. They were always either serving military or police personnel but to be honest when I thought about it I was not keen on joining the army and I could see that having an official briefcase handcuffed to your wrist could also a slight disincentive. Fortunately, perhaps for everyone Her Majesty's diplomatic service would not have accepted my meagre academic qualifications at the time and the recruitment of Queens Messengers was limited to a very small group of personnel whose jobs were never advertised in the Daily Telegraph on a Thursday. A number of embassies were entered over the years however and a number of diplomats met. Slightly surprisingly to me I got into and out of the Kremlin in Moscow quite easily enough but could not get into the British embassy on the other side of the river. The huge heavy wooden gates of the Spasskaya clock tower on Red Square opposite the GUM department store were about four metres wide and six metres high. They were also wide open. The only problem being the occasional Russian government car which whizzed in or out with horn blowing and lights blazing. They embassy however said that rather than me go to them they would come to me even although or maybe because I was in a small Scottish trade delegation. About three or four of the staff who were probably commercial and security met us in the Chamber of Commerce and gave us a long list of what to do in Russia which was actually list of what not to do. In Teheran the embassy on Ferdowsi Street seemed to sit in its own little tree lined area which backed onto the Russian embassy just across Nofel Lashato Street which sat in its own bigger forest. I could have got in to the embassy quite easily but was advised to go to a commercial office on the second floor of a building around the corner as several revolutionary guards were at that time threatening to climb over the railings. The embassy in Athens next to Saint Nicholas church at the bottom of Ploutarchou Street is now heavily fortified but when I was there it was just an old house with minimal protection. I am guessing that the shooting of Brigardier Saunders the British Defence Attache on his way to work by two Greek Marxists on a motor bike changed everything. In any case I preferred to go to the hamburger joint just round the corner. When I organised a big presentation in the Hilton both Milto and Leila insisted that we invite the British Ambassador and I agreed that they could. When the function was about to start a couple of guys who were second or third commercial attaches turned up and told me that the Ambassador would be fashionably late. This was fine but when they advised me that on arrival it was protocol that we all had to line up and be presented to his Excellency I told them that hell would freeze before that happened as I was slightly busy doing my bit for British exports. As it turned out in the end both the Ambassador and I could live with the compromise that I met him and introduced him to the assembled throng who he probably knew in any case so Milto and Leila mingled with him and the captains of industry making sure that his glass was always full. The British embassy in Bucharest was on Jules Michelet street and you will be suitably amazed to learn that I went there one night with Guy Fawkes not to blow it up but to join in the Thursday fun and games in the basement. These consisted mainly of darts, snooker, dominoes and Watney's red barrel with the ambassador who was from Edinburgh along with any other expats or visitors who were invited to attend. Getting past the Romanian police outside the gate was a pain in the gluteus maximus as they wanted names passport information and other details like accurate inside leg measurements. The huge warrant officer in civvies in the embassy gatehouse heartily welcomed us and advised that we should ignore them as they had no authority to hassle us anyway.

The British Embassy in Iceland was helpful during the cod wars but since then the Icelanders have opened an embassy and fourteen consulates in the UK to get their own back. In the Dominican Republic the gentleman who assisted me in business as agent was the Danish Consul and we used to run around the island in a Morris with diplomatic number plates because he also represented British Leyland.

SCRUFC

This not an anagram of scruff although in days gone by it might very well have been appropriate but now indicates the existence of Stirling County Rugby Union Football Club which formed and reformed several times from the year 1885. Promotion to Division 1 was gained at the end of season 1988/89. Six years later, in 1995, County achieved the unique distinction of being the first club to rise through the ranks from the depths of the seventh division and win the Scottish Championship. A further club highlight was when they played against the Barbarians at the new Forthbank Stadium in 1995 and were reportedly "narrowly beaten" by fifty-seven points to thirty-four.

The "Old Man" was very interested in sport all his life and had been the trainer and physio for Dunipace Juniors football club for many years. It was during this time that he wrote and had published his first book "A Medical Handbook for Football and Athletic Club Trainers". I take much pride in being one of the family, mentioned in the book's dedication along the lines of that "this book was written in spite of my wife and family".

It was some time after this that he acquired a much more colourful scarf and tie which had red in it as well as black and white when he first transferred his allegiance to Stirling County who much like Dunipace Juniors needed all of the support that they could possibly get. He was never the trainer of the rugger buggers whose training seemed mainly to be done at that time in the Old Original Bar in Port Street in Stirling but he was not averse to being a trainee every Thursday night before the team's next subsequent defeat almost every Saturday. The most popular position on the field at that time was full back because if it was organised properly, they could be the first person into the bath at the end of the game while it still had some clean hot water in it. Ironically the position seemed to be filled by Sandy "Pantry" who rarely seemed to get as mucky as most other players and whose nickname arose from often being found in the Pantry coffee shop which was the social centre around which downtown Stirling revolved. The muckyist player leaving the field was usually in fact my pal Tommy who was not only always covered in mud but often in blood although it was rarely his own blood. Tommy and I ran Stirling Judo Club which was for a time was based in Stirling Castle and was about one hundred metres from the Castle Hotel where we replenished our vital salts after each training session. This was generally instead of a hot shower as the squaddies complained bitterly that if we had a hot shower late at night they had a cold shower early in the morning not fully realising that this was one way in which the local army conspired to toughen them up in what was fairly Spartan environment anyway. I insisted with Tommy however whose motto on the rugby field seemed to be like the Royal Tank Regiment "From mud, through blood to the green fields beyond'" as per the brown, red and green colours on their

regimental tie that with the Argyles in Stirling castle that we should mainly aspire to
keep the blood off the white judo suits. As well as Tom's unique approach to the
gentle art of Judo it was very interesting to see how the squaddies occasionally forgot
the rules and fouled one of the junior officers by forgetting to stop strangling until the
referee broke their grip.

For a few years the "Old Man" was elevated to the upper echelons of the club
committee but still allowed to run the line if they were short of touch judges which
they always were when it rained or snowed or was blowing gale. One of his other
duties was to revisit whatever hotel was adjacent to the team's away fixtures and
return items such as chandeliers which someone may have inadvertently taken with
them onto the team bus on the way home. Incredibly one of my other friends was so
tired and unemotional that on exiting the bus he left his bagpipes on the rack and it
thus then became more of a search and rescue mission to reunite a deflated young
bagpipe player with his deflated bagpipes.

Any Port in A Storm

Whatever you do don't take a black cab is advice that you don't hear every day in the
UK even with all the minicabs and Uber clones that seem to exist in profusion these
days. It was standard advice to anyone going to South Africa in the eighties and also
the nineties as they were defined as a high risk in what could be a volatile situation. I
have to say that most of South Africa is a stunningly beautiful country and that I still
have several South African friends from many visits but there was no denying that it
was easy to get caught up in crime without even trying so that therefore sensible
precautions were definitely the order of the day. A company chairman whom I did not
particularly relate to asked me about arrival at Johannesburg airport and I confess to
telling him to take a black cab from the airport so that he could be hijacked on arrival
as this would save him the trouble of going downtown to be mugged later. Personal
security however was only one reason why when visiting Jozzi I usually stayed in the
Hilton in Sandton or maybe further out in Riverside and once on the road to Springs.

My friend Martin reckoned that his house in Sandton was relatively safe from most
burglars because as a successful international dog breeder he could have up to a dozen
large St Bernard dogs on the premises at any one time and I can attest that it is very
difficult to do much with one or more St Bernard's sprawling on top of you. One
night at dinner at another friend's house a young lady sitting at the table next to me
volunteered that she had passed her test that day. I congratulated her on being able to
drive but she corrected me saying that the licence was in fact for her .22 calibre pistol.
While staying in a guest house in Vereeniging I returned one night after dark and
nearly fell over the security guard who was squatting in the vestibule at the front door
hugging his rifle with his head against the barrel but apparently asleep which was
probably fortunate for both of us. My friend Tony told me next morning that his next
door neighbour had stopped outside his house in his Mercedes to operate the electric
gates when the car was approached on either side by two locals one of whom shot him
in the thigh while the other dragged him out of the car so that they could both drive

off in it. I don't imagine that they got very far and I would think that a blood-soaked driver's seat might depress the resale value but carjacking was far from being unusual.

Gregg's answer to the risks while driving was to lock the doors of his BMW M5 and always exceed the speed limit where possible while not necessarily stopping at red traffic lights or robots as the locals called them. He regarded the fines as a necessary business expense and gleefully recounted the story of one policeman with a radar gun crouching in the long grass at the side of the freeway who had been bitten by a snake. I have stayed in a suburban hotel to the east of Cape Town which had a Scottish and golfing theme and whose name I have long since forgotten but remember that it was very conveniently paced for a tour and lunch in the famous Stellenbosch wine region. The carpet in reception looked like a genuine tartan but again my memory fails me on this. The good thing about the carpet was that it led guests straight into the dark wood panelled lounge bar which had a couple of crossed golf clubs over the door and was certainly called the Saint Andrews. Looking out at the dry desert like terrain outside I remember thinking that it was like the biggest sand filled bunker that I had ever seen.

Not so very far away nestling on a sunny north facing slope of Table Mountain the Mount Nelson is probably the one hotel in Cape Town that no one could possibly ever forget and would always want to remember as it is a time warp from a distant era. The pink painted hotel sits in its own spacious grounds overlooking a large outdoor pool in a lightly wooded area. There are several quiet lounges and restaurants overlooking the spacious gardens serving up their almost legendary afternoon cream teas as well as the complete range of other really superb dining experiences at other times of the day. Very similar in its ambiance and excellence is the Elangani Hotel which faces onto a parade of palm trees overlooking the Indian Ocean and backs onto downtown Durban. It was the most perfectly apt place for me to first sample Turf and Surf as it straddles two different worlds with the ocean in front and the African veldt stretching away to the west at the rear. On a trip to the east coast where I visited some of the important clients in towns from Richards Bay in the north all the way down to Port Elizabeth in the Cape, we stopped off for a couple of days business meetings in Durban. The Hotel Elangani was a convenient and relaxed stopover. After a very pleasant dinner on the first evening our host Alastair summoned a young waiter over and ordered four large glasses of Cockburn's Port to round off the meal. This seemed to faze the young man who may never have heard of port but he returned shortly afterwards with four glasses of a slightly anaemic looking liquid which caused us all to exchange some concerned looks. Alastair insisted on tasting it before we all drank it and immediately exploded with rage asking the waiter what the hell was in the glasses. The waiter explained that it was definitely Cockburn's Port but that the bottle had been nearly empty and so he had topped up the four glasses up with tap water. This was not a stunt to try to pull on four world weary travellers including a Yorkshireman and two Scots We restrained Alastair as best we could in the circumstances and patiently explained to the hastily summoned restaurant manager that port was not drunk with mixers or on the rocks but normally savoured straight from the bottle or even the cask. The intervention won us four glasses containing double measures of best South African brandies but may have resulted in a slight rise in the unemployment rate in the Elangeni waiting or bar staff.

The Edinburgh Club sounds as if it might have been a swish watering hole for the upper echelons of the financial, legal and political classes in Edinburgh to unwind in each other's company. It is almost possible to envisage a number of mature men sitting around in subdued light in comfortable wingback armchairs with a glass of Port, a cigar and a copy of the playboy magazine concealed inside the Financial Times. If this is what the name conjures up for you then you would have the wrong end of the stick. It was actually quite Spartan premises at the time not the trendy themed collection of businesses that it is today around number 95. The Edinburgh Club sat behind the old original Georgian stone frontage on the street but inside it was a very basic judo dojo with changing rooms and a room for physiotherapy which frequently came in very handy although never for me I am happy to report. I still don't fully understand how the Dojo was about 6 metres wide and maybe 20 metres long with a low glass roof and fitted behind the original street façade. The thought did briefly pass through my mind that it had been a mortuary but very much more likely had been used to grow tomatoes. With the glass roof it could be pretty hot on summer and freezing in winter but since I was only in it once it was not a major problem which impacted on me very much.

One Saturday George Kerr with his Budokwai colleagues Sid Hoare and Saburo Matsushita ran a major event with demonstrations and competitions in Edinburgh and part of this was some intensive coaching in the Edinburgh club itself which generated a lot of perspiration. Overnight as the temperature dropped sharply the perspiration froze. When I arrived at the club early on Sunday morning for my black belt promotion examination the plastic tatami matting on the floor was covered with a very thin layer of ice. I imagine that this may have been the only time in the history of the sport that it was actually performed on ice but to be fair after a couple of dozens of us went thundering round warming up so did the most of the ice turn back to perspiration. I can confirm that at such times in my life I focussed entirely on what I was doing and so did not follow the fates of other entrants too closely. Neither did I know at that time that George had two of his own private pupils entered for the same black belt exam. Apparently as a professional he had coached them personally and promoted them from beginner to brown belt in less than a year. The normal timescale would have been nearer three and a half years. I had taken ten years although I had picked up a significant career along with a load of qualifications and a wife and family along the way. I could see that there was a mountain to climb and it would be me that was going to be struggling to the top.

My first two contests went well and I won them which would normally have qualified me for a line up of three other brown belts to finalise whether or not I would be promoted. I was called out however for a third individual contest with Maurice Allan one of George's proteges. I don't know whether this was because he had struggled in his contests or for some other reason that I could not possibly comment on. During the five-minute contest I knocked him down but was not awarded a score and at the end of the contest the club referee awarded a draw. I was not a happy bunny but was awarded a line up and went through it quite quickly winning all three contests because as I said I was not a happy bunny. At the end of the promotion examination three candidates George's two pupils and I were all awarded Shodan black belt status so I shouldn't moan. Shortly afterwards in the Edinburgh Evening News there was a short advertorial about the event which named only the two Edinburgh Club members. One was a local business man and the other whom I had fought was the commonwealth middleweight wrestling champion. Shortly after that there were reports in the Alloa Advertiser, Cumbernauld News, Falkirk Herald, and Stirling Observer, all of which surprisingly only featured my success at the event but as I say what's the point of being the Scottish Judo Federations press officer if you can't pull just a few strings and spin the news. Since there were probably less than fifty people in the whole of Scotland who read any of the reports anyway it never amounted to a hill of beans but gave quiet satisfaction.

The Edinburgh Club moved on to have a new name and a couple of new premises being currently located back in Leith. George moved on as well winning his Fifth Dan in competition in 1968 and finally his Tenth Dan in 2010 followed by an honorary degree at Heriot Watt in the same year plus the Edinburgh Award from the city council. In 2011 he was awarded a CBE by the Prince of Wales and in 2013 the Order of The Rising Sun by the Emperor of Japan. In September 2018 he celebrated his 80th birthday at a bash in the Waldorf Astoria in Edinburgh and I can imagine that there were a few bottles of Suntory emptied that non training night. All in all, "the boy done good". In fact, the boy done fantastic and wasn't held back in any substantial way from reaching the heights of his chosen path by the few early encounters with me off the mat naturally.

Road Rage

Ron was a geologist and spent much of his time peering down microscopes when he wasn't drinking coffee as he did not go in much for multitasking. He was relatively quiet and unassuming and often collected small semi-precious gemstone samples to polish in the lab before taking then home for he and his wife to make into jewellery which would sell at craft fairs and in the small ads section of the local newspaper. When he got behind the wheel of his car however a transformation came over him completely and it was quite normal to drive like the legendary Mr Toad of Toadhall. As a senior member of the laboratory staff he had qualified to get a Ford Corsair as his company car and while this was no Bugatti Veyron it could tootle along in the right hands but which everyone agreed was not his hands. He commuted every morning and evening from his home in Dunblane to the laboratory out in Castlecary, along what was at that time mainly the old A80 part of which was dual carriageway. Ron's journeys were all carried out around a fairly fixed schedule as were those of most other commuters heading up and down the same road to and from Glasgow. Over a very short period of time Ron identified another vehicle with which he decided he was going to have to duel with for supremacy. The basis of this decision may have been based on the make, model, colour or performance of the other vehicle or on nothing at all but the drivers of both cars soon developed a consuming hatred of each other. One sunny morning Ron cut up the other vehicle which was a BMW very badly on a roundabout and got within a coat of paint of a fender bender. The other driver was enraged and set off after Ron in a pursuit which got faster and faster as it rapidly progressed. When Ron realised that he was being pursued he got ever so slightly worried and left the dual carriageway at his usual exit more rapidly than normal and turned so rapidly left at the first "T" junction that he nearly rolled his vehicle over. On looking in his mirror however he realised that the other driver was still in hot pursuit and he did a quick right turn under the railway into the tunnel which formed the main entrance to the plant and laboratory. With growing horror, he realised that the other driver was still right on his tail. Since it was still relatively early in the morning he did not park at his usual parking slot at the lab and jump out to attempt to rush inside before he could be ambushed but continued to drive around the parking lot followed by the enemy as if they were a Spitfire and an Me109 in an aerial dogfight. In desperation he finally screeched to a halt outside the transport office where there was always someone on security duty, locked his doors and sat there blowing his horn and flashing his lights. The other driver did one more slow circuit of the car park and then peeled off and drove back out of the plant onto the main road to continue his journey to work as the clear victor in this confrontation. Ron eventually drove back up to the lab to park and got out of his car still shaking. As he scampered into the main door of the laboratory, a few of us in the office who had been attracted by the whole furious commotion gathered at various windows and applauded him into the building as it had made a break from the normal procedure of going into work on a sunny summer day. Oddly enough Ron found a compelling need to go to Brazil that day to inspect a new deposit of magnesite which the company was thinking of utilising in its product range. On his return fourteen days later, he took to travelling to and from work at slightly different times to those he had favoured prior to his little episode of lunatic driving.

In It for the Long Haul

Not quite up there with the meaning of life but on a long-haul flight do you go all the way or have stopover en route. Seventy-five years ago, you did not have the choice as a flight from London to New York could take up to 16 hours and might have at least three stopovers at for example Manchester, or Prestwick then onto Reykavik Iceland and again to Gander Newfoundland before finally landing at Newark airport. Even after the introduction of jets by BOAC in 1958 who operated the first service with a Comet and later Pan Am who operated a Boing 707 the "rules" were that only four engine aircraft could fly passengers across the Atlantic and they could never operate a leg where they were more than four hours from an airport in case of emergency. This was manly a problem flying west as there was almost always an adverse jet stream. This made for a quicker return journey and Concorde did it in two hours fifty-three minutes. The fastest that I have done it personally was five and a half hours from JFK to Prestwick in a VC10 with a seriously strong jet stream tailwind. A Norwegian Airlines flight has done JFK to Gatwick in five hours thirteen minutes in a Boeing 787 Dreamliner during January 2018.

Going to South America was even more problematical with flights going via Miami and down the coast until eventually a few brave souls in Europe went via Lisbon and the Azores or other West African airports. My friend Tony was flattered and pleased to be chosen by his company to organise and man a stand at an international trade fair in Sao Paulo Brasil. He was less pleased when he thought about it and realised that the show was in Brazil and he also remembered that he was terrified of flying. Glasgow to

London was just about bearable although he was shaking like a leaf at what was to follow. Somewhere between London and Lisbon he acquired a bottle of duty-free gin and somewhere between Lisbon and Rio he drank it. On arrival in the airport he collapsed in a heap as soon as he was hit by the November summer heat and high humidity. Shortly afterwards he became vaguely aware of lying covered by a thin white sheet in a space with white walls a bright white light overhead and soft music in the background. To his amazement and delight an angel in white was bending over him and mopping the sweat from his brow. Being a good catholic he knew then that he was dead and was in the waiting room for early admission to heaven. He was utterly amazed therefore when the angel told him in English that she was a nurse and that he was in the first aid centre at the airport. She advises him that he could leave when he felt able but that even if he had to wear his business suit that he should not also wear his heavy winter woollen coat in Brazil in Summer. Like many in Ally's tartan army before him Tony swore there and then to walk all the way back home to the UK even if like many of them it took him three or more years to do so.

One of my own very early long-haul flights wasn't quite so dramatic although it was on a round the world ticket. At that time frequent refuelling stops were the order of the day and is was not mandatory but the captain did everything possible to persuade passengers to get off the plane while this and some desultory cabin tidying took place.

This journey started in Prestwick and had a week long stopover in Sydney Australia but with refuelling breaks in New York, Los Angeles, Honolulu and Fiji on the way out and Manila, Hong Kong, Singapore, Delhi, Dubai and London on the return leg. I had a starboard window seat all the way so when I got home my right arm was flat on the bottom from leaning over to see out of the window and I guess I saw more types of clouds than I have ever seen since as I opted for a seat just in front of the wing. My seats were in what was laughingly referred to as tourist class. I was not POSH on this journey since Port Out and Starboard Home only worked to keep you in the shade when travelling east out of the UK and being from Scotland I had no aversion to a little bit of sunshine and in any case it gave me an excuse to wear my aviator sunglasses.

Kai Tak Heart Attack

Hong Kong's busy Kai Tak airport was replaced about twenty years ago by a new state of the art airport at Chep Lap Kok on Lantau Island but conveniently connected to the rest of Hong Kong and to the Chinese mainland by a major new bridge.

The original airport had one runway which started in downtown Kowloon and continued on a narrow strip of reclaimed land out into Victoria Harbour. All planes including jumbos had to start their descent over the harbour and then fly very low over the densely populated city where some of the higher flats in some apartment blocks actually looked down on the aircraft screaming past not so far away from them. When the plane reached a huge orange and white chequerboard sign on top of a small hill in a city park then the pilot had to execute a sharp 45 degree turn to the right which put him two miles from the end of the airports only runway jutting out to sea.

With a minimum air speed of two hundred miles per hour this meant about 30 seconds flying time away from landing before the wheels touched the tarmac and the brakes were slammed on to prevent overshoot into the harbour at the other end. A typhoon or even a half decent heavy shower of rain could make this event even more exiting. With more than thirty aircraft per hour trying to land and take off on Kai Taks single runway at busy times, pilots tended not to have a lot of time on their hands to worry. Most of the anxiety was left to the passengers especially those on the right-hand side of the plane who could see where they were going or was it maybe those on the left who could not see where they were going. The last of only a very few aerial mishaps occurred to a China Airlines Boeing 747 in 1998 which had to land during a typhoon when it overshot and ended up partly in the harbour. Fortunately, the several safety boats which were permanently stationed in the water on each side of the runway went into action immediately to evacuate all of the passengers and crew from the aircraft. I never gambled in any of the many casinos in nearby Macau but I gambled a few times at Kai Tak on landings and on take offs which if anything were even more hairy when the planes had to climb steeply before threading between Beacon Hill and Lion Rock. By comparison Chep Lap Kok is a dawdle, just along from Hong Kong's Disneyland.

Hong Kong airport used to be one of those which if you had any sense you actually listened to the in flight safety briefing especially the bits about bracing, releasing your seatbelts and putting your life jacket on before hopefully leaping down the escape chute into a waiting life raft and then getting a tot of rum before heading for the shore.

My arrivals in Hong Kong were always much more conventional affairs where you stumbled out of the plane into immigration and customs. Some passengers then slid into the back of a white rolls Royce which the Penninsula Hotel always sent for its guests while I made do with a taxi and the hair raising ride through the tunnel onto the island where I often stayed in the sky scraper Excelsior Hotel on Gloucester Road which was "only" the second best hotel in the colony. In those days you did not have to cross an eight-lane highway to get to Jardines Noon Day Gun. There are actually seven guns but only one goes bang at twelve noon each day and the other six are old cannons which were made in Carron iron works in Scotland. They say that "Mad dogs and Englishmen go out in the midday sun but here on Hong Kong Island they fire the Jardine's gun". Ok I wrote the last bit because Noel Coward was far too busy being a racist. Since I was always an early riser the gun never disturbed my sleep. I thought that there was a bit of one upmanship involved however because the gun at Edinburgh Castle never fires until one pm although because of the time difference this is actually about eight hours later. I suppose that the other good news is that although they fire the gun every day, they have so far not managed to hit the Star Ferry as it battles back and forth across Victoria harbour between the Island and the mainland in Kowloon.

The Iron Cross

The guy on the Hertz desk was very helpful. As well as the car keys he gave me a map and advised that the best route from Grenoble to St Jean de Maurienne was north north east up the A41 almost to Albertville then south, south east back down the A43. When I looked at the map however there seemed to be perfectly good if perhaps a slightly wiggly road designated as N 95 which dribbled more or less eastwards to my destination. Why drive two hundred miles in a rental car when I could drive fifty miles saving three hours and a tank of fuel on a beautiful summer's day in late June. The answer it transpired was that the wiggly road rose and then fell more than 2000 metres from sea level passing the summit of several French Alps and winding past the summit of the Col de la Croix de Fer which was still two metres dep in snow although to be fair a snowplough had cleared a narrow passage so that the car could wind between the high banks on either side of the narrow road but well paved road which was running with melted snow in the bright sunshine. I think that the snow plough crew were more surprised to see me than I was to see them but waved cheerily when they recovered from their surprise. Apparently, this route has featured almost twenty times in different Tours de France cycle race and maybe the snow plough crew were making sure the road was clear for that event. Anyone that can pedal 2000 metres up the Alps has my respect as the car was grinding up in second and third gear most of the way. Coming back down the zig zag roads on the other side was also a bit hairy and probably took a few mm off the surface of the cars brake pads and to be honest I could not envisage that journey on a bike although it was great experience in a car. I did not pass another vehicle during the traverse of the pass except for the snow plough so it was a bit adventurous for me although during the Tour de France the road was probably jammed with vehicles most of them full of medical equipment for the riders who might suffer a heart attack going up or even on the way back down the hill again. The unexpected shortcut gave me more time in Ste Jean de Maurienne so that I had a leisurely lunch with a large Salad Nicoise but stayed off the local vin blanc as I had to drive back again the same day. Slightly oddly to me the Alps also produce s few decent reds such as Sang Barbare from further east near Montana in Switzerland.

My colleagues in Ste Jean were apparently very impressed that I had driven over the top rather than around the local alp but I don't know if any of them had ever taken this route themselves or had just heard stories about it. In turn I thought that the beautiful setting in which they lived and worked was worth a few guineas a box in salary alone. On a separate visit I have also visited Albertville which is another charming little Alpine town close by and although at an elevation of less than five hundred metres still hosted the winter Olympics in 1992. The slightly surprising thing perhaps is that there is quite a lot of industry in the area powered by hydroelectricity but that most of it is well hidden to try to blend into the landscape as much as is possible although there are occasional thin plumes of smoke which indicate that something industrial is happening. Not so far East in Vallais in south east Switzerland is a long flat valley with steep mountains on both sides. On one side of the valley there are huge steel blast proof doors behind which the Swiss keep a few Northrop Tiger fighter aircraft hidden in some concrete reinforced caves and use the adjacent main road as a runway.

The Swiss military was recently described as "armed and dangerous but only during office hours" as they don't tend to get into too many scuffles and have not invaded another country since they went into France in 1815. They were two weeks late for the battle of Waterloo but this could just have been good tactics leaving most of the huffing and puffing to Wellington and his mates then turning up for the victory party. There are a couple of places on the French Swiss border where the road from France runs through Switzerland to get back into France a few miles further on. It's very interesting to note that Frenchmen have to show their passports entering and leaving or else drive on lengthy detours around these little bits of Swiss territories which are mainly composed on big lumps of limestone and of little strategic interest to anyone.

To be fair they did not let Hitler in either although Julius Cesar was more successful going west and Hannibal barged in with his elephants going the other way a bit later.

Do You Remember The 60's

In the late 50's there were two judo third degree black belt holders in Scotland. Rab Smith in the Tora Scotia (Scottish Tigers) club in Edinburgh which was located in a large hut in a back street in Leith and Dennis McQuaid in the Osaka Club in Glasgow which was housed in a first-floor hall in the old fruit market building in Albion Street near the Daily Express. There were probably four or five second degree black belts all of whom had qualified outside Scotland and perhaps as many as a dozen or so first-degree black belt holders some of whom would also have been trained externally. When I first joined Grangemouth Judo Club the instructor was Jack Cocker who was a blue belt at the time but obviously destined for better things as he was committed to the sport. After a few months of intensive training with him every Sunday afternoon with a week in between to attempt to recover I reached the dizzy heights of white belt. Around this time the double bus journey and two-hour round trip was palling slightly but I noticed to my delight that a new judo club had started in Stirling which was only twenty away minutes by bus and the club was running their slightly less intensive sessions on two evenings a week. I decided to go along and request to be accepted as a member. When I pitched up and asked to join there was strange reaction in that the committee went into a huddle. After some deliberations they emerged to tell me that my application was accepted but that since I was the only one to hold a valid current judo qualification, I would require to become the club coach. I negotiated terms with them and agreed that I would be an instructor as long as the existing coach big Tom Howie also continued in his role. This allowed me to concentrate on honing technique and Tom to concentrate on the more brutal but necessary aspects of physical training. The club secretary at that time was Walter Mitty who informed us that he had a blue belt but that he was not able to coach the club due to his war wounds. His blue blazer sported an RAF badge but I am not certain whether these injuries were suffered as he led his squadron of spitfires over the English Channel during the battle of Britain or whether they had arisen in hand to hand combat with Fuk Yew a communist insurgent in the Malaysian Jungle in a more recent theatre of war. So long as he just marked the register and collected the weekly dues, he was no problem but was replaced eventually in any case by an active member. The club then moved from the Boys Brigade hall in baker Street to the more spacious gymnasium of the REME in their local military depot and soon after to the even better-appointed Argyle and Sutherland Highlanders gymnasium in Stirling Castle and close to licensed premises across the esplanade. The final move when the army eventually vacated the castle after a major reorganisation was to the Tolbooth which was also one of Stirling's historic buildings at the top of the town. It was just outside the castle and equally convenient for even more pubs.

These premised hosted visits from senior coaches and successful Stirling students moved on to open new clubs in Bannockburn, Bridge of Allan and elsewhere locally. I myself also coached both in Falkirk and in Alloa for two local education authorities. While working for the Clackmannan District Council Education Authority based in Alloa I organised and took part in the demonstration classes organised for the Duke of Edinburgh on his visit to the new Laurencehill Academy. One of the weirder requests was from the council to run classes at Glenochill prison in Tullibody as I was not sure that they needed any further assistance in inflicting brutality on innocent members of the general public. Tom did this with me and exhibited a side of his personality that I had not fully been aware of. After the initial short introduction with demonstrations of typical throws we invited questions. The obviously most retarded and violent thug who was present in the small group of about twenty people asked what he could do to protect himself if someone attacked him for absolutely no reason whatsoever. Tommy beamed beatifically and invited the questioner to attack him in such a despicable way. The victim smiled an evil smile while a couple of the warders reached for their sticks. The victim lunged at Tom who took him round, up and over in a technique referred to as an arse hole winder only to crash him down heavily on his back. If you have never been winded you will not recognise the difficulty and pain in trying to breathe when your lungs have been very heavily impacted on your rib cage. The victim lay there in some agony for several minutes before he was helped out by two warders. I had to solemnly assure the rest of the class that neither Tom nor I would inflict any further serious injury or damage to any of the rest of them for the remainder of the session. I also decided to cut short the course to prevent serious harm to any more of the local criminal fraternity. Another teaching session was in Majorca long before I spoke any Spanish and the members of the club spoke more than a few words of English so we got by on a smattering of Japanese and an exaggerated mime. No bulls were harmed during the entire session and they must have appreciated my efforts as I was presented with a flag emblazoned with two judokas in action and the words Judo Club De Palma. I also acquired a pennant commemorating the England Scotland home international in 1967 at Crystal Palace in London. As P.R.O of the impecunious Scottish contingent I double as first reserve for the five-man team. Scotland were beaten three contests to two by a much superior English team and since no one was injured I did not need to pile into the fray and make in four to one for England. Next morning which was a Sunday we all took part it a friendly punch up in an open session before returning home. Brian Jacks a professional fourth dan who had just returned from Tokyo the previous week decided to warm up chasing me around the mat. He did not manage to throw me with his main contest technique but of course was well able to resort to one of the many others he had mastered after two years in Japan to bring the short unequal struggle to a conclusion in his favour. Shortly after that he married Sharron Davies the Olympic swimmer but that didn't last long so you win some you lose some I say. Perhaps my most prestigious award was the gold medal I got on my second visit to the birth place of Judo the Kodokan in Tokyo during a very exciting session of the Asian Games competition which was held because Judo at that time was not yet part of the list of sports approved for the

Olympics. Ok I admit that I did not win the gold medal after vanquishing half a dozen orientals and in fact I bought it in the Kodokan shop. It went well however I thought with the cufflinks and lapel badges that I had bought on previous visits to the Judo shop in Rue de la Montagne in Ste Genevieve in the fifth arrondeissement in Paris although normally I don't wear the medal round the house.

California Flakes Fruits and Nuts

I honestly believe that you have to be a bit different if you deliberately choose to live your life in a location with a medium to high chance that it could end quite suddenly any day. The San Andreas Fault runs from close to the Mexican border just east of San Diego in the south to San Francisco in the north. It runs more or less south east to north west and neatly bisects most of the state of California which sits astride two different geological plates which are constantly crushing against one another until one gives way resulting in earthquakes of different magnitudes. In the last fifty years I have heard it said many times that California is overdue to suffer another major earthquake. At the time of writing in June 2018 various experts are predicting a big another big one up to 8.0 on the Richter scale at the southern end. Being experts of course they couch it in terms of a seventy-five per cent or more probability of a major earthquake within thirty years. I am no expert but I predict a lot of tremors of less than a magnitude of eight but all still more than capable of considerable destruction. I experienced the aftermath of one in the middle of October 1989. I was in San Francisco just after it was struck by the so-called World Series Earthquake because it occurred during the World Series baseball and as a result was actually televised more than it might have been otherwise. The high rent Marina district of the city on the north shore around Ghirardelli Square was hard hit by the 6.9 strength quake. All of the houses and apartments in that area are constructed with vertical joints of about one inch between the buildings so that they all move individually. Most of the destruction that I encountered was on the double decker Nimitz Freeway that crosses over from San Francisco though Yerba Buena Island and into Oakland on the Bay Bridge. The bridge itself appeared to be OK but the soft foundations that it sat on as the road entered Oakland had caused the collapse of most of the upper level on to part of the lower level. The local authorities had made a major effort to reopen the road very quickly although traffic weaved around big piles of rubble for a few weeks until more permanent repairs were established. I was happy not to have been in the city and its environs during the five minutes or so when the worst of the quake was taking place. I was especially glad not to have been on BART the Bay Area Rapid Transit system which ran under the bay to Oakland. California has always been a magnet for all sorts of people such as Mexicans, Chinese, Irish, Gold Diggers, Japanese, Hippies and Geeks who if they were not weird when they arrived soon absorbed weirdness and created much more of their own. Who I ask myself would willingly choose to happily live somewhere that might be destroyed quite suddenly and dramatically while sober and halucogenic substance free but might be less likely to fall on you if you are not. One long standing building and thriving business however is City Lights a bookstore on Columbus Avenue opened in the fifties and named after the famous Chaplin film. The shop was certainly selling some esoteric volumes when I dropped by in the late sixties at the height of "Flower Power" to source a rare book for my brother for his research. One young lady customer around that time even confessed to distributing her father's ashes in nooks and crannies around the poetry room because she said that it had become like a second home to him. There was also a fire alarm on one occasion when wisps of smoke were seen coming from the basement. It turned out however to be one of the ladies from Lusty Linda's a few doors up servicing a local while still puffing on her Marlboro.

Not all of the eccentrics however were home grown by a long way and the UK has contributed its fair share. Billy Connolly was a slightly scruffy young married man when I met him walking his dog on the beach in Balmaha on Loch Lomond but recently has sported a wispy purple goatee beard and windswept and interesting hair in the golden stat. Big Tam aka Sean Connery delivered milk to my grandmother in Gorgie Edinburgh for St Cuthbert's Coop until he worked his way up from Holyrood to stardom in Hollywood. Sheena Easton who as a young married woman lived briefly with her husband about a mile up the road from where I stayed in Larbert soon shot to fame and acquired several more husbands on the west coast of America. Rod Stewart who was born in London but with a football mad Scottish father became an honorary Scotsman when he recorded the Scottish team's world cup song for the competition in Argentina in 1978. When they lost, Rod became a long-distance Scotsman based in Los Angeles. As Billy Connolly observed people seem to become more Scottish the further away they are from Scotland and life in California is very far away from life in Caledonia.

On another visit to San Francisco a local took me out to lunch in a seafront restaurant called Rainwater near the Marina area. The theme was that as you sat at your meal artificial rain poured down on top of large umbrellas over each table while thunder and lightning was copiously added for good effect. I couldn't fault the burger and the beer was fine but as someone who normally lived at latitude 55 degrees north and was exposed to an annual minimum of 55 inches of rain each year I was seriously underwhelmed especially as it was also cold, wet, foggy and raining outside hard enough to fill a wire basket.

I was also underwhelmed while driving down the 1000-mile length of the San Andreas Fault and stopping for "gas" to be asked more than once which part of Australia I came from. At the southern end of the fault near San Diego I decided to visit the wine growing area in Temecula and took an organised trip in a Mini Bus along with my wife and ten others. The driver gave a running commentary on everything including himself. He claimed to be a close relative of Jack Nicholson, to be married to a lady who was said to be an ambassador to the UN which of course is New York based. He claimed to live in a two-million-dollar house in a north west San Diego suburb and naturally his own vehicle when he was not driving a mini bus for out of town tourists was a Cadillac. As he dropped everyone off at their hotels however, I noticed that the hand went out for gratuities and then shot back into his pocket with a fistful of Dollars. We were the last passengers to be dropped off at the end of the tour at our waterfront Holiday Inn. As the left hand helped my wife down from the "van" and the right hand again shot out I gripped it firmly, shook it and thanked him for an interesting and entertaining insight into the rich tapestry of life that is Southern California.

Close to the Edge

Since biblical times poets and songwriters have been going on a bit about the ends of the earth but I suspect that few if any have ever been there even if they all deserve to. In fact, it is quite a formidable task to get to the ends of the earth these days since it was discovered that the earth was round rather than flat and tends not to have an end. For me one of the remotest locations on earth is not in Stirling in Scotland in spite of rumours by people from Falkirk but it is actually on Stirling Point just to the south of Bluff near Invercargill in New Zealand. It is over twenty thousand kilometres from Stirling in Scotland and Stirling Point on the south of the South Island of New Zealand as the crow flies and not many of them do. I stood on the low cliffs and leaned forward into a stiff breeze which seemed to be coming up from the South Pole in Antartica across a grey coloured sea flecked with white waves. It is a good job there was a continuous stiff breeze as otherwise I might have fallen into the water. I can readily imagine that it is possibly one of the very best places on earth to fly your kite.

Just north at Tiwai point there was and hopefully still is a major aluminium smelter powered by hydro electricity from the Southern Alps. The joint venture between RTZ and Sumitomo has been struggling because of the business climate rather than the actual climate although both have headwinds and blustery conditions to contend with. Invercargill is served by air but also surprisingly to me by train which must make its station at 46 degrees latitude south the most southerly railway station in the world. The Railway Hotel built in 1907 is also probably the best hotel in town. It is situated on the main north south avenue in town which is extraordinarily wide for such a relatively small town. The story is that it was designed so that a waggon and team of horses could easily turn on the street but it currently has a central reservation now that the horses have gone and have been replaced by trucks which do three point turns if they have to although there are lots more roads to choose from nowadays. From Invercargill north to Christchurch a distance of almost three hundred miles as the crow flies and then on another hundred miles further on to Blenheim is the range of mountains known as the Southern Alps. Mount Cook towers towel over twelve thousand feet in their midst so there are very few crows on that route. Queenstown and a few other small resorts draw in the winter sports enthusiasts while Christchurch the main city on the coast at sea level was s a bit retro but a few earthquakes recently have for better or for worse remodelled it slightly. My main memory of the downtown area was the number of the very well-preserved old Morris Oxford and other British cars that were in everyday use although today I suspect that they are all Japanese cars. Although Chicago is often referred to as "the Windy City" New Zealand must be the "Windy Country" because the roaring forties whistle not only over it but through the Cook Straight between the north and south islands making it an invigorating location. There is not much dust settles in Wellington and in even in New Plymouth which is up the west coast and should be more sheltered there are some interesting cross winds.

On one flight in on a Fokker the Pilot decided that with the wind from the east and the runway configuration from SW to NE it was better to land across the runway with most of the touchdown on the grass field itself. The old Fokker F27 Friendship two engine turbo prop bounced around a bit a low altitude but the pilot definitely made the right call and landed it without too much distress to any of the passengers on board. Much further north and only thirty miles south of Auckland is NZ Steel at Glenbrook. It was easy to tell the prevailing winds in that area because a thin plume of iron oxide had been taken up from the stack and spread out and deposited west of the plant. In Auckland harbour itself there is often a stiff breeze which pushes the many small yachts along at a fast lick but still feels quite chill even when the sun is shining down. If you want to freeze and still get sunburn this makes the harbour the ideal place to go. The bridge over the harbour was opened in 1959 after four years in construction and was originally a four-lane road structure built by Dorman Long and Cleveland Bridge. Ten years later the bridge was widened to eight lanes by adding the "Nippon Clippon" consisting of an extra two lanes suspended off each side. With high winds combined with occasional earth tremors a bus ride over the bridge can provide an unwelcome cheap thrill. Much of the rest of the country can provide unwanted thrills as well with frequent earthquakes and big geysers that unexpectedly scoosh hot water all over the place when you are least expecting it and often where you would least anticipate it.

Big Easy

Some people like The Big Easy and I mean the city of New Orleans and not the faux American overpriced Crab Shack stuck in a corner of Canary Wharf. The restaurant is only a couple of hundred metres from Billingsgate fish market so it's pretty certain any crabs eaten come from there and not the Gulf of Louisiana but they still insist on trying to tie cheap plastic bibs on to all the diners in case they dribble and drop food. The real thing is a bit over the top as well in my opinion even when it is not flooded.

The city was constructed from the swamps by slave labour building raised banks of earth referred to as levees more than three hundred years ago in 1718 and has been French and Spanish so many times it should have been called the Big Yoyo. Most cities are built on foundations but New Orleans is claimed to be built on stories and a few of them might even be true but the trick is to figure which ones. There are a couple of cities which host all year-round Christmas shops but New Orleans is the only city I know of with an all year-round Halloween shop which not surprisingly does a roaring trade in pseudo Voodoo paraphernalia. It is a city that is so banal that it seems to think that no one would notice it unless every single aspect of it is thing is exaggerated to extremes. In the streets in the French quarter around Bourbon street they sell voodoo drinks called Zombies which seem to consist of a litre plastic container full of crushed ice liberally dosed with rum and some kind of fruit juice presumable to disguise the awful taste and near fatal effects.

It is the only drink that I know of that anaesthetises you from the feet up to the skull. It's useful at Mardi Gras however especially if you can't stand what is promoted as being a carnival but to me is just cynical superficial attempt at gaiety designed to relieve you of your money faster than a team of pickpockets. Next day on an early

Sunday morning walk down to the river I was surprised to see the number of people sleeping in doorways although it is certainly something not confined to New Orleans. Fortunately for New Orleans most people seem to differ with my views on the subject of a fab February. On one October visit we were staying at what is now the Crowne Plaza on Canal Street and were invited out to dinner with a group of people and their wives. We assembled in the cold outside the hotel at the appointed hour and were surprised by the arrival of a huge purple stretched limo. About sixteen of us climber aboard via the single door and were even more surprised to see that the seating was not in rows but arranged around the body of the car with everyone looking inwards at a glass and chrome cocktail bar. The vehicle set off but immediately executed a "U" turn on Canal Street which would have been an eight lane highway running down to the Mississippi river in the south of the city if it did not have train tracks running down the centre perhaps even covering over an old canal which emptied into the river. The driver then turned right at the first set of traffic lights and stopped to let us out at the restaurant. The whole trip including loading and unloading must have been less than two minutes and less than two hundred yards so we did not even have time to get the decanters of Bourbon out of the cocktail cabinet before were out in the cold yet again. The local delicacy served that evening was Oxymoron. Well to me Jumbo means very large and Shrimp means very small and so that must be an oxymoron cocktail. Shrimp itself has a fairly bland flavour so the locals take to loading it with lemon, garlic and haemoglobin red sauce which strips the skin from the mouth and throat. This is locally referred to as Cajun sauce because it is easier to spell than Acadian but in any case has little to do with the mainly self-contained small isolated communities descended originally from French Canadians still living in the swamps and still speaking a form of archaic French or so the legend goes if you choose to believe it.

The following evening, we took a cruise on what may or may not have been a paddle steamer apparently propelled by a large rear paddle wheel at the back. It was dark and cold and wet however with a stiff breeze so that the voyage was spent in the bar from where we could occasionally see the lights of various refineries as we passed them by. In May I also flew from New Orleans two hundred miles westwards across the huge Mississippi delta to Lake Charles Louisiana in a small commuter aircraft and although it was fairly early in the day the turbulence was fierce and flight uncomfortable from rising thermals over the swamps. The take-off too was weird in that as the aircraft taxied out to the runway it became covered in a black swirling mass of Mayflies or similar gangly insects which blocked the view from the windows as they attempted mass copulation prior to their imminent demise. Even had they not all been torn from the fuselage as the plane accelerated and took off, they have a very short life span in any case but en masse can make quite a mess especially on the cockpit windows.

Cars, Cars and Mair Cars

I like cars as much as the next auto maniac. I passed my driving test first time at eighteen to the utter amazement of my instructor and in a driving career spanning over sixty years have driven well over sixty different marques and models of automobiles around the entire world. Perhaps twenty of these were owned by me while the rest were leased, rented or borrowed. My first car was an Austin Mini which was as basic a car as it was possible to buy but very reliable. On a good day it could reach sixty miles per hour going downhill with a following wind not that it was often asked to. While driving this I came across a Simca Matra Baghera, which was launched in France and lusted after it from the day I saw it. It was an incredible two door, three seat, mid engined family sports car which preceded the launch of the Lotus Europa and was also a forerunner of the Porsche 924 all of which looked quite similar to one another. It had a 1300 cc Matra engine and incredibly was very modestly priced. I got so far as going into the Simca Showroom in central Paris but the sales manager was so impressed by my appearance that he would not even discuss the car with me. In pique I decided to buy British and ordered a Lotus twin cam Cortina from Ford in Stirling. The speedo went up to 150, the car went up to 118 but I never went above 104 all the time I had it which was only about a year as it was not cheap to insure maintain or operate. It actually reached 104 in mid-air as it negotiated a hump in the road whereupon it resorted to low flying only for me to notice a T junction about 200 yards in front. I can confirm that four-wheel disc brakes do not slow the car when it is already airbporne. I ran it once at Ingliston racetrack in Edinburgh under an RAC beginner's competition Licence. I was refused insurance for driving the car while it was on the track but had to pay insurance for the track itself and everything else on it and surrounding it and so drove it most incredibly carefully being lapped by MG midgets and even pushbikes if there had been any on the track. From here I graduated to a couple of 1100's one of which was an MG and then a company Cortina XL no less in fluorescent custard yellow so that when I was flying into Glasgow and Edinburgh airports I could see it in the carpark and save time trying to remember where I had left it. It should be noted that this strategy does not work at all in Montreal where the cars are covered in a foot of snow for 6 months every year and was often even a bit dubious in a wintry Scotland. I had to wait 40 years to move to England to have car stolen and a further year to have the same car stolen twice in three days. The first time it was from the obviously unsecure car park of the five-star George Washington Hotel and then the second time a couple of days later was from the Sunderland Police car pound. The car finally turned up on the beach in Whitley Bay twenty miles north on the other side of the River Tyne. The fuzz dropped me off on the esplanade and when they saw the doors were open and the battery flat wished me every success it getting home again 200 miles to the south in Chester. The AA proved to be the equivalent of the 7th cavalry and started the car on jump leads. Since the car had also had the ignition lock barrel removed, they also made certain that the ignition was properly hotwired so that I could tip toe home over a period of about five hours driving. I think that driving my Rover 800 SDI gave me one of my very few tickets for speeding in my many miles behind the wheel. I was driving north through Glencoe on the A82 on a fine Sunday evening in dry conditions with no other vehicles on the road. As I approached the shore of Loch Leven to turn west to South Ballachulish the speed limit dropped from 60 to 50 and I slowed down. Just before the road turned to run along the southern shore of the loch, I noticed a police car parked behind a building and thought that they must be having a fallow spell if they were out looking for wrongdoers. After proceeding for a further few miles within the limit I noticed blue flashing lights in the distance behind me and slowed even further. The police land rover came right up behind me with flashing headlights so I pulled immediately over and stopped. Two enormous bobbies invited me to join them in the back of their vehicle. The car had an English registration and my licence showed my current English address so I got a lecture on rich English tourists in huge powerful motor cars putting the life and limb of the honest god-fearing local Scots population in jeopardy. I carefully weighed up the situation and decided to say absolutely nada as I had obviously woken two sleeping SNP dragons from their slumber. Two weeks later I got a summons from the procurator fiscal in Fort William. The envelope was addressed to me but inside they had managed to put the documents for a local highland tinker who had been drunk and disorderly in a local shebeen. What infuriated me was that they were fining the tinker less than they were fining me for my alleged offence. The fastest that I have ever travelled in a car was at about 150 mph in a new BMW 7 series on the unrestricted Autobahn between Dusseldorf and Cologne but on this occasion I was an apprehensive passenger being driven by a portly German who had just go the car that day and couldn't it seems figure out where all the controls were as he appeared not to be able to find the brakes. One of the slowest drives was for a few kilometres on an Autobahn running from Germany into France near Saarbrucken. When we eventually got to the dual customs posts on the actual border it seemed that the officials on the French side were working to rule or at least their interpretation of their rule which was to stop every single vehicle and to gaze at it for a short while. This seemed to affect cars with non-French registration marks more than any with French registration. As we rolled up to the barrier as two furious Brits in a German registered Mercedes with a German in the back the official mistook us all for Germans and held his hand up imperiously for us to stop and be overawed by him. I guess that he spoke English because of the look on his face when I wound down the window and told him loudly and clearly that it was great pity that the French had not stopped the Germans so efficiently in 1940. As we drove on, I noticed in the mirror that Wolfgang sitting in the back was looking very puzzled. I asked him what the problem was and after some thought he told me that they had not actually used that road as Germany invaded France through Benelux which was much shorter. Who said that the Erics had no sense of humour? This guy was comedy gold standard.

David and Goliath

The meeting was set for two o'clock in their office in Auckland with the MD the Technical Manager and the Sales Manager to try to interest them in representation or even in licencing the product range from a US engineering Company that was on offer to them as New Zealand partners. Exactly on two I was ushered into the MD's office. He introduced himself and offered coffee which was readily accepted before picking up the phone and asking his two colleagues to come in and join the meeting with us.

When the sales manager appeared, he was so big that he had to duck slightly to get through the door. It took only a few seconds for each of us to recognise the other. Twelve thousand miles away and twenty years earlier he had been the office boy in the office of the company Scotland in which we both started work. At the mail meeting in the morning when the post was taken into the MD's office to be opened and discussed he was the biggest guy in the room and he was only about eighteen.

My lunch hour usually consisted of a quick snack in the canteen and then developing photographs in a make shift dark room or making my version of Brylcreem with Gum Tragacanth. This tended to make my hair so hard I did not need a helmet when I was on the back of someone's motorbike. Other options occasionally included cleaning metal ornaments with CTF4 which we used to fill the fire extinguishers but which was actually hazardous with or without a fire or making pseudo soap which unfortunately was brown and a bit smelly and which with its caustic soda content remove the skin from your hands if overused. We also had some forays into dipping base metal int liquid mercury to make it look like Silver. Unfortunately, this could have been even more hazardous than messing with CTF4 and in any case the reaction usually still continued to work over time until in the end the metal became contaminated again. Some time was also occasionally given over to foraging for tiny scraps of platinum wire from used thermocouples as this was worth considerably much more than gold. The proceeds of this venture always went back to the company who were credited with the scrap value as none of us were intimately connected with bullion dealers. Jim, I think used to take a packed lunch suitable for a giant like him and eat it at his desk. He also used to play the other office boy Alan at chess but Alan got fed up with Jim towering above him during the game and took to sitting opposite him on the top of the back of a chair with his feet on the seat to elevate him another foot in the air. This gambit came to an early end however when Alan fell got excited fell off the back of the chair and seriously sprained his wrist.

Jim's brother was also called Alan and he equally large with even their sister June who had been in my class at school being taller than me. On Saturday nights Alan would go into the local dance hall and pass his ticket out through the toilet window so that Jim could use it to gain entry free of charge. Jim decided to take things a stage further one night and actually tried to climb in through the toilet window. Unfortunately for him his dimensions did not match those of the window frame and he got firmly stuck.

I don't know what tale Alan told the management but after they and the local police managed to extricate Jim from his predicament both he and Alan were barred from entry to the establishment for about 6 months although their legendary and probably exaggerated status seemed to enhance their street cred with the local Stirling female population.

How and when Jim made it to New Zealand, I really don't know but he seemed to be doing OK when I met him and I guess that a few Kiwis remember him affectionately even if they only met him once. They did not go ahead with licencing or representation because I think their parent organization wanted them to focus exclusively on selling the production from their own Whangerei brick plant as they needed to move tonnage. Many years later the Japanese company Shinagawa made a foray into Australia and New Zealand and bought up all of the local manufacturers and suppliers but I doubt that Jim waited around for that and I am sure that he enjoyed a well-earned and happy retirement in a land where the sun rises at least two hours earlier than it does in the so called "Land of the Rising Sun".

Dan, Dave and Bud

Dan was the CEO and a fully qualified chartered accountant or CPA as they are often referred to on the other side of the pond. At least he was not an actuary as they have been described in the past as accountants with all of the humour surgically removed. He ran the family firm which had been founded some seventy years before with his father as Chairman still looking over his shoulder on the few occasions that the old man ventured into the office which was kept aside for him to read his Wall Street Journal in. Dan was also on the board of management of the local bank as well as playing an active role in the local council of the small Ohio community that he lived and worked in. He had a pretty full and active life and he and his wife whose family was Spanish were very sociable. Dan was a bullshit free zone to the extent that one day when I asked him some fairly complex technical questions about one of the company's product ranges he told me outright that he had no idea but arranged for me to spend a day with their technical guru for an in depth discussion on the entire issue.

Dave their Sales and marketing VP was also a bullshit free zone and when a new product range was developed and introduced, he told major customers about it but added that it would probably be too expensive for them to invest in. When they learned of the technical advantages for the new range however and computed the substantial cost savings for themselves, they formed an orderly queue to purchase it. Together with their VP of technology they arranged a number of international technical seminars for their associates and these were supplemented by generous bursts of hospitality which sometimes included dinner for sixteen at a good restaurant. The dinner at Rainwaters in San Diego was so good that it exceeded the remaining limit on Dave's Amex card but the day was saved Dan immediately stepped up to the stump with his superior financial firepower. In Essen in Germany we all set out to dinner with the group in several Taxis and Dan and I had a bet as to who could pay for the taxi but give the lowest possible tip. Dan won because he did not give the driver anything and I hesitated to ask the driver for a discount on the metered price. The fun did not end there however as we had chosen a small German restaurant for its choice of local ethnic dishes of Goulash, Sausages, Pigs Knee, Schnitzels and Apple Strudel although not all on the one plate. The beer, wine and brandy were not bad either. Consternation ensued however when Dave discovered that that the restaurant did not take credit or debit cards at all which was not entirely unusual at that time. Dan saved the day by getting everyone present to put all their cash in a pile in the middle of the table to pay the bill against the issue of IOU's for each person's share. It was a pleasantly warm night and the hotel was not particularly far so we walked back.

Unfortunately, Dan sold the company just around the millennium to some east coast venture capitalists so that he could minimise death duties for the family if his father should die. The venture capitalists appointed one of their management to be the Chairman of the Board and the CEO, VP Sales and VP Technology all resigned en masse shortly after meeting him leaving the senior management of the company in the hands of someone who knew little or nothing of the business and gave me the distinct impression that he had no intention of making any effort to try and find out. Even in international meetings with licensees and customers the Chairman sat and read the WSJ while the discussion carried on around him. This period preceded smart phones by quite some years otherwise I am sure that he would have found some other way to show contempt for his colleagues and customers. Maybe it was actually for the best. At an international exhibition in Germany several of us arrived before the designated opening time of 09:00 hrs for visitors although exhibitors were being allowed access to man their stands. The Chairman decided that although only a visitor decided he would not wait for the official opening time and announced that he would show us how it was done in New York. Seconds later as he was frogmarched back out of the entrance to the exhibition, German security showed how it was done in Dusseldorf. He subsequently told me that in addition to his onerous duties as Chairman he filled in his spare time by lecturing on international business at an unnamed east coast college. When he invited me to look him up on his international.com website and gain the benefits from his long and extensive experience I managed to resist the temptation. With tongue pressed firmly in cheek I decided to set up my own global.com website. Let browsers draw their own conclusions as to whether this was even ever so slightly amusing. This situation could not last however and he soon instructed the new CEO to convince me that I would be happier seeking fame and fortune elsewhere. In fact, perhaps to his surprise this was the one thing that he got absolutely right. Shortly afterwards however he approached me again in San Francisco and offered to make me rich beyond my dreams by helping him buy and sell companies. Once more I was able to resist the lure. On a further occasion he contacted me yet again requesting that I assist him in selling a range of products into the European steel industry. Whatever the shortcomings of the European steel I decided that they did not deserve this and it was third time unlucky for him but probably third time lucky for the steel industry.

The Runaway Train

Whichever way you went it was a long way from Larbert. It required a very early rise and a drive to the airport. Then followed the tedium of checking in going through several layers of security and then two hours sitting amongst the multiplicity of shops selling overpriced so-called tax-free goods which you didn't really need and would be mad to buy and to lug around the world all the way back home again. A nine-hour flight across the north Atlantic with a final swoop down over the Canadian tundra and the great lakes deposited you in Chicago O'Hare airport. Unfortunately, about a dozen other "heavies" from all the main European destinations all arrived between two and three in the afternoon as well which meant that about two thousand passengers were all trying to clear US immigration and customs at much the same time. This delightful experience often took some time to accomplish which is why I often spent the first night in a hotel which was actually in or preferably close to the airport before then continuing my journey the following morning. There was nothing wrong with the Hilton in the airport except that it was in the airport so I usually tried an alternative like the Marriott which was only a short cab ride away. I seem to recall that the hotel was entirely fronted in gold tinted glass which made it spectacular as you flew in especially when the sun was low in the west. The whole stramash would take over twelve hours although with the five-hour time change the local time would only be early evening by the time you had a burger, beer, bath and bed. It was exhilarating however to wake quite early. One morning I rolled out of bed shuffled over to the huge east facing window and pulled back the drapes only to be confronted by an enormous jumbo jet heading straight for my twelfth-floor bedroom. It certainly woke me up to an unusual experience and took me several seconds to realise that it was further away than I had first thought, slightly higher than I had first thought and on course to pass the hotel about a mile to the south so that I would probably survive. Later in a spare moment on one of the airport car parks roofs I computed that aircraft using Chicgo's triangulated runways for landing and takeoff appeared to pass through the same airspace as often as only eight seconds apart. You certainly have to hope that none of the air traffic controllers was having as sleepy a day as I had that morning.

When I checked out it was to make an early start because I wanted to make the drive within the speed limit and still arrive well before lunch. I left the Sheraton hotel at O'Hare by eight o'clock and since it was almost on an intersection, I was soon headed south on Interstate 294 for a couple of junctions before driving almost due west on I 88 to Sterling Illinois. It may have been a small Midwestern town but the company I was going to see was of some significance. North Western Steel and Wire employed some four and half thousand people, making many thousands of miles of barbed wire amongst other steel products. They had the distinction at that time of operating three separates four-hundred-ton electric arc furnaces which were the biggest in the world. At over twenty-five metres diameter they were enormous units and the roofs had bricks which were individually suspended on wires from a spider's web network of steel beams. Approaching the site, I was confronted by an enormous scrapyard containing all shapes sizes and types of ferrous scrap towering almost thirty feet high in places and waiting to be crushed and re-melted again into finished product. The plant had been the first steel plant in the United States to use steam locomotives to move raw materials in and finished product out of the plant as well as transporting molten metal internally. I was quite astonished however to see apparently adjacent to the scrap half a dozen huge old black steam locomotives looking as they had come straight out of starring in an old western film. The chairman PW Dillon had apparently bought up number of these old locomotives as they had been withdrawn from active service on several American railroads the theory being that that they were a cheap form of scrap. Apparently, he had not had the heart to destroy any of them however and had even had the oldest of them cleaned up, transported and installed on his front lawn on Broadway Avenue overlooking the Rock River. It sure as hell beats garden gnomes into second place for ornamentation and the house which was built in the 1880's is now a historical monument and museum. The offices were situated in a traditional one-story wooden building next to the main plant. On entering the office, I found myself in a little reception area at the end of a long corridor lined whose floor was covered in old brown linoleum and which ran back through the whole length of the building. Sitting to one side there was an old man with a plaid shirt, dungarees, cowboy boots and a baseball cap reading the Chicago Tribune. I thought that he might be the janitor but we greeted each other amiably and enquired of him where I might find Mr Dillon the CEO with whom I had an appointment. He directed me to go along the corridor and knock on the wood panelled door at the end.

The CEO opened it himself and ushered me in for a coffee and a discussion on future cooperation. He seemed quite positive about being able to do business but asked if I could give him a few minutes so that he would just run everything past the chairman. Perhaps rather presumptuously I suggested that since I had come so far to visit the company, I might be allowed to meet him and say hello during my visit. My second surprise of the day was to be told that I had already met him sitting in his rocking chair in reception reading his favourite newspaper. It seemed that I had passed scrutiny since I got some drawings and a sizeable enquiry against which to quote. Indeed, the only fly in the ointment the whole day was when I got back to O'Hare and could not find the correct exit which would take me back across the Interstate 294 into the slip road leading to the hotel carpark. After traversing the toll gates three times the tollbooth keeper took pity on me and let me into the secret of which turn to make so that I was able to make it to the bar in perfect time for the start of Happy Hour.

Don't Rain on my Parade.

I spent one Chinese New Year period in San Francisco with my wife and unwisely decided to watch the seemingly endless New Year's parade which that year was held during a period of freezing rain on a wet Saturday in February. We were staying for a week in a boutique hotel on Geary street immediately off Union Square so I got the brilliant idea of going across the square into Macy's department store and watching everything from the warm dry comfort of their first-floor ladies fashion department. If we had been American, we would have been watching from the second floor which is what the Americans designate the first floor because they have already called the ground floor the first floor. When we did not buy anything however store security threw us back out into the cold wet street. So much for good old American hospitality and the special relationship I thought as we wended our way back across the square to our hotel in the Handlery Building and sought out the warmth and comfort of the bar. The parade itself had been interesting in that it was not something that we saw every day but to be honest it seemed to go on for ever. Almost every politician in northern California went by in his Cadillac followed by everyone else in California who had a Cadillac and a lot who did not. Local clubs, sports teams and majorettes skipped on by followed apparently by the entire city's gay community who seemed determined not to miss any kind of a parade even if it was mostly pissing down with cold rain. The parade even manged to include a number of dragons as well as a few hundred Chinese people with lanterns and banners some of which were inevitably adverts for the many Chinese restaurants through the large carved ceremonial gate in Bush Street two blocks away where Chinatown was officially located. The whole kitsch noisy cacophony was topped off by the constant sound of firecrackers which some "eejits" were throwing from the upper floors of the many tall buildings along the route of the procession in spite of this being wholly illegal of course and making the entire SFPD very jumpy. Anyone who imagines that California is permanently bathed in golden sunshine will never have been in San Francisco in February which is regularly cold and wet or in July or August when some pretty thick cold wet fogs roll into the bay. Most of the rest of the year the city has mild warm weather although I remember on one occasion in November driving north out of the city through bush fires burning fiercely just north of Oakland to reach Lake Tahoe and returning a couple of days later to Sacramento while being pursued by heavy snowfalls of up to a metre deep. If the weather does not inconvenience visitors there is always the chance of a sizable earthquake shaking things up. The last big one was 1989 when parts of the Nimitz Highway at the Cyprus Street viaduct and Oakland Bay bridge both collapsed and caused 63 deaths, nearly 3,800 injuries, and an estimated $6 billion in property damage. The earthquake struck at five o'clock local time just before the start of the third game of the 1989 baseball World Series, which was being played in Candlestick Park between the San Francisco Giants and the Oakland Athletics. The occurrence during a major live television broadcast meant that news of the earthquake, was well publicized immediately and aerial views of damage seen from the Goodyear blimp.

When I drove over to Oakland the following week the viaduct was still completely out of action and all traffic had to wend its way slowly between the rubble on temporary roads which had been hastily bulldozed and surfaced before full reconstruction began.

San Francisco lies at the northern end of the Sab Andreas fault which runs 500 miles almost due south west to the Mexican border just to the east of the Tijuana crossing. I have driven the length of the fault and to my utter amazement the small town of San Andreas founded in 1850 has three petrol filling stations built right on top of the fault. The fault in question being the area where the north American plate grinds up against the Pacific plate along a large part of the west coast of the United States in a valley between the beach and the Sierra Madre Mountain chain. Even worse was when I stopped for fuel and was asked by the filling station attendant where in Australia I was from when I wasn't even wearing my bush hat with corks hanging from the brim.

The 2010 census records 2750 people living in town and claims that 6% of them live in institutionalised accommodation so maybe that also included the lady in the garage The local real estate companies advertise cheap property prices which are no doubt popular with people who know little of geology and don't follow the local news much or maybe are from out of town since at the time of writing in 2020 the next big one is forecast as already overdue. Maybe it would be advisable to avoid wine tasting in the Temeecula vineyards for a few more seasons if you don't want to spill your drink.

Where There is Smoke There's Fire

I was never a member of the IRA but for many years was a member of the IRE and was even the President of the Institute of Refractories Engineers for the millennium year 1999 to 2000. This was really pretty sophisticated by that time and the annual dinner dance was held in the Cutlers Hall in Sheffield and was attended by over two hundred and fifty people including all sorts of luminaries. Back in the sixties not long after formation of the Institute the annual branch dinner dance in Scotland was held in the Normandy Hotel in Renfrew which is less than five hundred meters from the end of the main runaway at Abbottsinch airport and within two hundred meters of the flightpath for all of the traffic which mainly lands from the southeast. On a calm summer evening the sound of a BEA Trident going into full reverse thrust could certainly be heard much further afield. Maybe it was the burgeoning popularity of James Bond at the time but the Chairman of the Scottish branch that year decided to swap his black bow tie and dinner suit for a white tuxedo with tartan bow tie and cummerbund. The effect was slightly spoiled however when some of the brickies and briquettes who did not know him mistook him for the Maitre D' and requested to be escorted to their table. Most people fell into bed after midnight but a few thirsty souls kept the bar open until two O'clock in the morning. No doubt unhappy that the noise of the aircraft had ceased for the night and most revellers had dropped into an alcohol induced deep slumber they decide that on the way to bed they would set off the fire alarm. If I had not been so drowsy and could have found the fire extinguisher more quickly, the idiots who set the alarm off would definitely have been covered in foam. This was the very first hotel fire that I was never in because there was no fire. The second occasion was also after an Institute of Refractories Engineers dance in Middlesbrough when everyone was bussed back from the function suite to a motel on the outskirts of the city. This time the fire alarm was accompanied by firemen banging on the doors and shouting on everyone to evacuate. The fire was in the kitchen of a restaurant in a separate main building but we were still turfed out into the car park in the middle of the night. Breakfast next morning was coffee and toast and they even managed to burn too. The third occasion was in a modern high-rise hotel in Leeds when on hearing the fire alarm one Sunday evening and looking down into the car park I saw a couple of fire appliances with flashing blue lights and evacuated like everyone else only to find it was false alarm. The fourth occasion was more dramatic and was in Charlotte North Carolina. I had arrived from the UK and feeling tired had gone to bed at about 21:30. By about 22:30 the fire alarm which was klaxon went off at well over 100 decibels. This was accompanied by a verbal instruction to evacuate over a public address system and the emergency lighting kicking on in all the public areas like corridors. My grandfather after whom I had been named had been in the royal navy and I believe served in the battle of Jutland. Two of his sons, my uncles had also been in the Royal Navy. One story that he had told me when I was very young was that when on active service naval personnel did not always undress to go to bed and always knew exactly where all their kit was so that they could dress and evacuate quickly in the dark. I was never in the Senior Service although I might have smoked one or two but the story stuck. When I checked into hotels, I always looked for the fire instructions that were usually tacked to the back of the door and very seldom ever completely unpacked. On that occasion I had only hand luggage so it took about 30 seconds to dress roughly and bail out into the corridor turn left and head down the fire stairs to reception and out onto the street.

The klaxon kept blaring and to be honest that was very stressful but the hotel guests made their way down the fire stairs in the concrete shaft in the centre of the building with no panic. At the bottom we were met by hotel staff and directed outside onto the wide "sidewalk. I thought that some of the other guests looked a bit weird in their various stages of undress. They probably thought that I looked weird fully dressed with my luggage but I had decided that I was not going to be leaving the hotel without clothes, money or passport since the time difference was only going to be a few seconds in any case. This too turned out to be a false alarm but was the nearest that I came to be being burned to the ground. I must say that the Charlotte fire department and hotel staff handled the situation with great professionalism and not as I feared like the Keystone Cops and Buster Keaton might have done forty years before.

Hello Sailor.

Four queens is certainly not the worst poker hand in the world that you can be dealt in a game but four queens in an elevator is not in my humble opinion the best situation ever to be found. They were each about seven feet tall because they all had six-inch heels and beehive coiffure. Each of them seemed to be trying to outdo Shirley Temple in atire, Dame Edna Everedge in delivery and Louie Spence in locomotion. My wife and I had just flown from Manchester via London to Los Angeles followed by an hour in customs and immigration and a further hour and a half in a limousine before finally reaching Queensway Drive on the seafront in Long Beach California. After more than 18 long hours in total in transit I just wanted to check in to a comfortable hotel room and relax. The last thing I wanted was to be surrounded by four big ugly shrieking pantomime dames in a lift. To be fair it was quite a big lift and we were fortunately not jammed codpiece to codpiece. We walked from the quayside across thick steel decking and into "R" Deck of the RMS Queen Mary before being transported up to the reception area two levels above on "A" Deck. We turned left to the reception desk and after quickly being checked in were shown to our firstclass cabin A004. Our temporary cabaret had gone full steam ahead to who knows where to splice their mainbraces, shiver their timbers, haul their keels or perhaps were headed to the stern of the ship where a mariachi band was giving it laldy at a Mexican wedding which was in full cucuracha on the small external sun deck area. Maybe they are all still all stowing away under the canvas covers of one of the 24 lifeboats. Our cabin was not large but was panelled in wood and with all the fixtures and fittings which were then available in 1934 with the addition of a modern telephone and a colour television. One of the portholes looked out over the main entrance where a large illuminated sign proclaimed the "Hotel Queen Mary". Built in 1934 in Glasgow by John Brown and their 300,000 workers and contractors the ship had experienced and made some epic events in its short existence life before being permanently installed in Long Beach harbour and opened in May 1971 as a fine luxury Hotel. It's certainly the only luxury hotel that I have stayed in so far as I know that boasted two 40,000 hp steam turbines which used to propel it and giving 13 feet to the gallon of fuel, driving through four propellers. It also has its own antiaircraft gun currently located just outside the main Observation bar at the front of the promenade deck. I clambered up into the gunner's seat one day and although I still don't know if it was a Vickers, Bofors, or Oerlikon, I know that it was a twin barrel gun firing two streams of 20 mm shells and fiery tracer rounds at a high rate of knots which would discourage almost everyone except maybe a Kamikaze. It's also probably the only ship in the world set into its own car park. I was also fascinated inside the bar where the bar counter seemed to be a very long continuous semi-circle with no hatch and the barmen had to vault the counter every single time that he needed to collect empties from tables. I much regret that I never actually saw him vault the counter to deliver a full tray of drinks to customers even although I spent time almost every evening looking forward to just such an event during a happy hour that always lasted for at least 120 minutes. There were various other bars and restaurants around the ship ranging from the Chelsea room where we ate breakfast to the Sir Winston which was where we had our anniversary dinner. The ship was itself surrounded by other attractions such as a captured Russian Skorpion class submarine where the food and décor and creature comforts were non-existent. Located nearby there was the billionaire, Howard Hughes Spruce Goose flying boat which featured a variety of eateries within its enormous domed hangar. They did not serve food on the plane itself although with its 200 tons fuselage they easily could have done. The Spruce Goose is fantastic although neither spruce nor goose. It was and still is one of the world's largest aircraft which cost about $300 million dollars in today's money to develop and build but only ever managed to fly for about one mile at a height of about 70 feet. The construction of the giant eight engine aircraft is mainly in laminated birch wood for maximum lightness and strength. The Hughes Aircraft Corporation H-4 registration No NX 37602 was built in sections and then assembled at a pier on Terminal Island Long Beach California which is today a modern container terminal. Its only flight took place on 2nd November 1947 in the bay at the mouth of the Los Angeles River. It was designed to be operated by a crew of three but its only short flight had twenty crew on board which was certainly not a major problem as it did not have a cockpit as such and the flight deck extended back into the main fuselage itself as there was no intervening bulk head. It had been first intended to ferry about 700 troops on each flight between the USA and Europe but effectively missed the war by two years. With a top speed of about 250 mph it would have taken about 14 hours to fly from New York to London although it could not have made it without a refuelling stop in any case and could not have been comfortable transportation for troops going into battle. Subsequently it was moored locally and maintained until after Howard Hughes death in 1976. In 1980 it was acquired by the Aero Club of Southern California and displayed in a vast hanger which Walt Disney used to shoot scenes for several films including "Titanic" but it now resides in the Evergreen Aerospace Museum near Portland in Oregon. When I visited the Spruce Goose it was in its Long Beach hanger next to the cruise ship terminal and was an incredible sight inside and out especially its vast flight ballroom like open flight deck.

Not content with the fantastic aircraft itself local entrepreneurs set up the Ports O' Call village called London one of whose attractions was a "Scotch" shop selling tartans, souvenirs and ancestral charts along with the inevitable burger's coffees and ice creams although seriously lacking in oatcakes bridies, mutton pies and Irn Bru. Seeing the plane and ship in close proximity it is even possible that many Americans really thought that the Queen Mary had been built in England or even that Scotland had been built in England since the Scottish heritage centre was inside London Towne To be fair although it was the largest shop they also had Mexican, Italian and many other varied retail theme experiences to hoover up maximum sales from every corner of the Globe even if it never had actual corners. Howard Hughes was incensed at its nickname and called it the H4 but after his death it reverted to Spruce Goose because who was going to pay good money to see an H4. It's indeed a wonder that they did not rename the RMS Queen Mary as Scary Mary but have gone at least part way by promoting supernatural viewing points in parts of the ship which are alleged to be haunted and where Ghosts may be seen. I can only guess that these are most probably old John Brown and his 300,000 subcontractors turning in their collective graves.

Look Maw Nae Hauns

One of the two standard approaches for the BEA Shuttle from Glasgow to Heathrow was to turn left and then go into a wide slow turn to the east over Maidenhead. It would then fly almost due east down the ILS instrument landing system flight path to land on the northern runway 09L/27R. This usually involved sinking slowly down into the clouds and then shortly afterwards remerging under them to get a good view of Windsor Castle on the left of the aircraft before touching down and deplaning in terminal one. On one such approach I was amazed to hear an American couple in the row in front discussing why the Queen had allowed Windsor Castle to be built so close to the flight path as the noise of the planes would surely be at the very least a minor inconvenience even if she was double glazed. It did not seem to be a problem on that morning however as the weather was pretty crap and underneath the clouds there was still what seemed to be a layer of thick dense fog so that Windsor castle was completely obscured from view as was everything else on the ground. I was not at all cheered up by this since I assumed that when the plane had descended to around one thousand feet of vertical height from the ground the pilot would give all three of the engines full throttle and we would be off to sunny Gatport Airwick to try to land on their overcrowded single runway. There was no way for me to gauge the height but I did brace my feet on the supports of seat in front since I knew from experience that we were close to a decision being taken and if implemented I anticipated the rapid acceleration and climb. Of the aircraft back out of the murk. Much to my considerable astonishment and relief however there was a gentle thud as the wheels touched the runway and the Trident engines were put into reverse thrust and flaps fully deployed. My surprise was even greater when instead of the steward announcing our safe arrival the pilot himself came onto the PA system to welcome us to Heathrow and to casually announce that we had just done a category three fully automatic landing where the vertical visibility had been less than 70 feet and the horizontal visibility less than 750 feet. This meant that at close to 200 mph on touchdown we had been less than five seconds flying time away from any large object on the runway. Fortunately, air traffic ground patrols in their bright yellow land rovers had ensured that no large objects like another aircraft or even extremely small ones like a stray goat had been left on the runway. This was one of the first fully automatic category three landings of a BEA Shuttle ever carried out although the system had of course undergone extensive proving tests before being deployed in the mid nineteen seventies on the paying public. I am not certain whether it was the pilot or me who was more relieved to be taxiing to the gate behind the land rover with the illuminated Follow Me sign. It had not always been as high tech and convenient as this however as some years before I had boarded a BEA flight in Paris Charles de Gaulle airport which was scheduled for London Heathrow which but which diverted to Le Touquet in north western France. Because Europe was cut off from the UK by a thick blanket of fog in the channel and over most of southern England we were then bussed to Calais and set out to return to England on an overnight cross channel ferry. This then ran the gauntlet of the busiest shipping channel in the world in a dense pea souper fog. When we were eventually able to disembarked from the freezing wet vessel in England, we had to take a taxi to Dover Priory station and then a train to London St Pancras, the tube to Heathrow and a shuttle flight onwards up to Glasgow as the fog had by that time largely dispersed. Such fun when Europe is totally cut off and isolated from the British Isles. Perhaps one of my other unconventional approaches to Heathrow was the time when I flew back from Greece with my trusty hand baggage and large additional plastic bag full of oranges. If you have never actually tasted a fresh orange plucked and eaten straight from the tree in a fragrant orange grove then you may not fully appreciate just how different it is from the one you buy in the supermarket a month later even if it is in a cardboard box and has leaf still clinging to its little stem. If you have never carried about ten kilos of fresh oranges the length of Heathrow you may not fully realise just how heavy they can become. The immigration officer had no reason to delay me at his desk and waved me through but I could see that the customs squad was going to be a different matter as I staggered towards them smelling like a vegan juice bar. To thwart there obviously eagerly anticipated interception en masse I swerved into the red channel and laid my two bags on the counter. I agreed that the bags were mine and that I had packed them myself but this was where customs started to run out of what I thought were sensible questions. I confirmed the officer's suspicion that they were indeed oranges. They looked at them, hefted some of them in their hands to gauge the weight of each, felt the texture and sniffed them. They got some magnifying glass from somewhere and examined the skins for signs of needle punctures or surface cuts. Around then they seemed to run out of ideas but I was still taking the fifth amendment as I had no idea if fruit was able to be legally imported into the UK far less any arcane regulations that might apply if and when it was. Apparently, the customs men didn't either and were disinclined to consult the Brussels Tariff Nomenclature documents available to them as they ran to several thousand pages and it was getting near to the end of their shift. Maybe the pack of beagles they employ to sniff drugs now hadn't been recruited in those days but in any case, I got the green light to make for the door. I had thought to offer them each an orange which would at least have lightened my load somewhat but I thought to hell with it let them source their own bloody oranges.

And Don't Come Back

There I was at La Guardia, New York's second airport. It was eight-o clock in the morning. I had checked out of the Hilton and had taken a yellow cab to the airport where I checked in with American Airlines for Santo Domingo. After getting my luggage off my hands I relaxed and went I search of a coffee to help me wake up and a newspaper to find out what was happening in the world. There had been many announcements over the P A system and eventually it was like electronic wallpaper there in the background but almost un- noticed as they relayed messages about arriving and departing flights. Eventually one of the announcements intruded into my thoughts however and I realised that they were repeating a message asking a Mr Jarvis to go to the nearest white courtesy telephone call to take a message. It could not possibly be for me because no one knew precisely where I was at that exact moment in time. Once more the message was repeated and I thought that I had better at least check if it was for me or for someone else with a similar name. When I walked up to the American Airlines desk the girl smiled and indicated a white telephone, which I picked up. No sooner had I put it to my ear than I was greeted with a torrent of abuse in Greek. This took me ever so slightly by surprise and it was some seconds before I was able to halt the flow of the person at the other end. Eventually I realised that it was a client and friend from Athens and that he was not a happy chappy. From the tone of the encounter so far however I was convinced that it was my ex client and ex friend but I still had no idea why. The explanation when he was able to calm down and give me it was simple. He had a very large order with us which had taken over six months to manufacture and was at that very moment sitting on the dock n Liverpool ready to be swung over the rail of a vessel headed for Piraeus. This was the tear however when Britain was suffering from raging inflation which briefly touched 25%. Since it had taken so long to process the order my boss had decided that he was justified in telexing the client to advise him the that the price had gone up by a modest 10% which would have to be agreed to before the goods were loaded. I told him that I had no inkling of this cunning ruse and advised him that since it was eight am in New York, one PM in Glasgow and four PM in Athens I would get back to him first thing next morning. As I phoned the UK, I tried to figure how he had been able to find me. Maybe he had a cousin who worked with Lieutenant Kojak. When I finally got through, I found my boss adamant that the price increase was fair and reasonable in the circumstances and I had to relay that back to Greece. The customer agreed to pay the increase and never bought another thing from us.

One the flight down to Santo Domingo the plane was subjected to enormous turbulence as we flew through the Bermuda Triangle and I was sure that it was a punishment from Zeus but that's another story.

Kelly's Mountain Sydney NS

We sat in the lounge at Dorval, which was Montreal's airport and we waited and we waited. We had already flown the Atlantic from Prestwick to Montreal in a BOAC 707. This was a six-and-a-half-hour flight with the sun which meant that when we landed at three o clock local time it was already eight o clock in the evening. It took a further hour to go through customs and immigration and to transfer from the international to the domestic terminal This made it four o clock local time and the Air Canada flight to Sydney was not until five o clock. Sydney I should explain was Sydney Nova Scotia not Sydney new South Wales. For years Sydney could only be reached by a three and a half-hour flight due east on an ageing four engined Britannia propjet. With the flight time and the one-and-a-half-hour time change between Quebec and the Maritimes I used to arrive at my final destination not knowing whether I was coming or going. On this visit however I was pleased to see that Air Canada were now operating one of their DC9 jets and this I calculated would knock at least forty-five minutes of the journey. This meant forty-five minutes earlier to bed when I eventually arrived and I looked forward to that. This was not to be the case today however as severe snowstorms had closed the airport down at Sydney and our jet still sat at the gate empty. Normally Sydney was easy to find from the air. A plume of orange red iron oxide dust, which emitted from the steel plant stack and spread eastwards on the prevailing winds, would streak the crisp white covering of snow. At twenty-four thousand feet you could see this from nearly fifty miles away on a clear day. This was not a clear day however. Dusk was falling rapidly and a blizzard was raging across a wide area on the eastern seaboard. Suddenly the flight was called and the plane rapidly departed. The weather forecasters were predicting a window where the gale would abate and the snow stop for a few short hours sufficient for the plane to reach its destination safely. About two hours into the flight the captain informed us however that the forecasters had been too optimistic and that the snow was again blanketing Sydney. Rather than return all the way to Montreal the captain proposed to divert to Halifax to refuel and to reconsider his next move. It was not snowing in Halifax but the temperature was well below zero and there was a stiff breeze blowing. When we alighted from the plane, we had been warned about the conditions but I was unprepared for the events of the next few minutes. I found myself with knees slightly bent and with arms outstretched to keep my balance being blown across the ice from the plane to the terminal building. Fortunately, someone opened the glass doors when I reached them and I sailed right into a bright warm lounge. By ten-o clock the captain had made up his mind to terminate the flight at Halifax for the night and to continue the next day if possible. He advised us all to find a bed for the night and to check again in the morning. After some discussion our party decided that instead of finding a hotel or motel, we would rent a car and drive the rest of the way. By midnight we had enjoyed a hot meal, rented a car and were heading out of the airport on our hundred- and fifty-mile drive to Sydney. In the UK this might have taken us three or four hours but not in this case. Years later I am still not sure whether we made the right decision. Much of the road we travelled was in bright moonlight and with the car heater at full blast we were not fully aware of how cold it was outside. When we got higher up into the mountains it was starkly beautiful but on reflection, we must have been stark staring mad. At some points we ran into small snowstorms where the wind drove the snow horizontal and made the driving even more hazardous. Not that we were driving fast even with chains on our tyres because the several inches of fresh snow on the road covered sheet ice. We crossed Kelly's mountain in the early hours of the morning and by six were coming down into the outskirts of Sydney just as it got light. In Sydney there was about nine inches of new snow and not even the snowploughs had been out to disturb it. As we made it to the motel, we were not surprised to find that our rooms were still available but the staff in the hotel were amazed to see us. After a few hours' sleep and a good breakfast, we were off to the steel plant to keep our appointment. The personnel there were no less amazed than the staff at the hotel and after a short discussion to clarify a few important points rewarded us with a very large contract.

States of Matter

Solid, liquid, gas and plasma, are four states of matter. I have seen all of the Great Lakes in North America in all of the first three forms but not necessarily all at the same time. I have visited most of them on both sides of the border between America and Canada during all four seasons of the year over a period of a number of years.

Looking east and north from Chicago over a frozen Lake Huron in the middle of each winter with the lake frozen solid. there are sheets of ice as far as the eye can see.

If you leave the Chicago Hilton and walk due east for about half a mile along the broad sidewalk of East Balbo Drive which runs through Grant Park to the South Lakeshore Drive and the parallel Lakeshore trail it takes you to within about 20 yards of the shore of Lake Huron. In the winter the temperature can drop to well below zero even on a sunny day and the wind coming off the lake can freeze your eyelashes and provide a sensation that every time you breathe you are being stabbed in the throat. In January average daily temperatures are about -12 degrees C but the wind chill factor makes it feel so very much colder. The wind also carries ice from the surface of the lake onto the shore and deposits it as a jumble of boulders several metres wide at the water's edge. This would prevent access to the Lake itself assuming anyone would be daft enough to want to go out onto the frozen surface. Not for nothing is Chicago known as the windy city but in the dead of winter with snow and ice the shore is transformed by ice random sculptures which needless to say are frozen very solid.

It is very pleasant cruising north from Port Clinton over a placid flat calm liquid Lake Erie reflecting the sun's rays off the surface of the water in late afternoon. It is most definitely a time for sunglasses and sun screen although you can be fooled because the jet powered catamarans can get up to 40 miles per hour as they speed across the water to Put In Bay in twenty five minutes. This is fast enough to ruffle your hair if you are on the top deck but not fast enough to ripple your drink if you are in the bar. The ferry disembarks its passengers at the main pier downtown in Put In Bay which has a few guest houses, small hotels and restaurants set in a pleasant rural area on the small Island of South Bass. The highlight of the visit for me was undoubtedly the fish and chips chased down by two pints of chilled lager in overlooking the marina. While the lowlight was perhaps the Perry memorial column which towered only 350 feet high on the edge of the village

This commemorates the defeat in September 1812 of a British fleet of six warships commanded by Scotsman Robert Heriot Barclay by an American fleet of nine vessels led by Oliver Hazard Perry. The British fleet was there to guard the supply lines between Port Dover in Ontario and Fort Malden south of Detroit Michigan. All I can say is that the Americans obviously had an extremely unfair advantage because the British ships would have had to have sailed from the UK, up the Saint Lawrence river and across Lake Ontario before going over the Niagara Falls to get to where the battle took place just south of Rattlesnake Island. I think that this might have had some small bearing on the outcome although naturally I am not biased in the very slightest. Interestingly for me the town of Jarvis Ontario is adjacent to port Dover so maybe an ancestor jumped ship after going over the falls and set up a little settlement to retire.

On an earlier occasion I flew north northwest from Toronto on Lake Ontario to Sault Ste Marie Ontario Canada which lies on the very southeast corner of Lake Superior.

The great lakes are just under 100,000 square miles and are the largest surface area of fresh water in the world, while amounting to about 20% of the world's fresh water.

They were formed by glaciation about 14000 years ago and some of them are quite relatively shallow in parts which leads to an interesting micro climate because of the relative heating and cooling of the water and the land.

On the day of my flight we were in a small Japanese YS11 twin engine turboprop operated by Transair, which made the flight at a maximum height of about 10,000 feet, which put us firmly in the middle of a huge aerial storm which sprang up quite quickly soon after we had left Toronto. The plane with about 40 passengers and crew was thrown around like a leaf in what was a considerable gale and nobody was enjoying any part of the flight. The windows on the Japanese plane were set lower down than in a western built aircraft presumably because Japanese people on average are not as tall as westerners. This resulted in us having a ring side seat of the lake and the sky which were extremely difficult to tell apart and most of the time the view was of water vapour swirling around like steam from a boiling kettle. I swore that if I survived the flight that I would rather walk the 450 miles back along the length of the Trans-Canada Highway. I did survive the flight and did not have to walk back because we returned on a larger Jet which flew at 30.000 feet above nearly all of the clouds after the storm had abated. In the words of the locals "If you don't care Fly Transair".

No, I have no anecdote covering Plasma the fourth state of matter except to say that occasionally in Summer I benefit like everyone else does from a few rays of sunshine.

Hot Cuisine

The average American it is said is struggling with obesity but so far as I can see none of them are struggling very hard as between them, they munch through over 20 billion US Dollars, worth of food each year, or is that each day. I have seen an American at a breakfast buffet in Phoenix Sky Harbour airport piling a plate so high with food that some of it was sliding off the edges of the plate back onto the table. I wondered if this was better or worse than half filling the plate and getting the exercise of going back to the table twice for more food. I was only relieved that I was not sitting next to him on the plane or even on the same flight as I might have been crushed against the window by the hulk or the aircraft might not even have got off the ground if there were two or more of them. Maybe Pratt and Whitney engines have more oomph than Rolls Royce.

A restaurant in Milwaukee called the Safe House and located at 779 W Front Street has been advertising themselves since 1966 as a secret restaurant for U.S. spies and other espionage operatives with hidden access and wall to wall spy décor. They claim that without the password it is impossible to gain entry through the door marked International Exports behind which lurks the chef Oh Oh Seven. Their claim is that on orders from the CIA their spy restaurant opened in 1966 and has remained a covert operation to hide spies ever since. To conceal high priority agents, they claim to have created an elaborate low-lit espionage destination full of hidden doors, with two-way mirrors, and secret labyrinths of corridors. To be sure you're not an enemy informant, a clearance test is required to enter, but don't worry, as they have never been known to turn away a hungry spy who had any kind of valid credit card or negotiable foreign hard currency. On the day that I visited them I had to enter through a reproduction red British telephone box set against an outside wall where you picked up the receiver and dialled the secret code to allow the wall to slide open to allow entry. The secret code was printed on a large placard on the wall of the telephone box so breaking the code took even less than five seconds as it was designed not to delay potential diners. It has to be said that the menu was totally uninspiring but no one has died yet as result of eating their burgers as far as I know. It is one of the few restaurants in the world where diner's reviews seem to concentrate on a bizarre imaginary theme rather than on the food.

Continuing on the theme of odd themes the Nagoya Japanese Steak House and Sushi Bar might not immediately be expected to be operating near Sandusky in Ohio. From the outside it certainly looks authentic and inside it also appears to be fairly authentic with an all Asian looking staff and dozen or so Hibachi grills as well as regular tables. Our group was seated around one of the Hibachis which are large stainless steel table tops heated from underneath by gas burners. The iced water Sake and salads were served and then the celebrity chef appeared on the other side of the table nonchalantly juggling several large razor-sharp knives. One of these he used to chop vegetables and then he mixed these with bean sprouts and oil and started grilling them. After a few minutes cooking out came the shrimps and these were added in for the last thirty seconds. To check if the shrimps were ready, he indicated that he would flip one on a spatula for one of the groups to leap like a seal and catch it in their mouth to general applause. For an encore he indicated that he would flip one to me but I shook my head and said "I am not an American". Undeterred he flipped it anyway and I moved my head so that it hit the wall behind me and fell onto the carpet. It is not true that Orientals are inscrutable as I can confirm to you that his face was seriously scrutable.

While heading for Inco at Copper Cliff to visit the smelter now owned by Vale the Brasilian company we stopped for lunch in Sudbury where Trip Advisor claims that a Restaurant called "Tommy's Not Here" is number 1 out of 300 joints. My visit however predated Trip Advisor at a time when I seriously suspect Sudbury only had one restaurant whose name, I don't recall but it was probably on the right side of Town. and may have been the forerunner of "Tony V's" which claims to do Canadian, Italian and Greek food with equal ease or difficulty. Not that it would have mattered as Inco had a stack which at a height of 1250 feet was the tallest in the world at that time, designed to take the sulphurous fumes far away to the Eskimos. The stack with its plume of poisonous white smoke could be seen for many miles so it was hard to get lost in that part of Canada. The restaurant was busy as it would be if there were not many around even though it was very basic. I don't remember a menu but the waiter told us that the special of the day was stuffed cabbage leaves although he was vague on what they were stuffed with. I asked him what else was on the menu and he confirmed that there were only stuffed cabbage leaves. Faced with this tough choice I

chose the cabbage leaves although I am still vague as to what they were stuffed with although in fact would probably prefer not to know even today as I can be squeamish.

Greased Lightning

It is reliably estimated that the planet earth is struck by more than 8000 large bolts of lightning in any 24-hour period. Most people's first reaction to this is to think that this is ridiculously high number and to dismiss it as hyperbole. If you calculate this on the basis of the total surface area of the earth then it is only one lightning bolt per 6400 square kilometres and if you consider that most of these strikes are in the tropics and seventy per cent of the earth's surface is water then this maybe explains why most people in the UK don't see lightning all that regularly. In America the Federal Aviation Administration estimates that commercial jet airliners in the US are struck by lightning once every 1,000 flight hours, or once each year, on average. Planes can even trigger lightning themselves by flying through ionized clouds and each flash can easily have up to a billion volts power. Lightning strikes on aircraft are almost never fatal unless you have a weak heart and not been told that they are almost never fatal. My strikes came in the late seventies and the early eighties and seemingly proves that lightning can strike twice although since then I have not been struck a third time due to cutting back on travel quite substantially and not standing under trees in the rain on golf courses or anywhere else for that matter.

In 1978 I was flying from Miami Florida to Kingston Jamaica which is a relatively short flight of less than 600 miles taking less than two hours in an Air Jamaica DC 9.

About half way through the flight when the plane was flying over central Cuba in the early evening the weather deteriorated and it got very dark very quickly. The plane was not flying very high and the cumulonimbus clouds started below us and towered above us to almost thirty thousand feet. As the thunderstorm started bolts of lightning flashed between clouds and lit up the interior of the plane with an intense white light. I don't know how the crew did it but they persuaded passengers to close the window blinds and put on an impromptu fashion parade to distract everybody from the bad weather outside. It worked very well until the plane was stuck by lightening directly and the entire cabin was brightly illuminated throughout even with the blinds shut. This was one occasion where the models would have been happy not to be in the spotlight.

In the early eighties I was travelling from Australia to New Zealand and chose Pan Am flight 002 which started in New York and flew eastbound round the world to San Francisco. Meanwhile flight 001 originated in San Francisco and then flew westbound round the world ending up in New York. Fortunately, they never met in mid- air partly because on different days they called at different cities on the way to maximise their business and neither flight was allowed to carry passengers over the continental USA. The Sydney to Aukland leg was operated as was the entire route by a Boeing 747 jumbo jet in gleaming aluminium with the Pan Am logo in blue and white high on the tail. I had gone for lunch in Sydney before boarding the plane and while waiting for the plane to embark and depart was quite surprised to see that the sky turned almost black very quickly. I think in fact that the plane loaded and left promptly or even early because of the deterioration in the weather. As we taxied out onto the runway the storm broke and all hell was let loose with torrential rain and thunder and lightning. The captain must have thought that his best option was to get the plane out of Sydney as fast as he possibly could and he gunned it down the runway on maximum throttle. With the engines roaring he headed south to take off over Botany bay before planning on making a sharp right hander to the east. At a height of maybe three hundred feet there was an enormous blue flash followed by an huge bang and the plane shook and shuddered for a couple of seconds which was long enough for me to think that I was sitting on about thirty tons of kerosene and that I would prefer not to be n a storm. The plane was still on full power and climbing but the captain levelled off slightly and was presumably running a few checks on his instruments and underwear. Both of those seemed to pass scrutiny however as he quickly resumed full power and kept climbing at maximum rate. After a while he came on the intercom and announced that the plane had been struck by lightning shortly after taking off. This for me fell into the category of what John Cleese would have classified as a statement of the bleeding obvious. He also announced that the flight attendants would shortly becoming through the cabin with the drinks trolleys none of which fortunately had suffered any damage.

On arrival in Aukland some three and a half hours later a number of the alighting passengers including myself deplaned down the front steps onto the tarmac and saw signs of the strike on the nose of the plane above the first-class cabin and below the flight deck. At this stage they were already calling in specialist engineers to check out the area of impact and other controls before the plane set out again for the seven hour flight to Nadi in Fiji with a fresh crew complete with fresh underwear as well as a replenished drinks trolley which had been pretty well depleted on the incoming leg.

The City of Rain

No not Rotherham but the city of Rasht the capital of Gilan Province in northern Iran. The city sits just a few kilometres south of a fairly narrow shoreline on the southern coast of the Caspian Sea and was encircled by the Soviet Union. It is not encircled by the USSR now of course but by Azerbaijan on the west and Turkmenistan on the east. In the early seventies it was bandit country where kidnappings and ransoming were not totally unknown although to be fair this entrepreneurial flair was unknown to me. One of the top four-star addresses in town today is the unfortunately named Shabestan Hotel but my abode at that time was a much humbler guest house recommended by the client company that I was visiting. Whether they had no restaurant or in a spirit

of adventure and stupidity not necessarily in that particular order I found myself in a taxi heading north to the Caspian coast, looking for somewhere for my evening meal. There are a few restaurants by the side of route 49 today some of which trip advisor promotes as good for casual dining. The one that I was dropped off at by the taxi was certainly one of those. So casual in fact that it had no tables or chairs but only a few cushions spread around on a what was obviously a Persian rug since I was in Persia.

The Maitre D' was quite obviously amazed and no doubt thrilled to have a foreigner stumble into his barn but on recovering invited me with exaggerated gestures to sit anywhere in the almost empty room. Fortunately, with the universal signage for "gies a drink" a large glass of Raki immediately materialised along with a jug of iced water.

This made ordering from the non-existent menu which would in any case have been scrawled on goatskin parchment in Farsi a very much simpler mime than it might otherwise have been. I don't recall the starter although it could have been caviar and beetroot soup due to the proximity of the Caspian and Russia as was. The main course however was undoubtedly fried Caspian seagull with cherry sauce although it could have been roasted Albatross with plum sauce since the Raki had numbed my taste buds and much else besides since I felt no pain at all while sitting on the thin cushions. I decided to miss out on the Baklava and black coffee since by this time a few young people from the nearest village had come in to see the unusual visitor. A few words of French and German mixed with even fewer words in English however established that we were all comrades even although we all saw the same sun but may not all have seen the same fun. Such good comrades in fact that they taught me my first Russian swear word Blin which in English translates as Pancakes and might possibly not offend either a bishop or an actress if inadvertently blurted out at home. Eventually I paid the Maitre D' in Iranian Rials and he gave me an imaginary Farsi receipt for my expenses. Somebody managed to conjure up a taxi that I managed to struggle into and made my way back to a good night's sleep in my hotel in Rasht. It seems that I was obviously not worth kidnapping or possibly deemed to be far too much trouble to incarcerate in any of their woodsheds. I confess however that I was slightly concerned at one point the following day when the manager of the plant that I was visiting asked me to stop and stand up against a pock marked stone wall. It seemed that he did indeed want to shoot me but only with new his Japanese 35 mm camera. It is possible that the photo when it was developed and printed was destined for the Savak secret police archives and if so, may by now be on the most wanted list in the Iranian Revolutionary Guard archives. If that is in fact the case I can solemnly assure them that not only am I still the same handsome figure that I was then but that the chances of me being back in their area are now very considerably slimmer than I currently am at my mature time of life and that they can surely relax on my account.

Voodoo You Think You Are

I have no real reason to disbelieve whoever it was who told me that Port Au Prince Haiti has an Airport although when I started to go there in the seventies, I would have described it perhaps more as an Airstrip. From memory it had no ILS instrument landing system and no runway lights although it did have a runway which was straight and more or less flat and long enough to handle a Boeing 707 with reasonably good brakes during daylight hours. The terminal which was a wooden hut had been replaced by a single storey concrete building on the other side of the runway which appeared as if it had originally been designed as a gent's toilet block although without the actual urinal. I can't say that it did not have windows but they were not glazed with expensive imported glass but were fitted with local hardwood louvred shutters. Major carriers like American Airlines and Eastern Airways did not mind putting the luggage of the few passengers that disembarked on a trolley them running it over to the door to be claimed while smaller airlines preferred you to collect your luggage at the aircraft hold as it was unloaded and trundle it into the building yourself.

I don't recall the immigration and customs officials being particularly bothered to check British passport holders who did not need a visa at that time nor their luggage. The whole scene was however usually under the surveillance of the Ton Ton Macoute with their uniform dark suits and even darker glasses. Possibly the most noteworthy thing in the airport was assign that announced "My father completed the cultural revolution and I will create the industrial revolution" signed Jean Claude "Baby Doc" Duvalier, who had appointed himself president for life on the death of his father Francois "Papa Doc " Duvalier in 1971. Good luck with that one I thought as I have seldom seen a country with such a widespread potential or need to be industrially developed.

Passing into the main arrivals and departures area in an open-air roofed area at the front of the terminal there was not the usual frantic rush to grab your bag and throw it into an unlicensed taxi there is in most third world countries. The few people who were there were kind of listless and not unfriendly but much restrained by the heat and humidity, the fact that most only spoke the local patois and the baleful stares of the lurking TTM through their dark sunglasses. The language spoken by most people went back in origin to when Haiti declared itself the first black republic in 1804 and overthrew mainly French colonialist rule to become free but still incredibly impoverished. Before during and since the revolution the natives had been and were still much into Voodoo which is deeply ingrained in society and encompasses aspects of religion, civil law, crime, health care, advice to the lovelorn and taking tourists to the cleaners and is much to be avoided if one wishes to eventually leave Haiti with life and money intact. After finding a taxi myself and making clear to the driver that I knew the score the trip into town was largely uneventful and reasonably competitively priced if not entirely comfortable. The roads were largely unmetalled with many potholes and strewn with regular obstacles to progress like the odd tree branch, stray animal or recumbent local. At various points there were little kiosks set up where local food could be purchased if you had stout heart and an even stronger stomach. The driver advised that the speciality was barbecued pork creole although the meat could just as easily have been goat or turkey or God alone knows what. It was accompanied by afters consisting of sliced mangos, bananas, avocados or other fruit supplied by children who went foraging in the jungle by the roadside. This was all washed down by Cremas which is a mixture of condensed and evaporated milk and any local spice that they were able find to hand.

I advised the driver that I would pass on all of these delicacies sumptuous though they no doubt were as my plans encompassed more conventional dining in what more closely resembled a conventional restaurant later on in the day after a rum or two. The journey back to the airport was different in that the food vendors all seemed to have evaporated into thin air and as we approached the terminal there were some weirdly dressed people selling voodoo dolls, artefacts and some quite elaborate large carvings from local craftsmen since it was well before the time when everything was mass produced in China. Most of the souvenirs would not have been allowed back into the

USA or indeed most other countries who generally disapprove of the general importation of disease pestilence and such. I also knew that some of the larger pieces would not have fitted aboard any of the local LIAT Leeward Island Airways Transport Norman Britten Islander aircraft which had fairly limited passenger and luggage space. Even Eastern Airways were not going to willingly check in a large wooden carving to fly in one of their DC9's as it is not the sort of thing that you want hurtling about in the hold should the aircraft experience turbulence. Nobody wants a voodoo totem pole jettisoned from the plane over Cuba or even delivered damaged at the destination. You certainly would not have got it onto Air Haiti since they only had two planes one of which was permanently parked at the airport and the other which was lost in a crash in the jungle.

The clincher was usually that the airline check-in staff would tell the traveller that the only way they could fly with their souvenir was to pay for an expensive one-way ticket to the destination and secure it in an adjacent seat with the aircraft seat belt. I am certain that this was against FAA regulations and that the pilot would not have taken off with one of these in the cabin but the price quoted was so obscene that no one took them up on the offer anyway. All of this always resulted in the tourist trying to find the artist who had made the sale to them and trying to sell him the same sculpture back at a greatly depreciated price. I calculated that some sculptures were being recycled to the benefit of the Haitian economy twice a day. Any tourist who was not put off by the cost was told by the airline staff that the artefact was covered by a voodoo curse that anyone taking it off the island risked a terrible fate such as an early and painful death. Even if you had not suffered the ultimate fate what on earth could you have said to the neighbours if an eight foot mulatto undertaker in a black top hat and tail coat was leaping about on your front lawn all day every day chanting loudly in Creole while waving a bunch of white feathers and what looked and smelled like chicken entrails. Much better just to pay the bribe I say if you had been stupid enough to buy some mumbo jumbo in the first place.

C eh N eh D eh

Pierre Trudeau the fifteenth prime minister of Canada who was Liberal prime minister for four parliamentary terms travelled a rough and rocky road during his interesting political career. He fought and won not only the Quebecois independence movement but worked hard on the Canadian national economy as well. At one point in time he was getting a real drubbing from the opposition parties just before elections were called and announced to all that there was no such thing as unemployment in Canada. He was right but he didn't mention that most of the jobs were very much closer to the Arctic Circle than they were to Ottawa.

Canada has vast mining and smelting complexes producing mainly copper and nickel at similar latitudes to Hudson's Bay where in the summer you can't access many of these sites easily because they sit on boggy tundra and you risk being picked up and carried off to be devoured by huge man eating mosquitoes. In the winter tracked road trains can gain access over the deeply frozen ground and of course planes can land at specially constructed airports and sea planes on any of the lakes providing of course they have not frozen over otherwise the plane would stoat. Flights in and out of these remote locations are often by STOL Boeing 737's. These have sharply raked back angles under the very rear fuselage so that the pilots can all operate short take off and landings by making steep approaches in and ascents out from the gravel covered runways. The sound of loose gravel spattering against the back of the fuselage of the plane is quite distinctive when you know what it is and can be quite concerning when you don't. Most of the few passengers on all of these local planes are company personnel going to and from their workplace and their own home. The locals tend to be mainly Eskimos or you might think long term fugitives from justice who can't go home because someone is looking for them if they ever go back. The overused and to me humourless joke is that it must be midsummer day when a salesman is spotted on one of these flights. Maybe I got so much business because I called on them throughout the entire year and not just the day in summer when all of the local guys from Toronto thronged into town to try to bag a whole year's orders. When you do arrive at the airport, there are always a very few taxis but if you want to hire a car you can do so provided you take whatever happens to be available. It is no use complaining that the windscreen is cracked because the replacement vehicle if there is one may exhibit cracks which are even worse because of the flying gravel. There is not much sightseeing anyway as the road generally goes from the airport to the town and then back again with only a very short diversion to the mine or smelter. I don't imagine that any of these cars have ever been stolen as eventually you could not give one away and if you did there is nowhere to drive it to outside of the town limits. There are a few branches of the Hudson's Bay Trading Posts distributed around in Northern Canada which sell a wide range of goods because the main streets are not exactly thronged with department stores or supermarkets. I was taken with a plaid shirt in one which I decided would be very warm to wear while looking cool to the casual observer. The effect was ruined slightly however when I discovered that the shirt was made in Taiwan and fitted at the collar but the sleeves were far too short. I now realise why Canadian lumberjacks always roll their sleeves up to their elbows. The main pace to socialise in most of these towns is the hotel bar which is usually bigger than the hotel itself. On a freezing cold winters night small fur clad and snow-covered figures trying to gain entry are often Eskimos while larger fur clad figures are sometimes Polar bears which are generally discouraged from entering the bar. Eskimo women also often seek entry but are obliged to use a separate door and to sit apart from hotel guests. Drinks can be ordered at the bar but only served at the table and no one can be served a second drink until everyone at the table has consumed their first one. I thought so Scotland is not the only place to have eccentric licensing laws the but the Canucks also have a slight edge on exotic alcoholic drinks. In the north west territories, a bloody beer would have tomato juice in it while in Scotland it would be more likely to have flecks of blood group A+ plasma. Lumberjacks and miners may be tough but I don't know any Scotsman who has ever ordered a Harvey Wallbanger of his own free will. I rest my case.

Another Mad Scientist

Thompson was a decent enough cove but I was seventeen and he was in his middle forties so to me he was definitely over the hill and on the greasy slope to the big old laboratory in the sky. For part of each day I would be engaged in preparing geological bore samples for evaluation. This had some similarity with working on a Texas chain gang since it involved shovels along with various pestles and mortars some of which were cast iron and some of porcelain to cone and quarter tons of clay before selecting final samples for chemical analysis. The prisoners had it easier in some respects because the warders might have encouraged the felons with a whip but certainly never spoke to them the whole time that they were slaving on the rock pile. I was still what could be called however a captive audience as Thompson worked alongside on the analytical bench. If he got repetitive or unduly boring, I could always crash the pestle harder but this could I suppose have been the origins of my current deafness 65 years later. He did tell me how he acquired his first name but I obviously wasn't listening and simply just assumed that he was called after the sub machine gun which could chatter out bullets almost nonstop. I was a country boy and although I had been to Glasgow a couple or more times by bus, he was definitely metropolitan and had not only been to Glasgow but had worked there in a public analyst. In spite of having been trained in public health he smoked nonstop with a cigarette permanently dangling from the right-hand side of his mouth. He must have trained in ventriloquism too as I never saw his lips move throughout the entire monologue while the smoke was drawn up his right nostril and expelled who knows where. Maybe this is how the phrase talking out of one's arse originated. Another phenomenon was that the nicotine made it appear that he was sun tanned but only on the right-hand side of his face like someone on a geriatric cruise travelling port out starboard home on the entire voyage to avoid sunshine. Some of what he told me did register however and involved nefarious scams which the trades people of his youth had devised to short change the righteous citizens of Glasgow. Its surely a long time since some greedy grocer had obtained a few grains of pure white Loch Aline sand and used it to adulterate the sugar which he was weighing out into individual half pound brown paper bags. A foolish farmer who apparently added some tap water to his milk churns before ladling it out to customers who brought their own cans to be filled from his waggon as he travelled around the streets every morning. I could have told him that I suspected that a few barmen were still watering down beer and spirits even although this crime could have led to crucifixion or worse in many parts of Glasgow where life was cheaper than whisky. There was the bad butcher who was a bit heavy handed with the sulphur dioxide that he added to his mince to disguise the fact that the meat was well hung. I never understood this one as sulphur dioxide is a gas with a smell like rotten eggs which would have been very obvious and even smelled much worse than the meat. Being a gas, it must also have been difficult to come by and administer even to mince so I am guessing that some alchemist was mixing sulphuric acid and common salt in his washing house boiler and selling it as a fine white powder so no change there then. I also heard all about the mean manufacturer who put some extra copper sulphate solution into his peas to make them look stunning when poured from the tin into the pan. It apparently did not do the pan any good either however. It went on and on until there was quite a range of food I either avoided or examined very carefully before ever consuming It seems that one of the few times the country bumpkins got their own back on the merchant classes was when they went poaching for salmon. Apparently, it was not unknown for the poacher to slip a few large rounded pebbles down the salmon's gullet so that it weighed more and was worth more money. Sometimes I thought that Thompson was the classic gamekeeper turned poacher himself as in his spare time he featured in a few money saving schemes in the laboratory himself. He would get the local butcher to supply us some large lumps of the finest beef dripping but very cheaply and ask me to treat it by mixing it with concentrated sulphuric acid in a litre beaker on a hotplate. This sulphonation was time consuming smelly dirty and dangerous but the end product was said to be essential as a component of detergents and also in the tanning process. I can assure readers that I never used it and don't know what he got up to with it either. To save money we also emptied and refilled all of our lab fire extinguishers each year. The bright red ones with some kind of sodium bicarbonate solution and the small brass ones used for dousing electrical fires with raw carbon tetrachloride which was a liquid which slowly evaporated and turned into a poisonous gas so we had no need of air fresheners but gas masks could come in handy. The carbon tetrachloride was also used in dry cleaning and I reckoned that we all had the cleanest and oddest smelling ties in central Scotland. One of his other specialities was personal grooming and I think that he saw himself perhaps as a serious competitor to Unilever with his hair products. His version of Brylcreem seemed to be a trade secret but I am certain was based on a mixture of 98% paraffin oil and 2% perfume of your choice. The downside however was that when applied it ran off your scalp and right down your neck which greatly reduced its attraction for me. Not to be beaten he replaced this with a preparation which I believe was a concentrated solution of Gum Tragacanth in alcohol which when applied soon went as hard as a brick when the alcohol evaporated. This latest formulation did have one advantage however in that when in the plant we did not have to wear safety helmets. A blend of the two was attempted but unfortunately this ran down his neck and made his string vest go rigid and so was thus deemed not to be a very commercial proposition. His work on silver iodide solutions was much more successful however and I saved a good few quid in not requiring Boots to develop and print the many black and white films I took and processed in my formative years as an alchemist. The balance room was regularly re scheduled as the dark room although this meant that all of the beer mats that I had stapled to the wooden wall were occasionally not available to view by the general public.

Sin City

Why does Las Vegas appear to have some sort of ring to it while The Meadows seems to fall just a little short in the excitement stakes. To be honest no one is ever likely to confuse the den of iniquity in Nevada for the open parkland about a mile south of

Edinburgh castle even although it is said to once have been home to oak trees wild boar, outlaws and local outcasts. Las Vegas is alleged to suck in about 40 million suckers a year, divest them of their money and spit them out again hopefully but not always still in possession of their car or return their tickets home. Arriving at McCarron airport you are enticed int a world of glamour by floor to ceiling TV screens showing the most elegant sophisticated and exciting panoramas of glitz and glamour where everyone is depicted as the most handsome or beautiful person on Earth. Nothing delays your progress into the strip in the city centre which is only four miles away. Entering the hotel that you have chosen from the thousands available you might think that the first thing that you will see is the reception desk but this is usually hidden behind hundreds of slot machines which you have to thread your way through while trying not to disturb any of the zombies feeding quarters into one or more machines. It is a bit disappointing to some of the punters that there are no slots in the lifts but no doubt someone is actively pursuing this. Coming back downstairs you are confronted by the hotels main casino which will have hundreds of slot machines all beeping and flashing to anaesthetise the players just sufficiently to prevent them leaving the building. The idea is to draw you further in to the gaming tables where you can lose money faster in a dedicated area with no windows and no clocks designed to distract you from the primary objective of giving them all your money. I have only barely skimmed through the maths of probability but I know and the casino will even tell you if you read the exceptionally small print that the odds are in favour of the house. Playing any slot machines is therefore pointless to me as even if you win the chances are very high that you will be seduced into putting your winnings back in to win the prominently featured jackpot. The roulette tables are similarly set to ensure that the casino always wins out over the long term. Even games involving some skill such as blackjack are weighted in favour of the house and if you want to get involved in big money poker you are encouraged to play other people and the house just skims a commission off. I developed a system for blackjack to increase the odds of my winning since the dealer is playing the table with perhaps six people involved and is not just playing against an individual. The system is a bit tedious and really does not make much money but I was still advised to sling my hook when making a cumulative gain of 10 dollars in about 2 hours at the table. The whole city which was built by mobsters like Bugsy Segal and Meyer Lansky in the forties still operates on the principle of holding you virtual hostage until you pay the ransom which is set for each person as all the money that you happen to have on you or that you can obtain locally by pawning anything of any value. Most American cities operate GrayLine tours but Las Vegas offers only the one to the nearby Red Rock Canyon which is a very modest canyon with a few red rocks and two ancient donkeys which form the focal point for all such tours. The very ancient history of the place is actually quite interesting but I think that I may be only person ever to have visited the metropolitan museum of natural history to find out about it and it was not even raining at the time and since the casinos operate 24/7 there were no shortage of alternative divertissements available. The strip itself is probably not much more than a couple of miles long but is lined on both sides with most of the big hotel and casino chains with their enormous neon lit structures. I am actually surprised that when driving along I was able to see any traffic lights against the background of millions of flashing lights which are mostly all illuminated for the entire 24 hours each day and which at night are pretty overwhelming and seem to cancel each other out. The main attraction for me was when I found out that there were busses ran up and down the strip all day and that travel was totally free so that I soon ditched the car to look around. I have stayed in at least three of the hotels and visited more than a dozen others to sample the free entertainment on offer inside and even out. Caesars Palace is right at the centre and one of the attractions for my wife was to be photographed between two huge negros dressed as legionnaires although I pointed out to her that at home in Chester she could be photographed with one small off white Centurion on the city walls on most dry summer days in any case. Treasure Island was a little bit more dramatic outside with a full-scale sea battle between the pirates and the navy taking place on a large artificial lake between the hotel and the sidewalk. I am guessing however that a number of drivers making their first trip down the strip had to claim on their insurance when loud volley of cannons was fired just a very few feet away. Circus Circus had an overhanging flat roof at the entrance to provide a little shade before entering. The awning had several round holes cut in it through which were suspended large bunches of red balloons making the approach look like a close up of huge raw haemorrhoids. Inside it was a bit better with a circus ring in the middle of the casino hosting mainly scantily clad trapeze artists. The Imperial Palace which was next door to my hotel the Flamingo Hilton featured a vintage car museum with Hitler's "Grosser" Mercedes in it which they claimed to have purchased for £175,000. In the Luxor Hotel you could and indeed I did have a drink on Cleopatra's barge, which they insisted on rocking gently in the faint hope that you might imagine that you were on the Nile. Later I skipped down the yellow brick road with Dorothy and the Tin man at the Excalibur. Oh, the fun you could have. It just went on and on. A further large resort type Hilton hotel which was situated half a mile back from the strip featured a fight between Joe Bugner and Mohamed Ali while I was there in 1973. I wandered down to the hotel but saw neither of them in or around the lobby or grounds. I think that Joe Bugner was in a hardware shop posing with two colt 45's which critics said he would need to stop Ali although in the event Ali only won on points. While there I was offered one of the few remaining tickets for the fight at the bargain price of $1200 dollars which is about £1200 in today's money but was able to decide that I could easily resist any faint urges to spend that kind of silly money. On leaving I found that they even had slots in all of the airport departure lounges and somewhat against my better judgement fed one with a quarter prior to boarding the plane. It didn't win any prize but it was probably worth 20p in the form of a quarter to prove that they were fixed.

Broken Glass

I have never been stabbed in the throat with a broken bottle and most assuredly don't intend to add It to my bucket list of things that I must do in future. If I had been, I imagine that the initial pain would probably be similar to that which I experienced that first night that I stayed in Canada. All that I had done was to step outside of my hotel through the large revolving doors onto the broad pavement outside. Unfortunately for me the hotel was in downtown Montreal and it was an evening in early February with the outside temperature at about minus 12 degrees centigrade and a cold wind blowing some light snow from the north west creating a further chill factor. I literally did not know what had hit me because the event was one that I had not experienced before. I imagined that my tonsils may have frozen solid and then snapped of. With the first stab of pain I spun round with my feet slipping on the icy sidewalk and dived headfirst back towards the evolving door. The door man who was completely wrapped up and eve to the extent of having a scarf across his face was inside the lobby but saw me coming and pushed the door to help propel me back into the warmth. It was not that I was not dressed for the cold with a thick padded ski jacket but it had not occurred to me to wear anything on my head and face. The doorman obviously had me placed as from out of state never mind out of town and possibly out of my mind as well. It took me a few minutes of agonised chest beating before I was able to breathe almost normally and I crawled into the bar for a double brandy to heat me up but not daring to ask for a Caribou which I judged to be an incendiary drink too far. As I sat in the bar, I could see Mansfield street out of the window with the snow ploughed and piled up at the side of the road to a depth of about two meters. I did not know then but during the night the city authorities cleared each day's snowfall and dumped it on top of the frozen St Lawrence river which was only half a mile away.

After a further couple of nightcaps, I enjoyed a good night's sleep in my pleasantly warm heated room. Next morning, I was initiated into underground Montreal and discovered that you could travel significant distances in the city through its extensive network of underground shopping malls and tunnels around the central train station. Being a Saturday I decided that I was very happy to see Montreal from underneath and leave the real world for Monday with my new woollen scarf and the hood of my ski jacket fully extended against the elements. If the local weather persisted as it would do until about April, I would have been perfectly satisfied to see the sights of Montreal on a set of postcards. One of the underground stores that drew my attention was Radio Shack which sold an enormous array of radios and all sorts of electric and electronic accessories and spares parts. Normally I would have headed straight to the CB radio section but I did not fancy lugging home a new CB radio in a Doc Martens size shoe box package and the six foot steel spring loaded antennae with a magnetic mount to fix to the boot lid of my car. Instead I was more taken by a miniature FM radio about the size of a matchbox which being so small needed an earphone to hear what was being broadcast. Miniaturisation is the norm today but this American made set was fairly unique at the time because of its exceptionally small size.

On the Sunday morning with the radio in my shirt breast pocket and the earphone in my left ear I went down to the lobby where I was pleased to see the Sunday Times on sale in the hotel shop. Either they had shipped it the papers overnight on a freight flight or they had electronically sent the contents to Canada to print and distribute locally. I took my paper int the restaurant for brunch and chose a vacant table to sit and read it while listening to music in the background. A smiling waitress very quickly appeared as I examined the menu. She leant forward and then to my surprise shouted into my right ear asking if I would like tea or coffee to start with. It immediately occurred to me that she had mistaken the radio and earpiece for some new kind of a hearing aid. If I wasn't deaf before then I certainly was now but after a few seconds with her request ringing through my head I carefully removed the plastic earpiece and explained the nature of the device to the well-meaning waitress as I very quickly switched the radio off and put the earpiece away to prevent any further injury. I am guessing that the presidents secret service detail never had problems like this and in addition they all had dark glasses and so could also have been mistaken for being blind although giving guns to blind deaf people to protect you was never a good idea. That three-week trip spanned started in Chicago Illinois which was on the Canadian border at minus 12 and ended up at Douglas Arizona on the Mexican border at plus 30 degrees so dressing for the local conditions was equally difficult at both extremities. It was cost and time effective however in terms of not having to whip back and forth across the Atlantic so often as I was never into airmiles for airmiles sake although I am not sure that my boss fully appreciated this. Shortly after my return to the UK and my office with its busy in tray he informed me that he needed my help for a business negotiating in Europe and that he had booked us out to Dusseldorf. We met at the airport and checking in and progressing through to the departure lounge I thought that he was being a bit odd. Finally, he could not contain himself and asked if the three-week trip I had just returned from had culminated in me sailing back to the UK on a Cunard luxury liner. This puzzled me for a few seconds until I jaloused his problem. He had spotted the luggage tags on my brief case and suitcase and immediately leapt to entirely the wrong conclusion that I travelled back luxuriously on the RMS QE2. I carefully explained to him although I really should not have had to tell him that when checking in to the Queen Elizabeth and other decent hotels the bell boy would deliver your bags to your room and in order to deliver them to the right room put hotel labels on each item with the rom number written on them. It was part of the unavoidable ritual which inevitably cost a dollar tip. Check my expenses John. Maybe he always insisted on dragging his own bags up twelve flights of stairs. After all he had once turned up at one of our major customers in San Mateo California on the local bus.

The Embra Festival

The Edinburgh International Festival is a world-renowned event because it is totally unique and had been growing in stature, size and popularity for over 70 years from its inception in 1947. It has become the largest showcase for music, art, drama, dance, photography, comedy, satire, street entertainers, military spectacle and eejits on and beyond the huge fringe. In 2018 the world's largest arts festival, spanned 25 days of events and featured more than 55,000 performances of 3,548 different shows in 317 venues and these are only the official ones as many more impromptu happenings happened all over the place on a 24/7 basis. New York was nicknamed the city that never sleeps by Frank Sinatra because the subway ran all night. Well Frank never appeared in the Edinburgh Festival until about twenty years after he died and even then, only as a tribute act so I think that he might have been more than ever so slightly surprised and Edinburgh doesn't even have a subway although it has an underground. Since it doesn't sleep it is Ok to have more visitors than hotel beds by a considerable margin and more performances than venues because the city covers over 200 square miles with lots of open spaces for drummers and dossers though not at the same time. I used to go to the fringe regularly either travelling in by car or if drink was to be taken by train so it was normally by train. At one point I formed the international subsidiary company of a division of an American group and had an office at the West end so I was very familiar with the city even when the festival was not in full swing. I have done the Rose Street bar crawl from Charlotte square to St Andrews square and unlike some international rugby supporters up for Murrayfield lived to tell the tale. On one occasion while taking my wife and some customers out for some culture I chose to stay in the King James hotel at the top of Leith walk where it joins Princess Street. As we came downstairs in the lift and entered the foyer, I bumped into an enormous portly figure figure in a multi coloured floral full-length evening gown which swept to the floor. I apologised and she turned round to reveal a thick black curly beard and hirsute chest. Being sober at the time it only took a few seconds to get over my utter astonishment and to recognise Demis Roussos who was waiting for his taxi to take him to the Usher Hall. Boy could he sing. He could hold onto a high note longer than the Bank of Scotland. He might have had a high voice but he got through four wives. Later in the same evening I thought that I saw another portly bearded figure in a fancy kaftan and it turned out to be Billy Connolly who was easily identified as I got closer and I noticed his signature footwear of two large yellow bananas. This proves beyond doubt that even people from Glasgow went to the festival. Connolly however could always be relied on to antagonise the locals by asking them what the difference was between an Edinburgh barman and a coconut. It was not the question that upset them so much as the answer which was that you could eventually always get a drink out of a coconut. One effect of the festival is that Edinburgh has seen the arrival of sores of new bars and restaurants. The Dome restaurant is outstanding and I would happily go again. There are also many that have gone or changed ownership and names and one that I recall although not its name is a basement bar at the east end of George street. Paul and I went there one night and I was astonished to see in the chilled cabinet some tins of Coors beer. At that time Coors was little known west of the Rockies and totally unknown east of the Rockies. I asked the barman how it was possible a few tins of Coors had appeared like magic in Edinburgh. His story was that some oilmen had had it exported to Texas to quench their thirst when they worked on the rigs. Someone had then taken some to Aberdeen which at the time was like the wild west and eventually a few tins had made it to Edinburgh although the best of my knowledge there are no working oil rigs in the city. My second astonishment however was the high price of

the round and I asked the barman if he had flown the beer in on Branniff with one can
in each first-class seat.

El Tel

Tel's academic career peaked he insisted on informing me when he was senior pupil
at the Fulham School for Backward Boys in 19 God was it that long ago. This was the
launch pad which inevitably propelled him onwards and ever upwards to be chief dish
washer at one of the late lamented Lyons Corner Houses originally launched in 1885
by Glickstein, Salmon and Lyons. He was seriously anatomically challenged to aspire
to be one of their many waitresses known and loved by all as "Nippy's" but judged
perfect for dish washing as he could reach the very bottom of the sink without having
to stand on a box was economically viable at about £2 per week and didn't need
supplied with any Marigolds. But Tel was a real grafter and from here he soon
graduated to be an ace export sales executive for Richard Thomas and Baldwin's,
steel and tinplate makers to the world based in South Wales since 1790. At its peak
RTB was the largest steel mill in Europe. If you remember RTB however then you are
showing your age since it has also been British Steel, Corus, and Tata before closing
its doors for the last time just after the millennium. You may also be old enough to
remember the epic film Tennessee Williams Cat on a Hot Tin Roof or at least
Elizabeth Taylor perspiring fragrantly in it or was it on it or probably more
realistically under it. The roof was in fact not made of tin but of mild steel sheet rolled
thin before being coated on both sides with a layer of tin to prevent corrosion. This
sheet was then gently corrugated to encourage rain to run from it down the gulleys
when it was installed at even a slight angle. This could be quite a noisy procedure and
led to the invention of earplugs and gutters and drainpipes the latter being a speciality
of steelmaker Stewarts and Lloyds. Tel soon picked up a small order for this type of
roofing from an RTB agent in West Africa and this was shipped forthwith. Nothing
much happened then for some time until a larger repeat order rolled in from the same
source and this was soon followed by several more. Tel's boss was intrigued by his
success and scenting the opportunity to grow a new market he sent him off on the next
British Caledonian Airways flight to suss out exactly what was happening in Africa.
On arrival the agent met Tel and took him back to his office. There was a very
considerable noise from the busy street in front of the office but an even greater din
from the small workshop in the yard at the rear of the premises making it difficult to
converse without shouting and waving arms. Tel was soon led out into the workshop
where to his amazement he saw the agent's workmen taking the corrugated tin plate
sheets from one pallet beating them more or less flat with hammers and then piling
them on anther pallet. It seemed that what the market wanted was flat tin plate steel
sheets for roofing but they did not know that the sheets started out life as flat strip
steel. Since corrugated steel roof sheets cost twice the price of flat steel roofing sheets
Tel instantly decided that he was not about to be the one to inform the agent of this
fact as it would inevitably cut his commission in half at a stroke. The better option
appeared to be to take the agent for a beer or three and then take more new orders.

Icelandic Cod Wars.

Being in a war zone is not something that most people aspire to although for travellers in far flung lands with funny peculiar languages it can be somewhere that you can all too easily find yourself in. Being in Berlin in September 1939 would not have been a good career move and possibly on a par with being on the 38th parallel when the KPA Korean People's Army supported by the Chinese and to a lesser extent Soviet Russia swept over the border into South Korea to liberate the rest of the fatherland as they saw it. Britain has been in a few wars in is time but to be fair we always strive to fight them in someone else's country as this tends to lessen the inconvenience very slightly. Apparently, the UK has been in four Cod Wars with Iceland in the last fifty years but these were all at sea to reduce the inconvenience to both warring parties even further. I guess that not many people know that as Michael Caine might have said. Even fewer people know that the score was four one in Iceland's favour and of course the winner has written the rules as always. To the best of my knowledge neither side has fired on the other but there have been over fifty occasions when vessels have collided. In 1976 the UK had twenty-two ships allocated to the punch-up although it was the case that there were never perhaps more than about half a dozen actually directly involved at any one time. If there had been more hardware then there would presumably have been a lot of more bent ships sailing around in the north Atlantic. Iceland didn't win by beating Britain in naval battles they just withdrew diplomatic relations with Britain and threatened to shut the important Keflavik NATO base. Since NATO was slightly more important than a few thousand tons of codfish, Britain backed down on the 200 miles exclusion zone. Iceland then backed down on the number of British trawlers that were allowed to fish within the limit and allowed the two diplomats expelled from Reykjavik to sneak back in again. I believe that the Icelanders took the situation much more seriously than most people in Britain ever did and I was very slightly concerned to be in Reykavik at the end of the third Cod War. An Icelandic gunboat the Vis Tyr had been rammed at high speed when a British frigate HMS Falmouth hit it at about 40 mph and it had limped slowly home seriously bent. When I saw the Icelandic gunboat in the harbour, I could understand that somebody had got a bit annoyed. The slightly odd but nevertheless very pleasing thing to me was that none of the Icelanders that I ever met on my several visits seemed to be inclined to be the least bit uncivil to me personally even although they were very well aware that I was not a Viking. Most of them were pretty reserved on the initial meeting possibly because the population of Iceland t that time was about 30,000 people and they did not actually meet a lot of foreigners who did not actually originate in other parts of Scandinavia. Like most of the rest of the world's population however they warmed up considerably after a drink or three had broken the ice. On one evenings excursion to the hotel Bar I was actually quite taken by surprise by a group of young Icelanders who I could only describe as all being completely off their heads on drink. On enquiring as to the nature of the special celebration I was told that it was some of the staff of a local mental hospital on a night out after attending a gig by a local band called "The Lonely Blue Boys" and was curious to know as to how it was possible to actually differentiate between staff and patients based on the friendly stramash that was taking place. Later after listening to a CD of the band I could see where some of the patients originated. I openly admit however that if I had to live six months a year in near to freezing almost total darkness, I might so easily have graduated to become a lonely blue boy myself. Eating herring airdried for some considerable period on outside wooden frameworks would probably not have helped my situation especially if it was washed down with locally and illegally distilled antifreeze. To be fair there was also some stewed lamb available at that time although I am sure it was imported as was most of the smoked salmon. In the original Swiss owned aluminium smelter on the island lunch for all levels of staff was served in military style pressed aluminium unitary plates with four equal sized indentations. One had a ladle of soup in it, one a pickled herring, one some lamb stew and the fourth some custard while one spoon finished off the ensemble with style. I was quire relieved that the coffee was served afterwards in metal mugs although the source of the milk was a puzzle having been formerly condensed or perhaps maybe evaporated from some unsuspecting Danish cow The cheap geothermal power led to the construction of another three huge internationally owned aluminium smelters but I am sure their cuisine was also international by then. The local caviar however came in several grades all of which were excellent and at a fraction of the price that it sold for in London which made it a no brainer as to what to take home. One small jar of caviar which I gave to my father was so well liked that he had the lot on toast one morning for his breakfast and to hell with poverty. He wasn't quite so wildly enthusiastic about the Icelandic folk music CD apparently however for some strange reason. Keflavik had one of the biggest runways of any airbase that I had ever seen and served as an emergency landing strip for any transatlantic aircraft that needed to land mid trip for any reason. It operated as an American air base between 1951 and 2005 when it closed but it apparently has reopened to help track down Russian submarines. It continued to operate as a civilian airport however during all of this time and many airlines run services from Europe to the Americas with lots of tourists stopping over. As you landed in Keflavik you were obliged to walk through a vast duty-free area called the Horn of Plenty which was handy for Icelanders who had drunk their duty-free booze on the plane on the way home. Since it was really an American base it also had its own TV station which Iceland itself did not. A few Icelanders tried to patch TV sets into the American services although during one period of communist government on the island this was severely discouraged although this did nothing for sobriety in society.

Did the Earth Move for You?

We set out from the Intercontinental hotel on the Pondak Indah and after weaving through interminable inner-city streets eventually joined Highway 1 which at that time was an almost deserted four lane toll road which ran from the northern suburbs of Jakarta to Cilegon on the west coast of Java. At that time however only the first 20 km or so of the 100 km road were upgraded to motorway or at least to dual carriageway status so the total journey probably took nearly three hours. On reaching Cilegon which was to be our final destination we actually passed through to the south of the town and headed further south about 20 km down highway 3 twhich was the coast road to the area of Karang Bolong beach. I say to the area, of since at that time there was virtually nothing there except when you looked offshore there was the remains of what was probably the world biggest volcano Krakatoa. Again, to be strictly accurate it was Anak Krakatoa (Child of Krakatoa) that we were looking at because in 1883 Krakatoa blew itself to pieces. The cone of the island volcano was originally about 2000 metres above sea level but the eruption carried about 21 cubic Km of rock into the atmosphere and distributed it as rocks and ash over about 800,000 square Km of the earth's surface for most of the following year. The bang was heard up to 3500 km away in Australia although there is no existing record of any Australians having their sleep disrupted or their orgasms enhanced by the phenomenon. With the difference in time and the speed of sound being as they are it was probably too early in the evening in Sydney to distract the local drongos because the pubs would not long have been open and they would have more serious considerations to address before closing time. Today Krakatoa is only about 100 metres high and is in fact three separate small isles sitting on the caldera of the original volcano. It is still very active but not on the day I was there. I almost feel guilty about not being more impressed and considered asking for my money back because there was not even a wisp of smoke or slight shudder that day. I managed to restrain myself however and instead was persuaded to visit a beach restaurant which proved to be a bigger mistake then visiting a volcano on the wrong day. In this particular restaurant I am willing to bet that every day was the wrong day. I should probably have suspected something when there was no fish on the menu of a restaurant on the shore of a tropical island. In fact, there was no menu and if there had been it would have been in Bahasa or one of the 700 other dialects and so would not have been entirely relevant to my needs. Instead a tour of the kitchen was offered which is not at all unusual in many small local restaurants off the tourist beaten track. In this case the last place the management should have taken a prospective diner was into the kitchen. It smelt like an abandoned blocked public toilet in Palma on the second or third night of the Glasgow Fair when they still accepted pesetas for Paella. The contents of a huge cauldron bubbled ominously as it sat precariously on a gas stove and immediately images of Macbeth and witches sprang ominously to mind. The beaming chef of the world's first and ultimate greasy spoon joint announced proudly via an interpreter that this was soup. Neither he nor I however was able to satisfactorily identify any of the ingredients in the swirling grey coloured plasma. As a direct result I decided that I was happy to forego lunch that day which was in fact an extremely unusual event as I have eaten exotic local cuisine around the entire world. I feared that even a small bowl of the soup might have resulted in my own not so little eruption and with a bumpy three-hour return car journey to the hotel in prospect this exciting culinary adventure was something that I was not even going to contemplate. When I did get back to the hotel and its air-conditioned interior there was enormous relief from the growing humidity of the air in and around the city. After an informal dinner in the hotel's coffee shop and a beer or three I repaired to my room on the top floor. From here with curtains open I was royally entertained for some time with Son et Lumiere to one of the fiercest tropical lightning storms I have seen in comfort and safety. I also had a quiz to entertain me as the hotel had provided a large bowl of fruit. I looked at this for a bit, scratched my head and wracked my feeble memory but I was still only able to identify about four of the fruits in the bowl. I can almost see the slight sneer on your face thinking about the stupidity of such a poor disadvantaged bewildered wretch. Now that we all watch MasterChef and shop in Waitrose and Partners of course we all have the servants ply us with Rambutans and Madagascar vanilla custard along with the odd glass of Taylors vintage port all day long. That's when we are not stuffing ourselves with Durian, or Jackfruit, or Lychee, or Longan or Mangosteen or Papaya naturally in between smoking sticks of rolled cinnamon and snorting ginger. Come to think about it who needs Krakatoa and volcanos anyway.

Big Sur

The Spanish when they occupied what is now California referred to the vast and relatively unexplored coastal region to the south of Monterey as "el país grande del sur", or the big country of the south. This was often shortened to "el sur grande" and naturally Americans went one further or maybe went one not so far and referred to it as Big Sur so that neither Spanish nor Americans today know what it really means. It generally refers to almost 100 miles of pacific coastline which starts about 150 miles south of San Francisco and ends about 300 miles north of Los Angeles. I drove this as part of a massive figure eight which started in San Francisco went up through the Napa Valley to Lake Tahoe, down through Sacramento to the Gold Country and on to Monterey. The Big Sur then took me south to Santa Barbara then on through Santa Monica to San Diego. Here I turned northwest again for Palm Springs via Tecmecula and back through Riverside and Annaheim to Los Angeles and in only 14 days.

When Clint Eastwood stopped being Dirty Harry, he put his Colt 45 and Mustang away and moved down to Carmel on the Monterey peninsula to be the mayor where he had his own police force to ensure the rule of law. This included a few dickless traceys on motortricycles who aspired to be mistaken for CHIPS the California Highway Patrol in their white brain buckets and mirror sunglasses. Every thirty minutes they would cruise slowly along the small streets with a piece of chalk on a long wooden stick. Without stopping they would mark each car's rear tyre with a chalk mark and if the car and chalk mark were still there on their next circuit, they would issue a substantial parking ticket. This was also slapped on the windscreen without the women police officers stopping or getting out of the saddle as it is a fixed penalty of $100. They also had a lane on many streets where drivers were fined $500 if there are not two people in the car. This resulted in one huge barney, where a pregnant woman was fined and started screaming that her and the embryo comprised two people. By the time the case went to court the woman had given birth so the judge dismissed the case but she was then charged with allowing two people to wear the same seat belt which was it seems an equally expensive mistake. Clint certainly made her day. Most of the crimes committed there today arise from the prices of houses and even goods in the shops although for all the tourists that I saw going into shops I never saw one emerge with any purchases. Since all the shops seem to sell are paintings done by the large artistic community maybe the canvasses were delivered later by liveried footmen in gold Cadillacs. I suppose that the Scots have to take some share of the blame for all the artists and assorted chanty wrestlers who have descended on the area since this was where Robert Louis Stevenson met and married his American wife Fanny van De Grift Osbourne in 1880. He did try to make some amends however as he started a forest fire which almost burnt the old state capital down before he quickly set out for San Francisco, the Napa Valley and eventually the south seas. Actually, we Scots might also be blamed for the influx of golfers to Pebble Beach on the seventeen-mile drive but when you see the prices there today again you won't be surprised by the total absence of any Scottish accents. John Steinbeck also dropped by and finding the area full of sardine canneries wrote Cannery Row.

Further south is Hearst Castle where the daughter of the family Patti was kidnapped by some terrorists and joined in so enthusiastically, she became much worse than they ever were. Just down the coast is the Madonna Inn which is described as a whimsical lodging near the Costco Wholesale close to the Van den Burgh air force base. One of my favourite locations however was Santa Barbara with its pier at Stearns wharf where there were more pelicans than tourists when I stayed there out of season. According to the American author Dixon Lanier Merritt,

A wonderful bird is the pelican,
His bill will hold more than his belican,
He can take in his beak,
Enough food for a week,
But I'm damned if I see how the helican.

Having seen the large number of fish each of these birds was hoovering up I think he got it about right and it might be one reason that the sardine canneries are now well out of business.   Could be that the guano business is booming and maybe why the vineyards are proliferating. From there it was down to Santa Monica, Venice Beach, Long Beach and through Torrance without stopping in the city of Angels on this occasion. There was a little side trip however from Long Beach by high speed jet catamaran to Catalina Island and Mount Ada the old Wrigley house on Wrigley road overlooking Avalon, owned by the Chicago chewing gum magnate and presumably named for his wife. Its actually one of a large number of Wrigley properties across America and all described as the houses built by Juicy Fruit at 99c a time. South of Long Beach and just down the coast in San Clemente is Richard Nixon's western White House or La Casa Pacifico as he called it and described as a Tuscan style villa or a Spanish Colonial Hacienda depending on which realtor you believe. Sleeping twelve and on the market for sixty million which at five million a bed is not too shabby a des res. it doesn't seem to have the desirable appeal that it might once have had and certainly none for me.

Making a Strong Case for Travel

I have never had a case with wheels like most normal people do. I have always lugged mine by the handles which was a great reminder if indeed one was needed to travel light. Having watched what baggage handlers all over the world do to cases I used to favour light waterproof flexible faux leather and to pack nothing breakable. If you think that the indestructible hard plastic models are better then you have never seen one that has been dropped one of its corners in a puddle from the aircraft hold and run over by a baggage truck. I always packed important stuff like medication, toiletries and business papers either in a small hard attache case with a combination lock or latterly in a tough black canvas holdall with a padlocked zip both of which travelled as hand luggage around the world. With bags checked through to the final destination which was not always the same one that you were travelling to it was useful to have what you really needed close at hand at all times. I probably subscribe to the theory promulgated by Mark Russell that the rings of Saturn are made up entirely of lost airline baggage. On one occasion I checked in for Tokyo and asked for my bags to be sent to Brussels. When the check-in staff objected that this was not possible, I pointed out that they had successfully achieved this only a short time before. BA however countered to point out that this had been on SABENA which they insisted stood for such a bloody experience never again rather than BA which was only bloody awful although constantly striving to achieve even worse. The hand luggage was sometimes used exclusively for very short trips but in any case, was useful for clearing a path when barging through crowded foreign terminal buildings. Especially in America people used to spill out of waiting areas all over the pier when a busy flight was called for boarding at one of the many gates. If you were unable to force your way through you could end up in an aisle seat going almost anywhere. On one such occasion in O'Hare airport in Chicago I was especially annoyed at the crowd who did not even seem to be boarding an aircraft but were milling about aimlessly. As I emerged from the back of the scrum a young lady handed me a leaflet and insisted it was important. I made for a quiet area and did quickly read it. To my amazement it was a legal disclaimer from a film company stating that although I had just walked through a scene being shot for the Twentieth Century Fox film Home Alone 2, that I would not be paid as an extra for some arcane reason. It had not at that stage occurred to me that I had even been in a crowd scene in a big budget movie or that I might be able to get a claim in because of it. What really pissed me off when I thought about it was that the scrawny little kid who had got lost was paid $4.5 million dollars and that that were filming it in Chicago when the film clearly tried to indicate that he got lost in New York. I was much more totally taken aback to learn that the film producer was a gentleman allegedly called Christopher Columbus. When the film was eventually released it grossed about $350 million at the box office worldwide, I was even more pissed off. I mean getting lost in an airport is not a crime but getting lost in an airport which is about a thousand miles from where you are supposed to be is at best careless.

I have stopped believing anything I see on a screen whether the screen is large or small much as I no longer subscribe to the tooth fairy or Santa Claus. If there is any justice in the world then perhaps it is illustrated by the fact that Donald Trump also had a cameo role in the film but that they cut his scenes out before the film was released in Canada whilst for all I know I am still in it with a scowl on my face while assaulting all and sundry with my hand luggage. But here is a thought to hold onto .If Donald's scene had not been shot in Trump Towers in New York where was he was filmed telling the scrawny kid that the lobby was just down the hall to the left then it is possible that he might have been struck in the groin by a small black canvas bag in Chicago. For all anyone knows this could have changed the course of history and the resulting hernia could have resulted in the election of Hilary Clinton fourteen years later to the dizzying heights of POTUS. That's pretty scary when you think about it.

Transport for Scotland

A lot of travel in Scotland was designed for pedestrians with ancestors only three generations ago walking up to 50 miles at a time unhindered by horseless carriages and pantechnicons. Wee Wullie, ran all the way from Bonnybridge to Denny with his cleek and gird, or hoop and hook as its known in posh circles (geddit hoop – circle). When he reached Denny Cross, he went into Ferrari's for a bag of chips and some miscreant stole his gird from outside the shop so that in fact he was unable to travel home and may still be in Denny until this day for all I know. Still there are a lot worse places to spend your entire life than Denny aren't there? - aren't there?

Senga met big Lachie at Barrowland one Friday night. When she asked him what he did for a living he confided to her that he was a mariner. She in turn then confided in him that she had always wanted to sail away into the west to America. He offered to smuggle her aboard his vessel on condition that she shared his cabin and didn't wander around outside during the voyage. Thus, it was, that they boarded his vessel later that night in the dark and next morning she heard the engines burst into life. After a about a week on the vessel she enquired if they were getting near to New York and was informed that they still had some way to go. Feeling weary at being in the cabin for so long she ventured out after dark for some fresh air and was quite surprised to see that the vessel was in a large river and even more so that she was on the Silvers Marine Renfrew Ferry moored in Yoker. Still she was possibly more fortunate than the lone Celtic fan being chased through Govan by Rangers football fans after an Old Firm game at Ibrox. Reaching the Govan ferry quay, he could see the MS Ellen's Isle ferry was already a few of feet out on the river so he gave the chasing crowd one last big obscene gesture before making a giant leap onboard. "That was close," he cheerily told the skipper. "Not really," replied big Hamish. "We're just coming in to land and tie up at Govan pier. "Jings, Crivens, Help ma Boab are you sure? "What big teeth you have grandma" thought little green riding hood leaping into the Clyde and swimming for the south bank as fast as his little arms and legs could thrash the foaming water leaving all the blue noses disappointed on the pier.

Travel in the London area is a bit different as the underground alone has eleven lines with 270 stations carrying over 5 million people a day over an area of over 600 square miles. The first line the City and South London opened in 1890 followed by two other companies to form the "twopenny tube" with a mixed steam and electrified service where the atmosphere in the tunnels and stations was promoted as being good for your health. This was before you add in the overground lines, DLR, all the big red busses Boris bikes, BA Wheels and Emirates Skylon. London to my surprise is only the twelfth busiest underground system in the world not that I have ridden them all but I have managed to sample quite few for better or worse over time. Apparently, there are 180 subways in operation with almost 40 in China and almost another 40 under construction around the globe. Glasgow has the third oldest subway system in the world after London and Budapest and became operational in 1896. It has fifteen stations on a seven-mile circuit passing under the Clyde twice without so far filling with water. There are two lines with an outer circle running clockwise and an inner circle running anticlockwise. The clockwork orange transports about 38000 people a day on its narrow-gauge system with a railspan of about four feet. Maybe Glasgow people were always a bit smaller anyway with their Bunnets rather than Bowlers. Londoners and all other tourists should wherever possible avoid phrasing such as I am going to ride the tube as locally this is taken to mean that you will get a piggyback from a moron. It is possible that the main importance of the system is to allow people to buy a round trip ticket and get off at every station for a drink in the nearest pub all of which have perfected the art of quick service but not always having change available immediately for a fiver. Maybe the biggest subway I have ridden on is Shanghai with over 400 miles of track and some of the biggest carriages because it has only been in service for a few years. I was mildly impressed that in the carriage that I was in I was the only one not transfixed by my smartphone. I was more impressed that it connected with the Maglev from the airport which levitates and travels at up 300 kmph. Beijing subway is slightly bigger in its coverage but not as I recall so far as its carriage sizes are concerned. It only interconnects with a few bullet trains which also travel at up to 300 kmph but manage to do so with their wheels still on the track. Hong Kong MRT subway is smaller and slower all round but it is British built after all and has been around a lot longer. So why travel by subway and miss all the sights, actually there could be number of good reasons In Athens Bilbao and Madrid it just helps you miss the traffic although Athens and Bilbao seem to run downhill and back up again of course. In Berlin you miss the excitement of the Stasi and the stowaways mainly because they have knocked the wall down. In New York you can see the most highly decorated rolling stock in the world with fantastic Graffiti while in Moscow you can see the most highly decorated stations in the world with tiles and frescoes. In Paris you can play hide and seek with the pickpockets and muggers while in Brussels you can simply connect to trains and planes. In Chicago Copenhagen and Montreal, you can prevent freezing your follicles off in deepest winter while in Vienna you can dither to a never-ending zither. In San Francisco you can question the wisdom of riding BART when you feel the onset of an earthquake while in Detroit and Sydney you can marvel that they built all or most of their subways up on stilts above ground to take advantage of what views there are. Greektown in Detroit and China town and Darling Harbour area in Sydney. Of the new constructions the one I might want to see is Honolulu although to be honest why anyone would want to avoid the views of Waikiki Beach, Pearl Harbour and Diamond Head does puzzle me greatly. Maybe it is a cunning plot by the Uber drivers in Honolulu with a new marketing strategy to show tourists what they really came to see and experience in the first place instead of just the inside of a tunnel out of the airport to the AlaMoana Centre. Or maybe not as I am told that most of the subway will be on stilts like the DLR with driverless trains but at a cost so far of about half a billion dollars per mile of track so no wonder they can't afford any train drivers. Maybe I am missing a really big opportunity too by overlooking a huge potential market in Hawaii for hoops and hooks. After all they are already all half way there anyway with their hula hoops which they seem to be continually burling around their esparto grass skirts.

The Napoleonic Code

"Hi Dave it's Paul, Paul Hummer" said the distant voice as I picked up the office phone to stop the loud ringing noise from the cradle that many phones tend to make when someone dials you on your personal number. I was jolted awake but failed to immediately guess why the president was calling me at about 09:00 hrs his time presumably from his office in the mid-west of the USA. I say presumably because with my luck he might have been calling from Manchester Airport and looking for a lift into the office to give me grilling about something. "I just wondered what was in your schedule for Monday he said" giving me cause to reflect that whatever it was it sounded as if it was about to change. "I would really appreciate it if you were able to go over to Sarragumines for a couple of days for some meetings that we really very much need to be represented at and you seem to have the ideal qualifications. I think that he meant expendable. One qualification lacking at that point however was that I had no idea where Sarragumines was but I wasn't about to admit to such a piffling little problem to the boss who had such confidence in me. "Just email or fax the documents" I told him "and agree that we could talk then over again after I had read them and understand what might be involved. Thus, it was that I set out on a Monday before dawn for Manchester Airport and a flight to Paris CDG. I had looked up the location and figured that it had just avoided being in Luxemburg and was currently in France but that it yoyoed back and forth between France and Germany so many times that I better get there quick before it changed again and screwed up my travel plans. After looking at connecting flights which didn't and trains which required multiple changes, I decided to fly to CDG and blast east, north eastwards on the A4 Autoroute until I hit the Siegfried Line as this seemed to be the least worst option available. The A4 was memorable for many Polish cars with trailers heading west empty and many Polish cars with trailers loaded with cars heading back east. The speed that they were going at had to raise even a faint doubt if all of the cars heading east had been bought and paid for. They probably had co-pilots in the cabin with binoculars to warn the drivers of French motorcycle police (Motards) operating in pairs not so much to catch dodgy cars but to make a fortune in speeding fines. The flics lowered the speed limit if it looked like it might rain so they had a steady stream of victims of which I decided not to become one. If the cops didn't relieve you of all your ready cash in on the spot fines then the frequent siting of expensive toll barriers made sure to hoover up the rest and must also have inflated the cost of the cars heading for Poland by a few bob. After arriving at my destination and checking into my three-star abode followed by a quick lunch I made my way to the large petrochemical complex which was the site of the meeting. The gathering was in a large room which may have been part of their social club but with everything removed except chairs around all the walls. I was one of the first to arrive and as time went on the room slowly filled with lots of men of a certain age reeking of pate de foie gras, cognac and cigars. To my observant eye these were obviously lawyers who smelt money and blood for minimum effort. A chairman soon called the meeting to some sort of order which was made easier because some maitres were dozing quietly in their seats. It appeared that there were about a dozen parties present all with their legal teams except me of course since I was multitalented. After a bit of squabbling between them it transpired that a large reactor vessel had failed prematurely and they were all looking for someone topay large sums in compensation to the company so that the company could pay them. During a short lull in the babble one of them pointed at me and suggested that I should be given an early opportunity to confess my culpability. As I hesitated looking for the right words in French another leapt in with "Ah non, Monsieur il est Anglais" and waved his hand dismissively. To which I responded "Up yours Asterix and incidentally Monsieur, il est Ecossais". I was getting bored summaries briefly how forty years previously the French client had bought a chemical reactor from a leading American engineering company which included a set of drawings. They had currently invested now in a new reactor which was exactly the same as the old one except it would be twice as big, operate under much increased pressure and at higher temperature to produce double the amount of end product. They used the original drawings scaled up but omitted to ask my parent company for their recommendations for the high temperature lining and had simply ordered material similar to which had been used originally. It may or may not have been well installed and commissioned but cracked and failed within days. I suggested that they could probably squabble about reparation without my being present. The chairman suggested that since I was certainly the only engineer in the room that I could summarise my comments and submit them to a judge at the local court next morning. Over a gourmet Alsatian dinner, I wrote my comments on one side of one piece of hotel note paper and tucked it into a hotel envelope. On the other side of the dining room however I was interested to see a couple of the lawyers enjoying a glass or three of champagne. Apparently, they insisted that it be opened in the traditional way where the sommelier took a sabre off the wall behind the bar and swung it hard at the neck of the bottle just below the cork after removing the foil and wire cage. The theory was that the top was cut off cleanly and no broken glass entered the bottle because the pressure of the gas in the narrow neck prevented its entrance. I just hoped that they were better at lawyering than they were at chemistry and physics. Next morning, I drove to the old court building in the "centre ville" early so that I could be sure of parking. Driving in France is incredibly easy as there are only ever two directions that you can go in. These are "Centre Ville" and Toutes Directions". After parking and on entering the Bastille I was told to go upstairs and sit outside the courtroom on a seat until the judge pitched up. The seat was on a balcony with a good view of the main door and the grand sweeping staircase up to the first floor. There were very few people around but some short time later I was quite surprised and very amused to see a tall willowy but seemingly seriously bedraggled blonde staggering unsteadily into the entrance on high heeled shoes, shout bonjour and weave her way up the stairs. I uncharitably thought that if she had been a topless ventriloquist then no one would have been looking at her lips. I assumed that she might be a lady of the night who had somehow gone too far and was summoned to appear before the same judge as me. I was astonished however when on reaching the first floor she barged through a door marked in French "judges robing room". It was about then that I hoped that I had not been leering, laughing or looking too gobsmacked as she made her very dramatic entrance. Fortunately, indeed perhaps for me the judge that I soon appeared before was an old geezer who must have come in by the back door. After giving my name rank and number I gave him the deposition in an envelope which also contained my business card and he agreed that I need be detained no longer and was free to recommence spending toll money on the A4 heading back west for my Air France flight to Manchester. It was probably during one of my ABBA phases when because of something that had happened or maybe something that had not happened I decided that it was an Anyone but British Airways day. I feel obliged to be fair to BA they as they didn't take the top of Champagne bottles with a sabre even before all this recent security lark kicked in but neither were they too profligate in insisting that you had a plastic tumbler of champers as a condition of flying as one of their innocent victims.

Florida

Florida it seems was discovered and named by Juan Ponce De Leon in 1513 about 21 years after Columbus didn't discover America because he blundered on Hispaniola by mistake. No one can agree whether el Ponce called it Florida because there was an abundance of flowers there or because it was Palm Sunday when he stumbled on it. Around Easter in such a semi tropical climate would seem a good time to have an abundance of flowers in any case so it probably isn't critical. It was popular with the Spanish it seems who built the first permanent European settlement Saint Augustine in what is now the continental United States and almost 100 years before the English set up Jamestown in Virginia. Florida is popular with alligators who still outnumber the population as well as Cuban exiles and drug dealers who still must probably also outnumber the permanent population. The population rises in winter with many people escaping the snow further north and in summer with tourists who didn't realise how hot and humid it can be or they would have gone elsewhere. I transited through Miami many times before I got to know the state a bit better by starting off a real visit in Jacksonville in the north of the state named after Andrew Jackson and straddling the St John's River. It is actually the largest city in the USA by area if not by population and they claim the city with the youngest and hippest population whatever that means. If seems old Juan never found the fountain of youth but maybe its somewhere in Jacksonville. The Hyatt Regency on the north bank of the river near to the main street bridge is certainly cool or should I say fresh with a stiff breeze wheeching up and down the river depending on the season and the time of day. We drove down to Saint Augustine which is preserved in a bit of a time warp with its fort and original buildings including a sugar and rum distillery but we avoided the sugar which is said to be unhealthy. Our driver made the mistake of driving onto the beach but thought it would be more dramatic in the soft sand rather than on the wet sand near the water's edge. It was also more expensive because it cost him $100 dollars which he paid to a young lad with 4x4 who drove up and down to rescue all the idiots trying to drive on the soft sand on the beach. The entrepreneur who seemed to be a permanent feature around the beach to help passing idiots must be well on his way to being a millionaire or at least to paying off his truck rather soon. Orlando in central Florida is a bit unreal too but this is entirely intentional as it is the centre of Disney World, Universal Studios, Epcot and about a dozen other theme parks where you can easily avoid reality for the entire duration of your visit except the reality of queuing to avoid it of course which takes up most of the duration of your visit. You can always find a creek of course and be deafened by cruising around on a flat-bottomed airboat with an aero engine screaming at full power about a metre behind you. I actually wonder too if all of the many alligators sleeping on the muddy banks of the everglades are deaf since they don't even stir in their slumber as you scream by although if disturbed enough will happily bite the boat. Maybe that's why they head to the back gardens and golf courses for bit of peace and quiet. Alligators in fact seem to have a strong predilection for golfer's balls. One solution could be a heavy club between the eyes or alternatively you can even whack the alligator itself. My visit to Cape Canaveral in May 1969 coincided with the launch of Apollo 10 which was the fourth NASA crewed mission and a dress rehearsal for Apollo 11 which actually landed men on the moon. Apollo 10 just skimmed about eight miles above the surface as the landing module was too heavy to achieve lift off again from the moon's surface even with the greatly reduced gravitational forces in play. To ensure that the three-man crew did not go for a landing anyway the rocket was deliberately short fuelled and it seems they got the message as none of them really fancied a one-way trip. When I say I saw the launch I should also say that it was from about five miles distant from the launch pad away across the flat Floridan landscape as visitors were kept at a safe distance by security forces when they pressed the actual firing button and tons of liquid oxygen and other combustibles hurled the capsule atop a Saturn V rocket up into space. I did see the rocket on the pad before launch however as my US parent company made the heat resistant concrete to protect it from the sudden fierce blast on liftoff. I was not allowed anywhere near the command module but I did see all the bits and pieces of a previous mission on display in a hanger on the ground. My wife Sheena along with one or two other company wives actually had lunch in the canteen with at least one of the astronauts. When I asked her what he said she replied "not much" and when I asked which one, she said his name was part of the not much so it seems to have been an utterly memorable encounter. To be honest she seemed more

impressed by some of the gear at Epcot than she did with the whole Canaveral caper
although I was impressed at the chance to hold a piece of Moon rock. What I was not
especially impressed with was the Daytona international speed way just up the coast. I
find it hard to get excited at some big touring cars driving flat out in an endless loop
until one of them has covered 500 miles or they have all run out of tyres and fuel as I
inevitably run out of interest after the first two laps after which it seems to be a bit
samey. Our R& D manager was totally fascinated by it however and thought that he
had died and gone to heaven as the monsters screamed around the circuit. The only
really interesting feature for me was that part of the track lies within 300 yards of the
main runway of Daytona Beach International Airport which must have made it
slightly interesting when the cars and a Boing 737 appeared to be converging at a
combined speed of over 400 mph. When they say that Daytona Beach is one of the
most dangerous places to live in Florida, I don't think that they are referring to the
raceway but then you always have a wide choice of other dangerous places available
to live even when it not necessarily the hurricane season. If things get far too boring
in Miami Beach or anywhere else for your particular tastes then you always have the
option of launching yourself by sea or air into the nearby Bermuda Triangle

The Bit at the End

I never really set out to do things worth writing about but maybe along the way I have
written something describing experiences and characters that are worth reading about.
So, what lessons if any can be learned from the book dear reader? Well let's see if we
can distil something from this cauldron.

Never attempt to assist a minor Levantine official interpret his own byzantine rules
and regulations. They rarely have any sense of humour and who can honestly blame
them.

Never watch Greek television as the world does not need any more tragedies than we
currently have already.

Never fly in any plane that does not have at least one functioning engine since gliding
is strictly for the birds, especially over the sea, or over the land and most other places.

Never speak a foreign language when abroad as the natives of most countries very
seldom ever seem to be able to understand their own tongue when addressed in it.

I modestly admit that my musings may perhaps even be educational since I heard a
reviewer say to his colleague the other day "Well that certainly taught me a lesson".

I am quite excited really and can't wait as I look forward to the sequel dedicated to
the anonymous punter at the matinee of the Glasgow Empire who on realising that
Mike and Bernie Winters were a duo exclaimed "Aw f*** there are two of them".

Don't miss these unique bestsellers at your local bookstore or car boot sale.